Lecture Notes in Computer Science   3468

Commenced Publication in 1973
Founding and Former Series Editors:
Gerhard Goos, Juris Hartmanis, and Jan van I

Hans W. Gellersen Roy Want
Albrecht Schmidt (Eds.)

Pervasive Computing

Third International Conference, PERVASIVE 2005
Munich, Germany, May 8-13, 2005
Proceedings

Volume Editors

Hans W. Gellersen
Lancaster University, Computing Department, Infolab 21
South Drive, Lancaster, LA1 4WA, UK
E-mail: hwg@comp.lancs.ac.uk

Roy Want
Intel Research
2200 Mission College Blvd, Santa Clara, CA 95052-8819, USA
E-mail: roy.want@intel.com

Albrecht Schmidt
Ludwig-Maximilians-Universität München, Institut für Informatik
Amalienstr. 17, 80333 München, Germany
E-mail: albrecht.schmidt@informatik.uni-muenchen.de

Library of Congress Control Number: 2005925754

CR Subject Classification (1998): C.2.4, C.3, C.5.3, D.4, H.3-5, K.4, K.6.5, J.7

ISSN   0302-9743
ISBN-10   3-540-26008-0 Springer Berlin Heidelberg New York
ISBN-13   978-3-540-26008-0 Springer Berlin Heidelberg New York

Springer is a part of Springer Science+Business Media

springeronline.com

© Springer-Verlag Berlin Heidelberg 2005
Printed in Germany

Typesetting: Camera-ready by author, data conversion by Scientific Publishing Services, Chennai, India
Printed on acid-free paper   SPIN: 11428572   06/3142   5 4 3 2 1 0

Preface

Welcome to the proceedings of Pervasive 2005, *The Third International Conference on Pervasive Computing*. We were honoured to serve as chairs in this conference series, which was founded in 2002 and is now emerging as one of the most respected venues for publication of research on pervasive and ubiquitous computing. The conference is attracting research submissions of very high quality from all over the world, and from researchers representing a variety of disciplines and perspectives. We thank everybody who submitted their papers to Pervasive, demonstrating the extensive work going on in this area; and the Program Committee and our external reviewers who have spent countless hours providing feedback and guidance in order to create the final Program.

This year we received 130 submissions. By the end of the review process, we had 566 reviews on file, as well as long email discussion threads for each paper. In an initial phase we had each paper reviewed by two members of the Program Committee and two external reviewers. In a second phase, each paper was discussed by its four reviewers to reach consensus as to its technical merit. At the end of this phase, the top rated papers as well as those that were found to be most controversial were selected for discussion at the PC meeting and reviewed by an additional PC member. The result being that each paper discussed in the PC meeting had 5 reviews and was read by three people who participated in the meeting, leading to a very informed and lively discussion. In the PC meeting, 20 papers were selected for our single track paper program, a highly competitive 15% acceptance rate. Each accepted paper was then shepherded by a PC member to provide authors with guidance in the process of improving their papers before submission for inclusion in the proceedings.

We hope that the review process we adopted resulted in all authors receiving detailed and constructive feedback on their submission whether or not it was accepted for publication. We believe the process enabled us to assemble the best possible program for delegates at the conference. If you submitted a paper, we hope that you benefited from the feedback that your peers have provided, and if you attended Pervasive 2005 we hope that you enjoyed the program.

In addition to the technical sessions, we were delighted to have an inspiring keynote speaker. Rolf Pfeiffer, University of Zurich, was discussing intelligent artifacts and the interaction of brain, body, and environment. Pervasive 2005 also provided a number of other participation categories, including a doctoral colloquium, workshops on topics of special interest, posters for presentation of late breaking results, and videos and demonstrations as interactive contributions.

Several organisations provided financial and logistical assistance, and we are grateful for their support. We thank the University of Munich for hosting the conference and carrying the burden of local organization, and Intel Corporation and Microsoft Research for their sponsorship, which helped us provide an excellent conference experience for all attendees.

Finally thanks must go to all the authors who entrusted their work to us and to everyone who attended Pervasive 2005 and enjoyed the program we helped to assemble. None of this would be possible, or worthwhile, if it were not for your research in pervasive computing. Your continued support of this conference is most gratifying.

March 2005   Hans Gellersen, Roy Want and Albrecht Schmidt

Organization

Conference Committee

Conference Chair:	Albrecht Schmidt, University of Munich
Program Co-Chairs:	Hans Gellersen, Lancaster University
	Roy Want, Intel Research
Late Breaking Results:	Alois Ferscha, Johannes Kepler University Linz
	Rene Mayrhofer, Joh. Kepler University Linz
Workshops:	Antonio Krüger, University of Münster
Video Program:	Andreas Butz, University of Munich
Demonstrations:	Thomas Strang, German Aerospace Center
Doctoral Colloquium:	Anind Dey, Carnegie Mellon University
	Claudia Linnhoff-Popien, University of Munich
Publicity:	Rene Mayrhofer, Joh. Kepler University Linz
	Khai Truong, Georgia Institute of Technology
Local Arrangements:	Rainer Fink, University of Munich
	Paul Holleis, University of Munich
	Matthias Kranz, University of Munich
	Michael Krause, university of Munich
Webmaster:	Richard Atterer, University of Munich

Program Committee

Jakob Bardram, University of Aarhus
Michael Beigl, University of Karlsruhe
Gaetano Borriello, University of Washington and Intel Research Seattle
Nigel Davies, Lancaster University
Maria Ebling, IBM T.J. Watson Research Center
Alois Ferscha, Johannes Kepler University Linz
Ken Fishkin, Intel Research Seattle
Lars Erik Holmquist, Viktoria Institute
Stephen Intille, Massachusetts Institute of Technology
Gabriele Kotsis, Johannes Kepler University Linz
John Krumm, Microsoft Research Redmond
Marc Langheinrich, ETH Zurich
Kenji Mase, Nagoya University and ATR
Friedemann Mattern, ETH Zurich
Paddy Nixon, University of Strathclyde
Daniel Russell, IBM Almaden Research Center
Bernt Schiele, Darmstadt University of Technology

Chris Schmandt, Massachusetts Institute of Technology
Lyndsay Williams, Microsoft Research Cambridge

Reviewers

Gregory Abowd, Georgia Institute of Technology
Fahd Al-Bin-Ali, University of Arizona
Chris Baber, The University of Birmingham
Christian Becker, University of Stuttgart
Alastair R. Beresford, University of Cambridge
Mark Billinghurst, HIT Lab NZ, University of Canterbury
Alan Blackwell, University of Cambridge
Andreas Butz, University of Munich
Matthew Chalmers, University of Glasgow
Dan Chalmers, University of Sussex
Christian Decker, University of Karlsruhe
Anind K. Dey, Carnegie Mellon University
Simon Dobson, University College Dublin
Mark D. Dunlop, University of Strathclyde
Christian Flörkemeier, ETH Zurich
Adrian Friday, Lancaster University
Tom Gross, Bauhaus-University Weimar
Paul J.M. Havinga, University of Twente
Mike Hazas, Lancaster University
Ken Hinckley, Microsoft Research
Steve Hodges, Microsoft Research
Eric Horvitz, Microsoft Research
Liviu Iftode, Rutgers University
Matt Jones, University of Waikato
Jörg Kaiser, University of Magdeburg
Henry Kautz, University of Washington
Nicky Kern, Darmstadt University of Technology
Scott Klemmer, Stanford University
Gerd Kortuem, Lancaster University
Albert Krohn, University of Karlsruhe
Mik Lamming, HP Labs Palo Alto
Koen Langendoen, Delft University of Technology
Scott Lederer, UC Berkeley
Paul Lukowicz, UMIT Innsbruck
Panos Markopoulos, Eindhoven University of Technnology
Rene Mayrhofer, Johannes Kepler University Linz
Archan Misra, IBM T J Watson Research Center
Donald J. Patterson, University of Washington
Trevor Pering, Intel Research

Matthai Philipose, Intel Research
Claudio Pinhanez, IBM T J Watson Research Center
Tim Regan, Microsoft Research
Bradley Rhodes, Ricoh California Research Lab
Kay Römer, ETH Zurich
Dieter Schmalstieg, Graz University of Technology
James Scott, Intel Research Cambridge
Howard Shrobe, Massachusetts Institute of Technology
Marc Smith, Microsoft Research
Daby Sow, IBM T.J. Watson Research Center
Yasuyuki Sumi, Kyoto University
Tsutomu Terada, Osaka University
Sotirios Terzis, University of Strathclyde
Yoshito Tobe, Tokyo Denki University
Kristof Van Laerhoven, Lancaster University
Harald Vogt, ETH Zurich
Daniel S. Weld, University of Washington
Andrew D. Wilson, Microsoft Research
Ken Wood, Microsoft Research
Allison Woodruff, Intel Research

Sponsors

Intel Corporation
Microsoft Research

Table of Contents

Location Techniques

Activity and Context

Location and Privacy

Handheld Devices

Sensor Systems

User Interaction

Audio Location: Accurate Low-Cost Location Sensing

James Scott and Boris Dragovic

Intel Research Cambridge,
15 JJ Thomson Avenue, Cambridge CB3 0FD, UK
james.w.scott@intel.com
boris.dragovic@cl.cam.ac.uk

Abstract. Audio location is a technique for performing accurate 3D location sensing using off-the-shelf audio hardware. The use of off-the-shelf hardware allows audio location deployment to be low-cost and simple for users, as compared to other currently available centimetre-scale location sensing systems which have significant custom hardware and installation labour requirements. Another advantage of audio location is the ability to locate users who are not carrying any special location-enabling "tag", by using sounds that the user themselves can make such as finger clicking. Described herein are the various design parameters for audio location systems, the applicability of audio location for novel 3D user interfaces based on human sounds, and a quantitative evaluation of a working prototype.

1   Introduction

Location-aware computing [1] covers many different location granularities, from applications requiring city-scale location accuracy (e.g. online yellow pages), to others which operate on the centimeter or even millimeter scale (e.g. augmented reality). At the heart of location-aware computing is the body of research in location sensing, which has mirrored the wide range of location granularities, from systems such as RightSPOT [2] offering kilometer-scale accuracy to highly accurate systems such as the ultrasonic Bat [3] with its 3 cm accuracy.

However, high accuracy is not the only metric by which to judge location systems. The coverage of a location system is also of great importance. As one would expect, the most accurate location systems also exhibit the lowest coverage; for example, the Bat system is deployed in a portion of a single building, while GPS has worldwide coverage. Recent work on the Place Lab system [4] has focussed on providing high-coverage location information using WiFi-based location, in which the previous work was confined to single buildings [5]. However, such radio beacon–based location is limited in accuracy to tens of metres.

A location system with centimetre-scale accuracy and wide coverage has not yet been achieved. This is due to the high costs inherent in the non-standard hardware required for such systems, and in the installation and maintenance of this hardware. These costs pose too steep a barrier for many potential location-aware application user communities, outweighing the benefits of the applications. The work presented in this paper is motivated by the desire to reduce the deployment costs for potential users of

H.W. Gellersen et al. (Eds.): PERVASIVE 2005, LNCS 3468, pp. 1–18, 2005.

location-aware applications, and thereby enable the wide deployment of high-accuracy location-aware systems.

This paper presents "audio location", a technique enabling standard audio hardware to be used to locate people and objects with centimetre-scale accuracy. One defining feature of audio location is that it is possible to implement both "tagged" and "untagged" location systems using this technique, i.e. systems where users are required to carry special devices ("tags") in order to be tracked, as well as systems which have no such requirement and operate by making use of sounds the user themselves produce.

Section 2 will explore the design space for audio location systems, and previous work in this area. Section 3 will present a prototype system using audio location to implement a 3D user interface based on human sounds such as clicking fingers, including experimental results concerning the accuracy of audio location in this context. Section 4 will conclude the paper and outline future work in this area.

2   Audio Location

Audio location is a process whereby the time-of-flight of audio is used to determine the accurate location of people and/or devices. This section addresses the design parameters found in audio location.

2.1   Related Work

Sound source localization has been widely studied by the signal processing community. Two useful introductions to this work can be found at [6] (making use of microphone arrays), and [7] (using sensor networks). However, much of this body of work makes use of custom hardware, and is therefore unsuitable for low-cost and easily deployable location sensing. In contrast, this paper focuses on location sensing using off-the-shelf audio hardware; this area has been looked at by comparatively few research groups.

Girod et al. have developed a system for fine-grained range estimation [8, 9], making use of tags to produce sounds. The tags emit wideband chirps in the audible spectrum together with a RF reference signal to allow the receivers to estimate the time-of-flight accurately. The authors provide an in-depth discussion of the issues of audio signal propagation, chirp sequence correlation and sources of timing errors as well as an extensive set of evaluation results. However, untagged location is not discussed.

The work of Rosca et al., which does consider untagged operation, regards 3D audio-based positioning as a side-effect of a speech interface for use in virtual reality scenarios [10]. However, their discussion is purely theoretical and lacks an evaluation of the difficulties of implementation, in particular the difficulties of extracting a narrow feature of the audio signal for time-of-arrival calculation, and is based on an idealised scenario that may not stand up in real-life use.

Finally, the use of off-the-shelf audio hardware for context-aware applications in a pervasive computing setting, including coarse-grained location sensing, was recently presented by Madhavapeddy, Scott and Sharp [11]; the research presented in this paper was heavily inspired by their work.

2.2   Tagged Versus Untagged

Accurate location systems often require that the objects to be located be "tagged" with small devices which interact with the sensing infrastructure. There are many forms a tag can take, two examples being ultrasonic transmitters hung around the neck of a user or velcroed to a device, and visual barcode tags which can be attached to users' clothes or stuck to devices. Audio location can make use of tagged location sensing, using mobile or wearable devices such as phones to send or receive audio signals.

It is also possible to construct "untagged" systems, in which the user or device is located purely by means of their intrinsic properties or capabilities. One example is the Active Floor [12], which senses a person's body weight using load sensors under the floor. Not requiring tags has a number of advantages: hardware costs may be lower, users of the system do not have to remember to wear/affix tags, and new users do not need to be assigned tags to participate. One disadvantage of untagged audio systems is that the accuracy is likely to be worse than for tagged systems, in which the data exchanged between the mobile object and the stationary infrastructure can be well-defined (e.g. a high-contrast pattern in barcode-like systems such as TRIP [13]) as opposed to relying on what is available (e.g. the colour of the shirt a user is wearing, as used by the Easyliving system [14]).

Audio location may be used for untagged location sensing, since users are capable of generating sounds (e.g. finger clicking). An untagged audio location system will have to cope with two performance-degrading factors, namely the difficulty of detecting a suitable audio feature that can be identified at each microphone, and the lack of synchronisation as the time-of-send of the audio signal is not known. At least one previous research system, using the Dolphin ultrasonic broadband hardware presented by Hazas and Ward [15], has achieved unsynchronised fine-grained location, in which the time-of-send of the signal is determined during the location calculation.

2.3   Infrastructure

The infrastructure used to achieve audio location could involve the use of microphones in the environment and sound generation by the users/devices, or sound generation by speakers in the environment while users carry devices with microphones. This research focuses on the former technique, the most important reason being that this facilitates untagged operation while the latter technique does not.

In order to implement this type of audio location system, a number of microphones must be present in the environment, and they must be linked to one or more devices capable of processing the sound data to determine location. The simplest method of achieving this is to connect a number of low-cost off-the-shelf microphones to a single PC (which may already be in the room), and run the software on that PC. While the hardware cost may be quite low, this infrastructure may require the installation of long wires so that microphones can be optimally placed around the room.

In spaces where multiple computers are already present, e.g. shared offices, it is possible to consider making use of the sound hardware in all computers, where each computer provide only one or a few microphones. Since many PCs are already outfitted with a microphone for multimedia applications, this potentially reduces the cost of an audio location system, perhaps even to zero when deployed in a space that is already densely populated with PCs with microphones. This infrastructure also reduces audio wiring requirements, assuming that the PCs are spread across the space to be instrumented and that the PCs are networked.

2.4   Audio Feature Generation and Detection

In order to determine location, an audio location system must detect sounds as they appear in the data streams from multiple microphones. Furthermore, the system must identify a single feature of the sound which can be localised in each data stream, enabling the collection of a set of times-of-arrival for the same instant from the sound.

For tagged systems, the tag and infrastructure will communicate via radio. This allows the tag to inform the infrastructure of information such as its unique id, the characteristics of the signal it is sending (which may be implicit from the id), and the time-of-send of the signal. The infrastructure can then use this to search for the signal in the sound streams, to associate this signal with the correct tag, and to determine location more easily since the time-of-send is known.

For untagged systems, the infrastructure operates under much harsher conditions. While a tag-generated signal might conform to an easily-detectable format, a user-produced sound will not be so easy to detect. This means that the infrastructure must be able to detect a much broader class of signals, e.g. including sounds such as clapping/clicking of fingers which might be made deliberately for the benefit of the location system, and also sounds such as speech, typing, and others, which may be made by the users during their normal activities. One consequence of this is that the "noise floor" may be much higher, and might include sounds such as music, devices beeping or humming, vehicle noise, and so on. Possible signal detection methods might be based on monitoring each stream for amplitude spikes (e.g. for finger clicking), or on performing continuous cross-correlation between the sound streams, looking for spikes in the correlation coefficient to indicate the arrival of the same sound.

2.5   Location Determination

Timing information from multiple microphones must be gathered to determine location. In order to get some idea of how many microphones are required, one can regard the location problem as a set of equations in up to four variables: the 3D position of the sound source, and the time-of-send of the sound. Naively, a tagged system would require three microphones (since the time-of-send is known, only three variables need to be solved for) and an untagged system would require four. However, this gives no room for error resilience; an erroneous time-of-arrival at one of the microphones would pass undetected, and result in an erroneous location. With one extra microphone, an error situation could be determined, since the times-of-arrival would not "agree". However, it is difficult to determine which was the erroneous microphone without using external data such as the previous known location of the sound source.

To calculate the location, a non-linear system of equations is constructed in the time-of-send of the sound tos, times-of-arrival toa_i at each microphone i, microphone locations $\mathbf{micpos_i}$, the location of the sound source $\mathbf{soundpos}$, and the measurement errors err_i.

$$toa_i = tos + \frac{|\mathbf{micpos_i - soundpos}|}{speed of sound} + err_i \tag{1}$$

The known quantities are then substituted, and the unknown quantities (sound location, and, in untagged systems, time-of-send) are found using an algorithm such as the Levenberg-Marquardt method [16] to minimize the errors err_i. This approach is similar to that used, for example, in the ultrasonic Bat location system.

2.6 Issues Affecting Location Accuracy

To obtain a precise location, attention must be paid to the placement of the microphones in the room. If all the microphones are co-planar (which may often be the case, e.g. when mounting them against a wall or ceiling), there are always two possible locations for the sound source: one on each side of the plane. This ambiguity can often be resolved by looking at the location of the walls/ceiling/floor of the room, if this is known, as one of the locations may be outside.

Another issue that influences placement of microphones is Dilution Of Precision (DOP). This issue concerns the relationship between the accuracy of a positioning system and the angular relationship between the transmitter and receivers. If all receivers occupy the same narrow angle from the point of view of the transmitter, then small errors in the distance estimates will translate into large errors in the 3D position. To combat this, microphones should be widely distributed in the sensing space so that they have a large angular separation from any position where a sound source may be located.

Location precision is also affected by the speed of sound, which varies according to many factors [17], but most significantly according to temperature and humidity. The change in speed is as much as six percent between cold and warm air, and up to half a percent between dry and humid air. Whether this is regarded as significant or not depends on the location accuracy demanded by applications for which a given system was deployed, and also on the ease of statically predicting these figures based on, for example, the time of day. If it is significant, then computer-readable thermometers (and possibly hygrometers) could be deployed with the microphones.

2.7 Surveying

"Surveying", i.e. the discovery of information about the environment, is important for fine-grained location systems in two ways. Firstly, a survey of the infrastructure (for audio location, the microphones) is required for location determination to function correctly. Secondly, a survey of the characteristics of the environment, i.e. the locations of walls, doors, furniture, fixed electronics, and so on, is needed to enable location-aware applications, e.g. the nearest-printer application needs to know where the printers are. Since surveying can potentially be very time-consuming, and therefore be a discouraging factor for fine-grained location deployment, these topics are described below.

Surveying of the infrastructure can be achieved in a number of ways. Manually measuring the locations with respect to a reference point in the room is the simplest method, but may be time-consuming, subject to human error, and the microphones would have to be firmly fixed since moving them would mean re-surveying is required. Automatic surveying systems are feasible, e.g. using laser range-finders or theodolites. However, such methods require expensive equipment, and again the microphones must be fixed. Finally, "self-surveying" techniques [18] can be used, by which a location system can construct its own survey given enough raw data. For real deployments, this means that the system would not return valid locations when it was activated, until enough data points were gathered for the system to survey itself. This time depends on how much "surplus data" is present in the system, which is proportional to how many extra microphones are installed over the minimum number described previously.

Environmental surveying can also be conducted entirely manually, but again this is a very time-consuming process, and furthermore is likely to be made out-of-date due to objects being moved. Semi-automatic methods such as using the location system to manually indicate the vertices of objects such as rooms and furniture are possible; while quicker than typing in locations manually, this also suffers from falling out-of-date. A final possibility is to use audio location to automatically detect and monitor objects in the room, either because they make sounds during use (e.g. speakers, printers, keyboards, mice), or because they reflect sounds (e.g. walls, large items of furniture) such that the reflections can be detected by the system (the latter method was described by Rob Harle for the ultrasonic Bat system in [19]). The advantages of automatic methods are that they are transparent to installers/users, reduce the deployment overhead, and that they can automatically maintain up-to-date locations. However, mature, reliable and scalable methods for performing environmental surveying have not yet emerged.

2.8   Identification

While the location of sounds is useful in itself, discovering the identity of the sound's producer and associating it with that location enables a number of additional applications. This can be accomplished in tagged systems by simply having the tag declare its identity over radio, and provide enough information such that the infrastructure can determine which sounds it is making, which may include the time-of-send as well as information on the characteristics of the sound. For untagged systems, determining identity is much harder. One possibility is to use the sounds made to infer the identity of the object making them, e.g. performing voice pattern recognition on speech, using characteristic sounds such as the gait pattern during walking, habitual sounds such as tapping of fingers or distinctive laughter, and so on. However, these methods are not likely to identify users based on many common types of sound, e.g. clapping.

To solve this problem, sensor fusion methods can be used to draw from other sources of information, particularly those which provide accurate identification and inaccurate location (i.e. the complement of untagged audio location's characteristics). One example of sensor fusion used in this way was shown by Hightower et al. [20], in which coarse-grained RFID tag identification was combined with a very accurate but anonymous laser range-finder. This technique could also be applied to audio location, and in this way both the audio-based identification methods above and other identification methods using technologies such as RFID, Bluetooth, and so on can be combined to generate highly accurate locations for identified entities.

While the above discussion shows that it is possible to design audio location systems which identify users, some may regard that not including this functionality is in fact desirable, for privacy reasons. For example, if audio location were used to control an information kiosk in a shop describing their products, many users may wish to use this facility anonymously, and might refrain from using it if they felt they were leaving themselves open to tracking.

3   3D Interfaces Using Human Sounds

Out of the design space for audio location described above, one application area was chosen to demonstrate some of the novel possibilities of audio location, namely 3D interfaces using human sounds. This is inherently an untagged system, since humans themselves are generating the sounds.

A sound-based 3D interface would enable new types of computer-human interaction, moving away from physical input devices (e.g. keyboards, remote controls, etc), and toward a situation where physical input devices are not required, and the user interface is implicit in the environment. When a user makes a sound at one or more 3D locations in a pre-defined pattern, the environment can perform actions such as controlling appliances (e.g. lights), navigating through data presentation interfaces (e.g. on a wall-mounted display), and so on.

In order to guide the user to make sounds at the correct locations, these locations can be highlighted by marking that place, e.g. using printed paper affixed to surfaces such as walls or desks. Given that such markers cost very little, and that the cost of the audio location hardware is low and is only incurred once at install time, this makes for a very low-cost input method, as compared to the cost of fitting a new device at every location. The audio interface is also easily reconfigurable, in that controls can be added or changed easily. Furthermore, audio interfaces benefit from not requiring physical contact; this is useful in environments where such contact is to be avoided, e.g. in hospitals to avoid the spread of infection.

3.1   Related Work

There are many 3D user interface input methods developed by the research community as well as available commercially. Many of these require users to be equipped with special hardware such as gesture-recognising gloves or ultrasonic Bat tags in order to function. Steerable user interfaces [21] have no per-user device requirement, but rely on expensive cameras and projectors. Tangible user interfaces [22] use cameras to detect movement of physical objects and thereby cause actions on virtual objects, e.g. rotating a map display in an image, but this relies on appropriate physical objects being present and on the user knowing how to manipulate each object to control the environment according to their wishes.

Vision-based gesture recognition systems [23] are perhaps closest to audio location, in that the user does not need any special hardware or devices, and in that it is possible to consider using cheap "webcams" to produce low-cost 3D interfaces (though much of the research presented uses top-of-the-line cameras with significant cost). The advantage of audio location is the very simple interaction method, allowing the user to have a good mental model of when the interface is activated. If the user does not make loud noises, they are sure that audio location will not be activated, whereas a non-expert gesture recognition user may be wary of accidentally making a meaningful gesture.

3.2   3D Audio Interface Primitives

There are various kinds of user interface components that can be achieved using audio location. The first and most obvious one is the "button", in which a user makes a sound at a specific location to indicate an action, e.g. the toggling of a light. A second type of interface could rely on simple gestures, where the user makes a few noises in succession, at slightly different points. An example of this would be clicking one's fingers at a given point, and then again slightly higher or slightly lower, with one potential application being a volume control. The starting point of a gesture could be precisely fixed, or it could be relaxed to a broader area, with the relative location of the two noises being used as the input primitive. While more complex types of interface are possible, e.g. based on making sounds with a changing tempo or amplitude, this may prove counterproductive as the interface becomes less intuitive for users.

It is also possible to consider dynamic audio location interfaces, in which audio location interface components are dynamically created in front of a computer display. These could be used to interface with computers using display types such as projectors, which are difficult to use alongside traditional input devices such as a mouse and keyboard.

To illustrate the potential uses of audio location for user interfaces, four possible application interfaces are shown in Figure 1, parts a to d, which respectively illustrate interfaces suitable for a light switch, a volume control, a web kiosk, and a photo album application displayed on a projector.

A 3D interface has previously been demonstrated using the ultrasonic Bat system for fine-grained location [24]. One advantage of using audio location is that no tag is required for each user. A disadvantage of audio location is that, by itself, it is not capable of identifying the user, while the Bat system does identify the tag being used at that location (and assumes that it is operated by its owner). However, as discussed in Section 2.8, the identification of users (if required for a given application) can be accomplished using other coarse-grained location methods, and the process of sensor fusion can be used to combine this information with the fine-grained information from audio location.

3.3   Prototype Implementation

An audio location prototype was implemented using a single PC with six low-cost PCI sound cards and six low-cost microphones. The total cost of the sound hardware required was around one hundred british pounds, orders of magnitude less than the custom components required by many location systems described earlier. No temperature sensor was incorporated in the prototype, since this would affect the cost and off-the-shelf nature of the system.

While location can be determined from just four microphones, the use of six microphones allowed the prototype to be robust against occlusion of the path to a microphone by the user, other people, or items of furniture. The provision of redundant data also enables detection and rejection of erroneous sightings.

The software architecture was implemented in Java as an extensible object-oriented framework. Signal detection uses a dynamic amplitude-threshold scheme, whereby each sound stream is monitored for a sound sample with amplitude significantly greater than

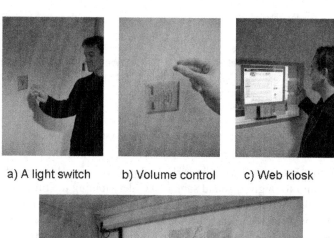

a) A light switch   b) Volume control   c) Web kiosk

d) Photo album application using dynamic
interface on a overhead projector

Fig. 1. Four examples of 3D interfaces based on audio location

the current background amplitude[1]. Location determination is then accomplished by using the Levenberg-Marquardt algorithm [16] to find the location most closely matching the signals detected, by minimising the sum of squares of the errors in the relative distance estimates, using the Levenberg-Marquardt algorithm as described in Section 2.

The amplitude-threshold signal detection method was chosen since it is good at detecting impulsive sounds such as finger clicking or hand clapping, which users can choose to make when using the 3D interface. However, this algorithm does not detect continuous, low-amplitude, or non-impulsive sounds, including human speech, ambient music, and keyboard strokes. This property is invaluable for the 3D user interface application area, since a system sensitive to such sound sources would generate high levels of false positives when used in a normal home or office environment.

---

[1] For each sample time t, $BackgroundNoise_{t+1} = BackgroundNoise_t * 0.99 + Sample_t * 0.01$, and $Sample_t$ is marked as a "peak" if $Sample_t > 2 * BackgroundNoise_t$. Parameter values were found by trial and error, and might vary if using different hardware.

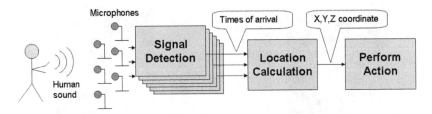

Fig. 2. Audio location–based 3D interface system architecture

One issue that became apparent in early testing was the problem of obtaining an accurate timestamp for a given sound sample, i.e. determining the time-of-arrival of a sound sample at the microphone. This is because there are potentially many delays and buffering points between the microphone and the Java application, including the delay for the hardware to raise an interrupt after its buffer becomes full, the delay for the interrupt to be serviced, and the delay for the Java application to be scheduled. In order to obtain an accurate timestamp, the driver for the chosen sound card[2] was modified such that it took a cpu-clock timestamp for new sound data at interrupt time, and made this available via the Linux /proc file system to the Java application. The modification required was modest, and is easily ported to other sound card drivers. Ideally, the sound card itself could maintain a timestamp; this would reduce the potential error in the timestamp from the current low value (the interrupt handling latency) to a negligible amount. It should be noted that Girod et al. [8] encountered similar timing accuracy problems, and suggested a similar solution.

3.4   Experiments, Results and Analysis

Two experiments were conducted in order to determine the performance of the system in one dimension and three dimensions. It is important to note that, in all of these experiments, actual human sounds were used — while recording and playback of such sounds using a speaker was considered, it was decided that this would not demonstrate the accuracy of the system as would occur in a real deployment.

1D Experiment. The 1D experiment investigates the performance of the prototype at the most basic level, namely the accuracy it exhibits in estimating a relative distance between a sound and two microphones.In addition, this experiment reveals how the microphones used perform at various ranges and various angles with respect to the sound.

The experimental setup is shown in Figure 3, and consists of two microphones placed 0.6 m away from, and pointing towards, a 7x6 grid of measurement points, with 0.6 m between each grid point. Both the grid and the microphones were at a height of 1 m above the floor. At each point on this grid, both a "finger click" and a "hand clap"

---

[2] The sound cards used were the C-Media 8738 model with the CMPCI chipset, chosen because it was the cheapest sound card available, at eight British pounds per card. For the same reason, the microphones used were the Silverline MC220G, also at eight pounds per unit.

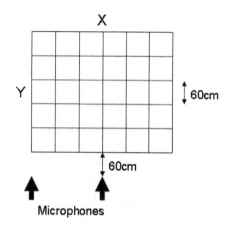

Fig. 3. Experimental setup for 1D experiment

noise was made twenty times, and the time difference of arrival at the two microphones was recorded. These time differences were then multiplied by the speed of sound to obtain estimates of the relative distance between the microphones and the grid point, which were then compared with the actual relative distance, resulting in a 1D distance error for each click/clap.

Figure 4 shows a surface plot of the median error in the relative distance over the 20 iterations, as plotted against each of the grid points used, with "finger clicking" used for sound generation. This illustrates the angular sensitivity of the microphones,

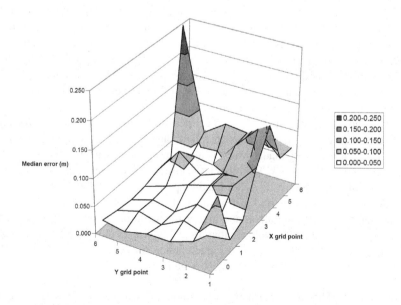

Fig. 4. 1D distance errors at each location: Clicking

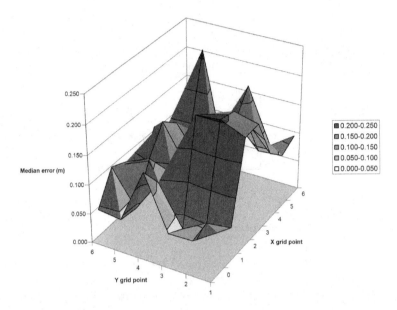

Fig. 5. 1D distance errors at each location: Clapping

as the tests at grid points with high X and low Y do not enjoy accurate relative distance estimates. Extrapolating from this plot, the microphones employed work best over an angle of around 60° either side of their axis; this information affects deployments of the prototype (allowing the installer to choose microphone locations well), and in particular contributed to the design of the 3D experiment described below.

The plot also shows that the microphones allow a location range of up to 4 m with low errors. The precise range of the system will depend on many factors, including the sensitivity of the microphones, the noise floor in the room (which was quiet during the tests presented), and the signal detection method used. In the conditions tested, errors appeared to increase at distances greater than around 4.3 m. These distances, however, are comparable to a typical office or home room. For larger spaces, it is possible to place more microphones around the room.

Figure 5 shows a similar surface plot for experiments using hand clapping for sound generation. It is obvious that the results are significantly worse. This is partly due to the character of the noise being made, which is less "impulsive" and hence harder to determine an accurate timestamp for. The other issue affecting location accuracy is the intrinsic location scale imposed by the use of hand-clapping — human hands measure 15 cm across; this imposes a precision limit of this order of magnitude. A human-imposed limit also applies to clicking, albeit at a higher precision of perhaps 5–10 cm. On this basis, the experimental results indicate that finger clicking is more suitable for location sensing; finger clicking was therefore decided upon as the sound generation method for both the 3D experiments and prototype deployments.

3D Experiment. The 3D experiment was conducted over a four-by-four grid with 0.6 m separating the grid points, and at each of three heights at 0.6 m, 0.9 m and 1.2 m.

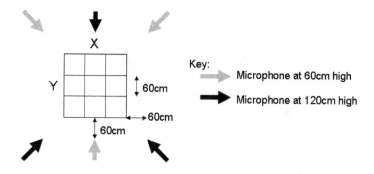

Fig. 6. Experiment setup for 3D experiments

Six microphones were used, three at 0.6 m high and three at 1.2 m high, facing towards this grid, as shown in Figure 6. This layout conforms to the range and angular sensitivity limits of the microphones determined in the previous experiment. At each location, twenty finger clicks were recorded; clapping was not performed.

Figure 7 shows the cumulative frequencies for various 3D distance errors. The rightmost line indicates that the prototype is capable of locating clicks with an absolute 3D accuracy of around 27 cm 90% of the time. In order to determine the various causes of this result, it is useful to examine the three other lines, which show the 3D distance error from the mean reported location, as well as the 2D (XY) errors (both absolute and relative to the mean reported location). Two observations can be made: there are sys-

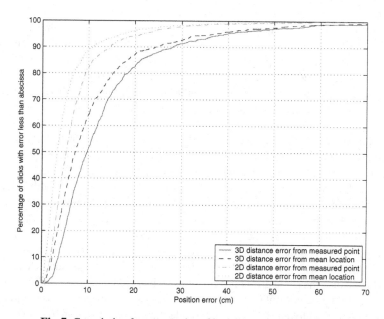

Fig. 7. Cumulative frequency plot of location error measurements

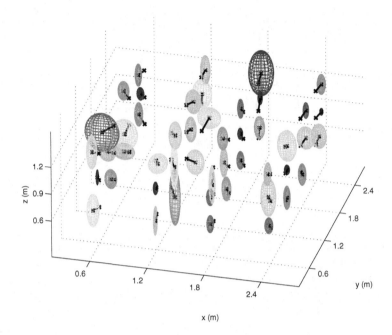

Fig. 8. "Lollipop" diagram showing mean and standard deviation of clicks at each test point

tematic errors of around 5 cm in the experiments, and the Z-dimension error accounts for around half the 3D position error. These are explained below.

Figure 8 shows a perspective view of the test grid including an ellipsoid for each test point with axes equal to the standard deviations in each dimension. This figure illustrates the higher Z-dimension errors well. These errors are due to the higher Dilution Of Precision (DOP) in the Z dimension, since the microphones are quite closely spaced in this dimension (a spread of 0.6 m as opposed to the 3.0 m range in the X and Y dimensions), thus reducing accuracy. The low spread was used since this may be the situation faced by real-life deployments of audio location systems, where microphones will be placed on objects in the room, and are therefore not freely placed over a wide Z range.

The systematic errors, illustrated by the lines from the centre of the spheres to the test points in Figure 8, may be due to such causes as experimental setup error, lack of temperature compensation, and with the position of the clicking hand as a prime suspect. As discussed above, it is difficult to make a clicking noise with a location accuracy of more than, say, 5-10 cm, because of the size of the hand.

When considering the application area of 3D user interfaces, it is not the absolute position error that matters, but the relative error between the position where a 3D button is defined and the position of the user's click on the button. Some sources of error are therefore tolerated well by a 3D user interface, namely those such as surveying errors which cause the same erroneous offset to be incurred each time. In addition, it is likely that 3D interfaces would be implemented against a plane such as a wall or desk, allowing the physical tokens to be affixed beside the button's location to help users. By organising 3D interfaces appropriately (depending on the layout of the microphones), the effect of DOP can be mitigated, thus providing a location resolution of closer to the lower bound displayed in Figure 7, and indicating that buttons can be as narrow as 20 cm wide while remaining usable.

3.5   Deployments

In order to test 3D user interfaces, a GUI was implemented allowing the audio location system and applications to be quickly deployed. This GUI is illustrated in Figure 9. To create a new configuration, a jpeg file is provided for the background, along with the coordinates of the corners. Microphones are then placed using GUI dialogs, and buttons

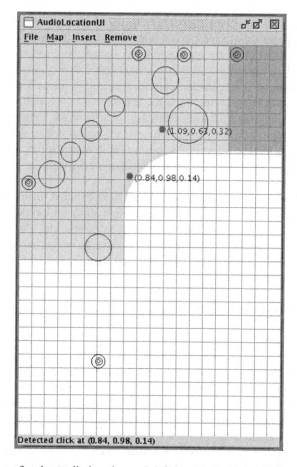

Fig. 9. GUI for configuring audio location and defining 3D user interfaces. A plan view of an office room with a corner desk is used for the background. The concentric circles represent microphones, the large unshaded circles represent buttons, and the small shaded circles represent finger clicks recently detected, along with their coordinates. Of the six microphones in the prototype, one is off the side of this plot and therefore not shown

can then be added either by clicking on the map, typing in coordinates, or by indicating a location by finger-clicking at the appropriate point 3 times. Buttons can be spherical, cylindrical, or cuboid, and an arbitrary shell command can be entered for execution when the button is triggered.

This interface has been used to implement a 3D finger-clicking interface controlling an mp3 music player (namely xmms) to demonstrate audio location. Over various occasions this has been set up at four different environments, with the setup time from a boxed to a working system being approximately 2 hours. The majority of this time is taken up in setting up the hardware and placing and manually surveying the microphones (automatic survey techniques described in Section 2 have not yet been integrated), with only a short time required to configure the buttons (play, stop, next track, choosing an album, etc) for the mp3 application.

While formal user studies have not yet been undertaken, it was observed that novice users are quick to understand the concept of "clicking" on a point in 3D space, which are marked with paper tags to indicate the virtual buttons. It was also discovered that few spurious location events are reported by the system even in very noisy environments. While such environments result in constant sound events across the various microphones, the location determination algorithm is able to discard the vast majority of these events as not representing the same sound, due to the high residual errors it finds when attempting to fit a 3D location to them. Furthermore, even when a rare false "click" is generated, it is unlikely to perform an incorrect action, since the majority of the 3D space is not marked as part of a button. These observations support the claim made earlier that the amplitude-threshold algorithm works well for 3D user interface applications.

Of the hundreds who have seen this system demonstrated, many (approximately half) were unable to click their fingers well enough to allow for location determination. This was overcome by providing cheap mechanical clickers, which have the disadvantage of introducing a hardware requirement for users. However, this clicker is easily shared, e.g. by leaving it next to the interface, and frequent users of the system could train themselves to click their fingers.

4   Conclusions and Future Work

This paper has described "audio location", a technique for low-cost centimeter-scale location sensing, which makes use of off-the-shelf audio hardware that is already deployed with many PCs, and cheap to add to PCs. The various design parameters for an audio location system were discussed, including the use of tagged (i.e. where the user carries some sort of locatable device) or untagged sensing, with untagged operation being identified as a key advantage over other types of location systems.

A prototype untagged audio location system was built, targetted at the novel application area of detecting human-generated sounds to enable 3D user interfaces. Experiments show that finger clicking can be detected with location errors of under 27 cm in 3D (14 cm in 2D) for 90% of the tests. This system does not suffer from the high cost and difficult installation of other centimeter-scale 3D location systems, with the audio hardware costing around one hundred British pounds, and installation being accomplished in a few man-hours. Audio location has therefore been shown as a viable technology to remove the barriers to entry for high accuracy location systems, opening the door to the wide deployment of location-aware applications relying on high accuracy location information.

There is much research left in the area of audio location. Topics for future work include the use of multiple PCs with fewer microphones per PC, a formal user study for the 3D user interfaces, and development of algorithms based on cross-correlating sound sources rather than amplitude-thresholding, which would for example allow the location of human voices.

Acknowledgements

The authors would like to thank Mark Williamson, Tim Sohn, John Krumm, Richard Sharp, Anil Madhavapeddy, and Mike Hazas for assistance during this research.

References

1. Hazas, M., Scott, J., Krumm, J.: Location-aware computing comes of age. IEEE Computer **37** (2004)
2. Krumm, J., Cermak, G., Horvitz, E.: RightSPOT: A novel sense of location for a smart personal object. In: Proceedings of UbiComp 2003. Volume 2864 of LNCS., Springer-Verlag (2003)
3. Ward, A., Jones, A., Hopper, A.: A new location technique for the Active Office. IEEE Personal Communications **4** (1997)
4. LaMarca, A., Chawathe, Y., Consolvo, S., Hightower, J., Smith, I., Scott, J., Sohn, T., Howard, J., Hughes, J., Potter, F., Tabert, J., Powledge, P., Borriello, G., Schilit, B.: Place Lab: Device positioning using radio becons in the wild. In: Proceedings of Pervasive 2005. LNCS, Springer-Verlag (2005)
5. Bahl, P., Padmanabhan, V.N.: RADAR: An in-building RF-based user location and tracking system. In: Proceedings of InfoCom 2000. Volume 2., IEEE (2000)
6. Brandstein, M.S., Adcock, J.E., Silverman, H.F.: A practical time-delay estimator for localizing speech sources with a microphone array. Computer Speech and Language **9** (1995)
7. Chen, J., Yao, K., Hudson, R.: Source localization and beamforming. IEEE Signal Processing Magazine **19** (2002)
8. Girod, L., Estrin, D.: Robust range estimation using acoustic and multimodal sensing. In: Proceedings of the IROS 01. (2001)
9. Girod, L., Bychkovskiy, V., Elson, J., Estrin, D.: Locating tiny sensors in time and space: A case study. In: Proceedings of ICCD 02. (2002)
10. Rosca, J., Sudarsky, S., Balan, R., Comanici, D.: Mobile interaction with remote worlds: The acoustic periscope. In: Proceedings of the AAAI 01. (2001)
11. Madhavapeddy, A., Scott, D., Sharp, R.: Context-aware computing with sound. In: Proceedings of UbiComp 2003. Volume 2864 of LNCS., Springer-Verlag (2003)
12. Addlesee, M.D., Jones, A., Livesey, F., Samaria, F.: The ORL Active Floor. IEEE Personal Communications **4** (1997)
13. López de Ipiña, D., Mendonça, P., Hopper, A.: TRIP: A low-cost vision-based location system for ubiquitous computing. Personal and Ubiquitous Computing **6** (2002)
14. Krumm, J., Harris, S., Meyers, B., Brumitt, B., Hale, M., Shafer, S.: Multi-camera multi-person tracking for EasyLiving. In: Proceedings of the Third IEEE International Workshop on Visual Surveillance. (2000)

15. Hazas, M., Ward, A.: A high performance privacy-oriented location system. In: Proceedings of PerCom 2003. (2003)
16. Press, W., Teukolsky, S., Vetterling, W., Flannery, B.: Numerical Recipes in C. Cambridge University Press, Cambridge, UK (1993)
17. Cramer, O.: The variation of the specific heat ratio and the speed of sound in air with temperature, pressure, humidity, and co2 concentration. The Journal of the Acoustical Society of America **93** (1993)
18. Scott, J., Hazas, M.: User-friendly surveying techniques for location-aware systems. In: Proceedings of UbiComp 2003. Volume 2864 of LNCS., Springer-Verlag (2003)
19. Harle, R., Ward, A., Hopper, A.: Single Reflection Spatial Voting: A novel method for discovering reflective surfaces using indoor positioning systems. In: Proceedings of MobiSys 2003, USENIX (2003)
20. Hightower, J., Brumitt, B., Borriello, G.: The location stack: A layered model for location in ubiquitous computing. In: Proceedings of the Fourth IEEE Workshop on Mobile Computing Systems and Applications (WMCSA 2002), IEEE Computer Society Press (2002)
21. Pingali, G., Pinhanez, C., Levas, A., Kjeldsen, R., Podlaseck, M., Chen, H., Sukaviriya, N.: Steerable interfaces for pervasive computing spaces. In: Proceedings of the PerCom 2003, IEEE (2003)
22. Ishii, H., Ullmer, B.: Tangible bits: Towards seamless interfaces between people, bits and atoms. In: Proceedings of CHI 97, ACM (1997)
23. Pavlovic, V., Sharma, R., Huang, T.S.: Visual interpretation of hand gestures for human-computer interaction: A review. IEEE Transactions on Pattern Analysis and Machine Intelligence **19** (1997)
24. Addlesee, M., Curwen, R., Hodges, S., Newman, J., Steggles, P., Ward, A., Hopper, A.: Implementing a sentient computing system. IEEE Computer **34** (2001)

Using Sound Source Localization in a Home Environment

Xuehai Bian, Gregory D. Abowd, and James M. Rehg

College of Computing & GVU Center, Georgia Institute of Technology,
801 Atlantic Drive Atlanta, Georgia 30332
{bxh, abowd, rehg}@cc.gatech.edu

Abstract. In this paper, we examine the feasibility of sound source localization (SSL) in a home environment, and explore its potential to support inference of communication activity between people. Motivated by recent research in pervasive computing that uses a variety of sensor modes to infer high-level activity, we are interested in exploring how the relatively simple information of SSL might contribute. Our SSL system covers a significant portion of the public space in a realistic home setting by adapting traditional SSL algorithms developed for more highly-controlled lab environments. We describe engineering tradeoffs that result in a localization system with a fairly good 3D resolution. To help make design decisions for deploying a SSL system in a domestic environment, we provide a quantitative assessment of the accuracy and precision of our system. We also demonstrate how such a sensor system can provide a visualization to help humans infer activity in that space. Finally, we show preliminary results for automatic detection of face-to-face conversations.

1 Introduction

Since the early 1990's much research effort has been focused on how to acquire, refine, and use location information [11]. Location-sensing systems rely on either explicit tagging of individuals or objects that facilitate tracking, or they leverage implicit characteristics. Most implicit localization systems use computer vision to track users. We are interested in the use of sound source localization (SSL), techniques that extract the location of prominent sound events, in the home environment. Sound events are often associated with human activities in the home, but few have exploited location of sound as context, particularly in a home environment.

There are appropriate social concerns when sensing video and audio in the home environment. However, when the actual information retrieved is not the rich signal that a human would see or hear, there is potential for alleviating those concerns. We designed a SSL system to locate sound events in the environment using microphone arrays. The only information extracted in this case is the location of sound sources. Our system is based on a standard SSL algorithm which uses the time of delay method and PHAse Transform (PHAT) filtering in the frequency domain to locate sound sources [15]. In Section 3 we describe the engineering modification we made to this standard algorithm to make it function more robustly in the public space of a

H.W. Gellersen et al. (Eds.): PERVASIVE 2005, LNCS 3468, pp. 19–36, 2005.

realistic home setting. The system runs continuously (24/7) and feeds the detected sound events into a database that can be consulted by a variety of applications for the home. For example, in other recent work, we have empirically established the link between face-to-face conversations in the home and availability to external interruptions from distant family members [18]. With this motivation, in this paper we wanted to explore whether temporal and spatial patterns of SSL events might be used to infer face-to-face conversations automatically.

To demonstrate the feasibility and usefulness of a home-based SSL system, we will describe how we engineered a solution based on previously published algorithms, focusing our discussion on modifications that would happen in any home environment. We will demonstrate how good the SSL system is in practice through experimental validation of its accuracy and precision over a large public space in a home, including kitchen, dining and living room areas, but with a controlled sound source. We will try to provide an honest appraisal of the SSL system we built, and attempt to discuss what advantages and disadvantages exist for this technology. Inferring activity, such as conversation, can be done by humans through visualization of the SSL data over relevant intervals of time. More automated forms of conversation detection will not be as robust, but we will show some initial promise in this area that leverages simple spatio-temporal heuristics. We believe this is a promising start, which points to more sophisticated activity recognition based on audio sensing.

2   Motivations: Sound as an Implicit Location Source

An interesting distinction between location-sensing technologies is the reliance on explicit means of marking the people or objects to track. We give a brief overview of location solutions, divided between those that require explicit tagging and those that function based on more implicit means of identifying tracked objects or people.

2.1   Explicit Location Systems

Many explicit localization systems, requiring users to wear extra passive tags or active devices, have been developed since the 1990's. Hightower and Borriello's recent taxonomy of current location systems mainly focuses on explicit localization systems [11]. The Active Badge system, one of the first successful indoor proximity location systems, required users to wear a badge that emitted infrared ID information giving zone level location information [9]. With the improved Active Bat system, users carried a 5cm by 3cm by 2cm Bat that received radio information and emitted an ultrasonic signal to ceiling-mounted receivers. This provided location accuracy of 9cm with 95% reliability [10]. The Cricket location system requires user to host the Listener on a laptop or PDA and obtains the location granularity of 4 by 4 feet [19]. However, these systems are generally expensive to deploy and maintain.

We designed our own indoor location service using passive RFID. Users wear passive RFID tags which are queried by RFID readers at fixed locations to obtain a unique ID [1]. RFID tags are small and passive, and hence, easy to carry and do not require batteries. However, instrumenting an environment with enough readers to obtain decent location information can be expensive. An alternative method is to tag the environment and place the RFID reader on a person, as suggested by the iGlove used in the SHARP project at Intel Research [14]. Although the iGlove is used to detect hand-object proximity in order to infer activities of daily living (ADLs), this approach also infers locations.

By taking advantage of existing radio beacon infrastructure, such as WiFi access points, wireless positioning systems use the signal strength of access points received by a wireless network card to determine the location of mobile users with an accuracy of 1-3 meters [4]. This technique has been explored at length in the mobile and ubiquitous computing communities and has been used on several campuses such as the Active Campus project at UCSD and CMUSKY project at CMU.

For outdoor localization, users can carry a GPS receiver and get the global position at the accuracy of 1-5m. Many projects use GPS as the primary outdoor positioning system, including Lancaster's Guide [6]. Intel Research's Place Lab effort leverages different methods of localization including GPS, WiFi, Bluetooth and GSM cell towers to provide increasingly ubiquitous location services [13].

Explicit systems generally tend to be more robust than implicit systems, and almost always provide identification information (e.g., unique tag ID) in addition to location. In more formal environments such as the office, the wearing of an explicit tag or badge can be mandated. However, our experience deploying a passive RFID in a home laboratory showed that one important reason why the system was not extensively used is that some users forget to wear or even lost their tags. Another drawback of explicit location systems from the user's perspective is the size and weight of the tag or device they must carry. Many devices require a certain amount of local computation or signaling capability. GPS receivers need a processor to compute their location after receiving satellite signals, while beacons must expend enough energy to be detected. The requirement for computation and/or broadcast power adds to the size and weight of the device.

2.2 Implicit Location Systems

These disadvantages of explicit location tracking techniques motivate others to consider more implicit forms of location sensing. Here, technologies take advantage of natural characteristics of the users to sense their location, including visual cues, weight, body heat or audio signals. Implicit tracking does not require users to wear tags or carry devices, which pushes the tracking technology, for better or worse, into the background.

Motion detectors and floor mats open supermarket doors, and motion sensing flood lights and sound activated night-lights ease light pollution while still providing illumination when needed. Although these simple appliances do not track the location of specific users, they implicitly know the location of whoever has activated them for a brief period of time. Simple sensors (motion detectors, contact switches, accelerometers) can be spread throughout the fixed infrastructure of a home (walls, cabinets, etc.), and the data from these sensors can be used to infer where human activity takes place [23].

With the development of artificial intelligence and increasing computing power, more perception technologies are used to support a natural interaction with the environment. Vision-based tracking and SSL are two important location strategies that have the ability to monitor large spatial areas passively with only modest amounts of installed hardware. In contrast to motion detectors and contact-based floor sensors, they provide greater resolution and discrimination capabilities.

Techniques for tracking people using multiple cameras treat the body holistically as a single moving target [8], often using a "blob" model to describe the targets' appearance. In a home setting, multiple users can be tracked in real-time using ceiling or wall-mounted cameras. The region corresponding to each user in each of the camera images is described as a blob of pixels, and it can be segmented from the background image using a variety of statistical methods [8, 17, 26]. By triangulating on the blob's centroid in two or more calibrated cameras, the location of the user can be estimated in 3-D. In the EasyLiving project at Microsoft Research, the blob's location was updated at 1-3Hz in a room environment with two cameras for up to 3 users. Vision requires significant processing power and broadband networking infrastructure in order to get satisfactory real time location updates [17].

Passive sound source localization provides another natural tracking method that uses difference in time of flight from a sound source to a microphone array. With computer audio processing, sound source location can determine the location of sound events in 3-D space. We will discuss SSL in more detail in Section 3.

Because users do not need to carry tags or devices, these systems allow for implicit interaction, but may not provide identification information. With the help of face recognition, fingerprint, or voiceprint recognition, computer perception based location systems can provide identity information in addition to location.

2.3 Implicit Vision-Based Tracking Versus Sound Source Localization

Vision-based tracking and SSL are potentially more accurate than other simple implicit location systems, such as contact based smart mats or motion detectors. Computer vision systems usually use multiple cameras to circumvent visual obstacles or provide continuous tracking for moving objects over multiple rooms. Vision systems require significant bandwidth and processing power, as a typical color camera with 320x160 resolution at 10 frames per second generates about 1.54 Mbyte of data per second.

In comparison, the data throughput of a microphone array is significantly less than a camera system. One microphone generates about 88.2 KByte of data per second for CD quality sound with 16 bit sampling resolution. Because of the relatively low bandwidth, data collection and processing of an array of 16 to 32 microphones can be easily performed on an Intel PIII-class processor. Because of lower bandwidth requirement of audio, projects like "Listenin" report the ability to monitor remote environments though a wireless IP connection in real time [22].

Current vision-based location tracking systems suffer from variance in circumstantial light, color, geometric changes of the scene and motion patterns in the view, while sound source localization systems suffer from environmental noise. A sound localization system can more easily detect activities that have specific sound features such as a conversation or watching TV, which might be difficult to detect using computer vision alone. However, sound source localization also has obvious disadvantages. Only activities which generate sounds (which may be intermittent) can be detected by the system.

An active research community is addressing the problem of fusing audio and video cues in solving various tasks such as speaker detection [20] and human tracking [5]. For example, the initial localization of a speaker using SSL can be refined through the use of visual tracking [25].

2.4   Sound Source Location as Important Source of Context

One important context from the audio is the capability to detect the sound event's location with some accuracy. We can find a cordless phone when it rings based solely on sound source location. Among the activities which take place in the home, identified by Venkatesh [24], many are connected with sound events, such as when we converse, watch TV, listen to the radio, talk on the phone, walk across the floor, move chairs to sit down for dinner, set plates on the dinning table, cook dinner, wash dishes, use utensils and chew during a meal.

In domestic environments, different activities are often conducted in particular locations. Leveraging this activity localization, a semi-automated method can be used to divide the room into activity zones and provide interaction based on status with regard to different zones [16]. Similarly, a previous study suggests availability for interruption from outside the home is strongly correlated to activities within the kitchen [18]. For instance, individuals preparing food at the kitchen counter indicated they would be accessible, but not available when helping a child with homework at the kitchen table. Sensing systems with only room location and presence context do not provide enough information to distinguish these differing states. SSL could provide precise location and sound event data to help a remote family member distinguish the different activities, without revealing the actual content or identities.

If the system observes sound events from the kitchen and stove for thirty minutes, followed by sound events surrounding the dinning room table, it can make a good prediction that a meal is occurring. Thus detecting kitchen activities, such as cooking and washing dishes etc., will have promise in predicting availability for inter-home communication. Also if you analyze the height of the sound events, footsteps occur at floor level, sound events from the table may indicate that an object was dropped, while conversational noises are likely to be located at seated or standing heights.

SSL has potential to summarize activities that generate sound events over a period of time and providing answers to questions like: *When did we have dinner yesterday? Did I cook yesterday?* The update frequency of sound event location is fast enough to recognize some patterns of sound event sequences, like the switching between two persons in a conversation. Sound events can be used to determine the status of the users: *Is the user in a conversation?* It provides substantial information towards high level context such as interruptability determination in an office environment [12].

Despite the potential for sound location to support relevant activity context, there is little to no research designed to investigate the relationship between sound events and household activity.

3   Sound Source Localization in the Home

Sound Source Localization (SSL) systems determine the location of sound sources based on the audio signals received by an array of microphones at different known positions in the environment. In this section, we first summarize challenges for sound source localization in home environments. Then, we present the improvements to the standard PHAse Transform (PHAT) SSL algorithm as well as the design decisions we implemented to overcome these challenges. Finally, we report on the performance of our SSL system.

3.1   Challenges to Deploy SSL System in Domestic Environment

Sound source localization research started many decades ago; however, there exists no general commercial SSL system. Based on current SSL research literature [7] and our own experiences [3], the main challenges for deploying SSL systems in domestic environment are:

1. **Background Noise.** The background noise in home environments can include traffic noise, noise from household appliances and heating and air conditioners. For example, noise from the microwave will pose a problem for localizing the person talking at the same time.
2. **Reverberation.** (Echoes) Reverberation in the home is difficult to model and can lead to corrupted location predictions when indirect (bounced) sound paths interfere with direct sound paths.
3. **Broadbandness.** The speech signals and sounds generated from household activities are broadband signals. The failure of narrowband signal-processing algorithms, applied in radar/sonar systems, requires the use of more complicated processing algorithms.
4. **Intermittency & Movement.** The sound to be detected is usually intermittent and non-stationary. This makes it hard to apply localization techniques that use stationery source assumptions, such as adaptive filtering localization [2]. Sound generated by a person tends to be fairly directional, since the acoustic radiation in some directions is blocked by the human body.
5. **Multiple Simultaneous Sound Sources.** When faced with multiple simultaneous sound sources, there would be multiple peaks in correlation between microphones. This decreases credibility of computed time of delay and increases location errors.

Despite these general challenges, our research system shows that it is feasible and useful to start investigating how sound source location can help to locate human generated sound events that can be used to infer activity both manually and automatically.

3.2   Fundamentals of Passive Sound Localization

SSL systems can be traced back to earlier active radar and sonar localization systems. An active localization system sends out preset signals to the target and compares it with the echo signal in order to locate the target, similar to how a bat locates its prey using ultrasonic pings. In passive localization, the system only receives signals generated by the targets, which are mostly human generated sound signal in our case. If a user wears an explicit tag (such as the Active Bat ultrasonic badge), the receiver can compute the location with high accuracy because of the high signal to noise ratio (SNR) in the narrow frequency range. However, for the implicit sound sources in a domestic environment we intend to explore, the signal is often noisy and with broader frequency ranges.

Different effective algorithms with an array of microphones are used in sound source localization. They can be divided into three main categories: steered-beamformer based locators; high-resolution spectral estimation based locators; and Time-of-Delay based locators [7]. Most current sound source location systems are based on computing Time-of-Delay using PHAT-based filtering, which is simple, effective and suitable for real-time localization in most environments. The Time-of-Delay locating process is divided into two steps:

- computing time delay estimation for each pair of microphones; and
- searching for the location of the sound source.

Different systems vary in the geometric deployment of sensors, pairing up, filtering and space-searching strategies. We will explain the design of our SSL system after a simple introduction to PHAT and correlation-based time of delay computations. More details are available in [3].

The incoming signal x received at microphone i can be modeled as

$$x_i(t) = \alpha_i s(t - \tau_i) + n_i(t) \tag{1}$$

where: $s_i(t - \tau_i)$ is the signal delay; $n_i(t)$ is the noise; α_i is the attenuation factor for microphone i. For every pair of microphones, we compute the correlation. This is usually done in the frequency domain in order to save time. However, because of noise and reverberation in the environment, some weight functions in the frequency domain are applied to enhance the quality of the estimation, such as the Phase Transform (PHAT), or Roth Processor [15, 21]. The general cross correlation with the PHAT filter is equation 2, where the first item is the frequency weighting filter.

$$\hat{R}_{x_1 x_2}(t) = \int_{-\infty}^{\infty} \frac{1}{|X_1(f)Conj(X_2(f))|} X_1(f)Conj(X_2(f))e^{j2\pi f t} df \tag{2}$$

$Conj$ is the complex conjugation function, and $X_1(f)$ and $X_2(f)$ are the Fourier transforms of $x_1(t)$ and $x_2(t)$. Ideally the maximum of equation (2) indicates the time offset of arrivals of the two signals if there is no noise. In practice, we compute the location of this peak by finding the time of occurrence of the maximum value of $\hat{R}_{x_1 x_2}(t)$.

3.3   Peak Weight-Based SSL and Other Design Decisions

We deployed our sound source localization system in an actual home setting and improved the location evaluation function to perform well in that environment. Figure 1 shows the floor map of the target area.

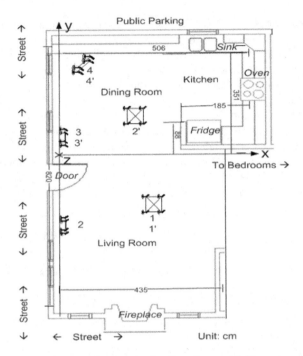

Fig. 1. 2D Floor map of covered space in the first floor with the primary "living room" setting(Quad 1,2,3,4) and "Kitchen" setting(Quad 1',2',3',4'). The only difference between the two settings is the location of the quad labeled 2 and 2'. Each Quad has 4 microphones

Deploying a working SSL system in a home environment introduces several challenges that many researchers do not consider when testing in a controlled laboratory environment. Below is a discussion of those challenges, and how we improved our system in light of those factors in the house where we deploy our system.

1) The house is close to a busy street and the noise level is variable throughout the day, so we dynamically update the noise threshold with equation (3) in processing before actual localization to ignore street noise.

$$Threshold_{t+1} = \alpha * Threshold_t + (1-\alpha) * Energy_t \qquad (3)$$

$Energy_t$ is the current sound energy and α is the inertial factor.

2) Our target area consists of a living room, dining room and kitchen. To cover the large space 16 microphones were used. The microphones were organized into 4 separate Quads (set of 4 microphones in a rectangle pattern). By only computing time of delay between microphones in the same Quad, it effectively limits the peak search range and rules out false delays.

3) To fully utilize the information from each Quad, we correlate sound signals between all six pair-wise combinations of the four microphones.

4) Quads which are closer to the sound source make better location predictions. Because of the high signal to noise ratio, a Quad selection strategy is needed.

Environmental factors such as noise and reverberation, etc., might corrupt the signal and generate maximum at the time other than true time of delay in equation (2). In addition to the above measures, we also found it is necessary to reflect the reliability of each Time -of-Delay estimation into the final localization goal function. We use the ratio of the second peak with the maximum peak in equation (4) to convey the reliability of computed Time-of-Delays. Specifically, we define the peak-weight of ith pair of microphones to be:

$$W_i = 1 - V_{\text{Second peak}} / V_{\text{Max Peak}} \qquad (4)$$

We discard the data items whose peak-weights (W_i) are less than some constant, chosen to filter about 60-80% of the measurements. In a home environment with a signal to noise ratio between 5 and 15 db we experimentally determined this constant to be 0.3.

In the second phase of searching for the sound source location, we use steepest gradient descent method in the 3D space during the process of minimizing the evaluation function. The final evaluation function E of each potential location is calculated by equation (5). Note that we consider the peak weight (W_i) in the final evaluation function.

$$E = \sum_{i \in PossilbePairs} [W_i (TDOA^{Exp}_i - TDOA_i)^2] \qquad (5)$$

$TDOA_i$ is the measured time of delay. $TDOA^{Exp}_i$ for a potential location is computed according to the distance to the ith pair of microphones divided by speed of sound. During the search for the location of a sound event, we added more initial searching points from the more probable sound source locations, like the kitchen area, dining and living room tables in addition to the previous detected sound source locations. By seeding the initial search points in this manner, we increase the responsiveness of the system to common sound events.

3.4   System Design in a Home Environment

Although our system design is not sophisticated enough to work in different environments, it does work well in our target home. The dimensions of the L-shaped area are shown in Figure 1, and the overall area is about 38 square meters. The environmental noise ranges between 60-70db during the day, which is probably more noisy than a typical residential house setting. Our home lab is close to a busy street with much traffic.

Figure 2 shows the pictures of microphones mounted in picture frames and ceiling tiles, each of which has exactly 4 microphones and is called a Quad. The microphone arrays are deployed in the connected areas including the kitchen, living room and dining room on the ground floor (see Figure 1). We are using 16 omni-directional pre-amplified microphones (cost: 10 USD each) that receive audio signals in the 20Hz to 16KHz range. For the initial primary "living room" placement of microphone quads, shown as 1,2,3,4 in Figure 1, our goal was to cover the whole space equally well. For that setting, one Quad is in the ceiling of living room, two are on the front wall and one is at the corner of the dining room that faces the dining room and kitchen.

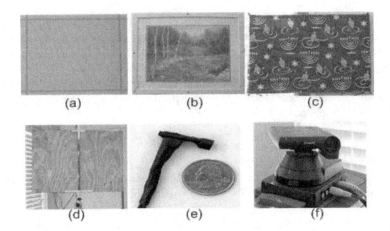

Fig. 2. (a)-(d) Microphone Quads, each has 4 microphones. (e) Single microphone with a quarter. (f) PTZ camera driven by detected sound location events

3.5 System Performance

In our home environment the current system can locate sound events from talking, footsteps, putting glasses on the table, chewing food, and clashes of silverware with dishes. For continuous talking that faces one of the quad arrays, we estimate the update rate as 1-5 seconds per reading. The system is especially responsive to crisp sound events such as clicking, eating, sniffing, or putting a backpack on a table. These crisp sound events generate high SNR signal which will help find correct Time-of-Delays between microphones.

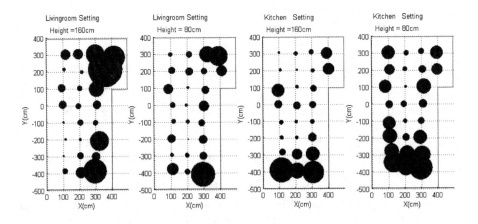

Fig. 3. Visualization of measured sound source location data at 1 meter by 1 meter grid for two different microphone Quad settings at heights of 80 and 160 cm

Table 1. The performance of SSL system for different settings with 25 measurements at each location. ERR is the average deviation with the true sound source location. STD is the standard deviation for 25 measurements

#	Grid Location		Living room 160cm		Living room 80cm		Kitchen 160cm		Kitchen 80cm	
	x	y	ERR	STD	ERR	STD	ERR	STD	ERR	STD
1	100	-400	19	16	27	34	25	73	72	60
2	100	-300	2	5	8	11	23	19	35	43
3	100	-200	14	7	4	24	15	12	30	43
4	100	-100	5	6	17	13	13	13	16	38
5	100	0	5	23	13	16	6	23	7	22
6	100	100	10	23	20	28	20	38	19	37
7	100	200	14	10	8	20	8	9	9	30
8	100	300	18	29	4	12	6	7	2	39
9	200	300	7	29	14	18	3	12	10	15
10	200	200	17	10	15	23	10	6	7	13
11	200	100	4	15	7	8	10	10	7	8
12	200	0	8	16	8	9	14	22	7	18
13	200	-100	9	17	6	11	6	10	4	12
14	200	-200	6	8	7	4	8	10	7	21
15	200	-300	7	19	6	13	12	31	14	46
16	200	-400	12	32	6	16	21	46	32	50
17	300	-400	29	71	14	72	24	65	24	70
18	300	-300	8	25	5	22	7	41	7	50
19	300	-200	45	57	9	25	4	25	8	40
20	300	-100	6	15	15	19	9	13	3	19
21	300	0	11	24	13	30	7	20	20	24
22	300	100	12	45	19	22	14	19	33	43
23	300	200	18	43	6	18	7	12	11	22
24	300	300	3	56	31	46	10	14	9	17
25	400	300	25	67	32	57	10	33	23	38
26	400	200	40	104	11	31	9	34	12	33

To test the accuracy and precision of our deployed SSL system, we created a 1 meter by 1 meter grid on the floor of the kitchen/dining/living room area and systematically placed a controlled sound source at two different heights (80cm, approximating table height, and 160cm, approximating standing height), for a total of 26 data collection points. At each sample point, we collected 25 independent SSL readings from a speaker on a tripod producing a crisp, clicking sound.[1] For the primary "living room" setting, we use microphone quad number 1, 2, 3 and 4 shown in Figure 1. In addition, we have tested the performance of a "kitchen" setting which includes microphone quad number 1', 2', 3' and 4' in Figure 1.

---

[1] This sound source was selected to allow for quick collection of data at the grid points. Using a more natural sound source, such as a recording of a person talking would not, in our opinion, change the results of the accuracy and precision readings, but would have greatly increased the time required for data collection.

The data collected is summarized in Table 1. Figure 3 shows a top-view visualization of the data collected to give a better at-a-glance demonstration of the accuracy and precision of our SSL system. For each grid point, a circle indicates the accuracy (how far away the center is to the grid point) and precision (radius of circle). We show this visualization at both heights (80cm and 160cm) for each setting of the microphone quads. Among all the measurements in our experiments, the mean of deviations from ground truth location is 13.5cm and 95% of the deviations are less than 33cm. We use the standard error of the 25 measurements to represent the accuracy of the system. Average standard error of all locations is 27.3cm and 95% of them are less than 68cm.

The experimental data verifies that to sense an area with less error and higher resolution, we need to put more microphones around that area. For example, in order to detect sound events better in the kitchen area, we placed a microphone quad in the kitchen ceiling. By doing so, we can enhance the SNRs of the signal and reduce the impact of reverberation. We can also see that between the height of 80cm and 160cm there is no systematically definable performance difference, though there are noticeable differences.

In general, our results demonstrate that the 4 microphone quad arrays give good coverage of this large area, and can provide data that can help determine activity in this space, as we will demonstrate next. This SSL system will help us to disambiguate the placement of relatively stationary or slow moving sound sources.

4 Using SSL to Detect Conversations

An initial application, developed to test how well the SSL technology works, drove a pan-tilt-zoom camera to show the area where sound was detected. While this kind of application might be useful for remote monitoring of meetings or for childcare, it was never intended to be the motivating application for our work. The advantages of the SSL sensing system we have created is that it covers a fairly large portion of the public living space of a home (kitchen, dining and living rooms) and offers reasonably good accuracy and precision for 3D location without requiring any explicit tagging. The SSL system also only records the location of the single loudest sound source every few seconds, without any other identifying characteristics being archived. Given the justifiable concerns with sensing and privacy in the home, this is a good feature of the sensor. The main disadvantage of this sensor is that location readings from the system are sporadic, with no guarantee of providing data at a fixed data rate. The same sound might not be consistently detected over time because of other environmental noise that cannot be controlled.

Given these advantages and disadvantages, we wanted to explore a use of the SSL technology that would play to its strengths. Using it for any real-time context-aware application would be unwise, given the sporadic nature of the data. However, it would be useful for near-term decision making, as the pattern of sounds in a home should reveal some important characteristics of activity. Previous research on communication support has revealed the potential for using near-term knowledge of home activity to determine whether the household is amenable to an outside interruption, such as an external family member phoning [18]. While the general capability of determining availability is so subjective as to be impossible to mechanize, this prior result does give some direction for applying our SSL technology. One specific finding in that work suggests that detection of face-to-face conversations, which we define as a conversation being held in the same room of a house, is a good first step.

We address this problem of conversation detection in two ways. First, we look at ways in which the visualization of SSL data over a physical space might inspire a human to make correct inferences about activity, whether looking for conversations or other patterns. Second, we look to implement simple spatial and temporal heuristics that might detect conversational patterns in a time series of SSL data. We present both of these uses of SSL in this section.

4.1 Visualizing SSL Data

In a domestic environment, the owner of a home might be interested in viewing what activities happened in his house yesterday morning, see a summary of activity over longer periods, or remotely access the house of another trusting friend or family member. We developed a sound event map to facilitate this. In the sound localization system described earlier, all the sound location data with timestamps are stored into a database server. The sound event map application connects to the server and retrieves the sound location history. Because each sound source location event consists of 16 bytes (X,Y,Z,Timestamp) and events detected are at most a few readings per second, the sound event map application requires very low bandwidth, meaning this information could be quickly transmitted outside of the home as needed.

The application, shown in Figure 4, allows a 3D manipulation of the floor plan, with SSL data points distributed throughout the 3D virtual space. It also supports top view, front view and lateral view to better determine what is happening in a particular area. We are assuming the user of the application is familiar with the space, so even if there is not very detailed information about furniture, and certainly without knowledge of who might be in the room at any given time, the distribution of sound events can still be meaningful.

The user can select a time interval of interest (e.g., 7:30am to 10:00am yesterday morning) or select an area of interest - the system automatically determines timeslots where activity in the chosen area (e.g., kitchen, dining table) occurred. Within a displayed interval, SSL events are colored from green (least recent) to red (most recent) depending upon their age. Another mode provides a form of replay so that the viewer can see a soundscape unfold over time, under their control. During the automatic replay, the current event is highlighted with the largest size dot, while the five previous events are rendered with smaller dots.

Though we have limited use of this application and cannot, therefore, report on how accurately a human can interpret activity in a familiar space using SSL data alone, our preliminary experiences reveals it is effective for summarizing activity over a reasonable period of time, usually from several minutes to several hours in duration. With this limited visualization, for example, it is possible to detect a moving sound source or alternating sound sources, as you would expect in a conversation. It is also possible to visualize and understand activity around special places, like a dining table. This visualization motivated us to look at more automated ways to detect these activities.

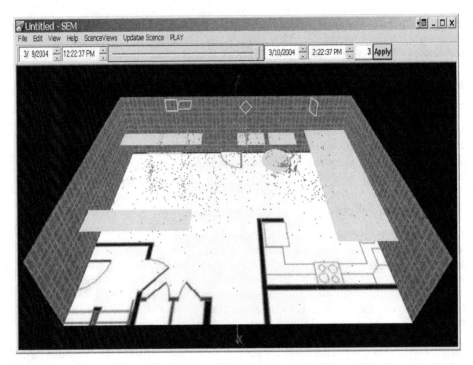

Fig. 4. Sound Event Map application, showing sound events (red/green dots) for a day in the home

4.2 Distinguishing Two-Person Conversations from Single-Person Talking

As previously discussed, the sound location context is usually associated with human activity. Certain household activities are usually linked with specific locations in the home, such as dining, cooking and watching TV. Currently, users examining the data we collect using the sound event map are able to recognize dinning activities manually by looking for events around the dining room table. Kitchen related activities are also easy to recognize. While this general direction for activity recognition is an interesting one to pursue, we focus on a simpler kind of activity, specifically how to differentiate between a single person talking and a two-person, face-to-face conversation.

To demonstrate that the data from our SSL system can differentiate between these two situations, we recorded 10 two-person conversations and 10 people talking over a telephone. These activities were distributed over the kitchen, dining and living room areas covered by the SSL system (using 1, 2, 3, 4 microphone quad configuration in Figure 1). The distances between the two people in conversation ranged from 0.5m to 5m. For a single person talking on the phone, we recorded 5 situations in which the phone conversation is relatively stationary (person sitting, but able to sway less than ·1m) and 5 situations in which the user paced around the house (representing a cordless handset). Three typical cases, with corresponding SSL data are visualized in Figure 5. Each black point in the graph represents a detected sound event. To better visualize the timestamp properties, we use both darkness and size to represent the age of each dot. The more recent events are drawn in larger sizes as well as darker colors. Each activity lasted between 2-5 minutes.

(a) One person sitting and talking   (b) One person talking while moving   (c) Two-person talking

Fig. 5. Three talking scenarios. The darkness and size of dots represent the age of sound events

Table 2. The clustering of 10 two-person conversations, 5 one –person talking cases at fixed location and 5 single-person talking cases while moving around

Cases	Total number of readings	Number of flip-flops	Distance between clusters(cm)	Classified as conversation?
2-person 1	79	23	191	Yes
2-person 2	29	16	160	Yes
2-person 3	32	12	202	Yes
2-person 4	47	15	118	Yes
2-person 5	59	17	120	Yes
2-person 6	44	16	440	Yes
2-person 7	44	12	258	Yes
2-person 8	51	17	150	Yes
2-person 9	44	12	134	Yes
2-person 10	79	23	191	Yes
1-person mv 1	32	2	340	No
1-person mv 2	32	5	118	No
1-person mv 3	43	2	322	No
1-person mv 4	22	8	201	Yes
1-person mv 5	35	7	283	No
1-person fix 6	48	22	69	No
1-person fix 7	34	4	101	No
1-person fix 8	31	12	97	No
1-person fix 9	39	18	61	No
1-person fix 10	36	19	64	Yes

To detect two-person conversations, we used a K-means clustering algorithm to separate the data points into two clusters. Then we counted the frequency of the back and forth between these two clusters with their timestamp information.

Our proof-of-concept algorithm uses the following two heuristic rules:

1. If (# of flip-flops between two clusters/ # all reading>R1 and distance < D)
       it is a conversation;
2. If (# of flip-flops between two clusters/ # all reading> R2 and distance >= D)
       it is a conversation;
3. else
       it is a single person talking;

Before our experiment, we assigned the parameters R1=0.5; R2=0.25; and D = 100cm. The meaning of these parameters is that when sound clusters are closer than D=100cm, we require 50% of the sound events to represent the flip-flop between the clusters before the activity is judged to be a conversation. When the sound clusters are farther apart than D=100 cm, then we only require 25% of the sound events to represent the flip-flop before the activity is judged to be a conversation.

When two persons are having a conversation, they will form two clusters of data points in the space and there should be sufficient flip-flopping between these two clusters. However, for a single-person talking around a fixed location, detected location events vary randomly around the true location. We choose D=100 cm to be larger than the maximum distance traveled by a swaying person plus sensing error.

The results in Table 2 show that all 10 two-person conversations were correctly categorized. Four of our five single-person fixed location cases and single-person moving cases were correctly categorized, while one of each was incorrectly judged to be a two-person conversation, giving our proof-of-concept algorithm an accuracy rate of 90% over all 20 cases.

We must point out that we are only using simple heuristic rules to distinguish conversations between two-person and a single-person talking on the phone in the home environment. More sophisticated linear dynamic models could be used to recognize patterns and provide inference for a dynamic number of people. But this work demonstrates the context information inherent within sound source location events, highlighting the potential for more sophisticated inference algorithms.

5   Conclusions and Future Work

In this paper we summarized two different categories of localization systems, explicit and implicit, and pointed out that implicit localization systems have advantages for deployment in a ubiquitous computing environment. By adapting current sound source localization (SSL) algorithms, we built a sensor system in a realistic home setting. We demonstrate the accuracy and precision of this 3D localization technology, resulting in a system that is accurate to within 13.5cm with an expected standard error of 27.3cm in average in a realistic home setting.

While this sensor system alone certainly has its limitations, based on the latency and potentially sporadic distribution of data for a noisy environment, the simplicity of the sensor (from the human perspective) and its socially appealing lack of archived rich data, motivated us to explore what value it might have on its own. We explored solutions that would use time series of SSL data points to help a human infer (through visualization) or be automatically informed of (through pattern recognition) the likelihood of human conversations in the home space. By capturing the sound event locations during conversation, we can dynamically cluster the points according to the number of people in the conversation. With more sophisticated modeling of conversations, we might also find interesting patterns such as who is dominating the conversation. Both as a single sensor modality, and in concert with other sensed data, SSL shows promise for the complex and compelling problem of automated domestic activity recognition.

Acknowledgments

This work was sponsored in part by the National Science Foundation (ITR grants 0121661 and 0205507) and the Aware Home Research Initiative of Broadband Institute at Georgia Tech. The authors thank our colleagues in the Ubicomp Group at Georgia Tech for their helpful input to this paper, particularly Jay Summet and Kris Nagel.

References

1. Abowd, G.D., Battestini, A., and O'Connell, T. The Location Service: A framework for handling multiple location sensing technologies. GVU technical report, Georgia Institute of Technology Technical Report (2002)
2. Benesty, J. and Elko, G.W. Adaptive eigenvalue decomposition algorithm for real-time acoustic source localization system. In *Proceedings of IEEE International Conference on Acoustics, Speech, and Signal Processing(ICASSP1999)*. (2001) 937-940
3. Bian, X., Rehg, J.M., and Abowd, G.D. Sound Source Localization in Domestic Environment. GVU center, Georgia Inst. of Technology Technical Report GIT-GVU-04-06 (2004)
4. Castro, P., Chiu, P., Kremenek, T., and Muntz, R. A Probabilistic Location Service for Wireless Network Environments. In *Proceedings of Proceedings of Ubicomp 2001*. Atlanta Springer Verlag, (2001) 18-24
5. Checka, N., Wilson, K., Siracusa, M., and Darrell, T. Multiple Person and Speaker Activity Tracking with a Particle Filter. In *Proceedings of International Conference on Acoustics, Speech, and Signal Processing*. (2004)
6. Cheverst, K. Developing a Context-Aware Electronic Tourist Guide: Some Issues and Experiences. In *Proceedings of Proc. 2000 Conf. Human Factors in Computing Systems*. New York ACM Press, (2000) 17-24
7. DiBiase, J., Silverman, H., and Brandstein, M., *Robust Localization in Reverberant Rooms*, in *Microphone Arrays: Signal Processing Techniques and Applications*, M.S. Brandstein and D.B. Ward, Editors. 2001, Springer.
8. Haritaoglu, I., Harwood, D., and Davis, L.S. W4: Real-Time Surveillance of People and Their Activities. In *Proceedings of IEEE Trans. On PAMI*. (2000)
9. Harter, A. and Hopper, A., A Distributed Location System for the Active Office. IEEE Network. **8**(1) (1994) 62-70

10. Harter, A., Hopper, A., Steggles, P., Ward, A., and Webster, P. The Anatomy of a Context-Aware Application. In *Proceedings of Int'l Conf. Mobile Computing and Networking (MobiCom 99).* New York ACM Press, (1999) 59-68

11. Hightower, J. and Borriello, G., Location Systems for Ubiquitous Computing. Computer,IEEE Computer Society Press. **34**(8) (2001) 57-66

12. Hudson, S., Fogarty, J., Atkeson, C., Avrahami, D., Forlizzi, J., Kiesler, S., Lee, J., and Yang, J. Predicting Human Interruptability with Sensors: A Wizard of Oz Feasibility Study. In *Proceedings of CHI Letters (Proceedings of the CHI '03 Conference on Human Factors in Computing Systems).* (2003) 377-384

13. Intel Research Place Lab Project. http://www.placelab.org (Downloaded on Oct. 6, 2004).

14. Intel Research SHARP Project. http://seattleweb.intel-research.net/projects/activity (Downloaded on Oct 6, 2004).

15. Knapp, C.H. and Carter, G.C., The generalized correlation method for estimation of time delay,". IEEE Transaction on Acoustics, Speech and Signal Process. ASSP-24. **24** (1976) 320-327

16. Koile, K., Tollmar, K., Demirdjian, D., Shrobe, H., and Darrell, T. Activity Zones for Context-Aware Computing. In *Proceedings of Ubicomp 2003.* (2003) 90-106

17. Krumm, J., Harris, S., Meyers, B., Brumitt, B., Hale, M., and Shafer, S. Multi-Camera Multi-Person Tracking for EasyLiving. In *Proceedings of IEEE Workshop on Visual Surveillance.* Dublin, Ireland (2000)

18. Nagel, K.S., Hudson, J.M., and Abowd, G.D. Predictors of Availability in Home Life Context-Mediated Communication. In *Proceedings of Computer Supported Collaborative Work, 2004.* Chicago, IL USA (2004)

19. Priyantha, N.B., Chakraborty, A., and Balakrishnan, H. The Cricket Location-Support System. In *Proceedings of Proc. 6th Ann. Int'l Conf. Mobile Computing and Networking (Mobicom 00).* New York, 2000 ACM Press, (2000) 32-43

20. Rehg, J.M., Morris, D.D., and Kanade, T., Ambiguities in Visual Tracking of Articulated Objects Using Two- and Three-Dimensional Models. Int. J. of Robotics Research. **22**(6) (2003) 393-418

21. Rui, Y. and Florencio, D. New direct approaches to robust sound source localization. In *Proceedings of Proc. of IEEE ICME 2003.* Baltimore, MD (2003)

22. Schmandt, C. and Vallejo, G. "LISTENIN" to domestic environments from remote locations. In *Proceedings of Proceedings of the 9th International Conference on Auditory Display.* Boston University, USA (2003)

23. Tapia, M., Intille, S.S., and Larson, K. Activity Recognition in the Home Using Simple and Ubiquitous Sensors. In *Proceedings of Proceedings of Pervasive 2004: the Second International Conference on Pervasive Computing.* Springer, (2004)

24. Venkatesh, A.: Computers and Other Interactive Technologies for the Home, in *Communications of the ACM.* (1996). p. 47-54

25. Wang, C., Griebel, S., and M., B. Robust Automatic Video-Conferencing With Multiple Cameras And Microphones. In *Proceedings of IEEE International Conference on Multimedia.* (2000)

26. Wren, C., Azarbayejani, A., Darrell, T., and A., P. Pfinder: Real-Time Tracking of the Human Body. In *Proceedings of IEEE Transactions on Pattern Analysis and Machine Intelligence.* (1997)

Tracking Locations of Moving Hand-Held Displays Using Projected Light

Jay Summet and Rahul Sukthankar

GVU Center and College of Computing, Georgia Institute of Technology,
801 Atlantic Drive, Atlanta, GA 30332
summetj@cc.gatech.edu
Intel Research Pittsburgh, 417 South Craig Street,
Suite 300 Pittsburgh, PA 15213
rahul.sukthankar@intel.com

Abstract. Lee *et al.* have recently demonstrated display positioning using optical sensors in conjunction with temporally-coded patterns of projected light. This paper extends that concept in two important directions. First, we enable such sensors to determine their own location without using radio synchronization signals – allowing cheaper sensors and protecting location privacy. Second, we track the optical sensors over time using adaptive patterns, minimizing the extent of distracting temporal codes to small regions, thus enabling the remainder of the illuminated region to serve as a useful display while tracking. Our algorithms have been integrated into a prototype system that projects content onto a small, moving surface to create an inexpensive hand-held display for pervasive computing applications.

1 Introduction and Related Work

Augmenting objects in the world with projected computer output is becoming more feasible as projector prices fall and quality improves. Projection screens made of paper, cardboard, or foam core board are so cheap as to be disposable, and could be distributed to visitors at a museum, art gallery or mass-transit system. By carrying one of these display boards under a ceiling mounted projector, the visitor could access background information about an exhibit, artwork, or train schedule, while the valuable infrastructure (projectors) remains secure from vandalism or theft.

However, projecting output onto objects has traditionally required a time-consuming calibration step, and projecting output onto moving objects has proved to be challenging. Vision systems such as the Visual Panel [9] can track quadrangles suitable for use as projection screens in real time, but difficulty arises when the quadrangle is simultaneously illuminated with dynamic content from a projector. The Hyper-Mask[8] used active IR-LED's and an IR-camera to track a white mask and project a character's face on it. The range of that system was limited by the power of the IR-LED's, sensitivity of the IR-camera, and ambient IR illumination.

Recent approaches to localizing objects using active embedded light sensors has greatly decreased the calibration time, but not yet achieved projection on moving ob-

H.W. Gellersen et al. (Eds.): PERVASIVE 2005, LNCS 3468, pp. 37–46, 2005.

jects. Raskar *et al.* [5] demonstrated the use of photo-sensitive electronic sensors to locate objects within a projection beam. Single pixel light sensors and radio boards were affixed to or embedded within objects of interest. After the projector sent a synchronizing radio signal, the sensors were illuminated by a location-encoding Gray code[2] from the projector, and could determine their location and radio it back to the projector system. Lee *et al.* [4] used similar technology, replacing the radio with a wired tether, to locate display surfaces within a projector's beam for user output purposes.

These previous methods have the following problems:

- **Brittleness to Sensing Errors.** If a light value is received incorrectly, the calculated location value is incorrect, and no indication of the error is given.
- **Sensor Cost.** Because the Raskar *et al.* wireless sensors required a radio receiver (for synchronization), in addition to a transmitter, this increases the cost and power requirements for each sensor. The tethered sensors in Lee *et al.* lack true portability, making them unsuitable for non-laboratory use.
- **Sensor Motion.** The previous approaches assume that the location of sensors does not change, and only needs to be measured once. This precludes using the technique on a mobile hand-held screen.

We aim to address these shortcomings in this work. The remainder of this paper is organized as follows: Section 1 describes our scheme for including error-controlling codes into the projected data pattern, and how this solves the first two problems mentioned above. Section 3 describes our approach to continuous tracking of sensors using projected light, while retaining the majority of the projection surface as a user display (Figure 1). Preliminary quantitative results confirm that our system is capable of reliably tracking relatively slow-moving hand-held display screens and objects.

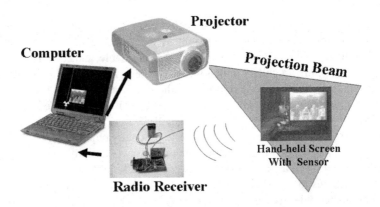

Fig. 1. System Diagram - While moving, a sensor on the hand-held screen detects location information from the projector and broadcasts it over the radio. A radio receiver returns this information to the computer, which adjusts the display accordingly to keep the projected image on the screen

2   Transmitting Location Data

Our sensor (shown in Figure 2), uses a low cost micro-controller, similar to those used in automotive remote key-less entry devices, with a built in radio transmitter, but no receiver[1]. We used an inexpensive photo diode as a single pixel light sensor. Lee et al. showed that using fiber optics connected to such sensors could be easily embedded in a white screen and the screen would provide "a light diffuser that helps bounce light into the fiber even at very shallow projection angles" [4].

Fig. 2. Left: Optical sensor (lower front), attached to rfPIC transmitter board. **Right:** Sensor (under thumb) mounted on the transmitter board (behind thumb), at the bottom left corner of a hand-held projection screen. With one sensor the system tracks the motion of the screen in two dimensions while preserving most of the display. This allows the image to remain centered on the surface during tracking. With four sensors, the surface can be tracked through arbitrary motions in 3D space (see Section 5)

When a single-pixel optical sensor receives data from a projector (which updates at 60Hz) it records a new intensity value every frame. Our system, like previous work, projects black and white patterns, delivering one bit value (zero or one) per projector frame. In the previous systems, the location was encoded with Gray codes. For example, when using 10 bits of location data, or the 1024 unique locations of a 32x32 grid, the (X,Y) coordinate (8,8) would be represented as {0,1,1,0,0,0,1,1,0,0} (in Gray Codes, 8={0,1,1,0,0}, and in this example the X and Y position would be independently encoded then concatenated).

Over the period of 10 frames, each of the 1024 different on-screen positions cycles through its own unique code series, producing a unique pattern of light and dark flashes. In this example, a sensor could determine its own location with only 10 projected frames/flashes (1/6th of a second), *if it knew where the beginning of the code was.*

---

[1] Radio receivers are more difficult and expensive to build than transmitters. The rfPIC 12F675 micro-controller costs $2.32 USD in quantities over 1600.

2.1   Error Controlling Code

In previous work, the sensors were either tethered to the projecting computer, making synchronization a non-issue, or a radio signal was used to indicate the beginning of the projected packet. But, an independent sensor without a radio receiver has no way of determining when a pattern has started.

One way to solve this problem is the inclusion of a framing pattern (which can never appear in a normal location pattern). Unfortunately, because Gray Codes use all possible patterns of ones and zeros, there is no appropriate framing pattern available that is shorter than the localization pattern. Additionally, a framing pattern does not solve the problem of bit errors.

Using a Hamming code[3], SECDED (Single-bit Error Correction Double-bit Error Detection), to transmit the data pattern allows an independent sensor to both synchronize with the data source, as well as detect bit errors. The SECDED code requires the use of $(log_2 N) + 1$ check bits for N data bits. We chose to use the SECDED code because it was straightforward to implement on an 8-bit micro-controller without floating point math support, and limited processing power and memory. The SECDED code can correct one bit of error, and detect (but not correct) two error bits. To increase robustness, we used it solely for error detection.

In our implementation, which delivers 16 bits of location information and uses 5 check bits, the SECDED code increases packet size and transmission time

Fig. 3. Single projected frame of Gray Code & Check-bit Code pattern

by 31%. This reduces our location data speed from a potential 3.75 packets per second to 2.85 packets per second, but gives us automatic synchronization and two bits of error detection per 21 bit packet (Figure 4).

2.2   Validating Received Packets

While receiving bits from the optical sensors, the rfPIC 12F675 micro-controller on our sensor examines the last 21 bits received, attempting to validate the packet. If the SECDED code indicates that a valid packet was received, the sensor knows that it is synchronized with the bit-stream and that no bit errors have occurred. It then decodes the data bits to determine its own (X,Y) location within the projection beam. In our system, the 16 bits were used to deliver 10 bits of location information (a 32x32 grid) and the remaining six bits were used for a projector ID, allowing up to 64 separate projectors to be identified.

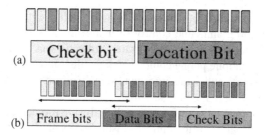

Fig. 4. (a) 21 bit location packet showing 5 check bits and 16 data bits, (b) A stream of three 8 bit tracking packets showing framing bits, data bits, and check bits. Arrows indicate the 10 bit pattern that is decoded, which includes framing bits at each end

Using an XGA projector, our 32x32 grid provides unique locations that are 32x24 pixels in size. The size of the physical area covered by a 32x24 pixel region depends upon the distance of the sensor from the projector, and does not represent a minimum accuracy of our system. If more accuracy is desired, the tracking pattern (in Section 3) can be used to "zero-in" on the sensor, down to a 2x2 pixel level of accuracy for DLP projectors[2].

2.3   High Scalability

Because decoding the stream of sensor values is done locally, the only data that needs to be returned to the infrastructure is the successfully decoded location packet (two bytes, including location and projector ID), and a three byte sensor ID. In our implementation this is a total of five bytes, which allows 32 projectors, and over 16 million sensors. By adding a few more bytes the number of projectors (and sensors) can be easily expanded.

Local decoding also allows the sensor to activate its radio and return location data only when it has successfully decoded a location packet, saving power and reducing the burden on the shared resource of the RF frequency. Additionally, the sensor knows when the last successful location packet was detected, and its own location, allowing it to take action independent of the infrastructure.

Sensors without on-board decoding must broadcast the data stream continuously, which can pose bandwidth problems over low power RF links, and must rely upon the infrastructure to inform them of their location.

2.4   Independent Operation

In our sample application, the micro-controller transmitted its location to the projecting computer, so that the infrastructure could switch to a tracking mode and display content on the hand-held screen attached to the sensor (See Section 3). However, if the sensor was only interested in determining its own location (similar to a GPS receiver), it would not need to divulge its observations to the infrastructure. The Office of the Future

---

[2] Due to automatic spatial dithering in the hardware of DLP projector, a computer cannot achieve accurate intensity control of pixel groups smaller than 2x2.

project [6] assumes that all lights in an environment will eventually be replaced with projectors, allowing programmable control over the illumination of every centimeter of every surface. If a location-providing infrared projector was mounted over a conference table, a person's mobile phone could switch to silent mode and be able to provide their spouse with location and status information in response to an SMS query, without revealing this information to the infrastructure.

Instead of providing location information directly, the projector could encode other data based upon the location of the optical sensor. For example, a projected electronic classified advertisement board could have a small flashing circle after every telephone number or URL in each advertisement. A user with a camera phone could use it as a single pixel optical sensor, and hold it under the flashing circle of a bankruptcy lawyer or mental health support group to quickly record the telephone number without notifying the infrastructure that the information had been recorded.

3   Tracking

As with the work by Raskar *et al.* and Lee *et al.*, when projecting a full-screen localization pattern, the projector cannot be used to display graphics. However, once the location of a sensor is detected, it is possible to switch to a "tracking" mode, which projects a small pattern over located sensors, but leaves the rest of the projection area free for user display purposes. Additionally, the tracking pattern can be used to "zero-in" on a static sensor, increasing accuracy (Figure 5).

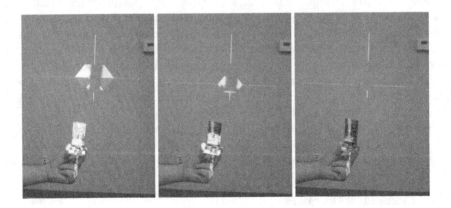

Fig. 5. Three frames from a video of the tracking pattern "zeroing-in" on a near-static sensor. The pattern size was artificially increased at the beginning of this sequence by covering the sensor for two seconds. For purposes of illustration our system is projecting red (horizontal) and green (vertical) lines which cross at the detected location of the sensor

Once the sensor is located, it is only necessary to detect if it moves, and if so, in which direction. Our system does this by projecting a hexagonal pattern with seven distinct areas. The central section covers the sensor if it does not move, and the six surrounding "wedges" indicate the direction of motion the sensor reports detecting. Identifying these seven areas require only three bits of data to be transmitted in each packet (The projector ID is known from the previously decoded localization packet).

We add two framing bits at the beginning of each packet, as well as three check bits, resulting in an 8-bit packet. We choose to alternate the framing bits of each packet between two zeros {0,0} and two ones {1,1}, enabling us to use both the framing bits from the current packet, as well as the framing bits from the following packet to synchronize and detect errors in the transmission channel. The current packet structure allows us to project 7.5 packets per second, which is just enough to track slow hand motions, approximately 12.8 cm/sec when 1.5m from the projector, as we will show below.

In Figure 2 (right) the system is projecting a hexagonal tracking pattern onto the sensor to track its location as it moves. The tracking pattern is intentionally difficult to see, as it is projected on a non-reflective portion of the hand-held screen. The system is using the detected location of the sensor to keep a photograph centered on the reflective display screen attached to the sensor[3].

Our system uses a quasi-static motion model, which assumes that the sensor remains at the last reported position, but varies the size of the tracking pattern (hexagon) depending upon its level of confidence in the accuracy of that location. The confidence metric is determined based upon the average frequency of location reports in the past and the time since the last location report was received, as follows:

- If we have not received a report for three times the average reporting frequency, we grow the tracker by a factor of 50%.
- If we receive a report that is either earlier than the average frequency or late by no more than 10%, we shrink the tracking pattern by 25% until it reaches a preset minimum size.
- If we have not received a location report for 2.5 seconds, we assume that the sensor has been lost, and we shift back to the global localization pattern.

These behavior rules accurately size the tracking pattern based upon the sensor's motion. Figure 5 shows the tracking pattern in the process of shrinking to locate a near-static sensor with greater accuracy.

Table 1. Measured successful tracking speeds and recovery times with projector pixels very close to 1x1mm in size. Recovery time is the time from the end of the motion until the tracking system had resolved the sensor's location with the highest level of accuracy available; the sensor's location was known with slightly lesser accuracy throughout the time the sensor was in motion

Speed - Distance (mm)	Recovery Time	Speed - Distance (projector pixels)
73 mm/sec - 314 mm	0.63 sec	74 pixels/sec - 319 pixels
77 mm/sec - 289 mm	0.50 sec	78 pixels/sec - 293 pixels
110 mm/sec - 349 mm	0.53 sec	112 pixels/sec - 354 pixels
128 mm/sec - 320 mm	0.53 sec	130 pixels/sec - 325 pixels

---

[3] Video: http://www.cc.gatech.edu/~summetj/movies/BurningWell320.avi.

Table 1 presents four typical "tracked movements", measured with a calibrated video camera, where the sensor moved from one stable location to another over a period of a few seconds. We chose to test the system with the sensor only 1.5m from the projector, which is reflected in the speed and distance given in millimeters, which is specific to our testing setup. At this distance, projector pixels were very close to 1mm in size. The motion distance presented in pixels is a more accurate measure of angular sensitivity of the system, which is invariant to changes in distance or focal length. For example, if we doubled the size of the projected region by moving the projector away from the sensor, the tracking speed in real units (millimeters) would double (to 25.6 cm/sec at 3m distance from the projector), while the location accuracy would be quartered. However, as the display can be located with no more accuracy than the projector provides, the degradation in accuracy is not a major problem.

4   Alternative Methods

One major advantage of using sensors to detect the (optical) projector output is that the calibration between the sensor locations (screen) and projector space is obtained directly. Alternative methods for calibrating a projector to a moving display surface involve computer vision using a camera or magnetic motion tracking sensors. The Visual Panel system can track a non-augmented quadrangle screen and translate finger motions over the screen into user interface events, but did not demonstrate projecting output on the screen [9]. By augmenting the surface with IR emitting LED's, the computer vision task is made much easier, but the IR camera and visible light projector must be calibrated [8]. Dynamic Shader Lamps project onto mobile surfaces by using tethered magnetic 6DOF trackers (affixed to the surface) which are calibrated to the projectors in a manual process [1].

5   Future Work and Conclusions

Figure 2 (right) shows an image projected onto a display surface which is tracked using a single sensor. Using a single sensor allows the surface to translate in two dimensions, but does not detect motion in the Z axis or rotations. By adding three more photo-diodes to the system (connected to the same micro-controller and radio transmitter) at the other corners of the display surface, an image could be projected upon it through arbitrary motions in space.

Additionally, as the board will already have an embedded micro-controller and radio transmitter, we intend to further augment it with a contact-sensitive film, for touch input. In addition to returning sensor location reports, the micro-controller can sense and return the location of user touch events on the board's surface, thus developing an extremely inexpensive mobile device which supports user interaction (with the support of environmentally mounted projectors). Such a board could be manufactured in quantities for $10 to $20 USD, and could be loaned or rented to the public with a negligible deposit.

Currently, the initial locating pattern is very visible and attention drawing, covering the entire projection area with a rapidly flashing pattern. This issue could be resolved by encoding the locating pattern in such a way as to be imperceptible to humans. For example, the projector could act as a lamp, throwing an apparently uniform white light which is modulated over time in a manner detectable to a sensor but not a human observer, allowing the system to share the optical sensory channel with humans [7]. Such a coding would slow the initial location acquisition, but could provide a much more user friendly experience.

6   Conclusion

In conclusion, this paper demonstrates a projection system that encodes location data within the projection and a sensor tag which has the following desirable and novel characteristics:

1. Ability to self-synchronize and independently decode location data solely from the optical signal.
2. Robustness to sensing errors due to the use of error detecting codes.
3. Ability to track a sensor while using the remainder of the projection area for graphical output.

Acknowledgments

The Intel Research Pittsburgh lab staff and Ubiquitous Computing Research Group at Georgia Institute of Technology provided valuable feedback on this research. The authors would like to thank Jason Campbell for technical support, Johnny Lee for technical discussions, and Gregory Abowd for editing assistance.

References

1. Deepak Bandyopadhyay, Ramesh Raskar, and Henry Fuchs. Dynamic shader lamps: Painting on real objects. In *The Second IEEE and ACM International Symposium on Augmented Reality (ISAR'01)*, 2001.
2. James R. Bitner, Gideon Erlich, and Edward M. Reingold. Efficient generation of the binary reflected gray code and its applications. *Communications of the ACM*, 19(9):517–521, September 1976.
3. Richard W. Hamming. Error detecting and error correcting codes. *Bell Systems Journal*, (29):147–160, April 1950.
4. Johnny C. Lee, Paul H. Dietz, Dan Maynes-Aminzade, Ramesh Raskar, and Scott Hudson. Automatic projector calibration with embedded light sensors. In *Proceedings of UIST 2004*, pages 123–126, 2004.
5. Ramesh Raskar, Paul Beardsley, Jeroen van Baar, Yao Wang, Paul Dietz, Johnny Lee, Darren Leigh, and Thomas Willwacher. Rfig lamps: Interacting with a self-describing world via photosensing wireless tags and projectors. In *Proceedings of SIGGRAPH'04*, volume 23, pages 406–415, 2004.
6. Ramesh Raskar, Greg Welch, Matt Cutts, Adam Lake, Lev Stesin, and Henry Fuchs. The office of the future: A unified approach to image-based modeling and spatially immersive displays. *Computer Graphics*, 32(Annual Conference Series):179–188, 1998.

7. Joshua R. Smith. Imperceptible sensory channels. *IEEE Computer*, 37(6):84–85, June 2004.
8. Tatsuo Yotsukura, Frank Nielsen, Kim Binsted, Shigeo Morishima, and Claudio S. Pinhanez. Hypermask: Talking Head Projected onto Real Object. *The Visual Computer*, 18(2):111–120, 2002.
9. Zhengyou Zhang, Ying Wu, Ying Shan, and Steven Shafer. Visual panel: virtual mouse, keyboard and 3d controller with an ordinary piece of paper. In *PUI '01: Proceedings of the 2001 workshop on Perceptive user interfaces*, pages 1–8. ACM Press, 2001.

Bathroom Activity Monitoring Based on Sound

Jianfeng Chen, Alvin Harvey Kam, Jianmin Zhang, Ning Liu, and Louis Shue

Institute for Infocomm Research,
21 Heng Mui Keng Terrace, Singapore, 119613
jfchen@i2r.a-star.edu.sg

Abstract. In this paper an automated bathroom activity monitoring system based on acoustics is described. The system is designed to recognize and classify major activities occurring within a bathroom based on sound. Carefully designed HMM parameters using MFCC features are used for accurate and robust bathroom sound event classification. Experiments to validate the utility of the system were performed firstly in a constrained setting as a proof-of-concept and later in an actual trial involving real people using their bathroom in the normal course of their daily lives. Preliminary results are encouraging with the accuracy rate for most sound categories being above 84%. We sincerely believe that the system contributes towards increased understanding of personal hygiene behavioral problems that significantly affect both informal care-giving and clinical care of dementia patients.

1 Introduction

The world is rapidly graying. Older adults already constitute one-fifth of the population of much of Western Europe and Japan [1]. Here in Singapore, it is estimated that one in five persons will be over 65 years old in 30 years' time. Older people are known to be the most expensive demographic group to be treated as longevity gives rise to costly age-related disabilities and chronic diseases.

A major challenge in ensuring sustainable healthcare costs and maintaining the quality of life for the elderly is to allow senior citizens to live independently in their own homes for as long as possible while facilitating informal care-giving. A critical element in ensuring the well being of the elderly, especially those afflicted by dementia and other forms of cognitive decline, is an accurate account of the subject's physical, behavioral and psychosocial functioning. This is achieved in some ways through a detailed understanding of their activities of daily living (ADL).

One class of ADL of utmost concern to both caregivers and clinicians is personal hygiene activities occurring within the private confines of the bathroom. It is quite common for people with dementia to forget about, or lose interest in, bathing and other personal hygiene activities. There were various reasons for this [2]: a) washing and cleaning oneself are intimate, private activities. People with dementia may feel particularly embarrassed if they are incontinent, and may refuse to bathe in denial of the problem; b) the person may feel uncomfortable. The room may be too hot or cold, or produce feelings of claustrophobia which confuses them; c) getting undressed, having a wash and brushing teeth can be overwhelmingly complex tasks because of

H.W. Gellersen et al. (Eds.): PERVASIVE 2005, LNCS 3468, pp. 47–61, 2005.

the many steps involved; d) some people with dementia may have a changed sense of perception of hot and cold water, caused by damage to the hypothalamus. They may also feel a different sensation from water; e) fear of falling may be another problem. Feeling out of control and powerless may add to a person shunning all personal hygiene activities within the bathroom altogether.

The understanding of personal hygiene behavioral patterns and problems thus significantly affect both informal care-giving and clinical care. The current practice in the field of elderly care is to obtain behavioral information through observer or self reporting. Direct behavioral observations of bathroom and toileting activities by clinicians or even family caregivers are embarrassing and even humiliating due to privacy reasons. Due to similar privacy reasons especially during the testing phase, the use of video sensors is inappropriate. Self-reporting meanwhile is not reliable for dementia patients suffering from cognitive decline.

The automated bathroom monitoring system we proposed in this paper is developed with the motivation to address the above unmet needs. The system is able to objectively capture behavioral patterns within the bathroom accurately and free from manpower constraints. Further benefits lie in the need for nighttime observations, such as in clinical studies of nocturia, nocturnal polyuria or nocturnal incontinence where self-reporting for even cognitively normal subjects is troublesome and highly inaccurate. Although less intrusive than using video, we acknowledge that the system may still result in some loss of privacy for the individual being studied. We will address this issue in depth further on.

1.1 Review of Related Work

Automated activity monitoring within bedrooms and bathrooms is not new. For example, motion sensors were used for activity detection within the confines of the bedroom and the bathroom [3]. These sensors could however only acquire limited information pertaining mainly to movement trajectories of the subject without being able to provide useful behavioral information relating to personal hygiene activities. In [4], various 'off-the-shelf' sensors were used to collect data on four different behavioural domains: medical adherence, movements throughout the house, bathroom use and meal preparation. While the above system permit continuous, unobstructive monitoring of certain ADLs, it is really the objects in the environment, e.g. pill bottle, the refrigerator door, a kitchen cabinet, that are electronically monitored, not the individual her/himself.

Activity recognition based on body worn sensors, in particular accelerators, has been demonstrated in [5]. This approach is unfortunately inappropriate for cognitively challenged dementia patients who will remove these sensors at will or is it suitable for monitoring activities such as bathing. In [6], the COACH system, which monitors progress and provides assistance in the washroom during hand washing, requires the wearing of a bracelet, which facilitates the tracking of user's movements. Besides being found to be obtrusive and bothersome, the system generated a fair degree of errors and false alarms.

More recently, a system which uses radio-frequency-identification (RFID) technology to infer the undergoing activities was proposed in [7]. Low cost RFID tags were embedded into representative objects that are highly relevant to the activities of interest. An RFID-detecting glove was designed to detect nearby objects and a probabilistic engine would infer activities from detected object-level interactions. This system could provide detailed information on the exact steps taken in performing a certain activity but the need to wear a glove probably makes it unsuitable for tracking personal hygiene activities such as bathing.

A vision of a Smart Home, which facilitates aging-in-place, was described in [8]. Under this vision, a wireless network of sensor motes will be installed ubiquitously within the home (including the bathroom) to monitor the activities of the subject. The type of sensor modalities that would be useful was however not discussed. Simple motion detecting, pressure-based or even water flow sensors may not be sufficient to delineate the subtly different personal hygiene and toileting activities. For example, a subject may be detected as sitting on the toilet seat but no meaningful conclusion could be inferred on exactly what the subject is really doing. Or a tap may be turned on but we will not know why. The gap between 'things happening within the home' and actual human activities taking place and specific behaviors being exhibited need to be bridged.

In spaces where the use of video surveillance is not socially acceptable, sounds may provide the alternative source of information regarding activities that are occurring and behaviors that are exhibited. This is especially true for personal hygiene and toileting activities within the private confines of the bathroom, each of which are typically associated with distinct sounds. Microphones that capture sounds with sufficient fidelity for automated processing are also much cheaper in comparison with other sensors. Finally, acoustics-based behavioral understanding systems work from a distance: they do not constrain subjects by requiring them to wear special devices; a prerequisite for individuals with dementia. It is therefore no surprise that computational auditory scene analysis (CASA), the understanding of events through processing environmental sounds and human vocalizations, has become an increasing important research area [9]-[12].

1.2 A Discussion on Privacy

One key question pertaining to the issue of privacy remains: will sound surveillance be socially acceptable in private places like the bathroom where the use of video is not? In attempting to answer this question, we quickly realized that we do not have a ready framework to address this issue. We felt that it would be necessary to return to basics and first attempt to understand what privacy really is. We will not be so bold as to define privacy, but we will attempt to qualify, within the scope of this work, the phrase personal privacy.

A useful term that can make this discussion more concrete is Palen and Dourish's [13] *genre of disclosures*, which are socially constructed patterns of privacy management involving recognizable, socially meaningful patterns of information disclosure and use. Amidst a given genre, people expect each other to disclose *this* information but not *that*, under *these* conditions but not *those*, to *this* but not *that* person, and to use information in *this* but not *that* way. Within this framework, the degree of perceived 'privacy loss' caused by the introduction by a new technological construct is related to its non-conformity to these expectations of disclosures within a given genre. With this, we can rephrase our original question more meaningfully, i.e.: does sound surveillance within the bathroom conform to the expectations of our societal genre of disclosures?

We do not have a clear answer to this question but will be using this framework to address this issue once again towards the end of this paper.

1.3 System Summary

In this paper, we describe an acoustics-based system that is able to detect, identify and selectively record activities occurring within the bathroom with the ultimate aim of automatically generating customized personal hygiene behavioral reports for the benefit of caregivers and geriatric clinicians. Personal hygiene activities that are studied and modeled include showering, brushing of teeth, washing hands and urination. The system is designed to present a list of detected and classified bathroom activities with associated details such the time of occurrence, duration and sequence of occurrence for each bathroom visit. All these information are also automatically condensed into a summarized daily report, with adjustable triggers for automatic alert notification based on customized definition of 'abnormal' behaviors.

Fig. 1. Photo of a typical Singapore Housing Development Board flat's bathroom (the very bathroom used for our full blown trial as will be described later on)

The targeted bathrooms for our system are those within Singapore Housing Development Board's flats, a typical structure of which is shown in Fig. 1. It will not be appropriate to install advanced sensor systems that take up precious space and unnecessarily increase the complexity of a system that needs to be as simple as possible.

For the remainder of the paper, we shall assume that, without the loss of generality, the system will be detecting activities performed by a single individual. For bathrooms frequented by more than one individual, we shall assume that there is an available identification system, based on RFID or other technologies, which helps resolve the identify of the subject being monitored.

The rest of the paper is organized as follows. In section 2, the sensor setup, system training and feature extraction methodologies, as well as the full operation of the system will be described in detail. Experimental results and performance evaluation of the system will be shown in section 3. We conclude and discuss further work in section 4.

2 System Description

The main sounds associated with activities occurring within in a bathroom include (a) showering, (b) washing-hands, (c) brushing-teeth, (d) flushing, (e) urination, (f) defecation, (g) human vocalizations (cough, laugh, sigh, etc), and various miscellaneous sounds such as footsteps, sounds of dressing/undressing, combing of hair, etc. In this paper, we shall describe the detection and automatic classification of sounds (a) to (e), as our work on defecation detection and human vocalization classification is still on-going.

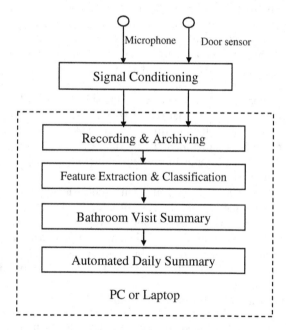

Fig. 2. Block diagram of system

2.1 Sensor Setup

The block diagram of our system is shown in Fig. 2 with the main sensor being a single miniature omni-directional microphone. A multiple microphone system as in [12] would unnecessarily complicate the sound-processing task due to the presence of strong reverberations within the targeted small bathrooms. Signal from the microphone is pre-amplified and routed into one of the two channels of the stereo *line-in* port of a PC sound card. To maximize overall signal quality of all major bathroom activities, we have found that the microphone is best installed near the washing basin to ensure that the weak sounds associated with brushing teeth and washing hands can be picked up clearly while in no way sacrificing the quality of the resultant more distant sounds of flushing, showering etc. which are typically loud.

An infrared door sensor is set up outside the bathroom to detect the subject entering the bathroom; its output being routed to the other *line-in* stereo port of the sound card, making this channel an 'entering/leaving' indicator. A simple energy-based detection scheme on this channel will be sufficient to notify the system every time the subject is entering or leaving the bathroom.

2.2 Methodology of Collection of Sound Samples for System Training

The exact nature of sounds arising from activities occurring within a bathroom are obviously a function of a bathroom's size and layout, material of the floor, type of shower and flushing system used etc. Proper training of the system using sound samples acquired from the same bathroom in which the system is to be installed is essential, analogous to the practice adopted for speech recognition whereby the system is individually trained on each user for speaker dependent recognition.

For clear audio-temporal delineation during system training, the sound capture for each activity of interest was carried out separately. A number of male and female subjects were used to produce the sounds of interest; each subject would typically go into the bathroom, generated the sounds of interest and leave. These steps would be repeated numerous times for each individual of the subject pool and for each activity of interest. It is important to note that in the generation of these sounds, associated 'background' sounds such as the shuffling of feet, undressing, application of soap, etc., are being simultaneously recorded. The variability in the captured sounds of the each activity provide realistic input for system training, and increase the robustness and predictive power of the resultant classifier.

Flushing sounds are generally loud and fairly consistent. Very few samples are typically needed to sufficiently train the classification model. Hands washing, on the contrary, exhibited a high degree of variability even for the same individual. The duration of the hand washing episodes varied significantly; sometimes the test subject applied soap and sometimes they did not. This required us to collect many more samples for hand washing sounds to capture the diversity of the sound of this activity.

2.3 General Observations of Bathroom Sounds

The typical waveforms of the sounds of four different bathroom activities are shown in Fig. 3. As can be seen, the flushing sound as depicted in the waveform of Fig. 3(a) is of short duration (about 5 seconds) and of rather high amplitude. It is almost unchanged every time. On the other hand, showering sounds will last for different lengths from a few seconds to more than an hour. Urination sounds (especially of a male subject) will be intermittent, lasting a couple of seconds long, while hand washing sounds are typically continuous but last for different lengths. Signals of human sighing are not displayed as it is difficult to find a 'typical' sigh.

The spectral of these typical sounds are analyzed and shown in Fig. 4. We can see that each sound has its distinct frequency distribution, corresponding to their distinct resonant frequency which is a function of the sound generation mechanism. For example, the flushing sound has a resonant frequency in the range of 265-285Hz, while for washing hand sound, the resonant frequency lies between 200-210Hz. Urination sounds have a strong frequency component at 600Hz while showering sounds shows a rather wide bandwidth of up to 6000Hz. For showering sounds, there are some strong frequency components between 100-300Hz, which can be explained as the low frequency splashing sound and their reverberations within the small shower enclosure of our bathroom. On the other hand, the high frequency components are contributed by sounds of water directly striking the floor. Generally, the major energy of these sounds is distributed below 5500 Hz and therefore a sampling rate of 11,025 Hz will be enough to preserve most features of these sounds.

2.4 Feature Extraction and Classification Methodology

It was obvious that simple frequency characterization would not be robust enough to produce good classification results. To find representative features, in [14], Cowling carried out an extensive comparative study on various transformation schemes, including the Fourier Transform (FT), Homomorphic Cepstral Coefficients (HCC), Short Time Fourier Transform (STFT), Fast Wavelet Transform (FWT), Continuous Wavelet Transform (CWT) and Mel-Frequency Cepstral Coefficient (MFCC). It was concluded that MFCC may be the best transformation for non-speech environmental sound recognition. A similar opinion was also articulated in [9]-[10]. These finding provide the essential motivation for us to use MFCC in extracting features for bathroom sound classification.

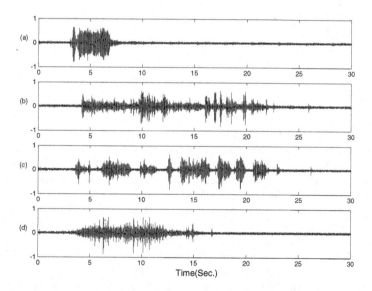

Fig. 3. Typical waveforms of four different sounds: Flushing, (b) Showering, (c) Urination (man), (d) Washing hands

An accurate and robust sound classifier is critical to the overall performance of the system. There are however many classifier approaches in the literature, e.g. those based on Hidden Markov Models (HMMs), Artificial Neural Networks (ANN), Dynamic Time Warping (DTW), Gaussian Mixture Models (GMM), etc. From these options, we have chosen an approach based on HMM as the model has a proven track record for many sound classification applications [15]. Another advantage is that it can be easily implemented using the HMM Tool Kit (HTK) [16]. It should be noted that HTK was originally designed for speech recognition, which meant we needed to carefully adapt the approach when applying in for sounds of our interest.

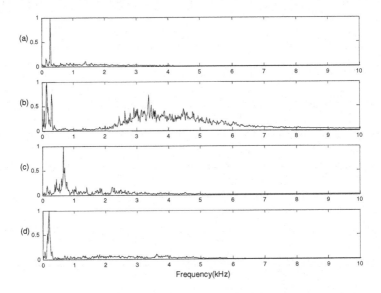

Fig. 4. Typical spectral of four different sounds: (a) Flushing, (b) Showering, (c) Urination (man), (d) Washing hands

Each sound file, corresponding to a sample of a sound event, was processed in frames pre-emphasized and windowed by a Hamming window (25 ms) with an overlap of 50%. A feature vector consisting of a 13-order MFCC characterized each frame. We modeled each sound using a left-to-right six-state continuous-density HMM without state skipping. Each HMM state was composed of two Gaussian mixture components. After a model initialization stage was done, all the HMM models were trained in three iterative cycles.

For classification, continuous HMM recognition is used. The grammar used is as follows: (<flush | shower | sigh | urination | wash-hand | silence >), which means that there is no predefined sequence for all the activities and each activity may be repeated for each bathroom visit. Special case was taken to avoid too many repetitive transcripts appearing in the final result for a single long event such as showering, while at the same time, ensuring that activities of short durations are recognized accurately.

As most bathroom sounds are intermittent, our classification system is unique that frequently, the resulting transcription number may not be equal to the number of predefined sound events. In other words, because sounds corresponding to urination or showering for example are intermittent in nature, there would be a number of 'urination' or 'shower' transcriptions being generated by the classification engine for these occurrences of these events. A general rule that we used to resolve this problem is that if a sound stops, and then restarts within a short time interval, it is considered to be a continuation of the activity of the previous instance.

3   Experimental Set-Up and Results

Experiments were carried out in two phases: a simplified scenario for proof-of-concept and a real continuous trial. The two phases were carried out in different bathrooms and involved different subjects. Common system components used for both phases included a miniature Panasonic microphone WM-034CY and its preamplifier, a commercial infrared door sensor and our software residing on a Windows platform laptop. Data was captured in real time at 11,025Hz sampling rate and 16 bits data resolution. All the data were then saved in the hard disk for post processing.

3.1   Simplified Scenario for Proof-of-Concept

The purpose of this phase is to test the performance of our system in recognizing the major bathroom events. The system was trained and tested to recognize the following 5 bathroom activities: showering, flushing, washing hands, urination (male) and human sighing. Four subjects, two males and two females, were involved in generating sounds of each activity except for urination which only the two male adults participated.

As explained earlier, the sound recording for each activity was carried out separately. For example, for showering, each subject entered the bathroom to take a shower and then leave, with this repeated a number of times for the same individual. The other subjects followed the same protocol and the entire process was repeated for each activity being tested. The resultant sound database is summarized in Table I.

The training data set was formed utilizing a '*leave-one-out*' strategy. That is, all the samples would be used for their corresponding models' training except those included in the signal under testing. Hence, each time the models were trained respectively to ensure that the samples in the testing signal were not included in the training data set.

Table 1. Composition of the 'simplified scenario' database

Activities	Samples	Total length (sec.)
1. Showering	39	724
2. Urination	12	144
3. Flushing	13	68
4. Washing Hands	49	715
5. Sighing	19	22

Since each sound file contains only a single sound event, we developed a statistical testing methodology to evaluate the system's performance on continuous sound streams of various sound events. 100 test signals were generated, each of which contained a mixture of all five sound events randomly selected from their respective classes and concatenated together with short periods of recorded background noise. For testing, the recognition accuracy rate is calculated using the following rules: the length of each segment is factored into account so that an error in transcripting a very short segment is scaled proportionately and vice versa. As a result, the final evaluation result is an accurate reflection of the true operating performance of the system.

Sound recognition results are presented in Table 2. The recognition accuracy is encouraging with most being above than 87%. The correct classification of sighing sounds was found to be very challenging due to the sounds' shortness in duration and weakness in strength, hence the increased frequency for them to be wrongly classified as a 'non-recognizable' sound event.

Table 2. Sound recognition rate for 'simplified scenario'

Class	Correct Rate (%)
1. Showering	92.57
2. Urination	88.82
3. Flushing	91.22
4. Washing Hand	87.89
5. Sighing	72.95

3.2 Real Continuous Trial

In the second phase, a trial testing the system's performance on actual bathroom behavior was conducted. The same system setup was used but on a bathroom different from that used for the first phase. For this trial, we concentrated on the following six activities: (1) showering; (2) washing hands; (3) urination; (4) defecation*; (5) flushing and (6) brushing teeth. Sighing was omitted because they occur too infrequently to provide meaningful statistical results. Four subjects were involved in the trial: a young man (32-year-old), a young lady (27-year-old), an old man and (62-year-old) an old lady (61-year-old). Bathroom visit activities were recorded for 10 full days with about **160** entries chalked up. Detailed number of bathroom activities records captured from each person and the number of samples used for training/testing are summarized in Table 3. The 'ground truth' of these activities was kept in a manual log-book against which our system will be benchmarked.

---

*Defecation was inferred through a set of heuristic logic rules operating on the relationship between the duration of a subject sitting on the toilet seat, the occurrence of urination and a flushing sound. As a temporary solution to detect someone seating on the toilet seat, we installed a simple mechanical whistle, extracted from a child's toy, under the toilet seat, which will emit a squeaky sound when someone sits down or stands up thereafter. We are using this as a 'workable hack' while searching for a more acceptable solution.

Table 3. Composition of the Database for Each Activity (unit: number of records)

Class	M1	M2	F1	F2	Training	Testing
1. Showering	23	15	18	12	24	44
2. Urination	25	37	21	52	64	71
3. Flushing	34	47	35	63	74	105
4. Washing Hands	59	75	52	78	99	165
5. Defecation	10	8	9	6	13	20
6. Brushing teeth	20	22	20	24	33	53

Note: M1- young man, M2-old man, F1-young lady, F2-old lady, Training/ testing: number of records or entries used for training / testing. (Training +Testing = M1+M2+F1+F2)

3.2.1 Special Consideration for System Training and Activity Classification

Due to the complexity of the trial set-up (the four subjects chosen are members of an actual family using their bathroom in the normal course of their daily lives), we utilized a slightly different approach for system training. Sounds recorded from the normal course of bathroom use for the first four days were used as data for system training, based on which the system's performance is benchmarked for the remaining six days of the trial.

Upon reviewing the recorded sounds after the first 4 days, we found lots of sounds generated by secondary events such as coughing, spitting, floor washing, towel squeezing, water flowing down the drain pipe, etc. The features of some of these sounds overlapped among themselves and even with some primary sounds of interest. These sounds needed to be modeled explicitly. The following integrative steps were taken to handle this challenge:

1) **Forming of 2 New Sound Classes:** Besides the six primary sound classes discussed above, three more classes were added: a) those generated by the human vocal system, such as coughing, laughing, spiting, sneezing etc., collectively grouped under the *vocal interference class*; b) those generated all other environmental sounds, such as footsteps, object dropping, floor being washed, towel being squeezed, water flowing, door opening, noise from outside the toilet outside etc., collectively grouped under the *environmental interference class*.
2) **System Training:** Sounds from the first four days of normal bathroom use were utilized as the training data. Each sound event was manually categorized into one of eight sound classes to be modeled. The same features extraction methodology described in section 2.4 was used to determine the HMM parameters of each sound class.
3) **Classification:** The grammar for the classification is broadened to include the two new interference classes.

3.2.2 System Performance for Real Continuous Trial

The overall recognition rates achieved by the system during final 6 days of the trial are tabulated in Table 4. Accuracy rates for defecation, flushing and showering are high as the sounds involved are either distinct or occur sufficiently long in real life to ease recognition. Urination and teeth brushing can be recognized reasonably well, leaving hands washing being the most challenging activity to recognize due to its relatively weak sound amplitude and in many times overlapping with other sounds.

Compared with the 'simplified scenario', the main reason behind the degradation of the recognition accuracy is the increased complexity of a real sound stream (as opposed to an artificial one) with lots more unpredictable sound interferences.

Table 4. The accuracy of recognition

Class	Correct Rate (%)
1. Showering	87.45
2. Urination	77.23
3. Defecation	93.60
4. Flushing	90.10
5. Washing Hand	68.67
6. Brushing teeth	84.23

4 System Operations

4.1 Using the System

Our Windows based software controls all functions of the system: sound detection, selective recording, recognition, consolidation and printing. The graphical user interface (GUI) of our system is shown in Fig. 5 for the benefit of our readers.

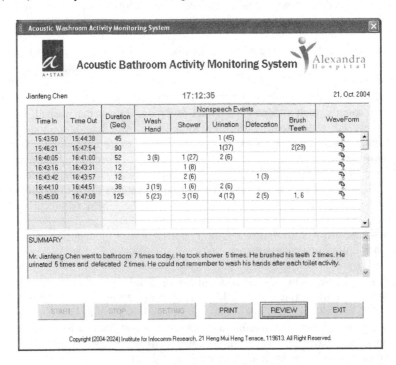

Fig. 5. Graphic User Interface of the System

Each time the subject enters the bathroom, the door sensor will be triggered and its audio output detected. The recording module is then immediately activated. Recording will continue until the subject leaves the bathroom as detected by the same door sensor. The entry time, leaving time and the duration of the bathroom visit will automatically be recorded in columns 1-3 of the GUI table of Fig. 5. The entire sound waveform captured during this period will be routed to the sound recognition and classification module which will detect and label each occurring sound event.

Detected activities will be denoted by a numerical digit indicating the sequence of its occurrence, 1 to indicate occurring first, 2 to indicate occurring second and so on. The duration of occurrence of each event is also captured and can be displayed as well if chosen to.

4.2 Automatically Generated Daily Summaries

On the stroke of midnight of each day, the whole day's activities are summarized and a daily behavioral report is automatically generated and archived in the hard drive for further reference. This report typically contains a consolidation of the frequency of occurrences of major activities of interest. Under the guidance of our geriatric clinician collaborators, normal baseline behaviors were defined, against which deviations are detected and highlighted in the 'comments' section. A series of pre-prepared words are used and intelligently strung together to form simple sentences that conform to the basic rules of English grammar. An example of this is shown below:

DAILY REPORT

Mr. Jianfeng Chen went to bathroom 7 times today. He took shower 5 times. He brushed his teeth 2 times. He urinated 5 times and defecated 2 times. He could not remember to wash his hands after each toilet activity.

Comments:

Normal but seems to have showered excessively. Recommend probing this possibly abnormal behavior.

The archival of these daily reports enables a caregiver or a doctor to review records very quickly and in the process, build a detailed understanding of the subject's bathroom behavioral patterns.

4.3 Revisiting the Issue of Privacy

We feel that it is appropriate if we return once again to the privacy framework introduced in section 1.2 and asked ourselves if it is socially acceptable for the type of information captured and the automated daily reports generated by our system be disclosed to care-givers and doctors who are caring for the monitored subject. Again we must acknowledge that we do not have a ready answer for this question. We can only hope that we have made some progress towards an affirmative answer by producing a solution that may actually be less intrusive than the alternative: the loss of independence that follows when a person is sent to a nursing home, partially due to a lack of understanding of the person's bathroom behavioral problems.

5 Conclusion

In this paper, we described a novel acoustic bathroom activity monitoring system that automatically detects and classifies major activities occurring within a bathroom. Carefully designed HMM parameters using MFCC features are used for accurate and robust bathroom sound event classification. Experiments to validate the utility of the system were performed firstly in a constrained setting as a proof-of-concept and later in an actual trial involving real people using their bathroom in the normal course of their daily lives. Preliminary results are encouraging with the accuracy rate for most sound categories being above 84%. We sincerely believe that the system contributes towards increased understanding of personal hygiene behavioral problems that significantly affect both informal care-giving and clinical care.

Besides further improving the recognition accuracy, we plan to enhance the capability of the system to identify different types of human vocalization, which provides useful information pertaining to the mental well-being of the subject. Urine flow sensors will also be integrated into the system to enable clinicians acquire better understanding in battling incontinence and lower urinary tract syndromes. The enhanced system will be shortly tested in a full-blown trial on the most needy dementia patients residing within the wards of a national hospital before evaluating its suitability as a benevolent behavior understanding system within the homes of these patients.

References

1. Cohen, J.E.: Human Population: The Next Half Century, Science, Nov 14, (2003), 1172-1175
2. Andresen, G.: Caring for People with Alzheimer's Disease, Health Professions Press, Baltimore, MD., (1995), 52
3. Chan, M., Campo, E., Esteve, D.: Monitoring Elderly People Using a Multisensor System, Proc. of 2nd International Conference On Smart Homes and Health Telematic, Singapore, (2004), 162-169
4. Glascock, A., Kutzik, D.: Behavioral Telemedicine: A New Approach to the Continuous Nonintrusive Monitoring of Activities of Daily Living, Telemedicine J., vol. 6, no. 1, (2000), 33-44
5. Lukowicz, P., Ward, J., Junker, H., Stäger M., Tröster G., Atrash A., Starner, T.: Recognizing Workshop Activity Using Body-Worn Microphones and Accelerometers, Proc. of Pervasive, Vienna, Austria (2004), 18-32
6. Alex, M.: Intelligent Environment for Older Adults with Dementia, http://www.agingtech.org/item.aspx?id=18&CAT=4&CA=1 (2004)
7. Philipose, M., Fishkin, K. P., Perkowitz, M., Patterson, D. J., Fox, D., Kautz, H., Hähnel, D.: Inferring Activities from Interactions with Objects, IEEE Pervasive Computing, Oct. (2004), 50-57
8. Philip, E. R.: Managing Care Through The air, IEEE Spectrum, vol. 12, (2004), 14-19

9. Okuno, H.G., Ogata, T., Komatani, K., Nakadai, K.: Computational Auditory Scene Analysis and Its Application to Robot Audition, International Conference on Informatics Research for Development of Knowledge Society Infrastructure (ICKS), (2004), 73–80

10. Eronen, A., Tuomi, J., Klapuri, A., Fagerlund, S., Sorsa, T., Lorho, G., Huopaniemi, J.: Audio-based Context Awareness - Acoustic Modeling and Perceptual Evaluation, Proc. of IEEE International Conference on Acoustics, Speech, and Signal Processing (ICASSP '03), vol. 5, (2003), V-529-532

11. Peltonen, V., Tuomi, J., Klapuri, A., Huopaniemi, J., Sorsa, T.: Computational auditory scene recognition, Proc. of IEEE International Conference on Acoustics, Speech, and Signal Processing (ICASSP '02), vol. 2, (2002), 1941-1944

12. Drake, L., Katsaggelos, A.K., Rutledge, J.C., Zhang, J.: Sound Source Separation via Computational Auditory Scene Analysis-enhanced Beamforming, Workshop Proceedings on Sensor Array and Multi-channel Signal Processing, (2002), 259–263

13. Palen L., Dourish P.: Unpacking "Privacy" for a Networked World, Proc. of CHI 2003 Conference on Human Factors in Computing Systems, Florida (2003), 129-136

14. Cowling, M.: Non-Speech Environmental Sound Recognition System for Autonomous Surveillance, Ph.D. Thesis, Griffith University, Gold Coast Campus (2004)

15. Rabiner, L. R., Juang, B. H.: Fundamentals of Speech Recognition, PTR Prentice-Hall Inc., New Jersey (1993)

16. Young, S.: The HTK Book, User Manual, Cambridge University Engineering Department (1995)

Simultaneous Tracking and Activity Recognition (STAR) Using Many Anonymous, Binary Sensors

D.H. Wilson and C. Atkeson

Robotics Institute,
Carnegie Mellon University,
5000 Forbes Ave.,
Pittsburgh, PA 15213
{daniel.wilson, cga}@cs.cmu.edu

Abstract. In this paper we introduce the simultaneous tracking and activity recognition (STAR) problem, which exploits the synergy between location and activity to provide the information necessary for automatic health monitoring. Automatic health monitoring can potentially help the elderly population live safely and independently in their own homes by providing key information to caregivers. Our goal is to perform accurate tracking and activity recognition for multiple people in a home environment. We use a "bottom-up" approach that primarily uses information gathered by many minimally invasive sensors commonly found in home security systems. We describe a Rao-Blackwellised particle filter for room-level tracking, rudimentary activity recognition (i.e., whether or not an occupant is moving), and data association. We evaluate our approach with experiments in a simulated environment and in a real instrumented home.

1   Introduction

Advances in modern health care are helping millions of people live longer, healthier lives. As a result, people aged 65 and older are the fastest growing segment of the US population (set to double in the next two decades) [5]. Current health-care infrastructure is inadequate to meet the growing needs of an increasingly older population. Clearly, there is a need to develop technological solutions.

One solution is to use automatic health monitoring to enable *aging in place*, in which elders live independently and safely in their own homes for as long as possible – without transitioning to a care facility. Automatic health monitoring uses data from ubiquitous sensors to infer location and activity information about at-risk occupants. Studies have shown that pervasive monitoring of the elderly and those with disabilities can improve the accuracy of pharmacologic interventions, track illness progression, and lower caregiver stress levels [13]. Additionally, [30] has shown that movement patterns alone are an important indicator of cognitive function, depression, and social involvement among people with Alzheimer's disease.

In this paper we introduce the simultaneous tracking and activity recognition (STAR) problem. The key idea is that people tracking can be improved by activity recognition and vice versa. Location and activity are the *context* for one another and knowledge of

H.W. Gellersen et al. (Eds.): PERVASIVE 2005, LNCS 3468, pp. 62–79, 2005.

one is highly predictive of the other. We seek to provide the information that is vital for automatic health monitoring: identifying people, tracking people as they move, and knowing what activities people are engaged in. This research takes the first steps toward solving STAR by providing simultaneous room-level tracking and recognition of locomotion (which we loosely categorize as an activity). Please note that in this paper we do not attempt to provide tracking at higher than room-level granularity, and activity recognition is limited to whether or not an occupant is moving.

Automatic health monitoring necessarily occurs in a home environment where privacy, computational, and monetary constraints may be tight. We proceed from the "bottom-up," using predominantly anonymous, binary sensors that are minimally invasive, fast, and inexpensive. We call a sensor anonymous and binary when it can not directly identify people and at any given time it reports a value of one or zero. These sensors can be found in existing home security systems and include motion detectors, contact switches, break-beam sensors, and pressure mats.

We employ a particle filter approach that uses information collected by many simple sensors. Particle filters offer a sample-based approximation of probability densities that are too difficult to solve in closed form (e.g., tracking multiple occupants in a home environment via several hundred anonymous, binary sensors). Particle filters are desirable because they can approximate a large range of probability distributions, focus resources on promising hypotheses, and the number of samples can be adjusted to accommodate available computational resources. We show that a particle filter approach with simple sensors can tell us which rooms are occupied, count the occupants in a room, identify the occupants, track occupant movements, and recognize whether the occupants are moving or not.

This paper is organized as follows: In section 2 we discuss our rationale for choosing simple sensors. In section 3, we introduce our approach, including the details of our learner. Section 4 contains experimental results from a real instrumented environment and from simulations. In section 5, we review existing instrumented facilities and discuss the state-of-the-art in location estimation and activity recognition. We discuss our findings in section 6. In sections 7 and 8 we conclude.

2   Instrumenting the Home

In this section we describe which sensors we use and why. First, we discuss several challenges faced when placing sensors in a home and describe the ideal properties of sensors. Second, we list the sensors used in these experiments and illustrate how they work together.

2.1   Sensor Constraints and Issues

In fieldwork, we have found that cost of sensors and sensor acceptance are pivotal issues, especially in the home. Many people are uncomfortable living with cameras and microphones. Laser scanning devices are anonymous, but costly and have limited range. We find that people are often unwilling, forget, change clothes too often, or are not sufficiently clothed when at home to wear a badge, beacon, set of markers, or RF tag. In particular, elderly individuals are often very sensitive to small changes in environment

[10], and a target population of institutionalized Alzheimer's patients frequently strip themselves of clothing, including any wearable sensors [11]. As a result, there is a great potential for simple sensors to 1) "fill in the blanks" when more complex sensors can not be used and 2) to reduce the number of complex (and possibly expensive) sensors that are necessary to solve a problem.

Like other researchers in academia and industry, we envision an off-the-shelf system installed and configured by a consumer [1, 6, 7, 28]. Ideally, the sensors we choose should offer solutions to the following issues: sensors and monitoring systems should be *invisible* or should fit into *familiar* forms. Sensor data should be *private* and should not reveal sensitive information, especially identity. Arguably equally important – sensors should not be perceived as invasive. Sensors should be *inexpensive*, preferably available off-the shelf. Sensors should be *easy to install*. Wireless sensors can be mounted to any surface, while wired sensors may require running cable to a central location. Processing sensor data should require *minimal computational resources* (e.g., a desktop computer). Sensors should be *low-maintenance*, easy to replace and maintain. Sensors will be neglected and should be robust to damage. Finally, sensors should be *low-power*, requiring no external power or able to run as long as possible on batteries. As a last resort the device may need to be plugged in or powered by low voltage wiring.

2.2   Our Sensor Choice

Sensors that are *anonymous* and *binary* satisfy many of these properties. Anonymous sensors satisfy privacy constraints because they do not directly identify the person being sensed[1]. Perceived privacy issues are minimized by the fact that anonymous, binary sensors are already present in many homes as part of security systems. Binary sensors, which simply report a value of zero or one at each time step, satisfy computational constraints. These sensors are valuable to the home security industry because they are cheap, easy to install, computationally inexpensive, require minimal maintenance and supervision, and do not have to be worn or carried. We choose them for the same reasons, and because they already exist in many of our target environments. (We typically use a denser installation of sensors than in a home security system, however.)

In this research, we chose four commonly available anonymous, binary sensors: motion detectors, break-beam sensors, pressure mats, and contact switches. These four sensors are selectively placed so that they are triggered by gross movement, point movement, gross manipulation, and point manipulation, respectively. In addition, we use an ID sensor to capture identity as occupants enter and leave the environment. In experiments, we replaced house keys with unique radio frequency identification (RFID) tags. Instead of a lock and key, an RFID reader near the doorway "listens" for the key (an RFID tag) and automatically records identification while it unlocks the door for a few seconds. (The RFID reader can detect multiple keys simultaneously from a distance of about a foot.) Afterwards, the door locks itself and the occupant need not continue to carry the key. See Figure 1 for an overview of a typically instrumented room.

---

[1] Our decision to use simple sensors provides inherent privacy at the physical layer, but does not directly address higher-level privacy issues, such as dissemination of information.

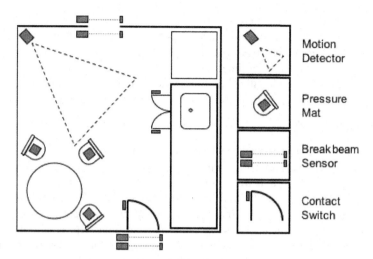

Fig. 1. Overview of typically instrumented room in which grey squares represent sensors

3   Approach

In this section we introduce the STAR problem, discuss why it is difficult to solve with simple sensors, and consider several simplifications. We discuss a Bayes filter approach and show why it fails to accomodate multiple occupants. We then describe a Rao-Blackwellised particle filter that is able to handle multiple occupants by performing efficient data association. Finally, we discuss how to learn model parameters both online and offline.

3.1   Simultaneous Tracking and Activity Recognition

There are two main problems when solving STAR for multiple people, (1) what is the state of each person and, (2) which person is which? In the first problem, observations are used to update the state of each occupant (i.e., their activity and location). In the second problem, identity of the occupants is estimated and anonymous observations are assigned to the occupants most likely to have generated them. Uncertainty occurs when several occupants trigger the same set of anonymous sensors. The tracker does not know which occupant triggered which sensor (i.e., which data to associate with which occupant).

There are several ways to simplify the problem. First, we could *increase the number of ID sensors*. This simple approach solves the problem by using sensors that identify occupants outright. Unfortunately, ID sensors are expensive, have significant infrastructure requirements, and/or must be worn or carried by the occupant. It is more desirable to employ many inexpensive sensors in lieu of expensive sensors. Second, we could *increase the sensor granularity*. Adding more sensors can reduce the ambiguity caused by multiple occupants, but may be expensive. Alternately, existing sensors can be placed so that they collect the maximum amount of information. In experiments, we intentionally placed sensors so that they would detect different properties, which increases granularity. For example, ceiling-mounted motion detectors detect gross movement while chair-mounted pressure mats detect static occupants. Similarly, noting which contact switches are out of reach of pressure mats can potentially separate two occupants when one is seated and the other opens a drawer. Third, we could *learn individual movement and activity patterns*. Over time, statistical models can represent particular habits of select individuals. Individualized motion models can help the tracker recover from ambiguity as occupants follow their normal routines (e.g., sleeping in their own beds).

3.2   Bayes Filter Approach

First, we address the question of how to update occupant state given sensor measurements. Bayes' filters offer a well-known way to estimate the state of a dynamic system from noisy sensor data in real world domains [14]. The *state* represents occupant location and activity, while sensors provide information about the state. A probability distribution, called the *belief*, describes the probability that the occupant is in each state $p(X_t = x_t)$. A Bayes filter updates the belief at each time step, conditioned on the data. Modeling systems over time is made tractable by the Markov assumption that the current state depends only on the previous state.

We estimate the state $x_t = \{x_{1t}, x_{2t}, ..., x_{Mt}\}$ of M occupants at time t using the sensor measurements collected so far, $z_{1:t}$. At each time step we receive the status of many binary sensors. The measurement $z_t = \{e_{1t}, e_{2t}, ..., e_{Et}\}$ is a string of E binary digits representing which sensors have triggered during time step t. The update equation is analogous to the forward portion of the forward-backward algorithm used in hidden Markov models (HMMs). See [25] for a detailed description of how HMMs work.

$$p(X_t = x_t|z_{1:t}) \propto p(z_t|X_t = x_t) \sum_{x' \in X} p(X_t = x_t|X_{t-1} = x')p(X_{t-1} = x'|z_{1:t-1}).$$

(1)

The *sensor model* $p(z_t|X_t = x_t)$ represents the likelihood of measurement z_t occurring from state x_t. The *motion model* $p(X_t = x_t|X_{t-1} = x')$ predicts the likelihood of transition from the state x' to the current state x_t. How these models are learned is discussed in section 3.4.

The graphical model in Figure 2 represents the dependencies we are about to describe. The state space $x \in X$ for occupant m is the range of possible locations and activities, $x_{mt} = \{r_{mt}, a_{mt}\}$, where $r \in R$ denotes which room the occupant is in, and $a \in \{moving, not\ moving\}$ denotes occupant activity. The raw sensor values are the only given information; the rest must be inferred. Each observation is composed of a collection of *events* and appear $z_t = \{e_{1t}, e_{2t}, ..., e_{Et}\}$. Event generation is straightforward. When a motion detector triggers a "movement event" is generated. Upon a state change a contact switch evokes a "manipulation event." While a pressure mat (on a chair) is depressed a "sit event" is generated. When a pair of break beam sensors are triggered, depending upon the order, "enter and exit events" are generated for the appropriate rooms.

Tracking multiple people causes the state to have quite large dimensionality, making model learning intractable. Currently, a simplifying independence assumption between m occupants means that the update equation is factored as:

$$p(X_t = x_t|X_{t-1} = x') = \prod_{m \in M} p(X_{mt} = x_{mt}|X_{m,t-1} = x'_m).$$

(2)

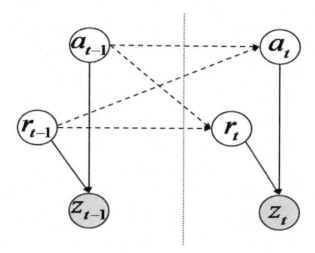

Fig. 2. A dynamic Bayes net describing room-level tracking and activity recognition. Arcs indicate causal influences, with dotted arcs representing causality through time. Circles represent variables. Shaded variables are directly observable, the rest are hidden

This assumption could be partially relaxed through the use of two models, one for occupants that are alone and another for multiple occupants. This abstraction avoids the exponential blow up resulting from joint models of combinations of specific individuals. A similar approach has been applied successfully to tracking multiple interacting ants in [19].

The Data Association Problem. The above approach works well for tracking a single occupant in a noisy domain (the Bayes filter is named for its ability to *filter* spurious noise). However, this approach struggles to track multiple occupants because other occupants do not behave like noise processes. The tracker becomes confused by constantly conflicting sensor measurements. We need some way to determine which occupant generated what observation. This is the data association problem, and in our domain it can become severe. For t seconds and m occupants each association has $m!^t$ possibilities. In a reasonable scenario with several dozen inexpensive sensors monitoring a handful of occupants for a week, there are too many data assignments to enumerate.

3.3   Particle Filter Approach

At each time step we wish to find the best assignment of sensors to occupants and to use this assignment to update the state of each occupant. Assignments between sensor measurements and occupants are not given. Therefore, we must now estimate the posterior distribution over both occupant state and sensor assignments.

We let θ_t represent a sensor assignment matrix such that $\theta_t(i, j)$ is 1 if event e_{it} belongs to occupant j and 0 otherwise. See Figure 3 for the updated graphical model. We must expand the posterior of Equation 1 to incorporate data association. We accom-

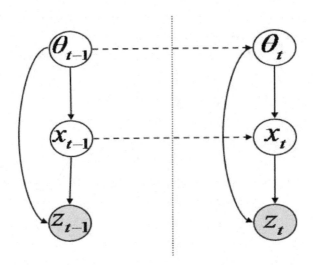

Fig. 3. A dynamic Bayes net describing tracking and activity recognition (combined into the state x) as well as data associations θ

modate our expanded posterior efficiently by using a Rao-Blackwellised particle filter (RBPF) [14]. By the chain rule of probability,

$$p(X_{1:t}, \theta_{1:t}|z_{1:t}) = p(X_{1:t}|\theta_{1:t}, z_{1:t})p(\theta_{1:t}|z_{1:t}). \qquad (3)$$

The key idea is to update the *state* $p(X_t = x|\theta_{1:t}, z_{1:t})$ analytically using the Bayes filter update already described, and to use a particle filter to generate a sample-based approximation of *assignments* $p(\theta_{1:t}|z_{1:t})$. This streamlines our approach by sampling only from the intractable number of possible sensor assignments and solving exactly for our (relatively) small number of possible state configurations.

The desired posterior from Equation 3 is represented by a set of N weighted particles. Each particle j maintains the current state of all occupants via a bank of M Bayes filters, as well as the sensor assignments and the weight of the particle.

$$s_t^j = \{x_t^{(j)}, \theta_{1:t}^{(j)}, w_t^{(j)}\}. \qquad (4)$$

Note that for filtering purposes we may store only the latest association $\theta_t^{(j)}$. $x_t^{(j)}$ is a distribution over all possible states of all occupants. The $\theta_t^{(j)}$ are updated via particle filtering, and the $x_t^{(j)}$ are updated exactly using the Bayes filter update. The marginal distribution of the assignment (from Equation 3) is therefore approximated via a collection of N weighted particles,

$$p(\theta_{1:t}|z_{1:t}) \approx \sum_{j=1}^{N} w_t^{(j)} \delta(\theta_{1:t}^{(j)}, \theta_{1:t}). \qquad (5)$$

where $w_t^{(j)}$ is the *importance weight* of particle j, and $\delta(x, y) = 1$ if $x = y$ and 0 otherwise.

Given the sample-based representation of assignments from Equation 5, the marginal of the state node is,

$$p(X_t|z_{1:t}) = \sum_{\theta_{1:t}} p(X_t|\theta_{1:t}, z_{1:t}) p(\theta_{1:t}|z_{1:t}) \tag{6}$$

$$\approx \sum_{\theta_{1:t}} p(X_t|\theta_{1:t}, z_{1:t}) \sum_{j=1}^{N} w_t^{(j)} \delta(\theta_{1:t}^{(j)}, \theta_{1:t}) \tag{7}$$

$$= \sum_{j=1}^{N} w_t^{(j)} p(X_t|\theta_{1:t}^{(j)}, z_{1:t}). \tag{8}$$

Given a sampled data association $\theta_{1:t}^{(j)}$ and an observation z_t, it is straightforward to update the belief $p(X_t = x|z_{1:t}, \theta_{1:t})$ exactly according to a slightly modified version of the Bayes filter from Equation 1. First, we show the predictive distribution, where information up to time step $t-1$ is used to predict the next state for particle j.

$$p(X_t = x|z_{1:t-1}, \theta_{1:t-1}^{(j)}) = \sum_{x'} p(X_t = x|X_{t-1} = x') p(X_{t-1} = x'|z_{1:t-1}, \theta_{1:t-1}^{(j)}). \tag{9}$$

We derive the full update equation given information up to time t according to Bayes rule.

$$p(X_t = x|z_{1:t}, \theta_{1:t}^{(j)}) = \frac{p(z_t|X_t = x, \theta_t^{(j)}) p(X_t = x|z_{1:t-1}, \theta_{1:t-1}^{(j)})}{\sum_x p(z_t|X_t = x, \theta_t^{(j)}) p(X_t = x|z_{1:t-1}, \theta_{1:t}^{(j)})} \tag{10}$$

$$\propto p(z_t|X_t = x, \theta_t^{(j)}) p(X_t = x|z_{1:t-1}, \theta_{1:t-1}^{(j)}). \tag{11}$$

Given these definitions we now discuss the overall RBPF approach. The following sampling scheme, called *sequential importance sampling with re-sampling*, is repeated N times at each time step to generate a full sample set S_t (composed of samples $s_t^{(j)}$ where $j = 1...N$) [14].

During *initialization* occupant location and identity are gathered by RFID and sensor measurements are assigned automatically. In each iteration there are four steps. First, during *re-sampling* we use the sample set from the previous time step S_{t-1} to draw with replacement a random sample $s_{t-1}^{(j)}$ according to the discrete distribution of the importance weights $w_{t-1}^{(j)}$. Next, we *sample* a possible sensor assignment matrix $\theta_t^{(j)}$. We discuss how to propose sensor assignments in the next section. Next, we use the association $\theta_t^{(j)}$ to perform an *analytical update* of the state of each occupant in sample j via Equation 10. Finally, during *importance sampling* we weight the new sample $s_t^{(j)}$ proportional to the likelihood of the resulting posteriors of the state of each occupant. This is equal to the denominator of Equation 10,

$$w_t^{(j)} = \eta \sum_{x} p(z_t|X_t = x, \theta_t^{(j)}) p(X_t = x|z_{1:t-1}, \theta_{1:t}^{(j)}), \tag{12}$$

where η is a normalizing constant so that the weights sum to one.

The Data Association Problem. During the sampling step a possible assignment of sensor readings to occupants (a data association) must be proposed for the new sample. Choosing an impossible association will cause that particle to have a zero weight and wastes computational time. For example, foolishly assigning two sensors from different rooms to the same occupant will result in a particle with negligible probability. A more efficient particle filter will propose data associations in areas of high likelihood. The better the proposals, the fewer particles necessary.

Assigning sensor readings uniformly (regardless of occupant state) is inefficient because it will propose many unlikely or impossible associations (e.g., one occupant given sensor readings from different rooms). A quick improvement is to use *gating* to eliminate impossible associations, but a gated uniform method is still inefficient because it ignores the current state of each occupant. Sensors are intimately tied to rooms and activities. Occupants that are in the same room as a sensor are more likely to have triggered it and occupants engaged in certain activities are more likely to trigger associated sensors. A simple heuristic takes advantage of these properties. We currently assign measurements based on the posterior $p(\theta_t | x_{t-1}^{(j)})$. The proposed assignment matrix θ_t is constructed by independently assigning each measurement to an occupant based on the probability that she triggered it $p(e_{it} | x_t) \forall i$. This method tends to choose likely assignments and usually avoids impossible assignments, but is not guaranteed to approximate the true distribution $p(\theta_t | z_{1:t})$.

3.4   Parameter Learning

Modeling the behavior of individual occupants can increase tracking and activity recognition accuracy and make data association more efficient. In a system with few ID sensors (like ours) these models are vital to disambiguate the identities of many occupants. Motion models describe individual tendencies to transition between rooms and activities. Sensor models describe individual tendencies to set off specific sensors (e.g., shorter occupants may use high cabinet doors less often). Models can be initialized generically for unknown occupants.

Motion Model. We wish to learn individual parameters for the motion model.

$$p(X_t = x_t | X_{t-1} = x_{t-1}) = p(a_t, r_t | a_{t-1}, r_{t-1}) \tag{13}$$

$$= p(a_t | a_{t-1}, r_{t-1}) p(r_t | r_{t-1}, a_{t-1}). \tag{14}$$

- $p(r_t | r_{t-1}, a_{t-1})$ is the probability of transition to a room given the previous room and whether the occupant was moving or not. Transition probabilities between contiguous rooms are initialized uniformly for moving occupants and set to small values for non-moving occupants.
- $p(a_t | a_{t-1}, r_{t-1})$ models the probability of whether or not the occupant is moving given the previous room and whether the occupant was moving during the last time step. This is initialized so that it is more likely for moving occupants to continue to move and non-moving ones to continue not to.

Sensor Model. Individual sensor readings, called *events*, are considered independent. For occupant m the sensor model can be rewritten:

$$p(z_t|X_t = x_t, \theta_t^{(j)}) = \prod_{m \in M} p(z_t|X_{mt} = x_{mt}, \theta_t^{(j)}) = \prod_{m \in M} \prod_i p(e_{it}|X_{mt} = x_{mt}, \theta_t^{(j)}).$$

(15)

This models the probability of observing each sensor measurement given the location of the occupant and whether or not the occupant is moving. This sensor model is initialized by assigning small probability to sensor readings occurring outside their designated room. Activity information contributes to the probability. For instance, motion detector readings are more likely from active occupants than from inactive occupants. Contact switches and break beam sensor readings are likely for active occupants but not inactive ones. Pressure mat readings are likely from inactive occupants but not active ones.

Training model parameters is simple when we know the true state of each occupant. When possible, we train parameters on data generated by occupants that are home alone. We assume that sensor readings are generated by that person or a noise process and use simple counting for parameter learning. However, this method ignores a significant amount of training data because occupants are often home together.

Multiple occupants introduce uncertainty that could hurt the accuracy of learned models. A common method to minimize this uncertainty is to use the Expectation-Maximization (EM) algorithm, an iterative approach to finding parameters that maximize a posterior density [9]. We use a version of the EM algorithm called Monte Carlo EM [20, 31], which takes advantage of the set of particles representing the posterior. In this version, both forward and backward updates are applied to the Bayes filter at each time step. At each forward and backward step, the algorithm examines each particle and counts the number of transitions between rooms and activities for each occupant (based on maximum likelihood estimates). The counts from forward and backward phases are normalized and then multiplied and used to update model parameters. The learning algorithm is introduced thoroughly for Monte Carlo HMMs in [29]. An application of this technique appears in [23] for learning the motion models of people walking, riding the bus, and driving in cars.

4   Evaluation

In this section, we evaluate the performance of our approach on simulated and real datasets. In every experiment, location and activity predictions are updated every second and accuracy is measured as the number of seconds in which the maximum likelihood predictions of the tracker match the labeled location tag. In simulated experiments the location of each occupant is known, but experiments in the real environment required hand-labeling. Results are reported for real-time, online tracker performance.

4.1   Simulated Data

We implemented a simple program to simulate the data generated by occupants in an instrumented environment[2]. The simulator can generate data from any number of mo-

---

[2] The simulator can be downloaded from *www.danielhwilson.com*

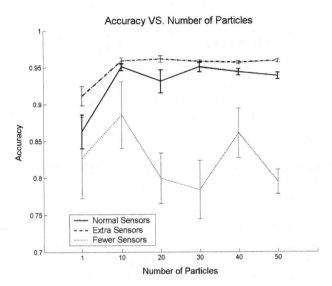

Fig. 4. Accuracy vs. number of particles for three simulated sensor infrastructures

tion detector, contact switch, and pressure mats per room, as well as break beam sensors on doors between rooms. The number of occupants, room structure, doorway location, and noise rates can be specified via command line parameters. "Noise" is defined as a random sensor measurement. Each occupant obeys an independent first-order HMM motion model that is set by hand or initialized randomly. Sensors also obey a hand-set sensor model in which the likelihood that a given sensor will trigger depends upon the number of occupants in the room and whether they are moving or not.

Simulated occupants are introduced to the environment from the same starting state and identified correctly from this state, to imitate an RFID set up in the entry way. Henceforth, each occupant is unlikely to re-enter this state. The simulation differs from reality in that simulated occupants behave truly independently. Simulated occupants were active (moving) approximately 15% of the time. There was a sporadic sensor reading about once every ten minutes. The particle filter tracker used the same sensor model for each occupant. Parameters of motion models were either learned offline via counting, or online (i.e., during the experiment) via the EM Monte Carlo method.

Small House Experiments. These experiments simulated a small house with ten rooms (three bedrooms, two bathrooms, a kitchen, living room, dining room, and hallways). Motion models for five occupants describe typical movements, with the first three occupants having their own bedrooms and the last two occupants as guests. Each experiment tracked occupants for one hour and was run for ten trials. In Figure 4, 5, and 6 the variance bars reflect variations over the ten trials.

Sensor Configurations. First, we looked at the impact of sensor configurations on tracking accuracy (see Figure 4). In this experiment we tracked two occupants with generic motion models, using three different sensor configurations: the *normal* config-uration contains one motion detector, contact switch, and pressure mat per room, the

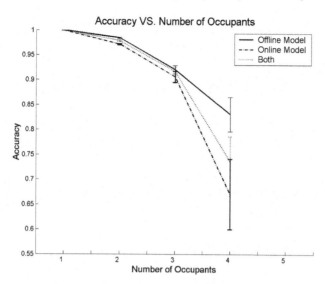

Fig. 5. Accuracy vs. number of occupants for three different parameter learning methods

extra configuration contains three of each type per room (i.e., more chairs and cabinets were added to the room), and the *fewer* configuration contained only one motion detector per room. In general, more sensors improve accuracy. The *fewer* configuration had so few sensors that the number of particles ceased to matter. Also, with fewer sensors come fewer measurements, and longer periods before tracker recovery. The number of particles will need to grow for sensor configurations with hundreds of sensors per room, which will pose a much more complex data association problem.

Parameter Learning. Second, we examined how different approaches to model learning affect accuracy (see Figure 5). In this experiment, the number of particles is set to fifty and we compare three techniques for learning motion model parameters. One method is to use simple counting to train a model using data from when the occupant is home alone. Alternately, we can use probabilistic methods to train a model online, while several occupants may be home. Three methods were used to train model parameters: (1) learning motion models off-line given one day of data generated by occupants that are alone (*offline*), (2) on-line via the Monte Carlo EM algorithm (*online*), and (3) a combination in which the MCEM online parameter learning algorithm was seeded by a model already trained offline on one hour of single occupant data (*both*). In general, the *offline* method had highest accuracy, followed by *both* and with *online* learning last. Although the offline method performed best, this is due in part to the simplicity of our simulator, in which occupants behave independently. We feel that the *both* method, of seeding a model with offline data and continuing to learn online, is the most promising real-world approach. As the number of occupants rises from two to three to four, we see the *online* method take a big accuracy hit. This is expected, as online model learning will be confounded by multiple interfering occupants.

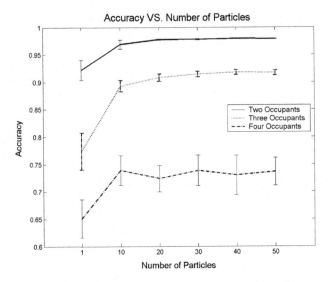

Fig. 6. Accuracy vs. number of particles for varying numbers of occupants

Number of Occupants. In Figure 5 we varied the number of occupants and used fifty particles, and in Figure 6 we varied the number of particles and used offline model learning. Accuracy plateaus as the number of particles are increased. As the number of occupants increases the step from one to ten particles is increasingly important. Due to efficient data association methods, the tracker does not need hundreds of particles. Accuracy does not drop linearly as more occupants are tracked simultaneously; the difference between one and two occupants is much less than the difference between three and four occupants.

4.2   Real Data

We conducted experiments using data generated by one to three occupants in an instrumented environment. The instrumented three story house contains twenty separate rooms, is 2824 square feet, and was home to two males (including the first author), one female, a dog, and a cat. The house contained one RFID reader located in the front doorway (the back door was not used during the experiment). There were twenty four motion detectors, with at least one per room. Twenty four contact switches were distributed to every doorway, the refrigerator, and in many of the kitchen cabinets and drawers. In these experiments we did not use break beam sensors or pressure mats. Sensor and motion models were learned before the experiment began (offline) using several days worth of data from when each occupant was home alone.

A human hand-labeled the location of each occupant using information gathered by eight wireless keypads. During the experiment, when anyone entered a room with a keypad they pushed the button corresponding to their name. The wireless keypads were placed on the front door, the kitchen, the living room, the study, the downstairs bathroom, the upstairs bathroom, and each of the two bedrooms. This process was unwieldy and has led our group to conduct further research concerning in-home data collection techniques [32].

Two Person Experiment. In order to understand how the tracker performs with occupants that are co-located versus occupants that are in different places, we scripted two ambiguous situations in which both occupants shared the same set of anonymous sensors and then separated. The scenario is as follows: two occupants enter the front door thirty seconds apart and move throughout the house without meeting. After fifteen minutes they meet in the living room. One occupant then moves to his bedroom and then returns to the living room. Next, the other occupant leaves to visit his own bedroom and then returns to the living room.

The tracker was accurate for over 98% of the thirty minute experiment. The bulk of the experiment was spent with occupants either moving separately (the first fifteen minutes), or co-located (meeting in the living room). We found near-perfect accuracy when 1) occupants were not co-located and had not recently shared the same sensors, and 2) when occupants were co-located. For example, it is easy to track two people while they watch television together. The difficulty arises when one or both occupants leave the room (the tracker must predict who left). There were two such ambiguous situations in this experiment, and in both cases the ambiguity was resolved as soon as the occupant reached his bedroom. In this case, the motion model contained information about who was more likely to visit a bedroom, and the tracker used it to recover identity. We ran the same experiment using identical generic motion models for both occupants, and found that one recovery was predicted correctly and the other not.

Three Person Experiment. We measured tracker performance over a five day period for all occupants. There were no guests during this period. When the house was not empty, on average there was one occupant at home 13% of the time, two occupants home 22% of the time, and all three occupants home for 65% of the time. During the experiment every occupant slept in the house. Two of the occupants shared a bedroom and one had a separate bedroom. Every occupant had a separate "study." The tracker used individual motion models for the three occupants. There were approximately 2000 sensor readings each day for a total of 10441 readings. We do not consider the time when no one was home.

On the whole, the tracker correctly classified 84.6% of the experiment. There was no significant difference in accuracy between occupants. The tracker was accurate 85.3% of the time when there was one occupant, 82.1% for two occupants, and 86.4% for three occupants. The system was quite good at tracking sleeping occupants (all three occupants were home each night). Accuracy for three occupants drops to 73.7% when sleeping periods (all data between midnight and 8 AM) are removed.

5   Related Work

Over the last several years much effort has been put into developing and employing a variety of sensors to solve key problems in the ubiquitous computing domain, including automatic health monitoring, activity recognition, and people tracking.

Automatic health monitoring is being explored via several stand-alone instrumented laboratories, using a variety of sensors to approach a set of highly-interrelated problems, mostly a subset of location awareness and activity recognition. The Aware Home project at Georgia Tech has built a house and instrumented it with a variety of sensors with the goal of helping elderly adults live independently [2]. Researchers at the RERC Center on Aging at the University of Florida instrumented a house with ultrasound localization and displays to provide timely information to (possibly confused) occupants [16]. Other groups have instrumented actual health care facilities with a variety of complex sensors such as cameras and microphones for a variety of experiments [4]. There is also significant interest from industry; existing companies already advertise ADL monitoring systems that use sensors such as motion detectors [1].

An impressive amount of research falls under the umbrella of activity recognition. In particular, researchers have used GPS readings to infer walking, driving and bus riding behaviors [23], laser range finders to learn motion paths in a home [8], and combinations of audio and video to recognize behavior in an office environment [22] and interactions between individuals [12]. Recently, researchers at Intel Research Seattle have used scores of radio frequency identification tags to recognize dozens of ADLs [24]. Simple sensors are also being explored; several research groups have instrumented homes with binary sensors and collected the resulting data. At the Tokyo Medical and Dental University raw data was made available to physicians who were able to pick out patterns of activity by hand [21]. Researchers at the Medical Automation Research Center (MARC) at the University of Virginia clustered sensor readings into rough groups based on room, duration, and time of day and demonstrated that many of the clusters corresponded to ADLs [6]. Finally, researchers with the House_n project at MIT have developed their own version of generic, simple sensors which they deploy for weeks at a time, collecting data that is later used for off-line activity recognition [17, 27]. Clearly, simple sensors have solid potential for solving activity recognition problems in the home.

People tracking is a fundamental problem in ubiquitous computing and has also been approached via a variety of sensors, including cameras, laser range finders, wireless networks, RFID (Radio frequency identification) badges, and infrared or ultrasound badges [2, 3, 8, 12, 18, 15, 26]. In a recent experiment, a particle filter implementation used laser range finders and infrared badges to track six people simultaneously in an office environment for 10 minutes [15]. The range finders provided anonymous, high granularity coordinates while the badge system identified occupants. We also use a particle filter approach to solve the multi-target tracking problem, however, we use ID sensors only at entrances and exits and rely upon individual motion and activity models to resolve ambiguity within the environment (in lieu of additional ID-sensors).

6   Discussion

We have shown that tracking multiple occupants in a home environment is feasible via a set of simple sensors. In summary:

- We found that highly predictive motion models improve accuracy, regardless of whether occupants behave similarly. In practice, the differences between motion models show up in private areas, like bedrooms and bathrooms, or during personal activities, like sitting in a favorite easy chair. The bigger these differences, the easier data association becomes and the more accuracy improves.

- Parameter learning is straightforward when an occupant is alone, however, occupants behave differently in groups. Learning models online could mitigate this discrepancy. In simulations, we found that the accuracy of models trained online falls as the number of occupants rises. One promising solution is to combine online and offline approaches.

- The number of particles required depends on the complexity of the data association problem. More particles are necessary for environments with many occupants and sensors. In particular, more particles are necessary for situations in which multiple co-located occupants separate. We found negligible accuracy improvements after twenty or so particles, even for up to five occupants. This number may change depending on the efficiency of the particle filter approach and the data association proposal scheme.

- More sensors will increase accuracy, regardless of the number of occupants. A low sensor density contributes to significant periods of time between readings (especially with only one occupant). During these "quiet" times no new information arrives to help the tracker recover from mistakes (such as the lag between entering a new room and triggering a sensor). Motion detectors are the most active sensors, and a lack of them hurts accuracy the most.

- More occupants will decrease accuracy, particularly if parameter learning is performed completely online and motion models are generic. The accuracy suffers most when data association becomes difficult, i.e., immediately after co-located occupants separate. In general, accuracy is high for co-located occupants and for occupants who have not come into contact with other for some time.

7 Conclusion and Future Work

We have introduced the STAR problem and shown the potential of simple sensors for providing simultaneous location awareness and activity recognition. Automatic health monitoring ultimately requires recognition of complex ADLs, and we intend to incorporate new sensors and models as needed in order to meet this goal. New models must span households with different sensor configurations and use training data that can be collected and labeled easily and quickly by non-experts. More advanced DBNs, such as hidden semi-Markov models, could better incorporate time information. Models should also easily incorporate new sensors, including those that can directly detect certain activities. Additionally, we are interested in determining just how far simple sensors can go towards solving the STAR problem. Through extensive simulation and precise instrumentation of real environments, we plan to reveal how many and what type of sensors are necessary to solve increasingly complex location and activity recognition problems. Finally, we recognize that simple sensors are best used in conjunction with more complex sensors. For instance, an RFID gate placed in a crowded hallway could improve the performance of a system that relies mainly on many simple sensors. We intend to explore which additional sensors should be chosen and where they should be placed, in order to maximize accuracy when used in conjunction with a network of simple sensors.

Acknowledgments

We would like to thank our anonymous reviewers for their valuable comments. Comments from Stephen Intille also helped improve this document. Thanks also to Jason Hong for a discussion on privacy. This material is based upon work supported by the National Science Foundation under Grant Numbers IIS-0312991 and DGE-0333420.

References

1. Living Independently - QuietCare system TM. www.livingindependently.com, 2005.
2. G. Abowd, C. Atkeson, A. Bobick, I. Essa, B. Mynatt, and T. Starner. Living laboratories: The Future Computing Environments group at the Georgia Institute of Technology. In *Proceedings of the 2000 Conference on Human Factors in Computing Systems (CHI)*, 2000.
3. M. Addlesee, R. Curwen, S. Hodges, J. Newman, P. Steggles, A. Ward, and A. Hopper. Implementing a sentient computing system. *IEEE Computer*, 34(8):50–56, August 2001.
4. S. Allin, A. Barucha, J. Zimmerman, D. Wilson, M. Roberson, S. Stevens, H. Watclar, and C. Atkeson. Toward the automatic assessment of behavioral disturbances of dementia. In *UbiHealth 2003*, 2003.
5. R. N. Anderson. Method for constructing complete annual US life tables, national center for health statistics. *Vital and Health Stat*, 2:129, 1999.
6. T. Barger, D. Brown, and M. Alwan. Health status monitoring through analysis of behavioral patterns. In *AI*IA 2003: Workshop on Ambient Intelligence*, 2003.
7. C. Beckman and S. Consolvo. Sensor configuration tool for end-users: Low-fidelity prototype evaluation # 1. Technical Report IRS-TR-03-009, Intel Research Seattle, July 2003.
8. M. Bennewitz, W. Burgard, and S. Thrun. Learning motion patterns of persons for mobile service robots. In *Proceedings of ICRA*, 2002.
9. J. Bilmes. A gentle tutorial on the EM algorithm and its application to parameter estimation for gaussian mixture and hidden Markov models. Technical Report ICSI-TR-97-021, University of Berkeley, 1997.
10. L. Burgio, K. Scilley, J. M. Hardin, and C. Hsu. Temporal patterns of disruptive vocalization in elderly nursing home residents. *Int. Journal of Geriatric Psychiatry*, 16(1):378–386, 2001.
11. L. Burgio, K. Scilley, J. M. Hardin, J. Janosky, P. Bonino, S. Slater, and R. Engberg. Studying disruptive vocalization and contextual factors in the nursing home using computer-assisted real-time observation. *Journal of Gerontology*, 49(5):230–239, 1994.
12. B. Clarkson, N. Sawhney, and A. Pentland. Auditory context awareness via wearable computing. In *Proceedings of the Perceptual User Interfaces Workshop*, 1998.
13. L. Davis, K. Buckwalter, and L. Burgio. Measuring problem behaviors in dementia: Developing a methodological agenda. *Advances in Nursing Science*, 20(1):40–55, 1997.
14. A. Doucet, N. de Freitas, and N. Gordon. *Sequential Monte Carlo Methods in Practice*. Springer-Verlag Telos, New York, 2001.
15. D. Fox, J. Hightower, L. Liao, D. Schulz, and G. Borriello. Bayesian filtering for location estimation. *IEEE Pervasive Computing*, 2(3):24–33, July-September 2003.
16. S. Helal, B. Winkler, C. Lee, Y. Kaddoura, L. Ran, C. Giraldo, S. Kuchibhotla, and W. Mann. Enabling location-aware pervasive computing applications for the elderly. In *First IEEE International Conference on Pervasive Computing and Communications*, page 531, 2003.
17. S. Intille and K. Larson. Designing and evaluating technology for independent aging in the home. In *Proceedings of the Int. Conference on Aging, Disability and Independence*, 2003.
18. T. Kanade, R. Collins, A. Lipton, P. Burt, and L. Wixson. Advances in cooperative multi-sensor video surveillance. *In Proceedings of DARPA Image Understanding Workshop*, 1:3–24, 1998.

19. Z. Khan, T. Balch, and F. Dellaert. Efficient particle filter-based tracking of multiple inter-acting targets using an mrf-based motion model. In *Proceedings of ICRA*, 2003.

20. R. A. Levine and G. Casella. Implementations of the Monte Carlo EM algorithm. *Journal of Computational and Graphical Statistics*, 2000.

21. M. Ogawa and T. Togawa. The concept of the home health monitoring. In *Proceedings of Enterprise Networking and Computing in Healthcare Industry. Healthcom 2003*, pages 71–73, 2003.

22. N. Oliver, E. Horvitz, and A. Garg. Layered representations for human activity recognition. In *Fourth IEEE International Conference on Multimodal Interfaces*, pages 3–8, 2002.

23. D. Patterson, L. Liao, D. Fox, and H. Kautz. Inferring high-level behavior from low-level sensors. In *Proceedings of UBICOMP 2003*, October 2003.

24. M. Philipose, K. Fishkin, M. Perkowitz, D. Patterson, H. Kautz, and D. Hahnel. Inferring activities from interactions with objects. *IEEE Pervasive Computing Magazine: Mobile & Ubiquitous Systems*, 3(4):50–57, October-December 2004.

25. L. Rabiner. A tutorial on hidden Markov models and selected applications in speech recognition. *Proceedings of the IEEE*, 77(2):257–286, 1989.

26. H. Sidenbladh and M. Black. Learning image statistics for bayesian tracking. *In IEEE International Conference on Computer Vision (ICCV)*, 2:709–716, 2001.

27. E. M. Tapia. Activity recognition in the home setting using simple and ubiquitous sensors. Master's thesis, Massachusetts Institute of Technology, September 2003.

28. E. M. Tapia, S. S. Intille, and K. Larson. Activity recognition in the home setting using simple and ubiquitous sensors. In *Proceedings of PERVASIVE 2004*, volume LNCS 3001, pages 158–175, 2004.

29. S. Thrun and J. Langford. Monte Carlo hidden markov models. Technical Report TR CMU-CS-98-179, Carnegie Mellon University, 1997.

30. K. VanHaitsma, P. Lawton, M. Kleban, J. Klapper, and J. Corn. Methodological aspects of the study of streams of behavior in elders with dementing illness. *Alzheimer Disease and Associated Disorders*, 11(4):228–238, 1997.

31. G. Wei and M. Tanner. A Monte Carlo implementation of the EM algorithm and the poor man's data augmentation algorithms. *Journal of the American Statistical Association*, 85(411):699–704, 1990.

32. D. H. Wilson and A. C. Long. A context aware recognition survey for data collection using ubiquitous sensors in the home. In *Proceedings of CHI 2005*, 2005.

Enhancing Semantic Spaces with Event-Driven Context Interpretation

Joo Geok Tan[1], Daqing Zhang[1], Xiaohang Wang[2], and Heng Seng Cheng[1]

[1] Institute for Infocomm Research, Singapore 119613
{tjg, daqing, hscheng}@i2r.a-star.edu.sg
[2] National University of Singapore, Singapore 119260
xwang@i2r.a-star.edu.sg

Abstract. One important functionality provided by a context-aware infrastructure is to derive high-level contexts on behalf of context-aware applications. High-level contexts are summary descriptions about users' states and surroundings which are generally inferred from low-level, explicit contexts directly provided by hardware sensors and software programs. In Semantic Space, an ontology-based context-aware infrastructure, high-level contexts are derived using context reasoning. In this paper, we present another approach to deriving high-level contexts in Semantic Space, event-driven context interpretation. We show how event-driven context interpretation can leverage on the context model and dynamic context acquisition/representation in Semantic Space as well as easily integrate into Semantic Space. Differing from the context reasoning approach, our proposed event-driven context interpreter offers better performance in terms of flexibility, scalability and processing time. We also present a prototype of the event-driven context interpreter we are building within Semantic Space to validate the feasibility of the new approach.

1 Introduction

Smart Spaces are environments where a variety of information sources such as embedded sensors, augmented appliances, stationary computers, and mobile handheld devices, are used to provide contextual information about the environment in which they reside. By making use of this information, applications in Smart Spaces can become context-aware, that is, they are able to adapt automatically and intelligently to the changing situation to provide relevant services to the user [1].

Context-aware applications are typically difficult to build since the developer has to deal with a wide range of issues related to the sensing, representing, aggregating, storing, querying and reasoning of context [2]. To address this, we have proposed Semantic Space [3], an ontology-based context-aware infrastructure where we exploit Semantic Web [4] technologies for explicit representation, expressive querying and flexible reasoning of contexts in Smart Spaces. Since Semantic Space abstracts and provides generic context-aware mechanisms as reusable components, application developers can leverage on Semantic Space to reduce the cost and complexity of building context-aware applications.

H.W. Gellersen et al. (Eds.): PERVASIVE 2005, LNCS 3468, pp. 80–97, 2005.

One important functionality provided by a context-aware infrastructure is context interpretation to derive high-level contexts. In context-aware systems, high-level contexts augment context-aware applications by providing summary descriptions about users' states and surroundings. They are generally inferred from low-level, explicit contexts which are directly provided by hardware sensors and software programs [1, 5, 6, 7]. For instance, the implicit high-level context pertaining to a person sleeping in the bedroom may be derived from these explicit low-level contexts provided by various sensors deployed in the bedroom: (1) the person is located in the bedroom, (2) the bedroom light level is low, (3) the bedroom noise level is low and (4) the bedroom door is closed [7].

Various approaches to context interpretation within a context-aware infrastructure have been proposed. In ontology-based context-aware infrastructures [5, 6, 7, 8, 9, 10, 11], context information are modelled with a formal context model using ontologies and kept in a context knowledge base. High-level contexts are derived by applying rule-based reasoning techniques over the context knowledge base. The advantage of this approach is that context reasoning, validation and querying can be easily supported as generic mechanisms in the infrastructure since the context information is explicitly expressed in a machine-interpretable form. Our Semantic Space falls into this category where we use a context reasoner to derive high-level contexts by performing forward-chaining reasoning over a context knowledge base. However, the centralized model of this approach may not scale so well when there is a large number of contexts to be handled. In particular, when the context knowledge base and/or rules set is large, context reasoning over the knowledge base may not perform well enough for time-critical applications [9]. Machine-learning approaches where useful context information are extracted and inferred from sensor data using Bayesian networks in a sensing service infrastructure have also been explored in [12]. Such machine-learning approaches have the advantage that they can be more flexible than static rule-based approaches, however, they may require a fair bit of training before they can become effective.

In this paper, we propose another approach to context interpretation in Semantic Space which is based on an event-driven distributed model of the context-aware system. Our approach, while retaining the benefits of using Semantic Space for context representation, reasoning, validation and query, can offer better performance in terms of flexibility, scalability and processing time when compared to context reasoning. We show how event-driven context interpretation can leverage on the context model and dynamic context acquisition/representation in Semantic Space as well as easily integrate into Semantic Space, co-existing with and complementing other context interpretation mechanisms (such as context reasoning) in the infrastructure, to provide a wide variety of high-level contexts for applications to use. In our event-driven context interpreter, we leverage on the event specification language and composite event detection algorithm found in active database research [13, 14] by extending them from a centralized database environment to a distributed context-aware system. We also extend the context model with an event ontology such that event information can be retrieved from the infrastructure in a consistent and semantic way using semantic queries.

The remainder of this paper is structured as follows. In Section 2, we give an overview of Semantic Space in terms of the various collaborating components present in the infrastructure. We then describe the context model of Semantic Space and extend it to specify events in Section 3. In Section 4, we show how dynamic context acquisition and representation is supported in Semantic Space and how these functionalities can be leveraged by the event-driven context interpreter. In Section 5, we describe in detail the design of the event-driven context interpreter and compare event-driven context interpretation with context reasoning. We present a prototype we are building to validate event-driven context interpretation in Section 6. Finally, in Section 7, we present our conclusions and future work.

2   Semantic Space Overview

Figure 1 illustrates the architecture of Semantic Space, our ontology-based context-aware infrastructure [3]. As shown in Figure 1, Semantic Space consists of a number of collaborating components, namely *Context Wrappers, Context Aggregator, Context Knowledge Base, Context Reasoners/Interpreters* and *Context Query Engine.*

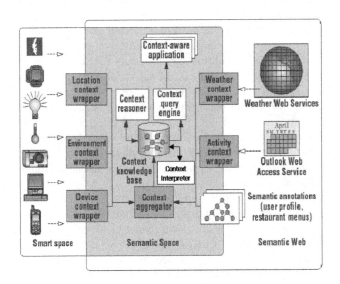

Fig. 1. The Semantic Space Context-Aware Infrastructure

Context Wrappers obtain raw data from software and hardware sensors, transform this information into a semantic representation based on the context model and publish it for other components to access. *Context Aggregator* discovers distributed wrappers, gathers context from them and updates *Context Knowledge Base* asynchronously. *Context Knowledge Base,* which serves as a persistent storage for context information, dynamically links context into a single coherent data model and provides interfaces for *Context Reasoner* and *Context Query Engine* to manipulate stored context. *Context Reasoners/Interpreters* are components that deduce high-level implicit context from low-level, explicit context using reasoning, learning and other techniques for context interpretation. The derived high-level contexts, likewise, are asserted into the *Context Knowledge Base*, where they can be queried through *Context Query Engine*. *Context Query Engine* is responsible for handling queries about both stored context and inferred, higher-level context.

Our Semantic Space has been built [3] using standard Semantic Web [4] technologies such as RDF (Resource Description Framework) [15] and OWL (Web Ontology Language) [16] for context modelling, and logic inference and semantic query engines from the Jena2 Semantic Toolkit [17] for advanced context reasoning, validation and query. Standard Universal Plug-and-Play (UPnP) [18] is used to support automatic discovery of context providing components.

As shown in Figure 1, Semantic Space can support various ways of performing context interpretation with different context reasoners/interpreters co-existing with each other in the infrastructure, and complementing each other by contributing to the set of available high-level contexts. This wide range of high-level contexts can be accessed from Semantic Space in a uniform way through standard query and subscribe/notify interfaces. The context reasoners/interpreters can leverage on the uniform context model and the generic services provided in the infrastructure (e.g., services from context wrappers, context knowledge base, etc) to support their context interpretation functionality as well as provide generic services to other components in the infrastructure. Context-aware applications, in turn, can retrieve different levels of context from Semantic Space in a uniform manner, without having to know how the different high-level contexts have been derived in the infrastructure, and utilize them to adapt their behaviours accordingly.

3 Context Model

Context representation is an important part of pervasive computing environments and an appropriate context model is the basis for context representation. We use ontologies to model contexts in Semantic Space as this enables context sharing, context reasoning and validation, semantic query and also knowledge reuse.

3.1 Context Ontology

Within the domain of knowledge representation, the term *ontology* refers to the formal, explicit description of concepts, which are often conceived as a set of entities, relations, instances, functions and axioms [19]. Among Semantic Web standards, OWL is used to define and instantiate ontologies that let distributed computing entities exchange and process information based on a common vocabulary.

For Semantic Space, we have defined an upper-level context ontology (ULCO) in OWL to provide a set of basic concepts common across different Smart Space environments. Among various contexts, we have identified three classes of real-world objects (User, Location and Computing Entity) and one class of conceptual objects (Activity) that characterize Smart Spaces (see Figure 2). Linked together, these objects form the skeleton of a contextual environment. They also provide primary indices into other associated contexts. For example, given a location, we can acquire related contexts such as noise, weather, and the number of people inside if we model these objects as top-level classes in ULCO.

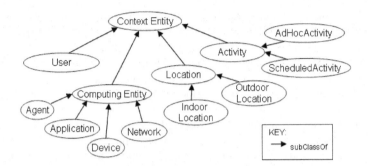

Fig. 2. Upper Level Context Ontology (ULCO) in Semantic Space

Our model represents contexts as ontology instances and associated properties (*context markups*) that applications can easily interpret.   Consider the RFID (radio frequency identification) indoor location system that tracks users' location by detecting the presence of body-worn tags.   When Grandpa enters the bedroom, the RFID sensor detects his presence and composes the following context markup:

<User rdf:about="#Grandpa"><locatedIn rdf:about="#Bedroom"/> </User>

Each OWL instance has a unique URI, and context markups can link to external definitions   through   these   URIs.   For   example,   the   URI   www.i2r.s-star.edu.sg/SemanticSpace#Grandpa   refers   to   the   user   Grandpa,   and   the   URI www.i2r.a-star.edu.sg/SemanticSpace#Bedroom refers to Grandpa's bedroom which have all been defined in the system.

3.2   Context from Events

Context information which are useful to applications fall into many categories [20]. We believe that one very important category of context information are those related to events occurring within the context-aware system.   When an event occurs at a computing entity in the system, it can trigger another event at another computing entity or combine with other events to generate a new event.   To support this type of context information, we propose another approach to context interpretation within Semantic Space which is based on an event-driven distributed model of the context-aware system.

We start by defining the various types of events. Events can be broadly classified into (1) Primitive Events and (2) Composite Events [13].

Primitive events are events that are pre-defined in the system and can be detected by a mechanism embedded in the system.   In the case of a context-aware system, primitive events are those low-level events which can be directly detected by sensors or other mechanisms embedded in the computing entities (which are typically the context wrappers) in the system.   Examples of primitive events are *sensed events* (e.g., when sensor readings exceed a certain threshold), *temporal events* (e.g., at 10 p.m. or 10 seconds after an event *E* occurs), *software events* (e.g., EOF when retrieving information from a file) and *network events* (e.g., event notification from context wrapper to remote computing entity which has subscribed to the event).

Composite events are events that are formed by applying a set of event operators to primitive and composite events. We leverage on the work on Snoop, an expressive event specification language for active databases [13, 14], by adopting its set of well-defined event operators for our event composition. Table 1 shows a summary of the event operators which can be used and their descriptions.

Table 1. Summary of Event Operators

	Event Operator	Description
1	OR (V)	Disjunction of two events E_1 and E_2, denoted by $E_1 V E_2$, occurs when E_1 occurs or E_2 occurs.
2	AND (Λ)	Conjunction of two events E_1 and E_2, denoted by $E_1 \Lambda E_2$, occurs when both E_1 and E_2 occur, irrespective of their order of occurrence.
3	ANY	The conjunction event, denoted by ANY(m, E_1, E_2, ..., E_n) where $m \leq n$, occurs when m events out of the n distinct events specified occur, irrespective of their order of occurrence. Also to specify m *distinct* occurrences of an event E, the following variant is provided: ANY(m, E^*).
4	SEQ (;)	Sequence of two events E_1 and E_2, denoted by $E_1;E_2$, occurs when E_2 occurs provided E_1 has already occurred. This implies that the time of occurrence of E_1 is guaranteed to be less than the time of occurrence of E_2.
5	Aperiodic Operators (A, A^*)	The Aperiodic operator A allows one to express the occurrences of an aperiodic event within a closed time interval. There are two versions of this event specification. The non-cumulative aperiodic event is expressed as A(E_1, E_2, E_3) where E_1, E_2 and E_3 are arbitrary events. The event A is signalled each time E_2 occurs within the time interval started by E_1 and ended by E_3. On the other hand, the cumulative aperiodic event A^* occurs only once when E_3 occurs and accumulates the occurrences of E_2 within the open time interval formed by E_1 and E_3.
6	Periodic Operators (P, P^*)	A periodic event is a temporal event that occurs periodically. A periodic event is denoted as P(E_1, TI [:*parameters*], E_3) where E_1 and E_3 are events and TI [:*parameters*] is a time interval specification with an optional parameter list. P occurs for every TI interval, starting after E_1 and ceasing after E_3. Parameters specified are collected each time P occurs. If not specified, the occurrence time of P is collected by default. P has a cumulative version P^* expressed as P^*(E_1, TI :*parameters*, E_3). Unlike P, P^* occurs only once when E_3 occurs. Also specified parameters are collected and accumulated at the end of each period and made available when P^* occurs. Note that the parameter specification is mandatory in P^*.

To illustrate composite event formulation, consider the following example of medical management for the elderly within the context of an assistive home environment:

1. *Send an alert to Grandpa to take his medication every 4 hours from the time he wakes up to the time he goes to bed.*

   Using the event operators in Table 1, we formulate the event expressions for this scenario as follows:

   status(Grandpa, isOutOfBed) = locatedIn(Grandpa, Bedroom) ∩
       status(Bed, Nobody)

   status(Grandpa, isBrushingTeeth) = locatedIn(Grandpa, Bathroom) ∩
       (ANY(3, status(Toothbrush, Moved), status(Toothpaste, Moved),
       status(RinsingCup, Moved), status(Comb, Moved), status(Towel, Moved)))

   status(Grandpa, hasWokenUp) = status(Grandpa, isOutOfBed) ;
       status(Grandpa, isBrushingTeeth) ; locatedIn(Grandpa, Bedroom)

   status(Grandpa, isInBed) = locatedIn(Grandpa, Bedroom) ∩
       status(Bed, Somebody)

   status(Grandpa, hasGoneToBed) = status(Grandpa, isBrushingTeeth) ;
       status(Grandpa, isInBed)

   The final high-level composite event we are interested in can be formulated as follows:

   P(status(Grandpa, hasWokenUp), 4 hrs, status(Grandpa,hasGoneToBed))

2. *If Grandpa has not taken his medication within a 10-minute period after the alert is sent, send a SMS message to alert the care-giver.*

   We detect if Grandpa has indeed taken his medication by checking if the pill drawer has been opened and the water flask has been pressed during a 10-minute interval starting from when the status(Grandpa, isAlertedToTakeMedication) alert is sent. The high-level event we are interested in can then be formulated as follows:

   status(Grandpa, hasTakenMedication) = A^*(status(Grandpa,
       isAlertedToTakeMedication, (status(PillDrawer, Opened) ∩
       status(WaterFlask, Pressed)), status(Grandpa, isAlertedToTakeMedication) +
       10 min)

   The example show how various primitive and composite events can be combined together, using event operators in the event specification language, to specify a wide range of high-level contextual events.

3.3   Event Ontology

To integrate event-driven context interpretation into Semantic Space context model (see Section 3.1), we propose to extend the context model with an event ontology to specify primitive and composite events. We therefore add another class of conceptual objects (Event) to the original ULCO. Figure 3 shows a part of the proposed event ontology in graphical format.

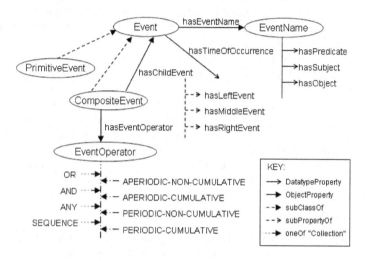

Fig. 3. Event Ontology (Partial)

The event ontology captures the key concepts of events described in Section 3.2. For example, primitive and composite events are modelled as subclasses of the *Event* class, thereby inheriting all the properties generic to events such as *hasEventName*, *hasTimeOfOccurrence*. Composite events, on the other hand, have additional properties such as *hasEventOperator, hasChildEvent, hasLeftEvent, hasMiddleEvent,* and *HasRightEvent* which enables the event expression associated with the composite event to be specified in the ontology.

With an event ontology as part of the context model, information about events can then be retrieved in a consistent and semantic way using semantic queries. For example, to find out all the parent child relationships of the events or to find out all the events which have occurred at a certain time, the following semantic queries coded in RDQL [21] format can be issued to the context query engine:

```
SELECT ?X, ?Y WHERE (?X, <owl:hasChildEvent>, ?Y)
SELECT ?X WHERE (?X, <owl:hasTimeOfOccurrence>, "20.05.04 13:00:41")
```

For a particular Smart Space environment where the ULCO has been further extended to model the specific Smart Space, additional linkages between various event objects to other objects in the context model can be defined. In our example, the User class is linked to the Event class by the ObjectProperty status, thereby enabling the various contexts such as status(Grandpa,isOutofBed), status(Grandpa, hasWokenUp), status(Grandpa, hasTakenMedication) to be modelled.

4   Dynamic Context Acquisition and Representation

The dynamism of a pervasive computing environment where sources of context can come and go warrants the need to support discovery and configuration of context sources (or their software wrappers). When a new context source joins the contextual environment, the context-aware infrastructure and applications should be able to locate and access it, and when the context source leaves the environment, applications should be aware of its unavailability to avoid stale information.

In Semantic Space, we employ standard UPnP as the mechanism for dynamic discovery of context sources. We provide a standard re-usable software wrapper with UPnP functionality which can be used to wrap context sources into context wrappers. Our context aggregator is then used to discover and aggregate the context information dynamically as context wrappers come and go or change their contextual information. In the following sections, we describe context wrappers and context aggregator in more detail.

4.1   Context Wrappers

Context wrappers obtain raw context information from various sources such as hardware sensors and software programs and transform them into context markups (see Section 3.1). Some context wrappers such as the RFID location context wrapper and the environment context wrapper (which gathers environmental information such as temperature, noise and light from embedded sensors) work with hardware sensors deployed in the Smart Space. Software-based context wrappers include the activity context wrapper, which extracts schedule information from Microsoft's Outlook 2000 and the weather context wrapper which periodically queries a Weather Web Service (www.xmethods.com) to gather local weather information.

To support explicit and uniform representation of context from a variety of context sources, wrappers in Semantic Space transform raw data (e.g. sensor data) into context markups based on shared ontologies used in the context model. As described in Section 3.1, context markups flowing within the Semantic Space are described in ontology instances, which can be serialized using alternative concrete syntaxes including RDF/XML and RDF/N-Triple. For example, a piece of context markup expressing the weather forecast of a city is serialized into XML (Figure 4(a) and triple format Figure 4 (b)).

```
<City rdf:id=http://...#Singapore>
<highTemperature>36</highTemperature>
<lowTemperature>28</lowTemperature>
<weatherType rdf:resource="http://...#Sunny"/>
```
(a)
```
(<http://...#Singapore> <http://...#highTemperature> "36")
(<http://...#Singapore> <http://...#lowTemperature> "28")
(<http://...#Singapore> <http://...#weatherType> <http://...#Sunny)
```
(b)

Fig. 4. XML and triple serialization of weather context

In Semantic Space, context wrappers publish context markups in the form of triples and other components can search for wrappers based on the matching of triple patterns. A triple pattern is a (subject, predicate, object) comprising named variables and RDF values (URIs and literals). To explicitly describe the wrapper's capability, each wrapper is associated with one or more triple patterns to specify the types of provided context. These triple patterns will be used as service description in wrapper advertisement and discovery. An example triple pattern for the location wrapper is:

```
(?user, http://...#locatedInRoom, ?room)
```

Once a wrapper is started, it periodically sends advertisement messages (with triple patterns) on the local network. Due to multicast and the periodic messages, other components in the system (e.g., context aggregator, context interpreter, context-aware applications etc) are notified about the presence of a wrapper, followed by the process of triple pattern matching and context subscription.

Our context wrappers have been implemented as UPnP services that can dynamically join a Smart Space, obtain IP addresses, and multicast their presence for others to discover. Context wrappers use the UPnP general event notification architecture (GENA) to publish context changes as events to which consumers (e.g., event-driven context interpreters) can subscribe. Since all context wrappers in Semantic Space are self-configuring components that support a unified interface for acquiring contexts from sensors and providing context markups, event-driven context interpreters in Semantic Space can easily leverage on context wrappers to provide the primitive events used in event-driven context interpretation. Since these primitive events can be dynamically added (and discovered) during runtime, the system is therefore able to evolve dynamically with new primitive and composite events being added at runtime.

4.2   Context Aggregator

Context aggregator discovers context wrappers and gathers context markups from them. The need for aggregation comes in part from the distributed nature of context, as context must often be retrieved from distributed sensors via various context wrappers. Aggregation is also critical for supporting knowledge-based management and processing tasks, such as expressive query and logic inference of context.

We implemented the context aggregator as an *UPnP control point* which inherits the capability to discover wrappers and subscribe to context changes. Once a new wrapper is attached to the Smart Space, context aggregator will discover it and register to published context. Whenever a wrapper detects the change in context, context aggregator is notified and then asserts the updated context markups into the context knowledge base.

To support event-driven context interpretation, we extend the context aggregator with an interface whereby information on the set of context wrappers (and their associated context) currently available can be retrieved. Rather than discovering individual context wrappers, primitive events available for composite event formulation can be made available from a single point, thereby simplifying the implementation of composite event formulation in event-driven context interpretation (see Section 6).

5   Event-Driven Context Interpretation

In this section, we look at the design of the event-driven context interpreter. We start by describing event graphs which are data structures representing composite events and explain the composite event detection algorithm used in event-driven context interpretation. We assert that event-driven context interpretation has a place in Semantic Space as another approach to context interpretation by discussing the advantages of event-driven context interpretation over context reasoning in Semantic Space.

5.1   Event Graphs

Event expressions contained in composite event specifications are converted into a collection of event graphs which are used in the composite event detection process.

An event graph is effective on a per computing entity basis. An event graph comprises non-terminal nodes (N-nodes), terminal nodes (T-nodes) and edges. N-nodes represent composite events and may have several incoming and outgoing edges. T-nodes represent primitive events and have no incoming edges, except those from remote computing entities which have been subscribed to for incoming network events, and possibly several outgoing edges. Figures 5(a) and 5(b) show the event graphs for the medical management example described in Section 3.2.

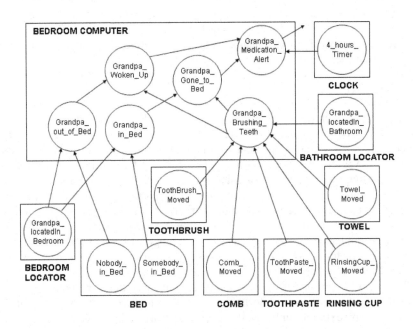

Fig. 5(a). Event Graphs for Example Context Interpreter 1

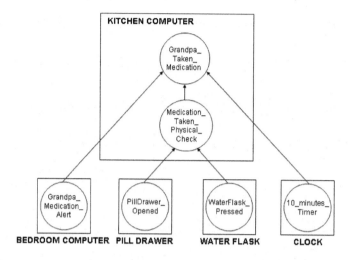

Fig. 5(b). Event Graphs for Example Context Interpreter 2

5.2   Composite Event Detection Algorithm

The composite event detection algorithm is an extension of the composite event detection algorithm in Snoop [14] so as to cater to a distributed environment where computing entities can subscribe to other computing entities in the system for events of interest to them.

When a primitive event occurs, it activates the terminal node that represents the event in the event graph. This in turn activates all nodes attached to it via the outgoing edges. When a node is activated, it evaluates the incoming event using the operator semantics of the node and if necessary, activates one or more nodes connected to it by propagating the event to them. An example of how the composite event detection algorithm operates for the "Or" and "Aperiodic" operators is shown in the flow chart in Figure 6.

5.3   Event-Driven Context Interpreter

Figure 7 shows the overall architecture of the event-driven context interpreter. A packet filter filters packets containing event graphs to the *Event Graph Processor* module and packets containing events to the *Primitive Event Detector* module. Upon receiving the event graphs, the *Event Graph Processor* merges new event graphs with existing event graphs in the *Event Catalog* and updates the *Event Catalog*. The *Event Graph Processor* then proceeds to subscribe to the context wrappers, context reasoners and/or other context interpreters for the events corresponding to the T-nodes in the event graphs, if the required subscriptions do not already exist. Upon receiving network events or when a local event is detected, the *Primitive Event Detector* sends an event notification (with its associated event information) to the *Event Queue*.

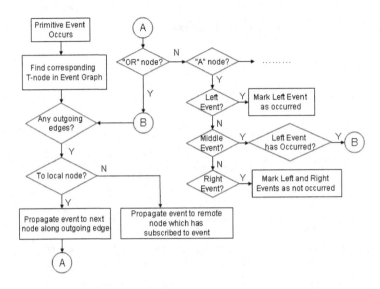

Fig. 6. Composite Event Detection for the "Or" and "Aperiodic" Operators

The *Composite Event Detector* retrieves each event from the *Event Queue* and processes it using the composite event detection algorithm (see Section 5.2) based on the event graphs stored in the *Event Catalog*. As the event graph is transversed, the *Event Dispatcher* will be signalled when graph nodes with event subscriptions are encountered. The *Event Dispatcher* will in turn send event notifications to the computing entities (e.g., other context interpreters or ECA Rule Service (see Section 6)) which have subscribed to the events.

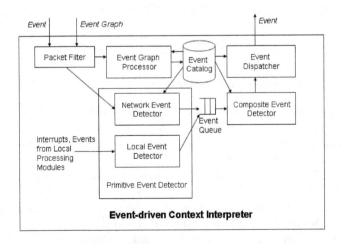

Fig. 7. Architecture of Event-driven Context Interpreter

5.4 Comparison of Event-Driven Context Interpretation with Context Reasoning

Figure 8(a) shows the model for our event-driven context interpretation. In this model, events corresponding to low-level contexts 1 and 2 generated by context wrappers 1 and 2 are propagated to context interpreter 1 where high-level context 1, specified in terms of low-level contexts 1 and 2 using the event specification language (see Section 3.2), is interpreted using the composite event detection algorithm (see Section 5.2). High-level context 1 is then propagated as an event to context interpreter 2. Low-level context 3 event from context wrapper 3 propagates to context interpreter 2. At context interpreter 2, high-level context 2 specified in terms of high-level context 1 and low-level context 3 is then interpreted.

Figure 8(b) shows a different model where context reasoning is used to derive high-level contexts. In this model, context wrappers propagate their low-level contexts to a context aggregator which stores the context information in a context knowledge base. The context reasoner, through the context knowledge base, can then derive high-level contexts 1 and 2 by reasoning over the knowledge base.

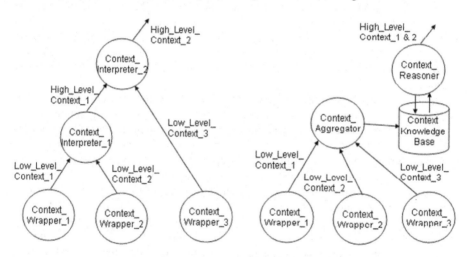

Fig. 8(a). Event-driven Context Interpretation   **Fig. 8(b).** Context Reasoning

By comparing the two models, event-driven context interpretation offers better performance in terms of flexibility, scalability and processing time. Being event-driven, processing can be triggered on demand in a flexible manner, thereby saving resources. The type of processing activated can also be selected based on previously received events. For example, in an environment where there are many sensors with power constraints, certain sensors can be active while the others are in sleep mode. When the active sensors detect a certain event, the others can be awakened to more accurately classify the situation. Distributed processing, which is more scalable than a centralized model, can be easily supported through the use of a number of context interpreters. The context interpreters, not only enable the processing load to be distributed, by having context interpreters close to its related context wrappers, the latency associated with deriving high-level contexts from low-level contexts can also be reduced. Event-driven context interpretation is also expected to perform better in terms of processing time when compared to reasoning since it is working with only a very small specific subset of the context information. In addition, with the proposed event specification language (see Section 3.2), temporal contexts, which are a very important category of context information [20], can be easily supported.

The tradeoff in event-driven context interpretation is increased communication overheads since event-driven context interpretation is based on a distributed model of the system whereas in context reasoning, communication is limited to accessing a centralized server.

6   Prototype

We are currently developing a prototype for validating event-driven context interpretation in Semantic Space (see Figure 9).   Besides the event-driven context interpreter, the prototype encompasses 2 other components, namely *User Interface* and *ECA Rule Service* which are designed to enable users to benefit from the ease and flexibility of configuring events and Event-Condition-Action (ECA) rules [22] associated with the events. We leverage on Semantic Space by making use of these generic components provided within the infrastructure: *Context Query Engine*, *Context Knowledge Base*, *Context Aggregator* and standard event subscribe/notify interfaces.

The *User Interface* component serves as the front-end to the user/programmer of event-driven context interpretation. Using this front-end, the user/programmer is able to (1) view all or selected events present in the system (both primitive and composite) and their corresponding context wrappers and context interpreters/reasoners,   (2) formulate composite events using drag-and-drop of events and event operators and (3) associate an ECA rule to a selected event. The typical sequence of user interactions is as follows. The user/programmer issues a semantic query about events in the system. The *Display Events* module retrieves the information by querying the *Context Query Engine* for event descriptions and the *Context Aggregator* for the network addresses of the context wrappers and/or context reasoners/context interpreters generating the events. The user/programmer formulates new composite events by drag-and-drop of selected events and event operators. The *Compose Events* module creates the event ontology associated with the new events and updates the *Context Knowledge Base*. The event ontology is also passed to the *Event Graph Generator* module which parses the ontology and translates each event expression there into an event tree. The *Event Graph Generator* exploits commonalities in event expressions and coalesces event trees into event graphs. The output of the *Event Graph Generator* is a set of event graphs for the various event-driven context interpreters in the system.   Each individual event graph is then sent to its corresponding context interpreter. If the user/ programmer wants to activate an action on the occurrence of an event, he/she can associate an ECA rule with the event by specifying the event handler and the ECA Rule Service which has the event handler installed.   The *Associate ECA Rule* module will then update the selected ECA Rule Service with the ECA rule information.

The *ECA Rule Service* component is intended to ease development of event-driven context-aware applications and can be considered as an instance of a context-aware application. With reference to the medical management example given in Section 3.2, the ECA rules can be formulated as follows:

On   P(status(Grandpa, hasWokenUp), 4 hrs, status(Grandpa,hasGoneToBed))
Condition   True
Action   Alert Grandpa and generate status(Grandpa, isAlertedToTakeMedication)
            event

On   status(Grandpa, hasTakenMedication)
Condition   False
Action   Send SMS message to care-giver

A packet filter at the ECA Rule service component filters packets containing ECA rules to the *ECA Rule Processor* module and packets containing events to the *Event Processor* module. Upon receiving ECA rules, the *ECA Rule Processor* subscribes to the context wrappers and context reasoners/context interpreters for the specified events and updates its *Rule Catalog* with the ECA rules. Upon receiving an event, the *Event Processor* will invoke the event handler for the event based on the information in the *Rule Catalog*. We plan to provide some common basic event handlers with the ECA Rule Service such as "Call X" or "SMS Y" which the basic users of the system can exploit. The more advanced programmer can implement a new event handler and install it in the computing entity running the ECA Rule Service, if the existing event handlers do not meet his/her requirements.

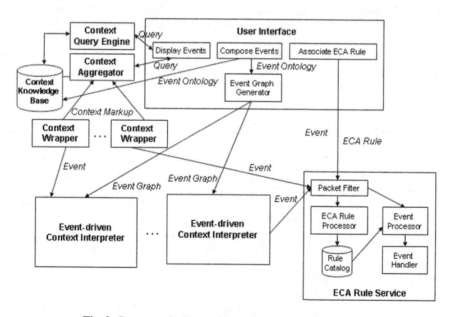

Fig. 9. Prototype for Event-driven Context Interpretation

7   Conclusions and Future Work

In this paper, we present event-driven context interpretation which is another approach to deriving high-level contexts in Semantic Space, a ontology-based context-aware infrastructure for Smart Spaces. We show how event-driven context interpretation can leverage on the context model and dynamic context acquisition/representation in Semantic Space as well as easily integrate into Semantic Space. Differing from the context reasoning approach, our proposed event-driven context interpreter offers better performance in terms of flexibility, scalability and processing time. We also present a prototype of the event-driven context interpreter we are building within Semantic Space to validate the feasibility of the new approach.

We intend to evaluate event-driven context interpretation with our prototype within Semantic Space in two dimensions: (1) Ease of development of event-driven context-aware applications using our generic event mechanisms and (2) Performance evaluation of event-driven context interpretation versus context reasoning. Our current model of event-driven context interpretation assumes that events can be detected with certainty. This is usually not the case in reality, particularly when sensors are involved. We plan to investigate further how composite event specification and composite event detection can be enhanced when events are detected in a more probabilistic manner.

We are providing event-driven context interpretation as a specific context interpretation mechanism within Semantic Space, which by design supports various context interpretation mechanisms co-existing within its infrastructure. We believe that event-driven context interpretation can be used to derive a wide range of useful high-level contexts, particularly when (1) the desired high-level context can be easily specified in terms of our event operators and (2) the desired high-level context is made up of many distributed contexts which can be derived in a hierachical fashion. As part of our future work, we would also like to further investigate and elaborate the specific scenarios in which event-driven context interpretation would be the preferred choice of context interpretation mechanisms.

References

1. Dey, A. K., and Abowd G. D.: A Conceptual Framework and a Toolkit for Supporting the Rapid Prototyping of Context-Aware Applications. Anchor article of a special issue on Context-Aware Computing, Human-Computer Interaction (HCI) Journal, Vol. 16 (2001)
2. Hong, J. I., and Landay, J. A.: An infrastructure approach to context-aware computing. Human-Computer Interaction (HCI) Journal, 16(2-3) (2001)
3. Wang, X., Zhang, D., Dong, J., Chin, C., Hettiarachchi, S. R.: Semantic Space: A Semantic Web Infrastructure for Smart Spaces. In IEEE Pervasive Computing, Vol. 3, No. 2 (2004)
4. Berners-Lee, T., Hendler, J. and Lassila, O.: The Semantic Web. Scientific American, May (2001)
5. Chen, H., Finin, T., and Joshi, A.: Semantic Web in the Context Broker Architecture. IEEE Conference on Pervasive Computing and Communications (PerCom) (2004)

6. Ranganathan, A., and Campbell, R. H.: A Middleware for Context-Aware Agents in Ubiquitous Computing Environments. In ACM/IFIP/USENIX International Middleware Conference (2003)

7. Wang, X.: The Context Gateway: A Pervasive Computing Infrastructure for Context Aware Services. Research proposal, http://www.comp.nus.edu.sg/ ~wangxia2, (2003)

8. Chen, H., Finin, T., and Joshi, A.: An ontology for context aware pervasive computing environments. Knowledge Engineering Review, Special Issue on Ontologies for Distributed Systems (2004)

9. Wang, X., Gu, T., Zhang, D., and Pung, H. K.: Ontology Based Context Modeling and Reasoning using OWL. Workshop on Context Modeling and Reasoning (CoMoRea) at IEEE International Conference on Pervasive Computing and Communication (PerCom'04) (March, 2004)

10. Gu, T., Pung, H. K., and Zhang, D.: A Service-Oriented Middleware for Building Context-Aware Services. Journal of Network and Computer Applications (JNCA), Vol. 28, Issue 1 (2005) 1-18

11. Gu, T., Pung, H. K., and Zhang, D.: Towards an OSGi-Based Infrastructure for Context-Aware Applications in Smart Homes. IEEE Pervasive Computing, Vol. 3, Issue 4 (2004)

12. Castro, P., and Richard, M.: Managing Context for Smart Spaces. IEEE Personal Communications, Vol. 7, no. 5 (October 2000) 21-28

13. Chakravarthy, S., Krishnaprasad, V., Anwar, E., and Kim, S.-K.: Composite Events for Active Databases: Semantics, Contexts and Detection. In VLDB (1994)

14. Chakravarthy, S., and Mishra, D.: Snoop: An Expressive Event Specification Language For Active Databases. Technical Report UF-CIS Technical Report TR-93007, University of Florida (1993)

15. Klyne, G., and Carroll, J. J., (eds.): Resource Description Framework (RDF): Concepts and Abstract Syntax. W3C Recommendation (2004)

16. McGuinness, D. L., and van Harmelen, F.: OWL Web Ontology Language Overview. W3C Recommendation (2004)

17. Jena2 Semantic Web Toolkit. http://www.hpl.hp.com/semweb/jena2.htm

18. Microsoft Corporation: UPnP Device Architecture Specification. Technical Report of Microsoft Corporation (November 1999)

19. Gruber, T.: A Translation Approach to Portable Ontology Specifications. Knowledge Acquisition, Vol. 5, no. 2 (1993) 199-220

20. Chen, G., and Kotz, D.: A survey of context-aware mobile computing research. Technical Report TR2000-381, Darmouth College, Computer Science, Hanover, NH (November 2000)

21. Miller, L., Seaborne, A., Reggiori, A.: Three Implementations of SquishQL, a Simple RDF Query Language. In Proceedings of First International Semantic Web Conference, Italy (2002)

22. Beer, W., Christian, V., Ferscha, A., and Mehrmann, L.: Modeling Context-aware Behavior by Interpreted ECA Rules. Proceedings of Euro-Par 2003, Springer Verlag, Vol. LNCS 2790, ISBN: 3-540-40788-X, (August 2003) 1064-1073

The Java Context Awareness Framework (JCAF) – A Service Infrastructure and Programming Framework for Context-Aware Applications

Jakob E. Bardram

Centre for Pervasive Healthcare,
Department of Computer Science, University of Aarhus,
Aabogade 34, DK–8200 Aarhus N., Denmark
bardram@daimi.au.dk

Abstract. Context-awareness is a key concept in ubiquitous computing. But to avoid developing dedicated context-awareness sub-systems for specific application areas there is a need for more generic programming frameworks. Such frameworks can help the programmer develop and deploy context-aware applications faster. This paper describes the *Java Context-Awareness Framework* – JCAF, which is a Java-based context-awareness infrastructure and programming API for creating context-aware computer applications. The paper presents the design goals of JCAF, its runtime architecture, and its programming model. The paper presents some applications of using JCAF in three different applications and discusses lessons learned from using JCAF.

1 Introduction

The idea of *context-aware computing* was one of the early concepts introduced in some of the pioneering work on ubiquitous computing research [28, 27, 13] and has been subject to extensive research since. 'Context' refers to the physical and social situation in which computational devices are embedded. The goal of context-aware computing is to acquire and utilize information about this context of a device to provide services that are appropriate to the particular setting. For example, a cell phone will always vibrate and never ring in a concert, if it somehow has knowledge about its current location and the activity going on (i.e. the concert) [22].

This paper presents the *Java Context-Awareness Framework* – JCAF. The goal of JCAF is to provide a Java-based, lightweight framework with an expressive, compact and small set of interfaces. The purpose is to have a simple and robust framework, which programmers can extend to more specialized context-awareness support in the creation of context-aware applications. Several projects have already been undertaken using JCAF, as discussed in section 6.

The paper starts by motivating JCAF and introduces the main design principles. Section 3 presents the JCAF runtime infrastructure and section 4 presents the programming model. Section 5 discusses the current implementation status of JCAF and the ongoing work based on the lessons learned so far. Section 6 presents how JCAF has been used and evaluated and presents two specific projects, discussing in detail how JCAF was

H.W. Gellersen et al. (Eds.): PERVASIVE 2005, LNCS 3468, pp. 98–115, 2005.

used and conceived by programmers using JCAF. Section 7 discusses related work and section 8 concludes the paper.

2   Motivation and Design

A common goal for programming frameworks for context-aware computing is to enable programmers to easily develop and deploy context-aware applications. Programmers can focus on modeling and using context information and functionality specific for their application while relying on a basic infrastructure to handle the actual management and distribution of this information. Requirements for context-awareness systems and/or frameworks have been widely discussed and described [11, 17, 15, 14, 16, 1, 8, 3].

JCAF incorporates many of the lessons from these previous contributions. But JCAF is also distinctive in at least three ways: (i) JCAFs service-oriented infrastructure is a distributed system based on the idea of dividing context acquisition, management, and distribution in a *network of cooperating context services*; (ii) JCAF embodies a general-purpose, robust, modifiable, event-based, secure *architecture*; and (iii) JCAF has a generic, extensible, and expressive *Java programming model* for the deployment and development of context-aware applications and context models.

The three distinctive features have emerged out of our analysis of the existing proposed context-awareness frameworks as well as from our empirical work within healthcare [3, 4]. In section 7 we shall discuss in more details how JCAF differs from the other related middleware support for context-aware applications.

2.1   Federated Context Services

The infrastructure of JCAF relies on having a set of distributed context services that cooperate in a loosely coupled peer-to-peer fashion. A context service is often dedicated to a specific purpose. For example, a context service might run in an operating room, handling specific context information in this setting, like who is there, what are they doing, who is the patient, and what is the status of the operation. This context service cooperates with context services in other parts of a hospital. Most context management is specific for the operating theatre, but occasionally it might become relevant to contact services running in the rest of the hospital. Therefore, the JCAF infrastructure consists of a network of loosely coupled context services, which cooperate in a peer-to-peer or hierarchical fashion. The exact topology of the context services are designed to fit the specific deployment of JCAF in a certain application.

2.2   Modifiable, Event-Based and Secure Architecture

A core software architecture quality [6] of JCAF is *modifiability*, i.e. support for adding, deleting, modifying, or varying functionality, capacity, or platform. The JCAF framework is designed to be highly modifiable and extensible at runtime – not at design and compile time as many other frameworks are. JCAF services, monitors, actuators, and clients can be added to the JCAF runtime infrastructure while running. The design principle of deploying a federated set of cooperating context services enables users of the framework to add special designed context services and register them in the infrastructure. For example, in a hospital where a set of JCAF context services may run as the core context-awareness infrastructure, a new context service responsible for context-aware application in the emergency department can be deployed at a later stage. This specialized 'emergency context service' serves context-aware application in the emergency department while cooperating and exchanging context information with the rest of the context services running in the hospital.

Many context-aware applications may only be interested in being notified about changes of context. Therefore, JCAF is based on an *event-based* infrastructure [9, 12], thereby ensuring a decoupling in space, time, and thread synchronization. The context service in JCAF has a publish-subscribe-notify interface notifying subscribers about changes in context. For example, a context-aware application showing relevant medical images during surgery would subscribe to changes in the context of an operating theatre. This application would be notified on the enterance of the patient and the surgeon, and is able to display appropiate images for the patient tailored to the preferences of the surgeon.

Context data, used e.g. in a medical setting, should be protected, subject to access control, and not revealed to unauthorized clients [7, 21]. Furthermore, establishing the credibility and origin of context information is key for some type of context-aware applications. Such cases may require an authentication mechanism for clients, and even a secure communication link between clients and services. However, in line with [20] we argue for supporting *adequate security* in a ubicomp environment. Hence, eavesdropping sensor information like temperature and location is seldom a major security issue – often it is easier to measure the temperature than listening in on low-power radio communication. JCAF supports a minimal set of default set of security mechanisms for access control and authentication. Additional support for security, authentication, access control, and encryption can be added to the JCAF framework by using the Java Security API.

2.3   Minimal Java API

The main goal of the programming model of JCAF is to provide the programmer with a framework that is extensible in a way that it helps him or her implement application-specific functionality by extending the JCAF framework. Hence, in the design of JCAF we have put special emphasis on providing only a minimal set of interfaces and classes that provides generic support for context modeling and handling while ensuring that these interfaces and classes (constructs of the programming model) are as expressive as possible. As we shall discuss in section 6 the constructs of the JCAF programming model have evolved over long period of time and incorporated experience in developing several types of context-aware applications for different settings.

Furthermore, applications are concerned with the quality of context information, including uncertainty [16, 24]. Therefore, the JCAF programming model encourage the programmer of context-aware applications to consider saving, revealing, and using quality measures for context information. Hence, the JCAF interface requires the programmer to implement methods on context information quality. For example, a clinical application trying to find relevant patient data during an operation might suggest to show more than one piece of medical data, if the sensing uncertainty is too high. Quality measures for context information are preserved from measurement, through any transformation to its use by applications.

3   The JCAF Runtime Infrastructure

The JCAF Runtime Infrastructure is illustrated in figure 1. Figure 1a illustrates a deployment situation with a range of *Context Services* which are connected in a peer-to-peer setup, each responsible for handling context in a specific environment like the operating room. A network of services can cooperate by querying each other for context information. All connections in figure 1 are remote and hence all components in JCAF can be distributed in a network.

3.1   Context Client Layer

Context Clients are the context-aware applications using the JCAF infrastructure by accessing one or more context services. Clients can access entities and their context; they can add or remove context information (and hence work as a context monitor, see section 3.3); they can add, query for, and use context transformers; and they can adjust the topology of the context service network. Clients can access entities and their context information in two ways. Either following a request-response schema, requesting entities and their context data, or by subscribing as an *Entity Listener*, listening for changes to specific entities. JCAF also supports *type-based* subscriptions of entity listeners, allowing a client to subscribe to changes to all entities of a specific type, e.g. patients. Context clients and entity listeners can access and subscribe to several context services.

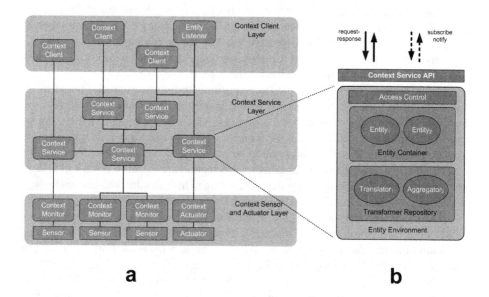

a   **b**

Fig. 1. The Runtime Architecture of the JCAF Framework. a – An example of a deployment situation of a set of context monitors, context actuators, and a set of cooperating context services. b – Details of a context service

3.2   Context Service Layer

Figure 1b illustrates the details of a *Context Service*, which is a long-lived service process analog to a Web Service, for example. An *Entity* with its *Context* information is managed by the service's *Entity Container*. An entity is a small Java program that runs within the Context Service and responds to changes in its context. The life cycle of an entity is controlled by the container in which the entity has been added. The entity container handles subscribers to context events and notifies relevant clients on changes to entities. An entity, its context and its life cycle are further discussed in section 4.2.

The Entity components in a Context Service work together with other components to accomplish their tasks. This is accomplished via the *Entity Environment*, which all Entities have a handle to when executing. The Entity Environment provides access to general resources like initialization parameters and logging facilities, and to user-specific resources, like databases, RMI stubs, shared objects, and other resources which are maintained across entities. Furthermore, the Entity Environment holds *Context Transformers*, which are small application-specific Java programs that a developer can write and add to the *Transformer Repository*. The Transformer Repository can be queried for appropriate transformers on runtime.

Access to a Context Service is controlled through the *Access Control* component, which ensures correct authentication of client requests. This component consists basically of two parts, namely an access control list, specifying what the requesting clients can access, and mechanisms for authenticating the client.

3.3   Context Monitor and Actuator Layer

There are two special kinds of context clients: the *Context Monitor* and the *Context Actuator*. A monitor is a client specially designed for acquiring context information in the environment by cooperating with some kind of sensor equipment, and associate it properly with an entity. A context actuator is a client designed to work together with one or more actuators to affect or 'change' the context.

The JCAF framework can handle the acquisition and transformation of context information in two modes. In the *asynchronous* mode monitors constantly deliver context information to one or more context services, which then can notify listeners or be queried. In the *synchronous mode*, the monitor is asked to sense context information. This is done when the context information for an entity is requested by a client. In this case, monitors associated with this context information are asked to refresh their context information. A user's current activity according to his calendar is an example where the activity monitor asks the calendar about the activity at the time of calling.

The interaction diagram in figure 2 illustrates the dynamics of this synchronous mode. First, a monitor registers itself at a context service by indicating what type of context information it can provide. When a client, who is an Entity Listener, is requesting context information by using the getContext() method, then relevant registered context monitors are called to acquire context information by calling their getContextItem() method. To avoid deadlocks (e.g. if the calendar system does not answer), the getContext() method starts a separate thread to handle monitors and returns immediately with whatever context information is available currently. When the Context Monitors starts reporting back (which might take some time), then clients

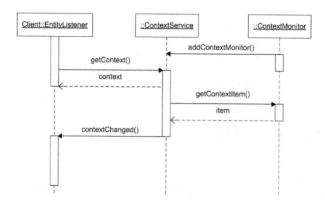

Fig. 2. Interaction Diagram for asynchronous context acqucition using Context Monitors registered at the Context Service

are notified using the `contextChanged()` method in the `EntityListener` interface.

Similarly, Context actuators can register at a context service by specifying what type of context items it is an actuator for. When a context item is changed in the context service (i.e. the `contextChanged()` method is triggered), then all context actuators registered as interested in this type of context item are notified with information about this new context information. This can, for example, be used to keep context information synchronized across a distributed network of JCAF components and applications.

4   The JCAF Programming Model

The JCAF programming model enables the programmer to create context-aware applications that are deployable in the JCAF infrastructure. The infrastructure both enables the programming model and makes use of it. The most important parts of the programming model is how to use the API of the context services, how to model context information for entities, and how to make use of the event-based infrastructure of JCAF.

4.1   The Context Service API

The `ContextService` interface has methods for adding, removing, getting and setting entities. The `getEntity()` method returns the service's copy of an entity object, whereas the `lookupEntity()` method contacts other known services trying to locate the entity object. The `lookupEntity()` method takes as arguments the id of the entity to look for, the maximum number of allowed hops between services in the search, and an `DiscoveryListener` which is called when the entity is discovered. The method is non-blocking and relies on notifying the discovery listener if a matching entity is found.

Embedded   in   the   context   service's   API   are   the   APIs   for   the `TransformerRepository`, containing methods for adding and getting transformers, and the `ContextClientHandler` interface, containing methods for adding and authenticating a clients, including context monitors and actuators. The `EntityListenerHandler` interface contains methods for adding, removing, and accessing entity listeners (see section 4.3). The `EntityEnvironment` is shared by all entities in a service and has methods for setting and getting attributes, accessing information about the local context service, and accessing the transformer repository.

4.2   Modelling Entity and Context

Context modeling in JCAF is done by making object-oriented models in Java. The core modeling interfaces provided by JCAF are the `Entity`, `Context`, `Relation`, and `ContextItem` interfaces. JCAF provides default implementations of these core interfaces. For example the `GenericEntity` class implements the `Entity` interface and can be used to create concrete entities using specialization. These are illustrated in figure 3.

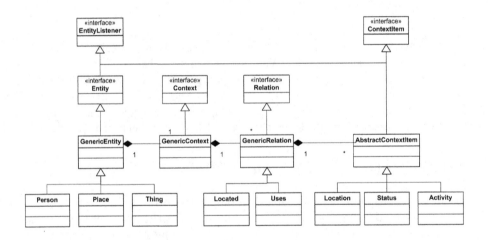

Fig. 3. The UML model of an `Entity` with a `Context` containing a range of `ContextItems`, each having a certain `Relation` to the context. Note that the an entity is also a context item

Persons, places, things, patients, beds, pill containers, etc. are examples of entities. A Hospital Context and a Office Context, each knowing specific aspects about a hospital and an office, respectively, are examples of context. Physical location, activity as revealed by a user's calendar, and the status of an operation are examples of context items. Examples of relations are 'using' or 'located'. Hence, we can model that '$person_X$ is *located* in *room.*333' where $person_X$ is the Entity, *located* is the relation, and *room.*333 is the context item.

The `ContextItem` interface is shown below. It is important to be able to judge the quality of a context item [16]. For example, how accurate is the location estimate. The `getAccuracy()` method is used for this purpose. Implementations of a context items returns a probability between zero and one. The `isSecure()` method is used to establish whether this context information originates from a trusted and authenticated context monitor.

```
public interface ContextItem extends Serializable {
  public long getSequenceID();
  public boolean isSecure();
  public double getAccuracy();
  public boolean equals(ContextItem anotherItem);
}
```

A subtle, but rather important aspect of entities is that they themselves are context items. Hence, in JCAF it is possible to add an entity as a context item for another entity. For example, in a Bang and Olufsen Home entertainment project we needed to model that a person is using a certain A/V equipment, like a TV or Radio. In JCAF both persons as well as the A/V equipment were modeled as entities and it was hence easy to model that "$person_A$ was using TV_x" by adding TV_x to the context of $person_A$ with a *using* relation.

4.3   EntityListeners and ContextEvent

The event-based architecture of JCAF is supported by the `EntityListener` interface and the `ContextEvent` class in the programming model. By implementing the `EntityListener` interface a client can subscribe to changes in context for an entity. Entity listeners can subscribe to changes in a specific entity or can subscribe to changes in a specific type of entities. For example, an entity listener can listen to all person entities. Clients interested in listening to context changes can implement the `EntityListener` interface shown below.

```
public interface EntityListener {
   public void contextChanged(ContextEvent event);
}
```

Entities themselves are aware of changes to their context by implementing the `EntityListener` interface (see figure 3). The central processing part of an entity is hence its `contextChanged()` method. This method is guaranteed to be called by the entity container whenever this entity's context is changed. This is a very powerful way to implement functionality handling changes in the entity's context and thereby create logic, which translates such changes into meaningful activities for users of the application. The `ContextEvent` object is a standard `java.util.EventObject` that gives access to the entity and the context item, which caused the change. A `RemoteEntityListener` interface exists as well, enabling clients to listen on changes to Entities in a remote context service process. This remote entity listener interface is also used across context services, thereby enabling one context service to listen to changes on entities in another context service. In the example where a special 'operating context service' is deployed in a hospital, this context service would listen to changes concerning e.g. persons who are in the operating room. Hence, in the AWARE framework developed on top of JCAF (see section 6.1), this operation context service would listen to changes to the context of the operating surgeon and may take appropriate actions, like revealing that he is busy operating or forward emergency calls only.

5   Implementation and Ongoing Work

JCAF is currently in a version 1.5 and is implemented using J2SE 1.4. The core functionality of JCAF as described above is implemented and working. Remote communication is currently implemented using Java RMI. A Context Service is looked up using the Java RMI Registry and accessed using RMI invocation. The lookup of entities in associated context services (using the `lookupEntity()` method) is also done using RMI. A configuration file contains information about known peers. Hence, there is no automatic discovery of other context services.

Security is implemented using an authentication mechanism based on a digital signature using the Java Authentication and Authorization Service (JAAS), which is a part of J2SE. This is currently used for context clients (including context monitors and actuators) and the authentication mechanism is part of the `ContextClientHandler` interface. Context information from authenticated monitors is labeled 'secure'. This security mechanism could be extended to include other types of context clients, like entity listeners and transformers added to the JCAF while running. Finally, security might be enhanced by using encrypted communication between a context service and a client, especially if sensitive (medical) data is transmitted. However, as discussed in section 2 we are very cautious about providing 'adequate security' and we are not sure if these latter security mechanisms are necessary. As for access control, a simple role-based access control mechanism is used currently: monitors can add context items (secure monitors can add secure items), and clients can query context information. From a privacy perspective, this access control mechanism is clearly a coarse-grained mechanism and we plan to extend it to real access control lists, which have a fine-grained specification of the rights of each client.

The projects that have been using JCAF have implemented a range of monitors for monitoring location based on RFID, WLAN, Bluetooth, and IrDA. Furthermore, monitors for monitoring activity in an online calendar and status information in an Instance Messaging system have been implemented. JCAF also contains several implementations of common entities (person, place, thing) and context items (location, status, activity, network capacity) as well as generic implementations of context clients and monitors.

6   Evaluation

A central research question is how to evaluate a programming framework. Our approach has been to use the JCAF framework in different situations – in different types of projects, including students and research projects, and in different types of application areas and for different types of applications within each area. Table 1 contains an overview of these projects. In this section we will discuss how JCAF was used in two of these projects: Proximity-Based User Authentication and the AWARE Framework. Both of these projects highlight different parts of the JCAF framework[1]. Furthermore,

---

[1] Each of these projects is motivated in our work on developing pervasive computer technology for the hospital of the future [2]. The design and evaluation of this technology have been done in cooperation with a range of clinicians, applying user-centered design methods like observations, design workshops, and prototyping.

Table 1. The use of JCAF in different projects, ranging from research projects (R) to students projects (S) in class

Project Title	Type	Description
Proximity-Based User Authentication	R	Enables a user to log in to a computer by physically approaching it.
Context-Aware Hospital Bed	R	A hospital bed that adjust itself and react according to entities in its physical environment, like patient, medicine, and medical equipment.
Bang & Olufsen AV Home	S	Using context-awareness to make B&O AV appliances adjust themselves according to the location of people and things.
AWARE Framework	R	A system that distributes context information about users, thereby facilitating a social, peripheral awareness, which helps users coordinate their cooperation.
Wearable Computers for Emergency Personnel	S	A wearable system for emergency workers, like ambulance personnel. Helps them react to changes in the work context.

in the end of this section we will discuss the feedback from programmers who have been using JCAF.

6.1   The AWARE Framework for Social Awareness

When people need to engage in a cooperative effort there is a risk of interrupting each other. For example, when calling people using a mobile phone or accessing them directly in their offices. People hence often tries to maintain a 'social awareness' of each other in order to align their cooperation to the work context of their colleagues. This social awareness relies on having access to the work context and when people are not co-located this access can be mediated using networked computers (including very small portable ones). The main purpose of the AWARE platform is to provide such social awareness by notifying and informing users about the working context of their fellow colleagues [4]. For this purpose JCAF is used to monitor the context of people.

Figure 4 shows the deployment of services, including context services, in the AWARE architecture. It illustrates the federation of JCAF context services into special-purpose context services. The AwareContextService in the AWARE architecture is responsible for managing context information for the users of the AWARE system. By using the lookup method and registrering as a (remote) entity listener, this AwareContextService replicates context information for users residing in other context services and maintains context information that is specific to the AWARE architecture. In our current implementation this includes location, status, and calendar information. In a typical deployment (as illustrated in figure 4), status monitors and calendar monitors add status and calendar context information directly to the AwareContextService, whereas location information is available in other context services in the network of federated JCAF context services.

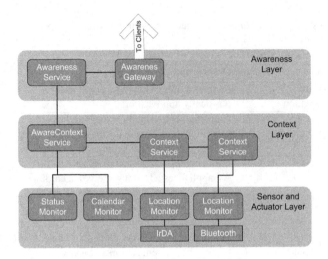

Fig. 4. The services in the AWARE Architecture, including the `AwareContextService` responsible for managing context information by cooperating with other Context Services

We have built two types of AWARE clients – a simple browser interface where a user can see context information about his fellow colleagues, and the AWAREPhone, which is a mobile phone client. The AWAREPhone implements a location monitor, using its built-in Bluetooth capabilities. Via the list of contact persons, a user can see the working context of a colleague and based on this information choose an appropriate cooperation strategy, like calling, sending a message, or not to disturb.

6.2   Proximity-Based User Authentication

Proximity-based user authentication [5] is a mechanism that allows users to log in to a computer just by approaching it and start using it. The system consists of two independent mechanisms. The first mechanism is a personal token with enough processing power to do public key cryptography. This token can be some jewelry (e.g. a ring, necklace, or earring), or it can be a personal pen used on the various touch screen embedded in a hospital. Currently we are using Java Smartcard technology as the personal token. When the user approaches a computer, this token can authenticate the user using public key cryptography. This is however not secure enough for use in hospitals – this token might be lost or stolen. Hence, when using e.g. smartcards in hospitals today, users are also required to enter a password or a PIN code. To avoid this, the second mechanism in our setup is to track the user's location via the context-awareness infrastructure. If the infrastructure can verify the location of the user in the same place as the token (and hence the computer) s/he is authorized. The location of the user can apply various methods based on e.g. something the user wear or trying to recognize the voice. Currently we monitor RFID tags woven into the clinicians whitecoats (see [5] for details).

In this application of the JCAF framework, two aspects become important. The first one is the security of the framework. If the context-awareness framework is used to verify the location of the users, it is of crucial importance that any adversary trying to gain illegal access cannot send a false "I'm here" message to the systems. Hence, we need to trust and hence authenticate the context monitors reporting on the location of users. A context monitor is authenticated to a context service using a public-key infrastructure. An example of a secure context monitor is shown below:

```
public class SecureLocationMonitor extends AbstractContextClient {

  SecureContextService scs

  public SecureLocationMonitor() {
    super();

    try {
      PrivateKey key = ... // holds this client's private key
      byte[] data = this.getClass().getName().getBytes();
      Signature sig = Signature.getInstance("DSA");
      sig.initSign(key);
      sig.update(data);
      byte[] signature = sig.sign();

      // tries to authenticate at the server.
      scs = getContextService().authenticate(this.getClass().getName(), data, signature);

      // If successful, then a secure context service is returned.
      if (scs!= null) {
        // Now use this secure service to provide some location information
        scs.setContextItem("1732745-3872", new Location("loc://daimi.au.dk/hopper.333"));
      }
    } catch (Exception e) {...}
  }
}
```

The only way to access a secure context service is through the authenticate method. When the setContextItem() method on the secure service is used, the context item is marked as secure. Hence, a client using this context information can ask if this item is secure by using the isSecure() method on the ContextItem interface.

The second aspect concerns the quality of the context data. It is of equal importance that the user authentication mechanism can judge the quality of the location data and decide whether the quality is sufficient to trust as a verification of the location of the user. Hence, the aggregation of quality (or uncertainty) measures is important in this application of context-aware computing, and thus relies on the getAccuracy() methods of a Context Item. In our current implementation of the Location context item, accuracy decreases by 1% pr. minute since the last measurement. In the User Authentication protocol there is a threshold, which determines how accurate the location estimation needs to be to verify the user.

6.3   Discussion

After each project we interviewed programmers about their thoughts on using JCAF. These interviews were often informal and were typically done while going through the code of their applications to see how they were using JCAF. Some of the things that was mostly appreciated in JCAF includes its event-based architecture, its modifiability, and its Java-based programming model.

The event-based architecture made programmers develop context-aware applications that were very loosely coupled and were reactive to changes in context. This style of application design and implementation was conceived by all programmers as a central benefit from JCAF.

The extensibility of the JCAF infrastructure and programming model was also highly appreciated by all programmers. The support for adding and removing context services, monitors, and actuators in a running infrastructure was used extensively. Often the event mechanism in JCAF was used to develop and deploy new modules in the infrastructure. For example, in the Bang and Olufsen project a 'Context-Aware Triggering' component were added, which were notified about changes in the environment and could trigger certain actions. For example, disallow children to watch PG-rated 16 movies on a B&O television. In another project, a history module was added. This module was listening in on relevant entities and a history update were triggered when an entity changed. This way of implementing new components as plug-ins to the existing infrastructure worked out well. In addition, such new components were working asynchronously with the rest of the framework by having the history or other modules run in their own threads (potentially on separate host machines), thereby not adding significant response latency to the rest of JCAF.

As for extending the programming model, all the projects implemented new types of entities, context, relations, and context items, which was a simple task for most programmers. Also new kinds of transformers were made and deployed. For example, filter transformers in the B&O project.

The Java programming model was also appreciated by most programmers. It was seen as simple and it was easy to start using. Also the programming model of JCAF conforms to the programming models of many other Java frameworks and experienced Java programmers hence find JCAF easy to understand and use. The Java programming model also helps integrate JCAF in other Java frameworks, like the Java Authentication and Authorization Service (JAAS) or Jini.

Some of the things that the programmers found problematic concern the deployment of context services in a network topology. To establish how to divide the infrastructure into different cooperating services was not always trivial. Furthermore, problems arose when an entity, like a person, had a representation and context information, which were distributed across several services. This introduced synchronization problems, which could be solved by having the distributed version of the entity in the different services subscribed to changes on each other. However, this still introduced some headache. A related problem was that information relevant for an entity – like a patients name and id number – often was in other systems, like a hospital information system. Hence, synchronizing such data was also problematic. This is, however, a more general software engineering challenges in many distributed systems and is hence not specific to JCAF.

Some programmers also found the modeling of context information in Java to be an overhead compared to just putting this information in a relational database and use SQL queries and triggers. Relational databases are clearly inherently good at handling relational data on the type of entity-relationships. However, many programmers also appriciated the pure-Java approach in JCAF and we have decided to stay within this model. We are, however, looking into how to address some of these challenges in the modeling capabilities of JCAF.

7   Related Work

As discussed in section 2, JCAF tries to incorporate the contributions from a wide range of related work within software frameworks for context-awareness. We shall hence concentrate on work specifically related to the core design principles in JCAF as described in section 2.

Creating support for context-awareness by having one server or infrastructure component is common in many context-awareness systems, like Schilit's mobile application customization system [25], the Contextual Information Service (CIS) [23], the Trivial Context System (TCoS) [17], and the Secure Context Service (SCS) [7, 21]. All of these act as the middleware that acquires raw contextual information from sensors and provides interpreted context to applications via a standard API. They can also monitor the context changes and send events to interested applications. This approach is often the simplest and most efficient way to ensure data integrity, aggregation, filtering, enrichment, etc. From a technical point of view, the use of one central server has its drawbacks in terms of having a single point of failure, scalability issues, and extensibility concerns. From a functional point of view, the collection of everything in one place makes a context-aware infrastructure hard to maintain while it grows in size and complexity. There is no way to separate responsibilities and concerns.

More distributed architectures have been proposed. For example, the Context Toolkit [11] has a range of loosely coupled distributed components and the architecture proposed by Spreitzer and Theimer [26] is based on multicasting context information to all members of a domain's multicast group. The Context Toolkit is distributed on a very low level of details and there is no way of collecting related context data and services into logical bundles. The disadvantage of multi-casting context information around is increasing computation and communication thereby paying a scalability penalty.

The federating context services approach in JCAF in a hybrid between having one server or a totally distributed infrastructure. This design principle is based on our different application areas. One the one side, the JCAF framework enables us to have a context-awareness infrastructure deploying in an organization (e.g. a hospital) where applications can discover and utilize this infrastructure when needed. On the other hand, the JCAF framework enables us to partition our infrastructure into separate but cooperating context services, each responsible for acquiring, handling, different kind of context information often in different localized settings. Hence, there is support for separation of concerns.

Many context-awareness systems incorporate some notification functionality. Infrastructures based on relational databases (e.g. [14, 17]) often use the triggering mechanisms in such databases and e.g. the Context Toolkit [10] supports subscriptions to state changes in a Context Widget. These approaches require their own specification language (e.g. in XML) to specify a subscription and only support subscribing for changes in low-level context information represented as native types are supported. In contrast to these approaches where subscriptions, notifications, and events are represented outside the programming environment, the event mechanism in JCAF is a part of the programming model. Hence, Java APIs for subscription and events exist and can be extended. The Rome system developed at Stanford [18] is based on the concept of a context trigger, much like context events in JCAF. However, Rome's decentralized evaluation of triggers embedded in devices does not allow context sharing and requires the device to have the capability to sense and process all of the necessary raw contextual information. In JCAF entities residing in a context service are notified on context events and can access each other locally and look up remotely located entities, without involving any clients. Hence, the JCAF event structure is not only used for client notification but also for triggering actions in the entities residing in the context services' entity container.

Despite the importance of security and privacy in ubiquitous computing [20] little work have been done here, with the Secure Context Service (SCS) [7, 21] as a notable exception. However, SCS is based on a Role-Based Access Control (RBAC) mechanism and is a closed system where the identity of all clients must be known to the system a priori. JCAF, on the other hand, supports a more relaxed security strategy where unknown context clients can access and provide context information, but this context information is labeled insecure. This strategy is more aligned with the basic purpose of JCAF, i.e. to provide the basic building blocks for experimenting with context-awareness.

Even though Java has been used as a programming language in many context-awareness systems, there is to our knowledge no Java Framework or API available for context-awareness. As a toolkit to be programmed in Java, the Context Toolkit [11] is what come closest. However, in the Context Toolkit, Java's basic abstractions for TCP/IP networking and hashtables of string-based context information is used. There is no object-oriented modeling of context information, nor any use of Java serialization of complex context data or the use of Java RMI. JCAF is an attempt to suggest a Java API for context-awareness, analogue to the APIs for e.g. service discovery in JINI. Some may argue that the use of Java in itself is not a virtue of context-awareness infrastructure that has to exist in a heterogeneous execution and application environment. However, we would argue – as also supported by our users (i.e. the programmers using JCAF) – that a pure Java-based framework is valuable because there is no need for dealing with special context modeling or markup languages.

8   Conclusion

Runtime infrastructures and programming models for creating context-aware applications and services are central in pervasive computing. This paper has presented the Java Context-Awareness Framework (JCAF), including its core design principles, its runtime infrastructure, and its programming model. JCAF has been used and hence evaluated in several research and student projects and we presented in some detail how JCAF was used in two projects in our research on creating ubiquitous computing support in a hospital setting. We discussed our experience from these two projects and more general experience from interviewing programmer, who have been using JCAF in different projects. When looking at related work, JCAF shares similarities with much of the research already done within creating generic support for the creation of context-aware applications. Distinct features of JCAF are, however, its support for distributed cooperating context services, its event-based middleware architecture, its support for a relaxed security model for authenticating context clients, and its Java-based modeling of context information.

The core feature of a framework is its extensibility and support for being used in several applications areas [19]. In our design and use of JCAF we have demonstrated that it is extensible both with respect to its runtime infrastructure and to its programming model. Hence, we believe that JCAF provides a comprehensive set of Java APIs and generic implementations which allow researchers, students, and programmers to start extending the framework and begin experimenting with context-awareness as a concept and as a technology. More information on JCAF, including a downloadable release, is available at http://www.daimi.au.dk/~bardram/jcaf.

Acknowledgments

The Danish Center of Information Technology (CIT) and ISIS Katrinebjerg funded this research. Henrik Bærbak Christensen was much involved in the early discussion on context-awareness in hospitals.

References

1. G. D. Abowd. Software engineering issues for ubiquitous computing. In *Proceedings of the 21st international conference on Software engineering*, pages 75–84. IEEE Computer Society Press, 1999.
2. J. E. Bardram. Hospitals of the Future – Ubiquitous Computing support for Medical Work in Hospitals. In J. E. Bardram, I. Korhonen, A. Mihailidis, and D. Wan, editors, *UbiHealth 2003: The 2nd International Workshop on Ubiquitous Computing for Pervasive Healthcare Applications*. http://www.pervasivehealthcare.dk/ubicomp2003, Seattle, WA, USA, Oct. 2003.
3. J. E. Bardram. Applications of ContextAware Computing in Hospital Work – Examples and Design Principles. In *Proceedings of the 2004 ACM Symposium on Applied Computing*, pages 1574–1579. ACM Press, 2004.
4. J. E. Bardram and T. R. Hansen. The AWARE architecture: supporting context-mediated social awareness in mobile cooperation. In *Proceedings of the 2004 ACM conference on Computer supported cooperative work*, pages 192–201. ACM Press, 2004.
5. J. E. Bardram, R. E. Kjær, and M. Ø. Pedersen. Context-Aware User Authentication – Supporting Proximity-Based Login in Pervasive Computing. In A. Dey, J. McCarthy, and A. Schmidt, editors, *Proceedings of UbiComp 2003*, volume 2864 of *Lecture Notes in Computer Science*, pages 107–123, Seattle, Washington, USA, Oct. 2003. Springer Verlag.
6. L. Bass, P. Clements, and R. Kazman. *Software Architecture in Practice*. Addison-Wesley, second edition, 2003.
7. C. Bisdikian, J. Christensen, J. Davis, II, M. R. Ebling, G. Hunt, W. Jerome, H. Lei, S. Maes, and D. Sow. Enabling location-based applications. In *Proceedings of the 1st international workshop on Mobile commerce*, pages 38–42. ACM Press, 2001.

8. L. Capra, W. Emmerich, and C. Mascolo. CARISMA: Context-Aware Reflective mIddleware System for Mobile Applications. *IEEE Transactions on Software Engineering*, 29(10):921–945, Oct. 2003.

9. G. Cugola, E. D. Nitto, and A. Fuggetta. Exploiting an event-based infrastructure to develop complex distributed systems. In *Proceedings of the 20th international conference on Software engineering*, pages 261–270. IEEE Computer Society, 1998.

10. A. Dey. *Providing Architectural Support for Building Context-Aware Applications*. PhD thesis, Department of Computer Science, Georgia Institute of Technology, USA, 2000.

11. A. Dey, G. D. Abowd, and D. Salber. A conceptual framework and a toolkit for supporting the rapid prototyping of context-aware applications. *Human-Computer Interaction*, 16:97–166, 2001.

12. P. T. Eugster, P. Felber, R. Guerraoui, and A.-M. Kermarrec. The many faces of publish/subscribe. *ACM Computing Surveys*, 35(2):114–131, June 2003.

13. A. Harter, A. Hopper, P. Steggles, A. Ward, and P. Webster. The anatomy of a context-aware application. *Wireless Networks*, 8(2/3):187–197, 2002.

14. K. Henricksen and J. Indulska. A software engineering framework for context-aware pervasive computing. In *Proc. PerCom'04*. IEEE, 2004.

15. K. Henricksen, J. Indulska, and A. Rakotonirainy. Modeling context information in pervasive computing systems. In M. Naghshineh and F. Mattern, editors, *Proceedings of Pervasive 2002: Pervasive Computing : First International Conference*, volume 2414 of *Lecture Notes in Computer Science*, pages 167–180, Zürich, Switzerland, Aug. 2002. Springer Verlag.

16. J. Hightower, B. Brumitt, and G. Borriello. The location stack: A layered model for location in ubiquitous computing. In *Proceedings of the Fourth IEEE Workshop on Mobile Computing Systems and Applications (WMCSA'02)*. IEEE Computer Society Press, 2002.

17. F. Hohl, L. Mehrmann, and A. Hamdan. A context system for a mobile service platform. In H. Schmeck, T. Ungerer, and L. Wolf, editors, *Proceedings of ARCS 2002: Trends in Network and Pervasive Computing*, volume 2299 of *Lecture Notes in Computer Science*, pages 21–33, Karslruhe, Germany, Mar. 2002. Springer Verlag.

18. A. C. Huang, B. C. Ling, S. Ponnekanti, and A. Fox. Pervasive computing: What is it good for? In *In Proceedings of the ACM International Workshop on Data Engineering for Wireless and Mobile Access*, pages 84–91. ACM Press, Aug. 1999.

19. R. Johnson. Documenting frameworks using patterns. In *OOPSLA '92*, pages 63–76, Vancouver, Canada, 1992. ACM.

20. M. Langheinrich. Privacy by Design – Principles of Privacy-Aware Ubiquitous Systems. In G. D. Abowd, B. Brumitt, and S. Shafer, editors, *Proceedings of Ubicomp 2001: Ubiquitous Computing*, volume 2201 of *Lecture Notes in Computer Science*, pages 273–291, Atlanta, Georgia, USA, Sept. 2001. Springer Verlag.

21. H. Lei, D. M. Sow, I. John S. Davis, G. Banavar, and M. R. Ebling. The design and applications of a context service. *ACM SIGMOBILE Mobile Computing and Communications Review*, 6(4):45–55, 2002.

22. T. Moran and P. Dourish. Introduction to this speical issue on context-aware computing. *Human-Computer Interaction*, 16:87–95, 2001.

23. J. Pascoe. Adding generic contextual capabilities to wearable computers. In *In Proceedings of the Second International Symposium on Wearable Computers*, pages 129–138. IEEE Computer Society Press, Oct. 1998.

24. M. Román, C. Hess, R. Cerqueira, A. Ranganathan, R. H. Campbell, and K. Nahrstedt. A Middleware Infrastructure for Active Spaces. *IEEE Pervasive Computing*, 1(4):74–83, Oct. 2002.

25. B. N. Schilit, M. M. Theimer, and B. B. Welch. Customizing mobile applications. In *Proceedings of USENIX Mobile and Location-Independent Computing Symposium*, pages 129–138. USENIX Association, Aug. 1993.

26. M. Spreitzer and M. Theimer. Providing location information in a ubiquitous computing environment (panel session). In *Proceedings of the fourteenth ACM symposium on Operating systems principles*, pages 270–283. ACM Press, 1993.

27. R. Want, B. N. Schilit, N. I. Adams, R. Gold, K. Petersen, D. Goldberg, J. R. Ellis, and M. Weiser. An overview of the parctab ubiquitous computing environment. *IEEE Personal Communications*, 2(6):28–43, 1995.

28. M. Weiser. The Computer for the 21st Century. *Scientific American*, 265(3):66–75, September 1991.

Place Lab: Device Positioning Using Radio Beacons in the Wild

Anthony LaMarca[1], Yatin Chawathe[1], Sunny Consolvo[1], Jeffrey Hightower[1],
Ian Smith[1], James Scott[2], Timothy Sohn[3], James Howard[4], Jeff Hughes[4], Fred Potter[4],
Jason Tabert[5], Pauline Powledge[1], Gaetano Borriello[4], and Bill Schilit[1]

[1] Intel Research Seattle
[2] Intel Research Cambridge
[3] Department of Computer Science, UC San Diego
[4] Department of Computer Science & Engineering, University of Washington
[5] Information School, University of Washington

Abstract. Location awareness is an important capability for mobile computing. Yet inexpensive, pervasive positioning—a requirement for wide-scale adoption of location-aware computing—has been elusive. We demonstrate a radio beacon-based approach to location, called Place Lab, that can overcome the lack of ubiquity and high-cost found in existing location sensing approaches. Using Place Lab, commodity laptops, PDAs and cell phones estimate their position by listening for the cell IDs of fixed radio beacons, such as wireless access points, and referencing the beacons' positions in a cached database. We present experimental results showing that 802.11 and GSM beacons are sufficiently pervasive in the greater Seattle area to achieve 20-30 meter median accuracy with nearly 100% coverage measured by availability in people's daily lives.

1 Introduction

Allowing users to discover and communicate their positions in the physical world has long been identified as a key component in emerging mobile computing applications [13]. Dozens of research and commercial location systems have been built using sensing technologies including ultrasonic time-of-flight, infrared proximity, radio signal strength and time-of-flight, optical vision, and electro-magnetic field strength. There have been many research and commercial efforts to improve accuracy and precision, shrink the size of the sensing hardware, simplify deployment and calibration of sensors, and provide more convenient middleware.

Despite these efforts, building and deploying location-aware applications that are usable by a wide variety of people in everyday situations is arguably no easier now than it was ten years ago. First and foremost, current location systems do not work where people spend most of their time; coverage in current systems is either constrained to outdoor environments or limited to a particular building or campus with installed sensing infrastructure. Applications like location-aware instant messaging fall flat if they only work for a fraction of users or only during a fraction of a user's day.

H.W. Gellersen et al. (Eds.): PERVASIVE 2005, LNCS 3468, pp. 116–133, 2005.

Second, existing location technologies have a high cost of entry to both users and application developers. Many location systems require expensive infrastructure, time-consuming calibration, or special tags, beacons, and sensors. The privacy cost to the many stakeholders is also typically ignored or considered only after deployment. These barriers leave location-aware computing in an unfortunate cycle: There are very few users due to a dearth of applications; developers are not interested in writing applications for nonexistent infrastructure; infrastructure investments are based on user demand, of which there is little. This cycle has not prevented researchers from prototyping and innovating in the application space. It has, however, prevented the widespread experimentation and adoption of these applications by real users. The result is that while we can give compelling demonstrations of location-based applications, few can be used in the places they are most useful: where we live, where we socialize, where we shop.

Place Lab addresses both the lack of ubiquity and the high-cost of entry of existing approaches to location. Place Lab is a fundamentally different philosophy compared to previous work because we focus on A) maximizing coverage as measured by the percent of time location fixes are available in people's daily lives and B) providing a low barrier to entry for users and developers. The Place Lab approach is to allow commodity hardware *clients* like notebooks, PDAs and cell phones to locate themselves by listening for radio *beacons* such as 802.11 access points (APs), GSM cell phone towers, and fixed Bluetooth devices that already exist in the environment. These beacons all have unique or semi-unique IDs, for example, a MAC address. Clients compute their own location by hearing one or more IDs, looking up the associated beacons' positions in a locally cached map, and estimating their own position referenced to the beacons' positions.

In this paper we show that existing radio beacon sources are sufficiently pervasive and can be mapped appropriately to meet Place Lab's goal of maximizing coverage in most people's daily lives. For example, Place Lab clients already have access to over 2.2 million mapped beacons situated in numerous cities and mechanisms are in place to scale well beyond this number. This paper will also show how Place Lab's use of commodity hardware and commitment to user's privacy lowers the cost of entry to users and how the high beacon coverage combined with flexible programming interfaces lowers the cost of entry for developers.

Precision of the location estimates, while important, is secondary to coverage, privacy, and cost in Place Lab. That is, we believe it is important to model location uncertainty and minimize it to the extent possible without requiring custom hardware or limiting the operation to controlled environments. This philosophy is similar to how ubiquitous wireless infrastructure remade telephony into an indispensable everyday tool. A cell phone with tremendous voice quality that only works in only one building has quite different affordances than one with passable voice quality that works almost everywhere. The former tends to lend itself to more niche problems like office automation while the latter finds a home in the hands of anyone who wants to socialize and conduct business throughout their daily activities. Although accuracy is not the primary concern in the Place Lab philosophy, it is clearly important to evaluate and understand the accuracy of a beacon-based approach to location. Therefore, this paper also presents experiments characterizing the accuracy of the

Place Lab approach as it relates to the types and densities of beacons in the environment.

Place Lab is released under an open source license. Binary and source releases for many platforms, as well as sample radio traces can be downloaded from http://www.placelab.org/. Adoption of Place Lab has been encouraging; as of October 2004 our system has seen around 500 downloads per month and a number of researchers are using Place Lab as a component of their projects.

This paper has three parts. First, we introduce the Place Lab architecture and show how it achieves the coverage and ease-of-use goals. Second, we present several experimental results quantifying the important relationships between beacon types, coverage, density, and accuracy. Finally, we discuss the future research problems and opportunities. This paper reports on the research contributions following the course laid out in our challenge paper which proposed using 802.11 beacons to create a global location system [11]. Specifically, we have designed a software architecture to make general beacon-based location a reality, implemented a system supporting multiple platforms and multiple beacon technologies, released the software through the open source community, and conducted coverage and accuracy experiments in the real world.

2 Related Work

Noticing the benefits afforded by high coverage and availability of a mobile service is not a new observation. Modern cellular telephone service providers stake their business on it. Moreover, many cellular providers are even starting to compute and offer the locations of the devices on their network as part of a push to branch out beyond basic telephony services. Separately, the Global Positioning System (GPS) is a location system which was designed to maximize coverage. Unfortunately neither cellular phone location nor GPS (nor any of the existing research location systems) provide both maximal coverage measured by percent of time that location fixes are available in people's daily lives and an extremely low-barrier to entry for users and developers.

GPS works world-wide and GPS capability can be added to existing devices using a variety of external dongles, cards, and corded accessories. The basic GPS scheme provides median accuracy of 10 meters, and various augmentation schemes have been added to improve this. GPS could be said to meet goal B of Place Lab in that it provides a relatively low barrier to entry (although an external card and antenna is still an additional cost over current commodity hardware). However, GPS fails to meet Place Lab's coverage goal because GPS receivers, while having high availability as measured by the percent of the earth's surface covered, have poor coverage measured by the percent of time they work where most people spend most of their time. GPS receivers require a clear view of the sky and thus they do not work indoors or under cover. They also work poorly in many cities where the so called "urban canyons" formed by tall buildings prevent them from seeing enough satellites to get a position lock. This limited availability severely constrains the class of applications for which GPS is an appropriate location technology. GPS is appropriate for and has been used successfully in navigation, tourism and search and rescue applications which primarily happen outdoors. Most individuals, however, spend the vast majority of their day indoors so day-to-day applications that rely on GPS location alone would have stretches lasting hours in which no changes in location would be reported. We present experimental results to verify this claim in Section 5.

Cell-phone companies have long been able to track phone users with network techniques like time-of-arrival or signal strength and handset techniques like assisted GPS that combine handset GPS receivers with network servers to assist in location calculation. E911 Phase II legislation in the US requires cell phone companies to be able to locate handsets within 150 meters by Dec 31, 2005. E112 initiatives in Europe are similar. Some cellular service providers have begun using the knowledge of handset location to offer users location-based services and applications. An example is AT&T Wireless' Friend Finder that is part of their mMode services. E911-like location services meet Place Lab's goal of high coverage since they work wherever normal cell phones do, but their success in providing a low barrier to entry is less encouraging. While Place Lab clients compute their own location, cellular carriers estimate a phone's location in the network and sell that information back to the user for a fee. The current fees of around $1 US per query substantially limit the application domains for which users will be willing to access these services. Furthermore, provider-driven location works only on cell phones whereas Place Lab can present the same location programming interfaces on phones, notebooks, and PDAs using any radio beacon technology.

A variety of previous device positioning systems use 802.11 access points as beacons from which to estimate location. The RADAR system showed that 1.5 meter accuracy could be obtained by constructing a detailed "radio fingerprint" of the available 802.11 access points and how strongly they could be heard along a one foot by one foot grid within an office building [3]. Ekahau (ekahau.com) sells a commercial software product that does very much the same thing with similar accuracies. These systems differ from Place Lab in two ways. First, products like Ekahau do not ship with any radio maps and require that the user collect this data himself. This violates our barrier-to-entry goal that a system can estimate location right out of the box. Second, deployment of these systems is only feasible in small environments (places measured in square meters, not square kilometers) due to the large amount of calibration data that needs to be collected and maintained. In contrast, Place Lab uses sparser calibration data that can be collected while walking or driving and is contributed by a community of users (and for this coverage and ease of mapping, Place Lab concedes an order of magnitude loss in accuracy as later experimental results will show).

Other similar systems that use specific radio sources in the environment include RightSpot and Laasonen et al's GSM based system. RightSpot showed that 15 kilometer accuracy could be obtained by using FM radio station strengths to predict location on a smart wrist watch device [6]. Laasonen et al. use changes in the set of nearby GSM cell towers to construct an abstract graph of places where the user goes [7].

Finally, there are numerous indoor location system that make use of ultrasonic [10, 15], infrared [12], ultra-wideband radio (ubisense.com). These systems all require that hardware infrastructure be installed in the environment to be monitored. These systems are generally expensive, costing thousands to tens of thousands of US dollars for a 1000 m^2 installation. These systems primarily focus on optimizing accuracy rather than wide-scale deployment and have accuracies in the 5-50 centimeter range. They have coverage constrained to a room, building, or campus environment. While this availability is sufficient for many home or office scenarios, limited coverage rules out many personal and social applications targeted at people's daily lives.

A wide variety of applications have been developed that utilize location-based technologies. Without having to disclose their location to others, users can run navigation-oriented applications that display their location on a map, highlight local points of interest, or plot a route to a destination based on current location (mappoint.com, streetatlasusa.com). Users that are comfortable disclosing their location to their social network have access to applications like dodgeball.com and mMode's Friend Finder (attwireless.com/mmode) that facilitate social interactions in the physical world. Finally, for users willing to disclose location information to institutions, useful day-to-day services like Yahoo Yellow Pages (yp.yahoo.com) and Google's Local Search (local.google.com) are available to anyone with a network connection.

3 The Place Lab Architecture

The Place Lab architecture consists of three key elements: Radio beacons in the environment, databases that hold information about beacons' locations, and the Place Lab clients that use this data to estimate their current location (See Figure 1). In the following subsections, we describe each of these elements and how they are designed to help meet Place Lab's goals of maximal coverage of daily life and low barrier to entry for users and developers.

3.1 Radio Beacons

Place Lab works by listening for the transmissions of wireless networking sources like 802.11 access points, fixed Bluetooth devices, and GSM cell towers. We collectively call these radio sources *beacons*. They all employ protocols which assign beacons a unique or semi-unique ID. Hearing this ID greatly simplifies the client's task of calculating their position. As we will show in Section 5, the coverage and accuracy of Place Lab is dependent on the number and type of beacons in range of the client device. Fortunately, wireless networking infrastructure is being deployed at a rapid pace in places that users spend their time. Most developed areas of the world have GSM coverage and cities and towns are becoming blanketed with 802.11 access points[1].

Place Lab devices need only interact with radio beacons to the extent required to learn their IDs. Place Lab clients do not need to transmit data to determine location, nor do they listen to other user's data transmissions. In the case of 802.11, receiving beacons can be done entirely passive by listening for the beacon frames periodically sent by access points. These beacon frames are sent in the clear, and are not affected by either WEP or MAC address authentication. Other technologies like Bluetooth

---

[1] Our measurements in downtown Seattle, for example, show an 802.11b density of 1200 access points per km^2.

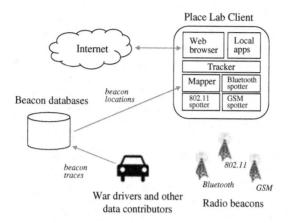

Fig. 1. Key components in the Place Lab architecture

require clients to initiate a scan in order to find nearby beacons. Due to restricted programming interfaces, detecting GSM cell IDs requires handsets to associate with nearby cell towers as they normally do when carried around and not on a phone call.

3.2 Beacon Databases

Place Lab has a critical dependence on the availability of beacon locations; if Place Lab knows nothing about a beacon, being in range does not improve our location estimates. In our architecture, the *beacon database* plays the important role of serving this beacon location information to client devices. We allow there to be multiple beacon databases and we do not specify whether beacon databases are private or public, how clients authenticate with a database or how many databases a client should load data from.

Many of these beacon databases come from institutions that own a large number of wireless networking beacons. Organizations like companies, universities and departments often know the locations of their 802.11 access points since this information is commonly recorded as part of a deployment and maintenance strategy. These data sets tend to be on the order of tens or hundreds of access points, and the maps are typically quite accurate. While these data sets were not originally built for doing beacon-based location estimation, it only requires a format-translation step to add this data to Place Lab and location-enable the institution's building or campus.

Other sources of Place Lab mapping data are the large databases produced by the *war-driving* community. War-driving is the act of driving around with a mobile computer equipped with a GPS device and a radio (typically an 802.11 card but sometimes a GSM phone or Bluetooth device) in order to collect a trace of network availability[2]. War-driving has become hobby for many radio enthusiasts and groups of

---

[2] The term *war-driving* is an allusion to the 1983 movie "WarGames" where Matthew Broderick's character David engaged in *war-dialing* by sequentially dialing blocks of phone numbers in an attempt to discover and establish a modem connection with interesting computers.

war-drivers have formed online and offline clubs to share and pool their trace data. Each war-driving trace is a time-coded sequence of records containing the latitude and longitude of where the record was taken, as well as the list of radio sources and associates signal strengths that could be heard at that time. By pooling their war drives together and applying some simple averaging, these groups have produced estimated locations for millions of beacons. Public domain war-driving software has been developed for most computing platforms, and there are many aggregation websites to which war-drives can be submitted. While war-driving has traditionally been performed in order to provide information about where nearby network access can be obtained, Place Lab uses these maps in reverse to infer where we are given a particular beacon is nearby.

Since the positions of beacons are being inferred from observations tied to GPS estimates, war-driving databases only contain *estimates* of beacons' positions. The error in these estimates translates into a decrease in the accuracy of location estimates made by Place Lab. However, what these databases lack in accuracy they make up for in coverage making them highly useful for Place Lab. As an example, wigle.net is the largest of the 802.11 war-driving repositories, and contains over 2 million known AP positions, and the recent "World Wide War-drive" added 275,000 new access points over an 8 day period (worldwidewardrive.org).

At this time, Place Lab clients have access to location information for approximately 2.2 million radio beacons, primarily 802.11 access points. These mostly come from wigle.net, but we have more accurate databases for UC San Diego and the University of Washington as well as some GSM tower locations imported from the FCC's database. To allow us to experiment with beacon placement algorithms, we also maintain our own database that currently has location estimates for around 40,000 GSM, 802.11, and Bluetooth beacons.

3.3 Place Lab Clients

The Place Lab clients use live radio observations and cached beacon locations to form an estimate of their location. To make client both extensible and portable, client functionality is broken into three logical pieces: spotters, mappers and trackers.

Spotters are the eyes and ears of the client and are responsible for the observing phenomenon in the physical world. Place Lab clients typically instantiate one spotter per radio protocol supported by the device. As an example, a laptop running Place Lab might have a Bluetooth and an 802.11 spotter, while a cell phone might run a Bluetooth and a GSM spotter. The spotter's task is to monitor the radio interface and share the IDs of the observed radio beacons with other system components.

An observation returned by a spotter is of little use if nothing is known about the radio beacons. The job of the *mapper* is to provide the location of known beacons. This information always includes a latitude and longitude, but may also contain other useful information like the antenna altitude, the age of the data, a learned propagation model, or the power of the transmitter. Mappers may obtain this data directly from a mapping database, or from a previously cached portion of a database. This cache can contain beacons for a large area, say the entire United States and Europe, or may, due to capacity concerns, just contain information for a single city.

The *tracker* is the Place Lab client component that uses the streams of spotter observations and associated mapper data to produce estimates of the user's position. The trackers encapsulate the system's understanding of how various types of radio signal propagate and how propagation relates to distance, the physical environment and location. Trackers may use only the data provided to them by the spotter and mapper, or may use extra data like road paths and building locations to produce more accurate estimates. As an example, Place Lab includes a simple tracker that computes a Venn diagram-like intersection of the observed beacons. This tracker uses very few resources making it appropriate for devices like cell phones. Place Lab also includes a Bayesian particle filter [1] tracker that can utilize beacon-specific range and propagation information. While computationally more expensive, the Bayesian tracker provides about a 25% improvement in accuracy and allows Place Lab to infer richer information like direction, velocity and even higher level concepts like mode of transportation (walking, driving, etc.). For more information on the intricacies and advantages of using probabilistic Bayesian filters in location systems, see Hightower et al. [5] and Patterson et al. [9].

3.4 Privacy

Privacy issues have had a strong influence on the design, implementation and use of Place Lab. Place Lab's key privacy principle is that devices should be able to position themselves based on passive monitoring of the environment. This principle gives the user control over when their location is disclosed, laying the foundation for privacy-observant location-based applications. Unfortunately, while it is theoretically possible to construct a device that senses GSM, 802.11, and Bluetooth passively, current devices are not as passive as we would like. For example, some 802.11 device drivers broadcast their existence to the infrastructure regularly. Similarly, we are not aware of any GSM cell phone that does not report itself to the infrastructure. Although the Bluetooth standard does not require that a device transmit its MAC address to neighboring devices when scanning, many of today's Bluetooth devices do so anyway.

Apart from passive scanning issues, another privacy trade-off is the manner in which mapping data is downloaded to clients from the mapping databases. Due to capacity issues, impoverished devices may only be able to load a small portion of the mapping database. However, if mapping data is downloaded for a small region, say a neighborhood, the operator of a mapping database has a reasonably fine-grained estimate of a user's location or potential location. Loading (and possibly discarding most of) a country or continent's worth of beacon locations gives the mapping servers less information about a user's location.

The war-drivers submitting their traces also have privacy considerations. War-drivers who submit their logs may not want a permanent record kept of the path they take while collecting a log. An approach to mitigating this problem is to have trusted entities anonymize and aggregate logs. For example, Place Lab has a design for a distributed backend database that slices up logs on a per-beacon basis and randomly distributes information about each beacon to a different node. Using this scheme, a contributor's war-driving path cannot easily be reconstructed yet the log is still useful for mapping. Of course any approach involving a trusted-entity still relies upon users trusting that entity.

Finally, we consider the privacy issues that affect the owners of the beacons used by Place Lab. Cell phone providers, coffee shops, and hotels probably do not mind if the existence and location of their network beacons are known. Individuals and corporations, however, may be wary in some cases of having information about their access points listed in a public database. They may be concerned about people attempting to steal network access or about revealing that they have computer equipment at a particular location. There are a variety of potential ways to mitigate these concerns. 802.11 and Bluetooth beaconing can be manually turned off, making them invisible to Place Lab. As stronger authentication becomes available for wireless networks, some concern about beacon visibility may simply disappear. Finally, there are possibly technical solutions to protecting beacon owners privacy in Place Lab such as using an encrypted hash of beacon identifiers so that clients must actually hear a beacon to resolve the true ID.

4   Implementation and Applications

With the exception of the small amount of native code that is written for each spotter, Place Lab is written entirely in Java 2 Micro Edition (J2ME). Place Lab currently runs on the following platforms and provides support for spotting the following beacon types. In addition, all platforms can access GPS devices for location and war-driving.

Operating Systems	Architectures	802.11abg Beacons	GSM Beacons	Bluetooth Beacons
Windows XP	x86	●	●[3]	●
Linux	x86, ARM, XScale	●		
Os X	Power PC	●		
Pocket PC 2003	ARM, XScale	●	●[3]	●
Symbian	Series 60 cell phones		●	●

The Place Lab APIs for spotters, mappers, and trackers are consistent across all platforms assisting developers in porting their applications to different platforms, *e.g.* from a full-featured laptop to a cell phone. To further facilitate low-effort development, Place Lab supports five ways of communicating location information to applications:

1. **Direct Linking.** Applications may link against the Place Lab Java library and invoke a single method to start the location tracking service.
2. **Daemon.** For lighter-weight interactions, Place Lab can be run in daemon mode and applications can query Place Lab via HTTP. This HTTP interface allows programs written in most languages and styles to use Place Lab.

---

[3] Place Lab supports GSM beacons on these platforms using a Bluetooth data connection to a paired Series 60 phone which actually receives the GSM beacons and forwards them to the master device.

3. **Web Proxy.** Place Lab supports location-enhanced web services by augmenting outgoing HTTP requests with extension headers that denote the user's location. By setting their web browser to use the Place Lab daemon's web proxy (in the same way one uses a corporate firewall's proxy), web services that understand our HTTP headers can provide location-based service to the user.

4. **JSR 179.** To support existing Java location-based applications Place Lab supports the JSR 179 Java location API [2].

5. **NMEA 0183.** Place Lab provides a virtual serial-port interface that can mimic an external GPS unit by emitting NMEA 0183 navigation sentences in the same format generated by real GPS hardware.

Several applications have been developed by both us and the Place Lab user community; we describe four of them below to illustrate the varied ways in which applications can interact with Place Lab.

- **Topiary.** Topiary is a rapid prototyping tool developed at UC Berkeley for designing location-enhanced applications [8]. A Topiary prototype can be run on one mobile device while the designer monitors the user's interactions from a second mobile device (Figure 2 is a screenshot of Topiary). In this mode, the user's location is determined Wizard-of-Oz-style by having the designer click the user's current location on a map. Topiary has been augmented to allow the designer to replace these Wizard-of-Oz estimates with live estimates from Place Lab running on the user's device. Topiary is using Place Lab as a GPS replacement, with the advantage that unlike GPS, Place Lab works both indoors and out.

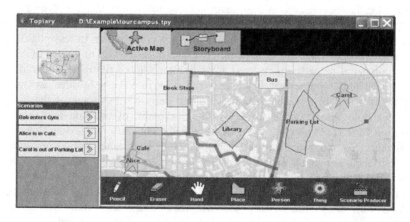

Fig. 2. A screenshot of *Topiary*, a prototyping tool for location-aware applications. Topiary uses Place Lab to allow the prototypes to use live location estimates

- **The PlaceBar.** We have developed a demonstration application called the *PlaceBar* that uses a browser toolbar to manage a user's interactions with Google's location-based search: http://local.google.com/. In addition to the query terms, Google Local accepts an address, or latitude and longitude and the results are filtered to return pages relevant to nearby places. Google determines page location by extracting information like addresses and phone numbers from the page content. When a query is performed in the PlaceBar, the user's location is obtained from Place Lab and is automatically used as the location for the query.

- **A2B.** A2B is an online catalog of web pages that allows users to add new geo-coded pages or query for nearby relevant pages (http://a2b.cc/). A2B can be queried by either manually entering a location or using a custom client that talks to a GPS unit. A2B extended their interface to support HTTP requests from by clients running the Place Lab web proxy. Devices running the Place Lab proxy can now talk directly to A2B in any web browser and automatically use their location-based lookup service.
- **Active Campus.** The Active Campus project is one of the most widely used 802.11-based location-enhanced systems [4]. Active Campus offers a suite of socially-oriented applications to students and classmates on the UC San Diego campus. The Active Campus project is currently porting their application suite to run on top Place Lab. The portability of Place Lab offers them more platforms than the small number that are currently supported. The large beacon database also offers them expanded coverage off campus in the surrounding cities.

5   Experimental Results

The coverage and accuracy of Place Lab depend on the number and mix of beacons in the environment, making it difficult to make absolute statements about the system's performance. However, certain high-level statements about the Place Lab approach are appropriate. First, due to the correlation of 802.11 and GSM beacon density with population density, Place Lab works better in urban centers than in less populated or rural areas. Second, Place Lab has better coverage in areas with ubiquitous GSM like Europe compared to partially covered areas like the United States. To quantify both the coverage and accuracy of Place Lab and how they vary by area we ran two experiments. First, to test our hypotheses about daily-life coverage of the different beacon technologies we outfitted users with an ensemble of small devices capable of monitoring GPS, GSM and 802.11 signals and had them carry the devices during their regular day. Second, we measured both 802.11 beacon density and corresponding Place Lab accuracy in an urban, a residential and a suburban area. Our coverage results were not surprising: both our user-time experiment as well as our density experiment show nearly ubiquitous GSM and 802.11 coverage whose density correlates with population density. Our accuracy results show that with sufficient density, 802.11 beacons alone can provide median accuracy of around 15-20 meters while GSM beacons alone provide accuracy of 100-200 meters.

5.1   Experimental Setups

We define the coverage of a location-tracking technology to be the percentage of time that the technology can produce a new estimate of the user's position based on what it senses from the physical world. If a GPS device, for example, has a satellite lock for 15 minutes and then loses its lock for the next 30 minutes and gets it back for 15 minutes, the coverage for that period would be 50% with an average gap of 30 minutes. Note that, consistent with the Place Lab philosophy, our formal definition of coverage is based on the user's time, not on geographic area.

To compare the coverage of GPS and the beacon technologies used in Place Lab, we outfit three users with a set of three mobile devices each and asked them to carry the devices throughout portions of a typical day. The devices included a Belkin wireless GPS, a Nokia 6600 and an Intel Stargate [14]. We logged, once per minute, the availability of GPS, 802.11 and GSM. All three devices were small enough to fit in a purse or backpack and had enough battery life to run for several hours. For our users we chose people from the authors' social network. None were computer scientists or students and the user's jobs included retail clerk, immunologist and a home maker. Between the three users we collected more than 30 hours of logs (10 for each of GSM, GPS and 802.11) that included work days as well as non-work days. Based on these logs, computing the coverage and coverage gaps of the various technologies was a straightforward task.

For the second experiment measuring beacon density its effect on accuracy, we gathered GPS, 802.11 and GSM trace data from three diverse areas:

- Downtown Seattle – a mix of commercial and residential urban high-rises
- Seattle's Ravenna neighborhood – a medium-density residential neighborhood
- Kirkland, Washington – a sparse suburb of single-family homes

For each locale, we drove around the areas for sixty minutes with a laptop, a GPS unit, and a Nokia 6600 cell phone. 802.11 scans were performed at 4Hz using an Orinoco 802.11 interface in the laptop. GPS readings were taken at approximately 1Hz using an external serial GPS unit. Finally, the GSM measurements were taken at 1Hz by the Nokia 6600 and relayed to the laptop via Bluetooth[4]. At all times we tried to navigate within areas in which GPS lock would not be lost as GPS forms the "ground truth" location to be used to estimate beacon positions and Place Lab's accuracy.

5.2 Coverage Results

The results of our user-time coverage experiment are shown in the following table:

Test Subject	GPS		GSM		802.11	
	coverage	avg. gap	coverage	avg. gap	coverage	avg. gap
Immunologist	12.8%	68 min	100%	-	87.7%	1.6 min
Home maker	0.6%	78 min	98.7%	2 min	95.8%	1 min
Retail clerk	0%	171 min	100%	-	100%	-
Average	**4.5%**	105 min	**99.6%**	1 min	**94.5%**	1.3 min

---

[4] Unfortunately, our Nokia cell phones only allow us to know the ID of the current cell tower with which the phone is associated, making it impossible to learn the full set of towers in range. While this allows us to know if coverage is available, it does not let us learn about density or Place Lab's accuracy if all towers in range were known. Thus all GSM-based Place Lab results are calculated using the *single* available cell ID.

In a real application, depending on the gap size it is often possible to apply smoothing, dead-reckoning, or various heuristics to try to fill in the gaps sensibly. This experiment ignores all gap-filling heuristics. Thus, we are not measuring the percentage of time that the application can make a meaningful guess at the user's location, but rather the fundamental coverage of the lowest-level estimation technology.

The coverage of GPS matched our expectations. It has poor user-time coverage and long gaps because satellites are cut off indoors or under cover where many people spend the vast majority of their time. Our subjects saw nearly ubiquitous GSM coverage. This is not surprising because once wireless carriers choose to offer coverage in an area, they strive to provide *complete* coverage. Even in places where the signal level may be too low to make an actual phone call, for example in an elevator or basement, it is still usually possible to see GSM beacons. The measured 802.11 coverage was slightly lower than GSM with similar gap sizes. From our data we can draw two conclusions. First, this data supports our claims that beacon-based location has the potential to provide user-time coverage which significantly exceeds GPS and is possibly ubiquitous. Second, comparing the coverage and gap sizes of GSM and 802.11 and assuming all other factors are equal, it seems GSM beacons are the ideal radio technology for Place Lab. However, all factors are not equal and the smaller cell sizes of 802.11 provide an opportunity for greater accuracy in Place Lab as the results will show in the next subsection.

5.3 Density and Accuracy Results

To confirm our intuition that beacon densities are correlated to population densities, we computed the distribution of the number of 802.11 access points in range per scan for each of the three areas we measured. The three histograms and accompanying satellite photos are shown in Figure 3. As expected, the highest density of APs were seen in the downtown urban setting with an average of over 3 APs per scan, no scans without APs, and a maximum of 15. Also not surprising, the suburban traces saw 0 APs (i.e. no 802.11 coverage) more than half the time and rarely saw more than one. The most interesting result came from the residential Ravenna data in which AP densities were higher than expected. With the exception of the approximately 10% of scans with no coverage, the AP density distribution for Ravenna fairly closely matched the downtown distribution. As we will explain shortly, the Place Lab accuracy in Ravenna actually exceeded that of downtown.

To evaluate the accuracy of Place Lab in our three neighborhoods, we divided each 60 minute trace into two halves: training and evaluation. The training trace was used to estimate beacon positions while the evaluation trace tests the accuracy of Place Lab. During training, beacon positions were estimated by averaging together all locations in which the beacon was observed. We then fed the evaluation trace into Place Lab and computed the accuracy of its estimate using only 802.11, only GSM, and fused 802.11 and GSM. To measure accuracy, the predicted estimates were compared with an interpolation of the two GPS readings closest in time. Note that GPS has an accuracy of 8-10 meters, bounding the accuracy of our measurements to this level of granularity. The position estimate was computed using a Bayesian particle filter tracker [5] with a sensor model that exploits the fact that observed signal strength and beacon-frame loss rate correlate with distance. Per-beacon signal and loss histograms are computed from the training data and these 50-100 bytes of calibration data are stored with each beacon's estimated position in the beacon database. These per-beacon parameters allow our tracker to predict location more accurately than our untrained models. The same technique works for both GSM and 802.11 beacons.

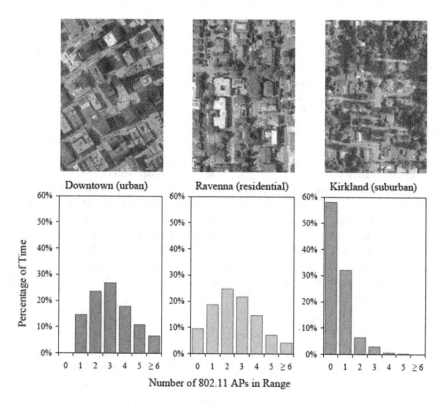

Fig. 3. Density of 802.11 access points (and photos) for the neighbourhoods in which we ran our experiments. For each area 7500 scans were performed at 250 ms intervals, while driving along surface streets. For each scan we recorded the number of APs in range. Satellite photos provided USGS through Microsoft's Terraserver

The following table shows the results of our accuracy tests.

	802.11		GSM		802.11 + GSM	
	accuracy	coverage	accuracy	coverage	accuracy	coverage
Downtown Seattle (Urban)	20.5 m	100.0%	107.2 m	100.0%	21.8 m	100.0%
Ravenna (Residential)	13.5 m	90.6%	161.4 m	100.0%	13.4 m	100.0%
Kirkland (Suburban)	22.6 m	42.0%	216.2 m	99.7%	31.3 m	100.0%

Two conclusions can be drawn from the results in this table. First, for single types of beacons, 802.11 outperforms GSM in accuracy although its coverage is worse in areas with sparser population. That is to say, when 802.11 beacons are in range, Place Lab's predictions are more accurate than with GSM alone. Given their relatively long range, GSM beacons play a high-coverage, low accuracy role in Place Lab. This tradeoff stands to reason because 802.11 has smaller cell sizes (shorter radio range) and, unlike GSM where cell placement is managed as a system to optimize coverage, 802.11 cells are deployed in small numbers by independent homeowners and institutions. Second, fusing 802.11 and GSM provides a good blend of accuracy and coverage. Consider the sparse suburban area of Kirkland where 802.11 coverage is only 42%. In Kirkland, fusing with GSM yields 100% coverage (up from 42% with 802.11 alone) with only an 8.7 meter decrease in median accuracy, despite the 216.2 meter accuracy of GSM alone in Kirkland. To explain this result, recall from the previous section that gaps in 802.11 coverage tend to be short. An effective location estimation algorithm like a particle filter can model the user's motion and allows GSM beacons to effectively fill in the gaps without the error ballooning.

To investigate the relationship between beacon density and accuracy we combined all data from the three areas and computed the median accuracy achievable by Place Lab using 802.11 alone. Figure 4 shows a graph comparing the accuracy of Place Lab as it relates to the number of unique beacons the client saw during the previous 10 second window. From this figure we can conclude that if 802.11 density is high enough for clients to see at least 3 distinct beacons during a 10 second window, the density is sufficient for Place Lab to achieve its "peak" median accuracy of 15-20 meters or approximately twice the error of unassisted GPS.

5.4 Bluetooth

The beacon technology notably absent from our results is Bluetooth. We found that non-mobile Bluetooth devices have not reached sufficient density where they are eminently useful for beacon-based location estimation in the wild. (Place Lab only looks for Bluetooth beacons likely to remain fixed such as printers, vending machines, and access points; we ignore nomadic Bluetooth devices like personal cell phones or laptops since their unpredictable mobility makes them harder to use to predict location.) Although our results do not report Bluetooth beacon densities, we did scan for them during our data collection and we saw virtually no fixed Bluetooth in any of the test locales. The sparseness of Bluetooth beacons is further exacerbated by the fact the each scan for nearby Bluetooth beacons takes approximately 10 seconds to complete. At this slow scan rate, a mobile device even moving only at human walking speed can miss a Bluetooth beacon it passes.

A simple experiment in our lab showed that due to their short radio range, fixed Bluetooth devices do improve Place Lab's accuracy. We deployed ten Bluetooth devices in our 1000 square meter lab and showed a Place Lab accuracy of slightly better than 10 meters using Bluetooth alone. This suggests that Bluetooth beacons could be deployed strategically in small environments to somewhat improve the client's location accuracy while preserving the Place Lab model of client-side location estimation with commodity devices.

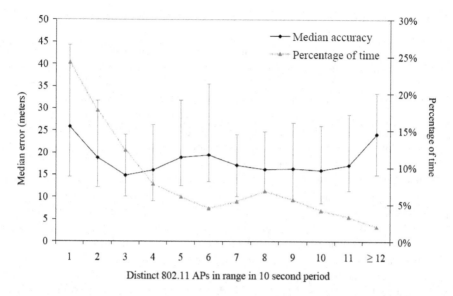

Fig. 4. This graph shows the effect AP density on Place Lab's accuracy. The graph includes all 22,500 measurements from the three neighbourhoods measured. The accuracy line is drawn through the medians, while the error bars represent the 1st and 3rd quartile readings. (50% of the readings fall between the error bars.) The second line shows how often we saw that number of distinct APs

6   Future Work

For many emerging location-aware applications it is much easier to utilize place names like "Bank", "Starbucks" or "Movie Theater", than geo-coordinates such as (48.43456, -122.45678). We are developing techniques that allow Place Lab to automatically learn and estimate places in addition to geo-coordinates. One step in this process is moving Place Lab to "2.5" dimensions. Place Lab currently only generates position estimates in two dimensions (latitude and longitude) and ignores the altitude component of location. This can present a problem in multi-story buildings where floor number is likely a key aspect of location. Our current belief is that generating "2.5" dimension estimates in which altitude is represented with a symbolic name such as "Parking Level A" or "3rd floor" are more meaningful than a coordinate-based altitude like 34.6 meters above sea level. We are planning to augment Place Lab to allow beacons and traces to be annotated with floor information and have our trackers predict this symbolic dimension along with latitude and longitude.

We intend to remove the reliance on GPS as ground-truth for war-driving and mapping new beacons. Given a map of a portion of the beacons, Place Lab should be able to use its *own* location estimates to map new beacons that are encountered in the environment. We plan to study the number of beacons which constitute a "critical mass" such that beacon trace logs *without* GPS can be used to grow and refresh the client's database as beacons are added, moved and decommissioned.

7 Conclusions

We believe that many emerging location-aware computing application are going to require 100% availability of location information in real people's lives, similar to the way cellular phones are held to a 100% availability standard. Place Lab provides the necessary features to move in this direction. In this paper we have shown that a beacon-based approach to location can A) maximize coverage as measured by the percent of time a location fix is available in people's daily lives and B) offer a low barrier to entry for users and application developers thanks to the use of commodity hardware, privacy awareness, and straightforward interfaces.

Our coverage experiment confirmed the intuition that GPS, often thought of as a pervasive location technology, in fact lacks availability in people's daily lives since people are frequently indoors or under cover, whereas 802.11 and GSM beacons are frequently available both indoors and out. This experiment was conducted by logging beacon availability using small recorders carried by people as they went about their daily routines.

To evaluate beacon-based location, we examined 802.11 and GSM beacon density and quantified the relationship between density and accuracy. In studying three distinct neighborhoods of the greater Seattle area (urban, residential, and suburban), we found that beacon density is sufficient to support the Place Lab approach. Specifically, for 802.11 beacons we can conclude that if density is high enough for client devices to see at least 3 distinct beacons during a 10 second window, Place Lab clients can achieve median accuracy of 15-20 meters. This accuracy is lower than GPS, but, unlike GPS, beacon-based location covers nearly 100% of users' daily lives. In the sparsely-populated suburban area we measured fusing 802.11 with GSM readings results in median accuracy just over 30 meters.

We believe Place Lab is a useful artifact for the research community. Binary and source releases of Place Lab are available for many platforms along with sample radio traces at http://www.placelab.org/. Adoption of Place Lab has already been encouraging; our system sees around 500 downloads per month and a number of research projects and web services are using Place Lab as a component of their system. Place Lab is an enabling technology because it is useful for developers and facilitates new research into location-aware computing such as exploring the meaning of place and the studying the utility of location-aware applications that can be deployed to real users.

References

1. *Sequential Monte Carlo in Practice*, DOUCET A. & DE FREITAS, N. (Ed.) (New York, Springer-Verlag).(2001)
2. JSR 179 Location API for J2ME, LOYTANA, K. (Ed.),(2003) http://www.jcp.org/en/jsr/detail?id=179
3. BAHL, P. & PADMANABHAN, V. RADAR: An In-Building RF-Based User Location and Tracking System *Proceedings of IEEE INFOCOM*, pp. 775-784 (Tel-Aviv, Israel).(2000)

4. GRISWOLD, W. G., SHANAHAN, P., BROWN, S. W., BOYER, R., RATTO, M., SHAPIRO, R. B. & TRUONG, T. M. ActiveCampus - Experiments in Community-Oriented Ubiquitous Computing, *To Appear: IEEE Computer.*

5. HIGHTOWER, J. & BORRIELLO, G. Particle Filters for Location Estimation in Ubiquitous Computing: A Case Study *Proceedings of the Sixth International Conference on Ubiquitous Computing (Ubicomp)* (Springer-Verlag).(2004)

6. KRUMM, J., CERMAK, G. & HORVITZ, E. RightSPOT: A Novel Sense of Location for a Smart Personal Object, Paper presented at the *UbiComp 2003.*(2003)

7. LAASONEN, K., RAENTO, M. & TOIVONEN, H. Adaptive On-Device Location Recognition, Paper presented at the *Pervasive Computing: Second International Conference.*(2004)

8. LI, Y., JASON, I. H. & LANDAY, J. A. Topiary: A Tool for Prototyping Location-Enhanced Applications, Paper presented at the *Symposium on User Interface Software and Technology - UIST'2004.*(2004)

9. PATTERSON, D. J., LIAO, L., FOX, D. & KAUTZ, H. A. Inferring High-Level Behavior from Low-Level Sensors *Proceedings of the Fifth International Conference on Ubiquitous Computing (Ubicomp)*, pp. 73-89 (Springer-Verlag).(2003)

10. PRIYANTHA, N. B., CHAKRABORTY, A. & BALAKRISHNAN, H. The Cricket Location-Support System *Proceedings of MOBICOM 2000*, pp. 32-43 (Boston, MA, ACM Press).(2000)

11. SCHILIT, B., LAMARCA, A., BORRIELLO, G., GRISWOLD, W., MCDONALD, D., LAZOWSKA, E., BALACHANDRAN, A., HONG, J. & IVERSON, V. Challenge: Ubiquitous Location-Aware Computing and the Place Lab Initiative *Proceedings of the First ACM International Workshop on Wireless Mobile Applications and Services on WLAN (WMASH).*(2003)

12. WANT, R., HOPPER, A., FALCAO, V. & GIBBONS, J. The Active Badge Location System, *ACM Transactions on Information Systems*, 10, 91-102. (1992)

13. WANT, R., SCHILIT, B., ADAMS, N., GOLD, R., PETERSEN, K., GOLDBERG, D., ELLIS, J. & WEISER, M. The ParcTab Ubiquitous Computing Experiment, in: Imielinski, T. (Ed.) *Mobile Computing*, pp. 45-101 (Kluwer Publishing).(1997)

14. WANT, R., PERING, T., DANNEELS, G., KUMAR, M., SUNDAR, M. & LIGHT, J. The Personal Server: Changing the Way We Think about Ubiquitous Computing, Paper presented at the *Ubicomp 2002.*(2003)

15. WARD, A., JONES, A. & HOPPER, A. A New Location Technique for the Active Office, *IEEE Personal Communications*, 4, 42-47. (1997)

Social Disclosure of Place: From Location Technology to Communication Practices

Ian Smith, Sunny Consolvo, Anthony Lamarca, Jeffrey Hightower, James Scott,
Timothy Sohn, Jeff Hughes, Giovanni Iachello, and Gregory D. Abowd

Intel Research Seattle,Intel Research Cambridge,
University of California, San Diego,
College of Computing & GVU Center, Georgia Institute of Technology, Atlanta, GA
{ian.e.smith, sunny.consolvo, anthony.lamarca,
jeffrey.r.hightower, james.w.scott}@intel.com
tsohn@cs.ucsd.edu
{giac, abowd}@cc.gatech.edu
jeffdh@cs.washington.edu

Abstract. Communication of one's location as part of a social discourse is common practice, and we use a variety of technologies to satisfy this need. This practice suggests a potentially useful capability that technology may support more directly. We present such a social location disclosure service, Reno, designed for use on a common mobile phone platform. We describe the guiding principles that dictate parameters for creating a usable, useful and ubiquitous service and we report on a pilot study of use of Reno for a realistic social network. Our preliminary results reveal the competing factors for a system that facilitates both manual and automatic location disclosure, and the role social context plays in making such a lightweight communication solution work.

1 Introduction

In many situations we use location, more specifically a notion of place, to communicate with friends, family and colleagues. People send postcards, teasing friends with catchy phrases like "Life's a beach in Biarritz" or "Thinking of you at the Grand Canyon." Even more often people exchange location information with people in their social network, using a variety of technologies, such as phone conversations, SMS, instant messaging, and email. User studies of SMS by teenagers in England [15] and Germany [18] agree that the top three uses are 1) to keep in touch with friends and acquaintances; 2) to coordinate and schedule physical encounters and phone calls; and 3) to chat. At least the first two of these uses suggest the use of location within the content of SMS messages.

Our focus is on an emerging class of pervasive computing application, the *social location disclosure application*, motivated by the explicit sharing of location information in social communication. One example of an existing social location disclosure application is Dodgeball [4]. Dodgeball helps cell phone users meet up with other members of their social network in the physical world, with a particular focus on the

H.W. Gellersen et al. (Eds.): PERVASIVE 2005, LNCS 3468, pp. 134–151, 2005.
© Springer-Verlag Berlin Heidelberg 2005

serendipitous encounter. Although Dodgeball has demonstrated value—it has approximately 1500 daily users—the space of social location disclosure applications is larger than just rendezvous scenarios.

Due to the large amount of shared social state between friends, co-workers and family members, the small amount of information contained in a place name is often sufficient to stand proxy for a wide variety of communications. We want to understand how people leverage social context using lightweight communication tools to share location. Furthermore, the emergence of technologies that allow mobile devices to learn and recognize their location reduces the overhead of sharing such information. This creates the opportunity to develop an application that allows users to exchange location information, manually or automatically, with other members of a social network. The design challenge is to create such an application with low interaction cost and high availability, without sacrificing the privacy or social control individuals want.

In this paper, we introduce Reno, a social location disclosure application that allows users to send their current location, manually and automatically, to other people in their social network as well as request the location of others. Reno runs on Nokia Series 60 mobile phones (such as the Nokia 6600) and uses cell-tower based location estimation to aid the user in defining and recalling places as well as triggering automatic disclosures. We describe our design, as well as the accompanying principles that helped us create a service that is both useful and respectful of people's privacy. We present the primarily qualitative results of a pilot user study of seven early adopters using Reno over the course of five days.

2   The Intended User Experience

The following scenario, adapted from a reported use in our pilot study, helps explain the basic capabilities of Reno. Figures 1 and 2 show screenshots of the user interface (UI) on a Nokia 6600 running the Reno application.

It's near the end of the workday, and as Phoebe prepares to go home, she wonders what she and her husband, Ross, will do for the evening. Ross should be heading home now too, but Phoebe thinks he may be in a meeting, so she doesn't want to phone him to ask. Instead she pulls out her mobile phone and, with a few quick clicks, sends a location query to Ross. Ross, in fact, is busy and working later than normal today. He sees Phoebe's request (Figure 1A), but chooses not to answer it.

His meeting ends about 45 minutes later, and while he is waiting at the bus stop near his office, Ross accesses Reno on his phone to send a location update to Phoebe (Figure 1B). The screen on his phone lists 4 place names that correspond roughly to his current location. His bus stop is outside Merchant Mick, a favorite store where he often buys dessert on his way home from work. When Ross sees that place name at the top of the list, he selects it, figuring that Phoebe will understand that he has left work and will be getting on the bus soon. Phoebe receives the message at home (Figure 1C) and is now eagerly anticipating Ross' arrival home.

When Ross gets off the bus, just outside the Easton Hotel, a location update is automatically sent to Phoebe, (Figure 2A) and she knows that he is only 10 minutes from home, so she sets out dinner just in time so that it is a warm welcome home for her husband. When Ross gets home, he smiles at the set table and says, "You are wonderful! I am late, and you already have dinner waiting for us!" Phoebe replies, "I made your favorite dish to go with my favorite dessert you just bought from Merchant Mick's." Ross, realizing that Phoebe misinterpreted the Reno message he had sent from the bus stop and feeling a bit embarrassed, admits that he didn't buy dessert tonight, because he was already running late. Seeing the disappointment in Phoebe's eyes, he decides to take her to Merchant Mick's for dessert after dinner. On the way home from dessert, standing at the same bus stop, Ross pulls out his phone and defines a new place in Reno that connects that place with the label "Bus stop by work," (Figure 2B), hoping to avoid the same confusion in the future.

Fig. 1. A, Left) Phoebe's request for location received by Ross. **B, Center)** Ross' list of nearby places he can send. **C, Right)** View of Phoebe's inbox after she receives Ross' location

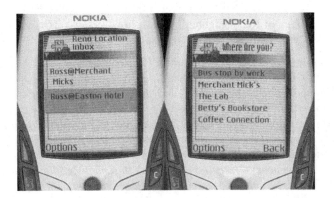

Fig. 2. A, Left) Phoebe's location inbox after receiving Ross' automatic disclosure. **B, Right)** Ross' list of nearby places after adding the bus stop

This scenario demonstrates four of the basic capabilities we built into Reno:

- explicitly and manually "push" a location disclosure to someone;
- automatic triggering of a location disclosure to someone else based upon entry or exit from a pre-defined and agreed upon location;

- explicit request of "Where are you?" to someone, with a subsequent, but not required location disclosure from that person; and
- ability to define new places that can be used for future location disclosures.

To allow the user to see queries for disclosures of their location, we use a common concept: an "inbox." The location inbox (see Figures 1C and 2A) contains a list of recent *queries*, marked with a '?,' and *disclosures*, sent manually or automatically, marked with an '@' character. These items can be "opened" with the phone's soft keys or joystick to see details; a detail view of a query is shown in Figure 1A. Query details include the time it was sent and the name of the requester; disclosure details include the time the disclosure was made, the full name of the place, and whether it was a manual or automatic disclosure.

In addition to clarifying how Reno works, this scenario also demonstrates how the communication of a place name is interpreted, sometimes incorrectly, within the social context of human discourse. It is precisely this leveraging of social context that makes Reno an intriguing research platform. While we are unable to provide a complete analysis of the implications of adopted Reno use over an extended period of time, our initial deployment study does reveal an interesting balance between the four functional capabilities and the social context of its use.

In the following section, we will review the guiding principles for designing, implementing and deploying Reno. We will then report on a pilot user study of its use over a 5-day period within a specific social network.

3 The Reno Application: Guidelines, Design and Implementation

Reno was designed with three guiding principles in mind: always-on service, avoid real or perceived privacy threats, and minimize deployment or acceptance barriers. By *always-on service*, we mean that Reno must be available 100% of the time, since otherwise users would not consider it robust enough to employ it for their day-to-day tasks. *Avoid real or perceived privacy threats* refers to the notion that users must be able to trust that Reno is not disclosing their location without their explicit consent, and it should avoid reliance on third parties who may not be perceived by users as trustworthy. To *minimize deployment or acceptance barriers*, Reno must be convenient for users, it must be low-cost and it must avoid relying on users to carry around hardware which they would otherwise not carry. It also should not interfere with the other hardware and services users already rely on. This also means that there should be minimal reliance on external infrastructure. Even though this infrastructure might improve the functionality of Reno, it presents obstacles to deployment that had to be avoided.

Certain principles were *not* prioritized in Reno. Location accuracy is useful, but wide coverage and availability is more important. Complex features (e.g., automatic detection of nearby "friends") might prove useful in some situations, but without a clear understanding of how basic social location disclosure is used in practice, it is unwise to design for those features at this point.

The principles above were used to make four key design decisions about Reno's platform, location sensing, place representation, and message transport. Regarding the message transport, Reno communications are entirely peer-to-peer, using the Short Message Service (SMS). This transport method was chosen because it is widely available, interoperates across mobile phone networks worldwide, has a clear cost model, and is already familiar to many users. The infrastructure that implements SMS is under the control of service providers and regulated by various national and international bodies. More importantly, the casual user of SMS understands it to be a person-to-person and private communication. Leveraging SMS for message transport, therefore, means that no real or perceived privacy threats are *introduced* by Reno, respecting the second and third of our guiding principles.

3.1 The Mobile Phone Platform

The mobile phone platform was chosen primarily because it is the most powerful computing platform which is already continually carried by many people. Requiring that a Reno user carries a PDA or other hardware would create deployment barriers, and threaten to make the service unavailable when users forget or do not bother to carry the extra hardware with them.

Reno is targeted at the Nokia Series 60 phone platform and is written primarily using Java 2 Micro-Edition (J2ME), with the Connected Limited Device Configuration (CLDC) and Mobile Information Device Profile (MIDP) APIs. All development and deployment was done using the Nokia 6600 phone, chosen for its large screen and good developer support. Disadvantages of this platform include the difficulty of debugging and the limited and slow persistent storage support.

The mobile phone platform satisfies some of the guiding principles mentioned earlier, but brings to the forefront a deployment barrier. Mobile telephony is a crucial function for many people—particularly for some of our pilot users with school-age children—so we were very cautious to avoid degrading the phone functionality of the device, e.g., by draining the battery or crashing the phone. Note that, in order for Reno to be able to send automatic location disclosures, it must always be running as a background task on the phone.

3.2 Location Sensing

There were a number of possible sources for determining the phone's location. The most widely commercialized location sensor, GPS, was rejected because it is not always available (indoors, in buses, etc), and the cost and extra hardware introduce deployment barriers. Another possibility would be to leverage location technology which is being implemented by some telecom operators to comply with "Enhanced 911" requirements [12]. Although network-based sensing is a compelling business case for operators, we have chosen to compute location on the handset because of the lack of standard methods for querying location from the network, and because we feel that this solution provides for simpler regulatory compliance in jurisdictions with strong location privacy legislation (*i.e.*, private use of others' personal information is exempt from most data protection provisions). Computing location on the phone also respects the user's control for disclosure.

A more promising option is Place Lab [2,21], which uses the known locations of visible radio beacons such as GSM cell towers and Bluetooth beacons to provide a current location estimate. However, Place Lab relies upon a user community having generated detailed "maps" of the radio beacons in a given area before location sensing works in that area. This goes against the principle of always-on service: even if large maps were gathered, users may move outside the mapped area. If, in the future, such mapping databases are well populated[1], a client-based location service such as Place Lab would be suitable for Reno.

Reno keeps track of the phone's currently associated cell tower, and each place defined in the phone includes a list of cell towers which have been seen while at that place. Location is determined entirely on the phone and does not rely on any special hardware or external service. This method has very high availability, introduces no new privacy threats, and does not hinder deployment, thus making it very suitable for a quick and realistic study. The biggest disadvantage is the relatively low accuracy of this technique, since cell tower footprints range from hundreds of meters to several kilometers.

Bluetooth beacons can be used in a similar way to GSM cell towers, potentially providing more accurate location information. However, we decided not to use Bluetooth in this study, for two reasons. Many Bluetooth nodes are mobile, and associating mobile Bluetooth beacons with a place will lead to false detections of that place. However, there is a deeper problem because there are adverse privacy implications in the (even unwitting) recording of the location and movements of other users carrying Bluetooth devices. While there are ways around this (e.g., allowing the users to specify particular Bluetooth beacons as being "stationary" and therefore usable), in the interests of simplicity and usability by novices, we did not do so in our initial study.

3.3 Representing Place

There are many ways to represent places. For use by humans, expressing places with mathematical coordinates or beacon IDs is not acceptable, regardless of how convenient it would be to implement. Furthermore, previous studies have shown that even symbolic names like exact street addresses are infrequently a user's first choice when communicating her location to other people [7]. As a result, we decided not to use pre-defined place lists (e.g., extracted from the web) in Reno, and instead required users to define their own places. This allows users to mark places with very personal labels (e.g. "10 minutes from home", "Phoebe's office"). Places in Reno consist of a user-defined name and a list of associated unique cell tower IDs, as shown in Table 1.

Table 1. Example of Place Definitions

Place Name	Cell Tower List
Ralph's Market	2561, 2221
Home	923
Bank	12087, 8921, 12071

---

[1] http://www.wigle.net is an example of a community-generated database which currently maps 1.8 million WiFi access points; phones with WiFi functionality have been announced by a number of manufacturers and may become commonplace.

A place is created when the user activates the "Record this place" feature. While platform restrictions mean that Reno is only capable of monitoring the currently visible cell tower, a list of all recently seen cell towers is maintained. When the user records a new place, this list is associated with that place. The user is also able to "Record this place" for already defined places; in such cases, the list of currently seen cell towers is merged into the place's existing list by taking the intersection of the two sets. Empirically, we have found a time limit of about two minutes for recently seen cell towers works well. This allows some smoothing of the GSM beacon environment seen by the mobile phone, while avoiding the accumulation of old GSM beacons.

4 Evaluation and Results

4.1 Management Burden for the List of Nearby Places

When a user selects "Tell someone I am here", a minimal list of nearby places is shown. We aimed to show the most probable nearby places in order of relevance to avoid requiring the user to scroll through a long list of places that have no current relevance. To validate whether this happens in practice, an experimental "walk" was conducted by one of our pilot users around a local shopping district. Using our nearby places algorithm, we sampled the returned list of results at each of the pre-defined places (triangles) and measurement (circles) points shown in Fig. 3.

In every case where the user was actually present at a place, the place received a non-zero score meaning it would have been on the user's list of nearby places. When the user was at a measurement point, the closest place was given as either the highest or jointly highest in each case. The highest or jointly highest rank place was given by the algorithm when at 6 of the 8 places. In the two cases where the algorithm did not put the user's true place as the highest scoring choice, it made significant errors in selecting the best choice; an error of about 350m at place 5 and an error of 550m when the user was truly at place 6. Further, the algorithm clearly offers no discrimination power between places 2, 3, and 4. These places are roughly all on the same block (distance north to south between place 2 and 4 is 205 meters). A check of the user's phone revealed that all these places were defined with the same, single cell.

During real use, we have found that our cell-tower-based algorithm works very well and has performance characteristics very similar to those shown in this section. One confounding factor in the experiment above involves Reno's cache of recently seen beacons. The current Reno system has no model of the speed of travel of the device it is running on. This means that the two minute decay of beacons has a very different effect when the device is in a car and when the user is walking, affecting both the definition of the place and the measurement of the environment to compute nearby places.

4.2 Pilot User Study

A pilot study of Reno was conducted in Fall 2004 with eight participants over five days. The participants were members of the research team and their families. We

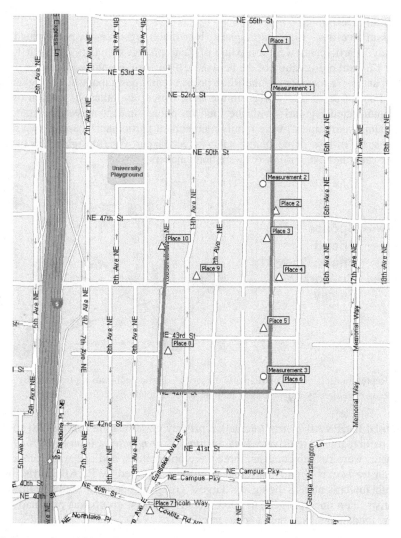

Fig. 3. Beacon Based Place Experiment. This figure shows an area 1170 meters wide by 1520 meters tall

chose this set of participants because they were part of an actual social group, yet would be forgiving of problems with both the technology and unintended and potentially awkward location disclosures to members of their social network. This group of participants provided a reasonable first pass at uncovering some of the social ramifications and privacy concerns that a social location disclosure application like Reno could create among co-workers, friends and spouses. A primary goal of this pilot study was to refine the study design and Reno for a longer term study with participants who are representative of the target user base.

We begin by describing the profiles of the eight participants and follow with the methodology used in the three phases of the pilot study. We then discuss key results.

4.2.1 Study Design

Participant Profiles. Eight participants (four male), aged 26-40, participated in the pilot study. Participants were a mixture of Reno project members and their families (see Fig. 4 for a representation of the network). Five were employed full-time, worked together, and were members of the Reno project team (participants a, d, e, g, and h in Fig. 4). Four of those five worked in the same office; the other (h) worked overseas but communicated regularly with the four via phone, instant messaging, and email. The remaining participants were family members of participants a and g: two spouses and one sister-in-law. One of the spouses was a part-time designer (f); the other spouse (b) and the sister-in-law (c) were homemakers.

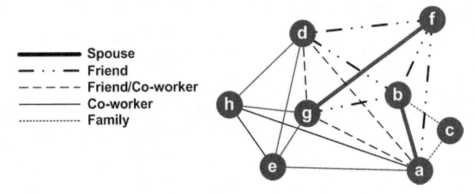

Fig. 4. Representation of the participants' network. Participants are represented by circles; letters are used to identify individuals. Lines show social relations

We used the P&AB-Harris Interactive privacy classification survey [28] to determine if participants were privacy *fundamentalists*, *pragmatists*, or *unconcerned*. Four participants were fundamentalists, three were pragmatists, and one was unconcerned. The trend we saw is slightly different than those reported by P&AB-Harris Interactive, with fundamentalists being the largest group in our pilot study, followed by pragmatists, then unconcerned (in 2003, P&AB's largest group was pragmatists, followed by fundamentalists, then unconcerned).

Pilot Study Methodology. The pilot study consisted of three phases: background, Reno deployment, and post-study feedback. In Phase 1, participants signed a release form, completed a couple of questionnaires, and worked with us to customize their Reno application. The questionnaires included basic demographic information, experience with a variety of technologies, the P&AB privacy classification survey, and exercises to explain how they knew and communicated with the other participants in the pilot study. To customize Reno, they each provided at least two triggers they wanted another participant to receive from them when they arrived at or departed a particular location and at least two notifications they wanted to receive about another participant. (They also provided a set of names for places they thought would be important during the five day deployment of Reno; the combined list of names from all participants was used to create a list of "Word Cheats." These cheats were simply a list of places that could be relied on to avoid typing in text on the phone, a task that several of our pilot users were unfamiliar with.) Once we received the trigger and notification requests, we asked the appropriate participants to accept/reject the requests.

For the Reno deployment (Phase 2), we supplied participants with Nokia 6600 cell phones with the Reno application pre-installed. Based on the customization exercises from Phase 1, their phones were already set up with the requested triggers that had been accepted. Participants were instructed on how to use the application, including how to "teach" their phone about places. Despite the triggers being set up in advance, each participant was responsible for teaching his phone about the relevant places (*i.e.*, even if participant h had a trigger set to notify participant g whenever h arrived at work, if h never taught his phone where work was, the notification would never be sent to g). Though we provided participants with cell phones, they used their personal SIM cards[2] and existing service.

During the Reno deployment which ran for five days from Wednesday through Sunday, participants filled out a daily email log that included several questions about their experiences with Reno and the other participants for that day. This set of questions was emailed to them every morning. They were asked to fill it out and send it in before going to bed that day. Participants received a reminder every evening. If they had not returned their daily email log by the next morning, they received a reminder to please fill it out and return it as soon as possible. The study concluded by returning the Nokia 6600 cell phone and filling out a post-study questionnaire which asked about their general reaction to Reno and their experiences during the study. Usage logs from the phones were extracted and analyzed.

4.2.2   Results: Basic Usage Results

The pilot study lasted for 5 days and we expected that the device would be with the person and on the vast majority of the time. Despite giving the participants fully configured phones and letting them keep their existing phone number, we met with mixed success on this point. We had an average of 53% for the amount of time the phone was on as a percentage of the 5 day (140 hour) study time, with a minimum and maximum of 22% and 85% respectively.

Fig. 5 shows the number of automatic and manual disclosures that were made by each participant over the course of the study. The total number of disclosures was 306 and an average of 38.25, or about 7-8 per day of the study. Fig. 5 shows that there is a significant difference between the systems heaviest and lightest users; although the two heaviest users shown, Ross and Joey, are developers of the system, their spouses, Rachel and Phoebe, used Reno a great deal as well, including a signifycant number of manual disclosures.

We expected that the amount of location disclosure would be correlated with the strength of a social relationship—the strongest of these being the spousal relationship. 45% of all requests for location (21 total requests) were sent to a spouse/partner. Similar requests to a colleague, a friend, and a "friend & colleague" were 23% (11), 17% (8), and 15% (7), respectively. Considering all location disclosures (automatic and manual) the percentage distribution between spouses/partners, colleagues, friends, and "friends & colleagues" was 44% (124 total disclosures), 34% (98), 4% (11), and

---

[2] One participant did not have a cell phone, so we provided her with a phone and service.

16% (46), respectively.   The spousal relationship did have the highest amount of location disclosures, but our data, both on real strength of relationship and amount of disclosures, do not allow us to draw any further conclusions.

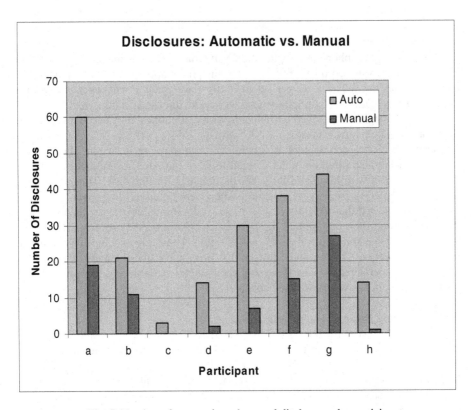

Fig. 5. Number of automatic and manual disclosures, by participant

4.2.3   Results: People's Context Makes Place/Location Communication Effective
Location information as we have defined it in Reno, is a relatively low data bandwidth channel. Reno makes it easy to share the user's location, either automatically or through user interaction, but what is shared is basically a few characters of text. Since we supplied users with a list of place names to avoid typing, very few places had names that were "customized" for the particular user, e.g. "Merchant Mick's" was chosen although better names might have "the Merchant Mick's on the 33rd street at 4th avenue" or "Merchant Mick's near my house."   Despite this relatively impoverished channel, a great deal of information flowed between the senders and receivers. Our pilot users had social relationships and these are relationships that are quite rich; the richness allowed a simple string to take on a great deal of meaning.

Quote 1: Day 2 (Thu), participant a: *Late tonight, [f] pushed her location to me from <anonymized> airport. That reminded me that some of her friends (also*

acquaintances of mine) were coming into town today. I wanted get together with them socially when they arrived. I had forgotten it was this weekend.

Quote 1 is completely dependent on the fact that *a* knew that *f* had friends coming into town and approximately when; the sender and receiver had significant shared context allowing what would otherwise be a seemingly random disclosure at a strange time to be interpreted correctly. It should also be clear from this example that the sender clearly *knew* that the receiver would interpret the message through the shared context.

Quote 2: Day 5 (Sun), participant f: *I knew [g] was coming home from work and when he was at McDonald's.*

Participant *f* in **Quote 2** is referring to two disclosures received from *g*, both of these involved *g*'s path. In the first case, an automatic disclosure revealed to *f* that *g* was nearly home from the office since the location was a place that would be passed on the route home. The latter was a manual disclosure that told the recipient that the sender would be home shortly with a fast-food dinner. In both cases, the context of the two participants allowed a simple place name to be taken for both a path as well as an approximate estimated time of arrival. Without shared context information, either of these could easily be misinterpreted by the receiver; for example, a different take on the latter disclosure is "He's telling me his diet is out the window."

We did see a number of instances where misinterpretation did occur. The types of misunderstandings of sender or receiver's context varied as did the consequences of the confusion. The scenario discussed in section 2 was based on an actual misunderstanding that occurred between *f* and *g*.

Quote 3: Day 1 (Wed), participant f: *"I saw that [g] was at <Merchant Mick's> but he was really waiting for the bus, and I was disappointed."*

As was discussed earlier the sender and recipient did not agree on the significance and meaning of the place in question. However, it is interesting to note that *neither* of the two participants took the place at face value. One was expressing the activity "waiting for the bus" and the other thought "buying dessert." We also note that the exact same message being exchanged between *a* and *d* of the same social group at lunch time between Monday – Thursday would mean, "If you want me to pick up a salad for you, call me" and on Friday during summer between any of *a, d, e,* or *g* would mean, "If you want me to pick something up for you for the barbeque, call me."

Quote 4: Day 1 (Wed), participant e: *I knew [a] was on the east side and I wasn't sure how close he was to being back. He replied with 'Home Depot' … I wasn't sure which Home Depot.*

After following up with *a* and *e* about the situation, we learned that *e* wanted to know which Home Depot because he thought *a* was trying to give him an indication of how close to the office he was, *i.e.,* that he was driving past a Home Depot, and *e* didn't know if he was at a nearby or east side Home Depot. However, what *a* was trying to communicate was "I'm done with work, so I'm taking a trip to Home Depot to run a personal errand. I'm finished with work for the day." Again, although this pair got their signals crossed, *neither* participant thought that this name would communicate the simple idea of *a*'s location!

We found that the location disclosures, both automatic and manual, were interpeted through the lens of the context shared between the sender and receiver. Since manual disclosures were sent *intentionally* by the sender, they were often able to achieve a higher level of abstraction, such as in **Quote 1**. The automatic disclosures, since they had no significance to the sender tended to be less significant to the receiver. Overall, we found that there were three types of interpretations commonly seen. These were, in increasing order of the use of the shared context, location, path, and activity. The first of these occurred most frequently when the sender and receiver were trying to rendezvous and the location of the sender could be interpreted literally. More frequently, the receiver used knowledge of the place transmitted and the local geography to understand the path of the sender, as in **Quote 2**. The last class of interpretations, activity, were quite amazing and varied dramatically in their level of understanding (or misunderstanding) as was shown in **Quote 1** and **Quote 4**.

4.2.4   Results: Automatic Disclosure is a Double-Edged Sword

There is a cost and a value to automatic disclosure. In our pilot study opinions varied significantly about the value of the automatic disclosures. **Quote 5** and **Quote 6** show that even within a single participant, opinions varied!

Quote 5: Day 2 (Thurs), participant a: *I had an 'anti-meeting' situation today in which Reno was VERY helpful. When [b] is out for the night I always let the kids stay up later than I should and she always gets peeved when she come home and finds them not in bed. I got my Reno alert that she was home and since she had to get stuff out of the car and walk up the flight and a half of stairs, I had the kids in bed before she opened the door. So Reno saved me some irritated spouse today.*

Quote 6: Day 3 (Fri), participant a: *When [b] and I went to our house together, we get cross-notifications, neither of which is useful at the time.*

The important point is that both were situations where *a* and *b* were in the same place—in the negative example, he wants Reno to not give the notification because it is useless. In the positive example, *a* is glad to receive the notification because he has a few moments to "clean up" his mess. Though *a* alludes to the fact that it might be when they arrive together being the problem, it's easy to imagine a situation in which *a* is not doing something wrong but is home before *b* is, receives the notification, and finds it useless. The key thing was that *a* was doing something he was not "supposed" to be doing. If *a* had been behaving properly so to speak, the notification would have been irritating, as in the negative example. The double-edged sword of automatic disclosures would have been even more pronounced had we been able to explain **Quote 5** to *b* and gauge her reaction!

Another example of the mixed feelings engendered by the participants can be seen in **Quote 7**. This quote shows that the participant did not fully understand the context in which this trigger might fire and when confronted with the unpleasant, privacy-invasive use of the trigger felt violated.

Quote 7: Day 2 (thurs), participant g: *My phone disclosed my location to [participant a] last night when I was out running an errand and was returning to my house ([a] has a trigger for my house). I'm now reconsidering that trigger because I felt* *weird about that one. I didn't feel weird when he got notified I was "home from work" but did about the late-night errand running."*

5 Related Work

Location-based services (LBS) have been hailed by telecom operators as the next killer app following the unexpected success of SMS [29]. However, marked success for LBS has lagged, in part due to lack of a clear regulatory framework and privacy concerns[3]. Japan has witnessed some success in this area: person-to-person LBS have been marketed by DoCoMo in the form of location-augmented iMode websites (used for, e.g., dating) [26]. Ubiquitous cell-phone tracking was commercially launched by KDDI with GPS MAP, a person finder service targeted at corporate customers, in 2002 [19]. This system works with GPS-enabled handsets that can be tracked through client software on PCs. Location information is stored on a server system managed by the operator.

A more general cell-phone based person-finder application has been developed by Kivera Inc. for AT&T Wireless (now part of Cingular). The system, called Find People Nearby (formerly known as Find Friends) [6] allows a user to build a buddy list, and to locate other service subscribers in any area covered by AT&T. After locating a friend, the user can call the person, send a message or invite him/her to some meeting point chosen from businesses in the AT&T Yellow Pages. The success of this application has been arguably limited by the lack of interoperability with other providers; Reno overcomes this limitation by leveraging the universal interoperability afforded by SMS. Another difference is that the Find People Nearby application is web-based: the location of the phone is sensed by the infrastructure and the application is accessed through a web browser on the phone, along with other AT&T-provided services. Reno computes user location on the device; given the different legal status of location information used for call routing as opposed to value added services in major world markets (e.g. the EU [1]), this simplifies information management on behalf of the operators and increases user control on their personal information. Finally, users of Find People Nearby cannot label locations: location names are predefined and typically refer to urban coordinates (e.g. street intersections).

Recently consumer-oriented person-finder applications (e.g. dating and child-tracking applications) have started to appear amidst mounting privacy concerns and a clamp-down on websites linked to high-profile 'horror' stories of abuse [3]. Several child tracking applications are currently available in the United Kingdom. For example, Mapamobile allows to track a phone with the precision allowed by cell-tower coverage. [24] As opposed to Reno, these services are marketed as single-purpose applications, are centrally managed, and subject to strict organizational oversight.

Apart from dating and child tracking, applications of location technology include mobile guides and games. In the Lighthouse location-aware museum guides by Galani and Chalmers [14], mobility is a resource for interaction as participants use motion to communicate between each other, to signal presence and to support contextual awareness. We observed that our participants also used location information as a resource for interaction, e.g. for planning, communication and coordination activities.

Mobile location-aware devices serve not only explicit interaction, but also more subtle purposes. In the WatchMe prototype [25] GPS location and activity information are used to provide users with awareness of each other, and to initiate explicit communication. Our observations indicate that participants use Reno for similar purposes, especially when location is disclosed automatically in "push mode" (through triggers). When a disclosure occurs, people reconnect the location information with prior knowledge of the other's activity; location disclosure thus acts as a reminder and awareness mechanism of the whereabouts of the other person. Finally, like WatchMe, Reno is build on a ubiquitous, always-available device.

In 'Uncle Roy All Around You' users self-report their location (by pin-pointing it on a map on a touchscreen. Interestingly, Benford et al. noted that, similarly to how Reno users use location to express activity and share context, players in their game used self-reported location to express intent (where they will be going) and history (places they had visited) [10].

In location-based games 'Can You See Me Now?' [13] and George Square [11], mobility also represents a tool for interaction. These systems use both GPS and WLAN beaconing to enrich the gaming experience and the imprecise nature of this kind of location sensing is exploited by the designers to enrich the game by creating uncertainty. Imprecision and ambiguity are very important in Reno, as they afford an essential space for privacy. Thus, the imprecise nature of cell-phone tower-based localization can be viewed as both a problem and an advantage.

Laasonen *et al.* show how cell-phone tower localization can be used in combination with user-based labeling schemes [20]. They also use predictive algorithms to recognize when a user is in a certain *base* (i.e., a recurring location such as workplace and home), or in *areas* (which are clusters of bases, *e.g.*, a neighborhood) and *routes* between bases. A different approach to movement prediction is followed by Ashbrook and Starner, who propose associating place labels to GPS information and Markov models to infer the user subsequent movements [5]. Reno uses cell phone tower location because such information is more available in buildings and dense urban environments than GPS readings. Despite the name, GPS is less ubiquitous than cell-phone technologies in places of human significance, because where there are humans there is an interest in providing cell phone coverage (e.g. subways, buildings, factories).

Harrison and Dourish have brought to the attention of the ubicomp community the long-standing distinction between space and place (i.e., a location associated with a meaningful semantic) [17]. Adopting their observations, Reno hides the spatial coordinates from the user. Rather, it provides tools for creating and using meaningful place names, instead of hard-to-understand geographical or urban coordinates.

The view of interpersonal privacy as a continuous negotiation process and a tool of social action dates back several decades. Goffman, for example, characterizes privacy as one of the fundamental instruments that enable people to create their social presentation [16]. Palen and Dourish have adapted this concept of privacy to information technology, and suggest that IT must provide the tools for finely managing this negotiation in order to preserve our ability to function as social beings [27]. This kind of negotiation clearly emerges from a web-based survey performed by Lederer *et al.* [23] in 2003, which shows that people tend decide whether to disclose information about their activities and location based on the identity of the requester more than on the situation in which this happens. This is confirmed by a precursor study to the present [7], which, in addition, indicates that the supposed reason for the request is a co-determinant for deciding whether to disclose, whereas current activity and mood have only secondary influence on the decision. This study also highlighted that based on that decision, users provide either the information that they think will be most useful to the requester, or none. The present work is directly influenced by these findings: Reno is designed to support fine-grained control on the projection of their social image.

Fine control over information disclosure has been the topic of much work in the security community; more security implies increased administrative burden. This balance has been inquired specifically for context-aware technology by Barkhuus and Dey, who have suggested that people are willing to forgive some control over their personal location information [8]. Our experience with Reno shows that users display similar feelings towards automatic disclosure of location information — what these authors term "active context-awareness". Feedback and control of information disclosure are central to the ubicomp community from the very beginnings of the field [9]. Recently Lederer *et al.* have stressed that successful designs must make information flows visible, provide coarse-grain control, enable social nuance, and emphasize action over configuration [22]. Reno's design confirms these guidelines; when Reno does not perform as expected by its users, it can be attributed to one of these pitfalls.

8 Conclusions

The social communication of location or place information is common, and we often co-opt a variety of technologies to facilitate this practice. In this work, we explored what it would mean to provide a purpose-built social location disclosure service that met certain criteria for rapid deployment and adoption. We introduced Reno as a prototype location disclosure service for a mobile phone platform, and we presented some significant results from a pilot user study of its use within a realistic social network.

While our implementation of Reno was not as available and transparent on the mobile phone as we would have liked, it did provide a simple means of communicating user-defined place information, both automatically and manually. When combined with the rich, shared social context among family, friends or colleagues, this simplified disclosure of place facilitates effective communication. The automatic disclosure of location, while at times valuable, suffers because the explicit communication act by the sender, and its accompanying knowledge of intended context for interpretation, is lost.

The advantages and disadvantages hinted at by our pilot study suggest deeper research questions which we intend to explore next. Specifically, we want to better understand whether unauthorized or unintended location disclosure will be restrained to an acceptable rate by a combination of algorithmic techniques, user interaction and pressure from social norms. Another important feature for any technology supporting social interaction is the extent to which it supports the human need for plausible deniability. Adoption of Reno, or of any similar location disclosure application, will engender denial practices, attributable to user activity, the supporting infrastructure, or even the operational or failure modes of the service. Understanding these denial and restraint strategies, and supporting them explicitly in new technologies, will be essential condition for the acceptance and, ultimately, the success of pervasive technologies.

Acknowledgments

The authors would like to acknowlege the support of the National Science Foundation's Graduate Research Fellowship Program and the MacArthur Foundation for their support (Iachello). We would also like to acknowledge the Intel corporation's support of academic collaborations (Iachello, Abowd). This work would not have been possible without the excellent technical work provided by James Howard, Jeff Hughes, and Fred Potter.

References

1. Directive 2002/58/EC of the European Parliament and of the Council of 12 July 2002 concerning the processing of personal data and the protection of privacy in the electronic communications sector (Directive on privacy and electronic communications) Official Journal of the European Communities (2002) 37-47
2. Placelab.[Online]. Available: http://www.placelab.org
3. What the Operators Are Doing. in Mobile Location Analyst, Oct 2003.
4. Dodgeball. Ubiquity Labs LLC, [Online]. Available: http://www.dodgeball.com/. Downloaded January 26, 2005.
5. Ashbrook, D., Starner, T.: Learning Significant Locations and Predicting User Movement with GPS. In: Proc. Int. Symp. on Wearable Computers (2002) 101-108
6. AT&T Wireless. Find People Nearby.[Online]. Available: http://www.attwireless.com/ personal/features/organization/findfriends.jhtml
7. Consolvo, S., Smith I., Mathews T., LaMarca A..: Location Disclosure To Social Relations: Why, When, & What People Want To Share. To appear: ACM Conference On Human Factors In Computing Systems (2005), Portland, Oregon.
8. Barkhuus, L., Dey, A.: Location-Based Services for Mobile Telephony: a study of users' privacy concerns. In: Proc. Interact 2003 (2003) 709 -712
9. Bellotti, V., Sellen, A.: Design for Privacy in Ubiqui-tous Computing Environments. In: Proc. ECSCW '93 (1993)
10. Benford, S., Seager, W., Flintham, M., Anastasi, R., Rowland, D., Humble, J., Stanton, D., Bowers, J., Tanadavanitj, N., Adams, M., Farr, J. R., Oldroyd, A., Sutton, J.: The Error of Our Ways: The Experience of Self-Reported Position in a Location-Based Game. In: Proc. Ubicomp 2004 (2004) 70-87
11. Chalmers, M.: George Square -- Demo Game at Mobile HCI 2004 Conference. (2004)
12. Federal Communications Commission. Enhanced 911.[Online]. Available: http://www.fcc.gov/911/enhanced/
13. Flintham, M., Anastasi, R., Benford, S. D., Hemmings, T., Crabtree, A., Greenhalgh, C. M., Rodden, T. A., Tandavanitj, N., Adams, M., Row-Farr, J.: Where on-line meets on-the-streets: experiences with mobile mixed reality games. In: Proc. CHI 2003 (2003)
14. Galani, A., Chalmers, M., et al.: Developing a mixed reality co-visiting experience for local and remote museum companion. In: Proc. HCI international, HCII2003 (2003)

15. Grinter, R. E., Eldridge, M.: 'y do tngrs luv 2 txt msg?' In: Proc. Seventh European Conference on Computer-Supported Cooperative Work ECSCW '01 (2001) 219–238
16. Goffman, E.: The presentation of self in everyday life. Anchor Books, New York (1959)
17. Harrison, S., Dourish, P.: Re-place-ing space: The roles of space and place in collaborative systems. In: Proc. CSCW (1996) 67-76
18. Höflich, J. R., Rössler, P.: Mobile schriftliche Kommunikation – oder: E-Mail für das Handy. Die Bedeutung elektronischer Kurznachrichten (Short Message Service) am Beispiel jugendlicher Handynutzer. Medien & Kommunikationswissenschaft 49 (2001) 437
19. KDDI. GPS MAP, a Location Service For Mobile Phones.[Online]. Available: http://www.kddi.com/english/corporate/news_release/archive/2002/0718/
20. Laasonen, K., Raento, M., Toivonen, H.: Adaptive On-Device Location Recognition. In: Proc. Pervasive 2004 (2004) 287-304
21. 21 LaMarca A., Chawathe Y., Consolvo S., Hightower J., Smith I., Scott J., Sohn T., Howard J., Hughes J., Potter F., Tabert F., Powledge P., Borriello G., Schilit B., Place Lab: Device Positioning Using Radio Beacons in the Wild, To appear: 3rd International Conference On Pervasive Computing (2005), Munich, Germany..
22. Lederer, S., Hong, J., Dey, A., Landay, J.: Personal Privacy through Understanding and Action: Five Pitfalls for Designers. Intel, IRB-TR-03-035 (2003)
23. Lederer, S., Mankoff, J., Dey, A. K.: Who Wants to Know What When? Privacy Preference Determinants in Ubiquitous Computing. In: Proc. CHI 2003 (2003)
24. Mapamobile. [Online]. Available: [http://www.mapamobile.com/].
25. Marmasse, N., Schmandt, C., Spectre, D.: WatchMe: communication and awareness between members of a closely-knit group. In: Proc. CHI 2004 (2004)
26. NTT DoCoMo. iArea: Location Based Services.[Online]. Available: http://www.nttdocomo.com/corebiz/imode/services/iarea.html
27. Palen, L., Dourish, P.: Unpacking "Privacy" for a Networked World. In: Proc. CHI 2003 (2003) 129-136
28. Privacy & American Business: Consumer Privacy Attitudes: A Major Shift Since 2000 and Why. 10 (2003)
29. UMTS Forum: Enabling UMTS / Third Generation Services and Applications, UMTS Forum Report 11. (2000)

A Formal Model of Obfuscation and Negotiation for Location Privacy

Matt Duckham[1] and Lars Kulik[2]

[1] Department of Geomatics,
University of Melbourne, Victoria, 3010, Australia
mduckham@unimelb.edu.au
[2] Department of Computer Science and Software Engineering,
University of Melbourne, Victoria, 3010, Australia
lkulik@cs.mu.oz.au

Abstract. Obfuscation concerns the practice of deliberately degrading the quality of information in some way, so as to protect the privacy of the individual to whom that information refers. In this paper, we argue that obfuscation is an important technique for protecting an individual's location privacy within a pervasive computing environment. The paper sets out a formal framework within which obfuscated location-based services are defined. This framework provides a computationally efficient mechanism for balancing an individual's need for high-quality information services against that individual's need for location privacy. Negotiation is used to ensure that a location-based service provider receives only the information it needs to know in order to provide a service of satisfactory quality. The results of this work have implications for numerous applications of mobile and location-aware systems, as they provide a new theoretical foundation for addressing the privacy concerns that are acknowledged to be retarding the widespread acceptance and use of location-based services.

1 Introduction

Privacy is internationally recognized as a fundamental human right [9]. Location-aware pervasive computing environments provide the ability to automatically sense, communicate, and process information about a person's location, with a high degree of spatial and temporal precision and accuracy. Location is an especially sensitive type of personal information, and so safeguarding an individual's location privacy has become an key issue for pervasive computing research.

This paper addresses the issue of protecting sensitive information about an individual user's location, at the same time as providing useful location-based services to that user. Our approach focuses on negotiating a balance in the levels of privacy and utility for a location-based service. Thus, in our model an individual may deliberately degrade the quality of information about his or her location in order to protect his or her privacy, a process called *obfuscation*. However, the quality of the location-based service an individual receives is directly linked to

H.W. Gellersen et al. (Eds.): PERVASIVE 2005, LNCS 3468, pp. 152–170, 2005.

the quality of information which that individual is willing to reveal about his or her location.

The primary contributions of this paper are the development of:

- a formal model of obfuscation and location privacy;
- an algorithm for efficient computation of a simple obfuscated location-based service; and
- a procedure for achieving a satisfactory balance of location privacy and location-based service quality through negotiation between an individual and a service provider.

Following a brief motivational example, section 2 situates this research within the context of the pervasive computing literature on location privacy. Section 3 introduces obfuscation, with particular reference to existing research related to this topic. Section 4 provides a precise description of the scenario addressed by this paper and the assumptions embedded within this scenario. Section 5 sets out the formal model of obfuscation in location-based services, and develops the mechanisms for obfuscating a simple location-based service. Section 6 concludes the paper with a summary of the results and an overview of current and future related research.

1.1 Motivational Example

In order to motivate this paper, consider the scenario illustrated in Figure 1.1.

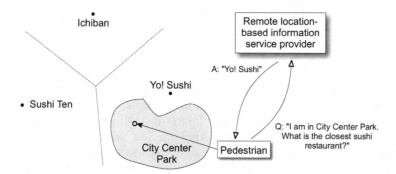

Fig. 1. Idealized example of an obfuscated location-based information service

A pedestrian wishes to access information about the address of the closest sushi restaurant, via a remote location-based service provider. Although there are three nearby restaurants, our hungry pedestrian would like to protect her privacy by providing only an approximate location to the information service provider. For example, the pedestrian can obfuscate her exact location by revealing only that she is in the "City Center Park." In this case, the service provider should still be able to correctly reply with the address of "Yo! Sushi," using basic spatial analysis algorithms (i.e., by constructing the Voronoi diagram for the sushi restaurants).

This example makes several simplifying assumptions, including a homogeneous Cartesian space with distance measured according to the Euclidean metric, and that the park does not overlap two proximal polygons. Nevertheless, this simple scenario does provide an intuitive example of a situation where it is possible to receive *high-quality information services using low-quality positional information*. It is this intuition that motivates this research.

2   Background

2.1   Location Privacy

Within a pervasive computing environment, failure to protect location privacy has been associated with negative effects across at least three distinct areas [12, 27, 18].

1. *Location-based "spam"*: Location could be used by unscrupulous businesses to bombard an individual with unsolicited marketing for products or services related to that individual's location.
2. *Personal wellbeing and safety*: Location is inextricably linked to personal safety. Unrestricted access to information about an individual's location could potentially lead to harmful encounters, for example stalking or physical attacks.
3. *Intrusive inferences*: Location constrains our access to spatiotemporal resources, like meetings, medical facilities, our homes, or even crime scenes. Therefore, location can be used to infer other personal information about an individual, such as that individual's political views, state of health, or personal preferences.

Concern about the effects of new technology on an individual's right to privacy is not new, having already surfaced, for example, with respect to GIS [23], the Internet [1], and collaborative user interfaces [16]. In most countries, there already exist legal frameworks that govern the fair use of digital information about an individual, including location (see [19] for a concise overview of the history and current status of privacy legislation and fair information practices internationally).

Regulation, whether legal or voluntary, will inevitably form the baseline for location privacy in any pervasive system. However, there are at least two reasons why regulation needs to be supported by other strategies for protecting location privacy in pervasive computing. First, new regulation often lags behind new technology and ideas. Second, regulation applies "across the board," making it is difficult to guarantee privacy protection for individuals without stifling technology and innovation.

2.2   Privacy Policies

Pervasive computing research into privacy protection is addressing the definition of policy and trust mechanisms for prescribing certain uses of location information. A variety of policy-driven approaches to location privacy in pervasive systems are reviewed in [10]. Much of this research draws on established or developing privacy policy frameworks, such as the W3C Platform for Privacy Preferences (P3P; e.g., [29, 20, 22]), the IETF draft geographic location privacy charter (GeoPriv; e.g., [24]), and personal digital rights management (PDRM, e.g., [13]).

Privacy policies are necessary in order to implement unambiguous computer-readable mechanisms for location privacy protection, and are also undoubtedly a long-term part of the landscape of pervasive computing technology. However, like regulation, privacy policies cannot offer a complete solution since such policies usually incur considerable information infrastructure overheads and are vulnerable to inadvertent or malicious disclosure of private information [12].

2.3   Anonymity and Pseudonymity

Anonymity concerns the dissociation of information about an individual, such as location, from that individual's actual identity. A distinction is often drawn between "true" anonymity, where an individual is indistinguishable from all other individuals in a set, and *pseudonymity*, where an individual maintains a persistent identity (a pseudonym) that cannot be linked to their actual identity [25]. A variety of research has addressed the problem of maintaining anonymity (e.g., [3, 11, 8]) and pseudonymity (e.g., [26]) within the context of location-based services.

However, anonymity and pseudonymity are, again, not a complete answer to privacy concerns in pervasive computing because:

- Anonymity presents a barrier to authentication and personalization, which are important for a range of applications [19, 15].
- Pseudonymity and anonymity are vulnerable to data mining, since identity can often be inferred from location [7, 3].

Thus, in this paper we argue that obfuscation is complementary to existing privacy protection strategies (regulation, privacy policies, anonymity, and pseudonymity) and demands further investigation.

3   Obfuscation

In this paper, obfuscation is defined as:

> the means of deliberately degrading the quality of information about an individual's location in order to protect that individual's location privacy.

3.1   Related Research

Obfuscation, or closely related ideas, have already been suggested in the literature. Hong et al. Within the Confab system, [15] use landmarks and other significant locations to refer to instead of coordinate-based geographic information. The effect of this "reverse gazetteer" is to provide less information about a user's exact location. Similarly, Snekkenes [29] suggests adjusting the precision of a individual's location as part of a mechanism for policy-based protection of location privacy.

Gruteser and Grunwald use a quadtree to explore the effects of adapting the spatial precision of information about about an individual's location according to the number of other individuals within the same quadrant, termed "spatial cloaking" [11]. Individuals are defined as k-*anonymous* if their location information is sufficiently imprecise in order to make them indistinguishable from at least $k - 1$ other individuals. The authors also explore the orthogonal process of reducing the frequency of temporal information, "temporal cloaking." Obfuscation, as presented in this paper, is broadly comparable to the spatial cloaking in [11]. Despite this similarity, there are several distinct differences in our approach when compared with the work presented in [11]. These differences will be noted as they arise. At this point, it will suffice to highlight that the overall aim of [11] was to guarantee an individual's k-anonymity. By contrast, in the model and algorithm presented in this paper, we aim to enable an individual's actual identity to be revealed (thereby facilitating authentication and personalization [19]) at the same time as maintaining that individual's location privacy.

3.2   Imperfection in Spatial Information

There exist clear parallels between uncertainty in spatial information and obfuscation in location privacy. The former focuses on imperfection as the result of the inherent limitations of the measurement and representation of spatial information; the latter focuses on imperfection as the result of the deliberate degradation of spatial information quality.

Three distinct types of imperfection in spatial information are commonly identified in the literature: *inaccuracy*, *imprecision*, and *vagueness*. Inaccuracy concerns a lack of correspondence between information and reality; imprecision concerns a lack of specificity in information; vagueness concerns the existence of boundary cases in information [31, 6, 32]. So, for example, the statement "Melbourne is in New South Wales" is inaccurate (Melbourne is in fact in Victoria). The statement "Melbourne is in Australia" is at the same time more accurate (it accords with reality), but less precise (it provides less detail about where Melbourne actually is). Thus, precision and accuracy are orthogonal, although these terms are often confused or conflated in the literature (e.g., [29]). Finally, the statement "Melbourne is in south-eastern Australia" is vague, since there exist boundary locations that are neither definitely in south-eastern Australia nor definitely not in south-eastern Australia.

Potentially, any or all of these three types of imperfection could be used to obfuscate an individual's location. For example, for "Agent X" located (accurately and precisely) at the corner of Flinders Street and Elizabeth Street in Melbourne city center, we might provide the following obfuscations of that agent's location:

1. "Agent X is located at the corner of Flinders Street and Spring Street" (inaccurate, since the statement does not accord with the actual state of affairs);
2. "Agent X is located on Flinders Street" (imprecise, since the statement does not specify at which of the many locations on Flinders Street the agent is located); and
3. "Agent X is located near Flinders Street Station" (vague, since there exist boundary locations that are neither definitely near nor definitely not near Flinders Street Station).

In this paper, as in [11], we only consider the use of imprecision to degrade location information quality. Future work will also address the use of inaccuracy and vagueness in obfuscation. Deliberately introducing inaccuracy into location information as part of an obfuscation system raises some difficult questions, since it essentially requires the obfuscation system to *lie* about an individual's location. Vague spatial terms, like "near" and "left," are commonly used by humans to communicate information about geographic space[1] and have been a particular focus of qualitative spatial reasoning research over the past decade (e.g., [34, 33]).

In summary, in this paper we consider the obfuscation of location information, using imprecision, in order to protect an individual's location privacy. With respect to regulation, privacy policies, anonymity, and pseudonymity, this approach has the advantages that obfuscation:

- is flexible enough to be tailored to specific user requirements and contexts;
- obviates the need for high levels of legal and policy infrastructure;
- enables an individual's identity to be revealed, facilitating authentication and personalization; and
- combats data mining by not revealing an individual's precise location.

4   Scenario

In presenting the obfuscation algorithms and formal model (section 5) we make several assumptions about the high-level architecture and usage scenario for the obfuscation system, detailed in this section.

4.1   Location Sensing

A location-aware system is a type of context-aware system that uses information about a mobile individual's current location to provide more relevant information

---

[1] Although Hong et al. [15] do use the term "near" in the Confab system as part of their location privacy protection system, the term is used in the paper specifically to refer to anything within 100m of the actual location (i.e., as an imprecise term rather than as a vague linguistic term).

to that individual. There exist a wide variety of techniques for automatically sensing an individual's location, including GPS, infrared proximity sensors, and wireless RF network triangulation. The different techniques are surveyed and classified in [14]. Using one or some combination of these techniques we assume that a user's current location, in the form of georeferenced x and y coordinates, is known with a high level of precision and accuracy. We deliberately leave unstated the details of how this location information is generated, in order to focus solely on the situation where reasonably precise and accurate location is known.

4.2   Architecture

We assume that a user wants to access information relevant to his or her current location from a remote location-based service provider via a wireless communications network. Further, we assume that the location-based service provider (LBSP) has no information about the user's location, other than the information that the user chooses to reveal to the LBSP. These assumptions taken together can at first sight seem somewhat strong, and so warrant further examination.

Infrastructure. The technical characteristics of many positioning systems demand that information about an individual's location must necessarily be revealed to the second-party who maintains of the positioning system infrastructure, such as the cell phone company (see [27] for a classification of positioning systems according to their privacy characteristics). This private information will undoubtedly need to be protected in some way, usually by legal or regulatory means. Irrespective of the positioning system, an individual may often wish to access a location-based service from some third party. It is exclusively this situation that we are addressing in this paper. The desire to access location-based services from third party service providers is not unusual in today's architectures, and we anticipate this situation will become increasingly common as pervasive location-aware systems become more commonplace.

Our obfuscation architecture allows an individual to connect *directly* with a third-party location-based service provider, without the need to use a broker or other intermediary (such as cell phone company or the "location server" used in [11]). As a consequence, our architecture is lightweight and distributed: it is compatible with mobile ad-hoc networks as well as more conventional client-server networks. Although the architecture presumes an individual acts as a client for the location-based service provider, these are simply roles that different agents fulfill. It is conceivable, for example, that the location-based service provider itself is in turn a mobile user who also acts as a client for other location-based services.

Communication. One way to protect sensitive location information is simply not to communicate this information to any third party service provider (cf. [21]). However, our scenario presumes that a user must communicate information about his or her location to a third party in order to receive useful location-based services [27]. The alternative, where users carry all the information they might need around with them in their mobile devices, is not viable for most location-based services for several reasons, including:

- Mobile devices typically possess limited processing and storage capacity, making it inefficient to perform complex calculations on voluminous spatial data directly on the mobile device.
- Despite advances in positioning systems, spatial data sets remain expensive to collect and collate. The companies who collect this data would usually be reluctant to make their valuable data sets available in their entirety to mobile users.
- Maintaining copies of the same data sets across multiple mobile devices inevitably leads to data integrity and currency issues.

Further, we assume that the location-based service provider does not derive any additional positioning information from the communication itself. For example, we assume that the location-based service provider cannot infer additional information about users' locations via their devices' mobile IP addresses (a separate issue that is already being addressed by the networking community, e.g., [4]).

4.3   Summary

Our architecture is deliberately simplified, in order to abstract away from the technical details of location sensing and communication in mobile networks. But we believe the architecture is not over-simplistic. In summary, the key assumptions made by are architecture are:

- A client device uses some combination of conventional location-sensing techniques to provide precise and accurate information about the client's location.
- That client device is able to communicate directly with a third-party location-based service provider (TPLBSP) via a wireless network to obtain some information service based on the client's current location.
- The information that the client chooses to reveal about his or her location constitutes the only source of information available to the TPLBSP about that client's location.

5   Obfuscation Model

In the previous section, we defined the scenario and architecture of our proposed obfuscation system. This section aims to provide a concise formal model of obfuscation and location privacy.

5.1   Geographic Space

As a first step, we adopt a discrete model of geographic space as a graph, $G = (V, E)$. Thus, geographic locations are modeled as a set of vertices, V, with connectivity or adjacency between pairs of locations modeled as a set of edges E, where $E \subseteq V \times V$. Graphs provide a highly flexible model of geographic space. For example, a graph is a natural choice for modeling a road network, with vertices as distinct locations on the network, edges indicating the presence of a direct road link between pairs of locations. Alternatively, vertices can be used to represent regions, with edges representing adjacency or neighborhood between pairs of locations. A function $w : E \to \mathbb{R}$ is used to associate a weight with each edge. This weight can be used to model proximity between vertices, including Euclidean distance or travel time.

In previous work on location-based services, geographic space is often modeled as the Cartesian plane (e.g., [11]). Adopting a graph-based model of geographic space offers several additional capabilities, primarily:

- Graphs can be used to model constraints to movement, such as a road network, and non-metric spaces, such as time-travel spaces.
- Graphs can be embedded within the Cartesian plane (e.g., the vector model used in many GIS and spatial databases) or higher dimensional Euclidean space (e.g, modeling the location of users in all three spatial dimensions).
- Graphs are computationally efficient discrete structures.

5.2   Obfuscation in a Graph

An individual's location in geographic space is represented as a vertex $l \in V$. An obfuscation of an individual's location l is represented as a set O, such that $l \in O$ and $O \subseteq V$. For every element $o \in O$, we say that o is *indiscernible* from l. The set O provides an imprecise representation of an individual's location. At any moment in time, the individual must be located at exactly one of the vertices in O, but which one remains unspecified.

Consequently, for an obfuscation O of an individual's location, one measure of the level of privacy (imprecision) is the cardinality of the set O, $|O|$ (the number of locations that are indiscernible from the individual's actual location). The larger this set, the less information is being revealed about the individual's actual location, and the greater the individual's privacy.

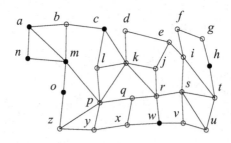

Fig. 2. Graph $G = (V, E)$ with example obfuscation $O = \{a, c, h, m, n, o, w\}$ (black vertices)

Figure 2 shows an example graph. An individual, located at one of the vertices in the graph, might represent his or her location using the obfuscation $O = \{a, c, h, m, n, o, w\}$, thereby not specifying at which of the vertices in O that individual is actually located. Note that the obfuscation O does not need to be in any sense contiguous (e.g., elements of O do not need to be connected in G). For ease of depiction, the graph in Figure 2 is planar, although planarity is also not a requirement of our model.

5.3   Proximity Location-Based Services

A simple but important subclass of location-based services concerns querying a spatial database in order to find information about features of interest that are nearest to an individual's location, which we refer to as *proximity queries*. Examples of such queries include, "With reference to my current location,

- "what is the address of the closest sushi restaurant?"
- "where is the nearest hospital?"
- "where is the nearest person waiting for a taxi?" (for a taxicab driver)

All these queries have the general form of finding the most proximal feature to a user's current location, usually returning some information related to that feature, for example the address, phone number, or price list. Data mining multiple such proximity queries could provide the basis for inferring the location (and so identity) of an anonymous or pseudonymous individual. Further, the final query might additionally demand authentication, where an individual is required to verify his or her true identity before being allowed to access privileged information (in this case, the location of a paying passenger). Obfuscation offers the ability to support authenticated location-based services, where a user cannot remain anonymous but still wishes to retain location privacy (see section 2.3).

In these queries, proximity may be quantified using a variety of different proximity measures, including Euclidean distance, network distance, or travel-time. In the graph, different proximity measures are represented using different weighting functions. Proximity queries are straightforward to answer if we know precisely where an individual is located. Even if an individual's location is not precisely known (i.e., under obfuscation), basic spatial analysis operations are enough to answer proximity queries in cases where Euclidean distance in a homogeneous Cartesian space is used (see section 1.1). The algorithm and negotiation process presented in the following sections provide a mechanism for responding to proximity queries in a weighted graph when an individual's location is not precisely known.

The discrete graph-based model of geographic space is general enough to be able to represent proximity queries in continuous Cartesian space. Thus, we can choose to represent the motivational example in section 1.1 as a weighted graph (see Figure 3). The locations of the three sushi restaurants and the pedestrian would be vertices of the graph. Edges between the pedestrian's location and the restaurants would assume as weights the Euclidean distance between these points

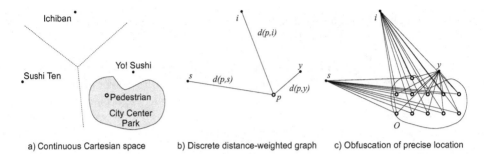

a) Continuous Cartesian space   b) Discrete distance-weighted graph   c) Obfuscation of precise location

Fig. 3. Representation of continuous Cartesian space using discrete distance-weighted graphs

(Figure 3b). By discretizing the "City center park" region as a set of points, we could further represent the obfuscated scenario, where the pedestrian's precise location is unknown (Figure 3c).

5.4   Negotiation and Quality of Service

We are now in a position to present an algorithm for negotiation between a mobile client and a TPLBSP. The negotiation process aims to provide the best quality of service possible, whilst revealing as little information as possible about the client's location.

Algorithm 1 provides a formal description of the negotiation algorithm from the perspective of the TPLBSP. The algorithm requires as input:

- the weighted graph $G = (V, E)$ representing the geographic environment (presumably stored in the location-based service provider's spatial database);
- an obfuscation $O \subseteq V$ of the client's location $l \in O$; and
- a set Q of query vertices $Q \subseteq V$, from which the client wishes to identify the closest vertex (e.g., Q might represent the locations of all the sushi restaurants in the geographic environment G).

The preliminary lines in Algorithm 1 (1.1–1.3) define the relation δ such that for all $o_1, o_2 \in O$, $o_1 \delta o_2$ iff o_1 and o_2 have the same query vertex $q \in Q$ as their most proximal. Proximity is determined using the shortest path between the two vertices in the graph. Thus, $o_1 \delta o_2$ can be understood to mean "o_1 is most proximal to the same query vertex as o_2." By stipulating that each element has a unique most proximal query vertex (line 1.2) δ becomes an equivalence relation (reflexive, symmetric, and transitive). In fact, an equivalence relation is not a requirement of the obfuscation model, and we could recast Algorithm 1 to permit non-transitive relations (important to allow for the case where two query vertices are equidistant from an element of O). However, making δ an equivalence relation yields a much simpler algorithm, and so is used here purely for reasons of notational convenience and ease of presentation.

Any equivalence relation on a set induces a partition on that set. As a consequence, O/δ is a partition on O. If O/δ has only one element (O), then the

---

Algorithm 1: Negotiation proximity query with obfuscation

Data: The geographic environment represented as a weighted graph $G = (V, E)$, the set of query vertices $Q \subseteq V$, and the obfuscated location of the client $O \subseteq V$

Result: The pair $\langle q, C \rangle$, where $C \in (0.0, 1.0]$ indicates the confidence that $q \in Q$ is the nearest target to the client's current location (the quality of service)

Define $d(v_1, v_2)$ to be the distance between $v_1, v_2 \in V$, measured using the shortest path through the graph G;

Define the function $min : O \rightarrow Q$ where $min(o) \mapsto q_1$ such that $\forall q_2 \in Q.d(o, q_1) \leq (o, q_2)$ (assume that $\forall q_1, q_2 \in Q.q_1 \neq q_2 \rightarrow d(o, q_1) \neq d(o, q_2)$);

Define the relation $\delta \subseteq O \times O$ such that $\forall o_1, o_2 \in O.o_1 \delta o_2$ iff $min(o_1) = min(o_2)$;

Construct the partition O/δ ;

if $O \in O/\delta$ **then**

    | Return the pair $\langle q, 1.0 \rangle$ where $q = min(o)$ for an arbitrary $o \in O$;

else

    if *Client agrees to identify for its current location l the equivalence class* $[l] \in O/\delta$ **then**

        | Return the pair $\langle q, 1.0 \rangle$ where $t = min(o)$ for an arbitrary $o \in [l]$;

    else

        if *Client agrees to identify a new obfuscation $O' \subset O$* **then**

            | Reiterate algorithm with O' in place of O;

        else

            | Return the pair $\langle q, C \rangle$ where $C = ||[o]||/|O|$ and $q = min(o)$ for some $o \in O$ such that C is maximized;

---

possible client locations in O must all be closest to the same query vertex (line 1.5). In this case, we can simply return the closest query vertex $q \in Q$ to some arbitrary element of O along with the confidence measure 1.0 (highest possible quality of service, total confidence in the result).

If O/δ has more than one element, then the next stage is to begin negotiations with the client. The TPLBSP now communicates with the client. The client knows its true location $l \in O$, and so potentially can identify the equivalence class $[l]$ in O/δ in which it is located. If the client is prepared to reveal this information, then it will again be possible to return the nearest query vertex with total confidence (lines 1.8–1.9). (Note that even if the client chooses to reveal this information, the TPLBSP will still not know the precise location of the client.) However, it is entirely possible that the client may not wish to reveal this much information about its location (especially if the cardinality of the set $||[l]||$ is much smaller than the cardinality of the set O). If so, then the client has two options.

First, if the client does not agree to provide any further information about its location, then the service provider returns the closest query vertex $q \in Q$ to an arbitrary location $o \in O$, along with a measure of the confidence that the returned query vertex is indeed the closest to the client's actual location (line 1.14). In our algorithm, we assume all locations in O are equally likely to be the client's location $l \in O$, and therefore for an arbitrary $o \in O$, the likelihood C that the closest query vertex to o will also be the closest query vertex to l is simply $|[o]|/|O|$ (the ratio of the cardinality of the equivalence class of o to the cardinality of O). The algorithm selects an $o \in O$ such that C is maximized, and so represents a "conservative" algorithm that returns the query vertex associated with the highest confidence level. Alternatively, the algorithm could also be adapted to select the $o \in O$ such that the distance from some $q \in Q$ to o is minimized (an "optimistic" algorithm) or that this distance is maximized (a "pessimistic" algorithm). Indeed, it is not too difficult to devise several more sophisticated ways of dealing with this case. For example, a further alternative would be to return the entire set Q of query vertices and leave the client to choose between them. However, in many cases a commercial location-based service provider might be unwilling to reveal such information, especially where Q represents high-value or high-volume data.

Second, the client can provide a new obfuscation $O' \subseteq V$ with which to reiterate the algorithm (line 1.12). At this point it becomes critical that the obfuscations O and O' are only imprecise and not inaccurate (i.e., O and O' definitely contain l). Since $l \in O$ and $l \in O'$, we know $l \in O \cap O'$. Consequently, the negotiation process requires that $O' \subseteq O$. Further, there is no purpose in a client reiterating the algorithm with the same obfuscation, $O' = O$, since that will return exactly the same result. Therefore, to continue the negotiation process a client is required to provide a strict subset of O, $O' \subset O$ (line 1.11). This is an important result, for two reasons. Since at every iteration the client is obliged to provide a strict subset of O in order to continue the negotiation process, we know that:

- the negotiation process must terminate (since O is finite); and
- the service provider needs to compute the shortest paths between locations in the graph only once, the first time the query is posed (all future iterations can reuse the same information).

5.5   Efficient Shortest Path Computation

One further aspect of importance is the complexity of the shortest path computation needed to construct the relation δ. A naive approach would be to compute the shortest path from every element of O to every element of Q. In general, single source shortest path algorithms, like Dijkstra's algorithm, have a computational complexity of $O(n^2)$. As a result, the naive approach would require m iterations of the shortest path algorithm to compute this result, where m is the cardinality of O. As the size of $|O|$ increases (m approaches n), the complexity of this naive algorithm approaches $O(n^3)$, the complexity of the all pairs shortest path algorithm. Thus, a naive approach significantly increases the computational complexity of this task. (A similar reasoning holds for the related task of computing the shortest path from every element of Q to every element of O.)

However, it is possible to use a single pass of Dijkstra's algorithm to compute all the shortest paths needed for the entire negotiation process in Algorithm 1, as described in Algorithm 2. Algorithm 2 is based on a multisource shortest path algorithm (e.g., [28]). Given a set of source vertices, a multisource shortest path algorithm computes the shortest of all shortest paths from any source vertex to every other vertex in the graph. Algorithm 2 is essentially a multisource shortest path algorithm which finds the shortest of all shortest paths from an element of Q to each element of O. (We assume the graph is not directed, so the shortest path from a to b is the same as the shortest path from b to a, although it would be simple to modify the algorithm to also deal with directed graphs.)

Algorithm 2 accepts the same inputs as Algorithm 1, but returns the equivalence relation δ. The first step is to add a new dummy vertex, s, to the graph G, such that there exists an edge from s to every query vertex $q \in Q$, each with zero weight (line 2.1). This step is included in the standard multisource shortest path algorithm. Figure 4 illustrates this step, showing the addition of the dummy vertex s to a graph with $Q = \{q_1, ..., q_5\}$ and $O = \{o_1, ..., o_6\}$.

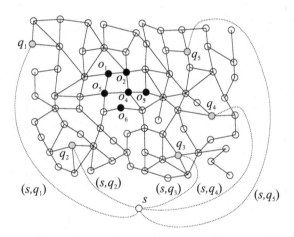

Fig. 4. Addition of dummy vertex s to obfuscated multisource graph algorithm, with $Q = \{q_1, ..., q_5\}$ (gray vertices) and $O = \{o_1, ..., o_6\}$ (black vertices)

Next the algorithm performs a single pass of Dijkstra's algorithm to yield the shortest paths from s to every other vertex in the graph (line 2.2). Finally, we compute the equivalence relation δ from this information (lines 2.3–2.4). Every shortest path begins at s and must have one element of Q as its second vertex. For each element of $o \in O$, this second vertex represents the most proximal element of Q to o. Therefore, all the information needed to compute δ can be obtained using a single pass of the Dijkstra algorithm, with computational complexity $O((n + 1)^2) \approx O(n^2)$ (the same computational complexity as the conventional case, where no obfuscation is used).

Algorithm 2: Computation of the relation δ

Data: The geographic environment represented as a weighted graph $G = (V, E)$ (with weights $w : E \to \mathbb{R}$), the set of target locations $Q \subseteq V$, and the obfuscated location of the client $O \subseteq V$

Result: The relation $\delta \subseteq O \times O$ such that $\forall o_1, o_2 \in O.o_1\delta o_2$ iff $min(o_1) = min(o_2)$ (see Algorithm 1 line 1.3);

Construct a new graph $G' = (V', E')$ using a dummy vertex s such that $V' = V \cup \{s\}$, $E' = E \cup S$, and $\forall e \in S.w(e) \mapsto 0.0$, where $S = \{s\} \times Q$;

Using Dijkstra's algorithm, compute the shortest paths from s to all vertices in G';

Define $second : O \to Q$ such that $second(v_o) \mapsto v_q$, where v_q is the second vertex of the shortest path from s to v_o (note that the second vertex must be an element in Q);

$\forall o_1, o_2 \in O$ define $\delta = \{(o_1, o_2) \in O \times O | second(o_1) = second(o_2)\}$;

5.6   Summary

The obfuscation model and algorithms given above provide a mechanism to balance an individual's location privacy with that individual's need for a high quality location-based service. The more information an individual is prepared to reveal, the higher the quality of information service an individual can be provided with. The importance of such a balance between privacy and utility has already been noted in the literature (e.g., [2]). Further, the aim of this approach is to use only just enough location information to provide a location-based service: the so-called "need to know principle" [17, 29] or "principle of minimal collection" [11].

The analysis of the algorithms above shows that obfuscation can be highly efficient, in the sense that the computational complexity of answering proximity queries can be the same for the obfuscated case, where an individual does not reveal his or her precise location, as for the conventional case, where an individual's location is known by the TPLBSP. The negotiation process may incur an additional communication overhead, where the service provider requests more information from the client. However, the additional communication is bounded, because at each iteration an individual must provide a more precise specification of his or her location.

An important unanswered question concerns how a client selects the initial obfuscation O to start the negotiation process (section 5.4). There are a number of natural choices for answers to this question. A client could begin by being completely imprecise and giving no information about their location (i.e., $O = V$, the obfuscation is the entire set of vertices in the graph). The efficient shortest path computation ensures this strategy is computationally practical, although it may lead to an extended negotiation process, so increasing bandwidth and communication overheads. Where applicable, an alternative strategy would be to utilize the precision characteristics of the location sensing infrastructure. For example, if a user's location is determined within a cell phone network, the set of all locations within the same cell as the user could be used for O. More alternatives involving further research are discussed in section 6.

Finally, there are several extensions to the algorithm that were not included in the discussion above, but nevertheless could easily be introduced, including:

- extensions to allow obfuscation on a directed graph;
- extensions to fully automate the negotiation process, by setting a minimum privacy threshold for the client, in terms of the size of O;
- extensions to provide a more sophisticated confidence measure, for example a confidence interval specifying the range between the best and worst possible answers.

6   Discussion and Future Work

This paper has argued that obfuscation is an important component of an overall approach to location privacy. Obfuscation provides a framework for the provision of high quality location-based services based on low quality location information. A detailed formal model for obfuscation is presented in the paper, with respect to a simple location-based service. The model includes algorithms able to achieve a balance between location privacy and location-based service utility, using an efficient negotiation process.

In developing our obfuscation architecture in this paper, we have attempted to set out our assumptions in a clear, formal, and methodical way. Planned future research has the objective of relaxing the model assumptions in the following ways.

Spatial Configuration of Obfuscations. In addition to the alternatives in section 5.6, another strategy for initializing the obfuscation O would be for a client to define an arbitrary threshold n, such that O contains n distinct locations, $|O| = n$. However, the spatial distribution of locations in O must be carefully chosen, in order to ensure the client's true location cannot be simply deduced from analysis of O. (For example, the client's true location would be easy to compute from O if it is known that the client always initializes O as the n closest locations to the its actual location.) Current research is investigating the effects of different spatial configurations for O. Following on from this, future research will aim to determine in advance what obfuscation will provide the best balance of location privacy and quality of service to a client.

Invasions of Privacy. For information to be worth protecting, it must also be worth attacking. Ongoing research aims to analyze the techniques a hostile agent might employ to circumvent obfuscation and attempt to discover a individual's exact location, so invading that person's privacy. Beresford and Stajano [3] have already shown how effective heuristics can be as a means of invading location privacy. Our initial approach to this problem is to categorize, and then formalize as an algebra, the different heuristics that a hostile agent might apply to a series of obfuscations (for example, using assumptions about an individual's maximum and/or minimum speed of movement). However, current models of location privacy are limited by their fundamentally static nature (i.e., modeling the movement of an individual as a sequence of static snapshot locations). To overcome this limitation, our longer-term research aims to move toward a truly spatiotemporal model of location privacy, based on approaches developed for moving object databases or process-oriented models of geographic information (e.g., [30]).

User Models for Obfuscation. This paper has focused on the underlying architecture and algorithms for obfuscation. However, research is practically motivated, and current work is implementing and testing the formal model; extending the obfuscation techniques into further types of location-based services (such as wayfinding services [5]); and developing user models and usable interfaces for obfuscation systems. With respect to this last aim, we have argued throughout this paper that the negotiation process should be based on balancing the level of location privacy against the quality of location-based service. We envisage these parameters, level of privacy and quality of service, will form the basis for users to configure an obfuscated location-based service to their personal requirements. Therefore, future work will also develop improved indicators and measures of level of privacy and quality of service that can be easily understood and manipulated by non-expert users. For example, the size of the obfuscation set, $|O|$ is the simple but naive measure of location privacy used in section 5.2. A more sophisticated measure of location privacy would need to reflect the spatial properties of locations in O (for example, the accessibility of the locations, or the number of other individuals at those locations) in order to adequately represent the level of location privacy to an obfuscation system user.

Acknowledgements

Dr Duckham is partially supported by an Early Career Researcher Grant and a Edward Clarence Dyason Fellowship from the University of Melbourne. Dr Kulik is partially supported by an Early Career Researcher Grant from the University of Melbourne. The authors are grateful to the four anonymous reviewers for their thorough and constructive comments.

References

1. M. S. Ackerman, L. F. Crannor, and J. Reagle. Privacy in e-commerce: Examining user scenarios and privacy preferences. In *Proc. 1st ACM conference on Electronic Commerce*, pages 1–8. ACM Press, 1999.
2. M. S. Ackerman, T. Darrell, and D. J. Weitzner. Privacy in context. *Human-Computer Interaction*, 16(2, 3, & 4):167–176, 2001.
3. A.R. Beresford and F. Stajano. Location privacy in pervasive computing. *IEEE Pervasive Computing*, 2(1):46–55, 2003.

4. R. Dingledine, N. Mathewson, and P. Syverson. Tor: The second-generation Onion router. In *Proc. 13th USENIX Security Symposium*, 2004.
5. M. Duckham, L. Kulik, and M. F. Worboys. Imprecise navigation. *Geoinformatica*, 7(2):79–94, 2003.
6. M. Duckham, K. Mason, J. Stell, and M. Worboys. A formal approach to imperfection in geographic information. *Computers, Environment and Urban Systems*, 25:89–103, 2001.
7. S. Duri, M. Gruteser, X. Liu, P. Moskowitz, R. Perez, M. Singh, and J-M. Tang. Framework for security and privacy in automotive telematics. In *Proc. 2nd International Workshop on Mobile Commerce*, pages 25–32. ACM Press, 2002.
8. F. Espinoza, P. Persson, A. Sandin, H. Nyström, E. Cacciatore, and M. Bylund. GeoNotes: Social and navigational aspects of location-based information systems. In G. D. Abowd, B. Brumitt, and S. Shafer, editors, *Ubicomp 2001: Ubiquitous Computing*, volume 2201 of *Lecture Notes in Computer Science*, pages 2–17. Springer, 2001.
9. General Assembly of the United Nations. Universal declaration of human rights. United Nations Resolution 217 A (III), December 1948.
10. W. W. Görlach, A. Terpstra and A. Heinemann. Survey on location privacy in pervasive computing. In *Proc. First Workshop on Security and Privacy at the Conference on Pervasive Computing (SPPC)*, 2004.
11. M. Gruteser and D. Grunwald. Anonymous usage of location-based services through spatial and temporal cloaking. In *Proc. MobiSys '03*, pages 31–42, 2003.
12. M. Gruteser and D. Grunwald. A methodological assessment of location privacy risks in wireless hotspot networks. In D. Hutter, G. Müller, and W. Stephan, editors, *Security in Pervasive Computing*, volume 2802 of *Lecture Notes in Computer Science*, pages 10–24. Springer, 2004.
13. C. A. Gunter, M. J. May, and S. G. Stubblebine. A formal privacy systems and its application to location-based services. In *Proc. Workshop on Privacy Enhancing Technologies*, Toronto, Canada, 2004.
14. J. Hightower and G. Boriello. Location systems for ubiquitous computing. *IEEE Computer*, 34(8):57–66, 2001.
15. J. I. Hong and J. A. Landay. An architecture for privacy-sensitive ubiquitous computing. In *Proc. 2nd International Conference on Mobile Systems, Applications, and Services*, pages 177–189. ACM Press, 2004.
16. S. E. Hudson and I. Smith. Techniques for addressing fundamental privacy and disruption tradeoffs in awareness support systems. In *Proc. ACM conference on Computer Supported Cooperative Work*, pages 248–257. ACM Press, 1996.
17. D. Hutter, W. Stephan, and M. Ullmann. Security and privacy in pervasive computing: State of the art and future directions. In D. Hutter, G. Müller, and W. Stephan, editors, *Security in Pervasive Computing*, volume 2802 of *Lecture Notes in Computer Science*, pages 284–289. Springer, 2004.
18. E. Kaasinen. User needs for location-aware mobile services. *Personal and Ubiquitous Computing*, 2003.
19. M. Langheinrich. Privacy by design—principles of privacy-aware ubiquitous systems. In G. D. Abowd, B. Brumitt, and S. Shafer, editors, *Ubicomp 2001: Ubiquitous Computing*, volume 2201 of *Lecture Notes in Computer Science*, pages 273–291. Springer, 2001.
20. M. Langheinrich. A privacy awareness system for ubiquitous computing environments. In G. Borriello and L. E. Holmquist, editors, *UbiComp 2002: Ubiquitous Computing*, volume 2498 of *Lecture Notes in Computer Science*, pages 237–245. Springer, 2002.

21. N. Marmasse and C. Schmandt. Location-aware information delivery with com-Motion. In *Proceedings 2nd International Symposium on Handheld and Ubiquitous Computing (HUC)*, pages 157–171, Bristol, UK, 2000.
22. G. Myles, A. Friday, and N. Davies. Preserving privacy in environments with location-based applications. *Pervasive Computing*, 2(1):56–64, 2003.
23. H. J. Onsrud, J. Johnson, and X. Lopez. Protecting personal privacy in using geographic information systems. *Photogrammetric Engineering and Remote Sensing*, 60(9):1083–1095, 1994.
24. J. Peterson. A presence-based GEOPRIV location object format. http://www.ietf.org/internet-drafts/draft-ietf-geopriv-pidf-lo-03.txt, September 2004.
25. A. Pfitzmann and M. Köhntopp. Anonymity, unobservability, and pseudonymity—a proposal for terminology. In H. Federrath, editor, *Designing Privacy Enhancing Technologies*, volume 2009 of *Lecture Notes in Computer Science*, pages 1–9. Springer, 2001.
26. T. Rodden, A. Friday, H. Muller, and A. Dix. A lightweight approach to managing privacy in location-based services. Technical Report Equator-02-058, University of Nottingham, Lancaster University, University of Bristol, 2002.
27. B. Schilit, J. Hong, and M. Gruteser. Wireless location privacy protection. *IEEE Computer*, 36(12):135–137, 2003.
28. R. Sedgewick. *Algorithms in Java, Part 5: Graph Algorithms*. Addison Wesley, 3rd edition, 2003.
29. E. Snekkenes. Concepts for personal location privacy policies. In *Proc. 3rd ACM conference on Electronic Commerce*, pages 48–57. ACM Press, 2001.
30. M. F. Worboys. Event-oriented aproaches to geographic phenomena. *International Journal of Geographic Information Science*, 2005. In press.
31. M. F. Worboys and E. Clementini. Integration of imperfect spatial information. *Journal of Visual Languages and Computing*, 12:61–80, 2001.
32. M. F. Worboys and M. Duckham. *GIS: A Computing Perspective*. CRC Press, Boca Raton, FL, 2nd edition, 2004.
33. M. F. Worboys, M. Duckham, and L. Kulik. Commonsense notions of proximity and direction in an environmental space. *Spatial cognition and computation*, 2004. Accepted.
34. M.F. Worboys. Nearness relations in environmental space. *International Journal of Geographical Information Science*, 15(7):633–651, 2001.

A Conceptual Framework for
Camera Phone-Based Interaction Techniques

Michael Rohs and Philipp Zweifel

Institute for Pervasive Computing,
Department of Computer Science,
Swiss Federal Institute of Technology (ETH) Zurich, Switzerland
rohs@inf.ethz.ch

Abstract. This paper proposes and evaluates interaction techniques for camera-equipped mobile phones. The proposed techniques are based on a visual code system that provides a number of orientation parameters, such as target pointing, rotation, tilting, distance, and relative movement. Our conceptual framework defines a set of fundamental physical gestures that form a basic vocabulary for describing interaction when using mobile phones capable of reading visual codes. These interaction primitives can be combined to create more complex and expressive interactions. A stateless interaction model allows for specifying interaction sequences, which guide the user with iconic and auditory cues. In using the parameters of the visual code system as a means of input, our framework enhances the currently limited input capabilities of mobile phones. Moreover, it enables users to interact with real-world objects in their current environment. We present an XML-based specification language for this model, a corresponding authoring tool, and a generic interpreter application for Symbian phones.

1   Introduction

Today's camera-equipped mobile phones and PDAs combine a large number of features and provide computing and communication capabilities comparable to those of earlier desktop PCs. Yet much of this functionality is hard to use. If we consider the input capabilities of camera phones, we soon discover that mobile device technology has outgrown the ability of the interface to support it. For example, small keypads are ill-suited for input tasks of moderate complexity. These input problems are only slightly mitigated with the integration of joysticks and touch screens.

What is missing is an interface that takes mobile users' constantly changing context into account and allows for spontaneous interaction with physical objects that users encounter while on the move. If we can provide a simple way to access information services associated with these objects, then we can create a more useful mobile Internet. Also, if we can provide a consistent interaction model for objects in the user's environment, then we can greatly increase the usability and functionality of mobile devices.

H.W. Gellersen et al. (Eds.): PERVASIVE 2005, LNCS 3468, pp. 171–189, 2005.

In this paper, we show how camera phones can be used as versatile interfaces to real-world objects. Our goal is to create an expressive means to "bridge the gulf between physical and virtual worlds" [1] for mobile users. To this end, we augment mobile phones with physical gestures, such as those reported in tangible [2] and embodied [3] user interfaces. We show how integrated cameras can act as a powerful input channel for mobile devices and turn them into interaction instruments for objects in the user's vicinity. In this way, camera phones can be used as enhanced input and control devices, e.g. for large-scale displays [4], and physical/virtual intermediaries at the same time.

In our conceptual framework, we propose and evaluate a number of physical gestures that form a basic vocabulary for interaction when using mobile phones capable of reading visual codes. These fundamental *interaction primitives* are based on camera input and simple image processing algorithms. The primitives can be combined to form more expressive interactions that provide rich input capabilities and effectively structure the output space. An interaction specification language defines rules that associate conditions of certain phone postures to actions, such as textual, graphical, and auditory output, which are performed by the mobile device. As described in detail below, these interaction primitives can be used in visual code image maps, augmented board games, product packaging, posters, and large public displays.

The visual code system described in [5] and [6] forms the basis for the proposed interaction techniques. The recognition algorithm has been designed for mobile devices with limited computing capabilities and is able to simultaneously detect multiple codes in a single camera image. In addition to the encoded value, the recognition algorithm provides a number of orientation parameters (see Figure 1). These include the rotation of the code in the image, the amount of tilting of the image plane relative to the code plane, and the distance between the code and the camera. The algorithm also senses the movement of the camera relative to the background. No calibration step is necessary to compute the orientation parameters.

An essential feature of the visual code system is mapping points in the image plane to corresponding points in the code plane, and vice versa (see Figure 1,

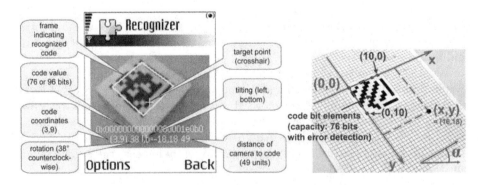

Fig. 1. Visual code parameters (left) and code coordinate system (right)

right). With this feature, the pixel coordinates of the camera focus (the point the user aims at, indicated by a crosshair during view finder mode) can be mapped to corresponding code coordinates. Each code defines its own local coordinate system that has its origin in the upper left edge of the code and is independent of the orientation of the code in the image. Areas that are defined with respect to the code coordinate system are thus invariant to projective distortion.

The following section gives a brief overview of related work. Section 3 outlines a number of application scenarios. Section 4 discusses interaction primitives, their combinations, and how they are indicated to the user. In Section 5, we define our user interaction model, which describes how to create visual code image map applications. Also, we describe an XML-based specification language, an authoring tool for visual code image maps, and a corresponding parser and interpreter on the phone. In Section 6, we report about a usability study in which we evaluated our interaction techniques. We wrap up with a number of conclusions and ideas for future work.

2   Related Work

Several projects have investigated linking physical objects with virtual resources, using technologies such as RFID tags or infrared beacons [1, 7]. However, these projects were mainly concerned with physical linking per se or with the infrastructure required for identifier resolution. They were limited in the richness of user interactions and typically allowed just a single physical gesture (for example presence in the reading range of an RFID reader) and thus just a single action per object. We, in contrast, allow the semantics to be a function of both the *object* and the *gestural sequence*.

A number of projects focused on improving interaction with the device itself rather than with the user's environment. No objects in the environment were integrated in the interaction. In 1994, Fitzmaurice et al. [8, 9] prototyped a spatially aware palmtop device with a six degrees-of-freedom tracker to create a porthole window into a large 3D workspace. The actual processing was done on a graphics workstation. The palmtop sensed its position and orientation in space and combined input control and output display in a single unit – thus integrating "seeing" and "acting". One could explore the 3D workspace with the palmtop using an *eye-in-the-hand* navigation metaphor. The goal was to step out of the "claustrophobic designs and constraints" imposed by the form factor of handheld devices. While this was a vision in 1994, similar interfaces can be built today with handheld devices and interaction techniques as presented in this paper.

Our work can be seen as an instance of an *embodied user interface* [3], in which the user directly interacts with the device itself – for example by tilting it – and both the manipulation and the virtual representation are integrated within the same object. Tilting of a handheld device has been explored as an input parameter for menu selection, scrolling, navigation, text entry, and 3D object manipulation [10, 11, 12, 13, 14, 15]. Readability problems of tilted displays, which we also experienced in this work, are described in [11] and [12].

In [2] Fishkin analyzed the idea of a physical grammar, and in [3] he addressed the issue of multi-gesture command sequences. Bartlett [12] used gestures – like tilting, snapping, shaking, tapping, and fanning – as a vocabulary of commands for a handheld electronic photo album. Our work tries to build compound interactions from a vocabulary of interaction primitives.

Bartlett [12] commented on some of the limits of embodied user interfaces: "perceived motion on the screen is the sum of the motion of the embodied device and the changes made to the display by the device. As you interact with the device by moving it, the orientation of the display to the user changes, then in response to that motion the display contents move on the display." This effect is especially severe for fast movements; however such movements are not required in our design. Rather, our work is more concerned with subtle yet easily and manually controllable changes.

Our interaction model allows us to define state spaces of phone postures in 3D. These issues are similar to those experienced with augmented reality environments and with 3D input devices [16, 15]. In our case however, our 3D environment is the physical world perceived through the camera lens. The Video-Mouse [15] is an optical mouse for 3D input based on video sensing and although it shares some similarities with our system, it is different in that it provides only very limited height sensing.

3   Application Scenarios

As outlined in the introduction, our system enhances the general input capabilities of mobile devices and provides a way to access mobile information services related to physical objects within a user's vicinity. Our system allows fine-grained control and access to various information items and services that can be physically hyperlinked [7] to objects in the environment. Typical objects that a mobile user might encounter include product packaging, vending and ticketing machines, posters and signs, as well as large electronic displays [4]. A few application scenarios are outlined below.

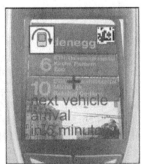

Fig. 2. A tram stop (left and middle) and a vending machine (right) equipped with visual code image maps

- **Tram stop.** The left and middle sections of Figure 2 show a tram stop information panel tagged with a visual code which allows users to access tram arrival times and to obtain further information by rotating the phone. To obtain information about the route of interest, users focus on the corresponding route number.
- **Vending machine.** The right part of Figure 2 shows a vending machine tagged with visual codes. To purchase products and confirm the purchase, users aim at the desired object. Of course in this scenario, a payment method needs to be in place.
- **Campus map.** Visual code image maps can help to find the location of an event on a campus map. A visitor to the campus could focus on an area labeled "current events" to get information about conferences, talks, and other events. The location of the event could then be highlighted on the mobile phone screen.
- **Augmented board games.** Computer-augmented board games are another good candidate for using visual code image maps since such games could benefit from a wide range of interaction possibilities that do not tie the user to a desktop computer.

4 Interaction Techniques

This section introduces the interaction techniques that are used in visual code image map applications. These techniques rely on sensing visual codes from different perspectives. We describe how interactions are combined from basic building blocks and how interaction cues guide users in the interaction process.

4.1 Interaction Primitives and Interaction Cues

Combined interactions are constructed from basic building blocks, called *interaction primitives*. *Static interaction primitives* require the user to aim their camera phone at a visual code from a certain orientation and to stay in that orientation. We defined two kinds of *dynamic interaction primitives*, which either involve "sweeping" the camera across a visual code or simply moving the phone relative to the background.

To facilitate information access and guide users in their interaction flows, each interaction primitive is associated with one or more *interaction cues* in the form of an icon. They appear on the mobile device's display and provide users with an indication of the possible interaction postures. Visual cues can optionally be combined with auditory icons.

For instance, the leftmost *rotation* interaction cue in table 1 indicates to users to rotate the mobile phone either clockwise or counterclockwise in order to access more information. The rightmost cue for the *distance* primitive means that more information can be obtained by moving the phone closer to the code – relative to the current posture.

An interaction cue should be both intuitive when encountered for the first time and easy to remember. Interaction cues should also be unambiguous so that it is easy to distinguish between different interaction primitives. In our design of interaction icons, we use color extensively since it facilitates distinguishing between different interaction primitives, and color displays are available on all camera phones. We restrict icon size, since the interaction cues must occupy only a small part of the phone display. They have to be rather simple and plain in order not to unnecessarily distract the user or clutter the interface.

4.2   Input and Output Capacity

Static interaction primitives map certain orientations of the mobile phone, also called *postures*, to individual information aspects. The posture of the device is determined with respect to a visual code in the camera image. With the term *input capacity* we denote the number of discrete information aspects that can be sensibly encoded in each of the interaction primitives. The input capacity is a measure of how many discrete interaction postures can be easily and efficiently located and selected by users. An important performance aspect is the time it takes a user to locate an individual information item among a set of available information items. This time depends on the kind of interaction primitive, the number of available postures, as well as the quality of feedback that is provided to the user. For static interaction primitives, discrete postures are possible, like focusing a particular information area, as well as more fine-grained forms of input, like the continuous adjustment of a value by moving closer to or away from a code. For each interaction primitive, we will give an estimation of its input capacity, which has been obtained experimentally and during user testing. In this work, discrete postures activate associated information aspects. It would also be conceivable to use voice commands for this purpose. In addition, voice commands can be taken as a way to get further input once a certain posture has been reached. This combination of postures and audio input would realize a multi-modal user interface.

The output capabilities of mobile devices are limited due to the small screen size. Thus, the amount of textual and graphical information that can be shown on a single screen is limited. Fortunately, the interaction postures are very well suited for structuring the presentation of data by distributing it across several related interaction postures. With the proposed approach, text and graphics can be overlaid over the camera image as known from augmented reality applications. Graphical elements can be registered with objects in the image, i.e. shown at the same position and resized and adapted to the viewing perspective. This makes the connection between the physical object and the information shown on the display more obvious to the user and avoids its isolated presentation without any other context.

Output can also be used to realize a feedback loop to the input side, which has an impact on the input capacity. To create the feedback loop, characteristic icons can represent interaction primitives and indicate interaction possibilities to the user. Mobile devices typically have an audio output channel which can be also used for establishing a feedback loop. Characteristic audio cues ("earcons" [17]) can be permanently associated to different information or interaction types. Auditory cues have the advantage that they do not take up any space on the device display. Designing audio feedback needs to be done with care, because it has privacy repercussions or might be distracting to some users. Another interesting option to support the feedback loop between output and input is available with the phone's vibration feature ("tactons" [18]).

4.3   Static Interaction Primitives

Static interaction primitives are based on the parameters of the visual code system, as well as the focused area, key presses, and the time stayed in a given interaction posture. For the user, this means finding a posture in view finder mode guided by the interaction cues, staying in that posture, and optionally taking a high-resolution picture to "freeze" the current posture. The "information freezing" feature stops the view finder mode and shows the information related to the last captured phone posture. The available static interaction primitives, their estimated input capacity, and the associated icons are shown in table 1.

Table 1. Input capacity and interaction cues of static interaction primitives

Static interaction primitive	Input capacity	Interaction cues
pointing	number of information areas	information area is highlighted
rotation	7	
tilting	5 (+4 if using NW,NE,SW,SE)	
distance	8	
stay	unlimited (time domain)	(icon has a highlighted display)
keystroke	12 (keypad) + 5 (joystick)	(icon has a highlighted keypad)

Pointing. The *pointing* interaction primitive requires targeting an area with the crosshair shown on the device display in view finder mode. The area is defined in terms of code coordinates. The input capacity is only limited by the number of areas that can be reached with the crosshair while the associated visual code is in the camera view. Section 5.5 presents techniques for extending the scope of reach. The borders of an area are highlighted when the associated visual code is recognized and the focus point is inside that area.

Rotation. The *rotation* interaction primitive associates rotation regions with discrete information items. For usability purposes, the rotation of the phone should be limited to ±90° from the upright position. To improve legibility, text should be aligned vertically if the rotation is greater than 45°. Users can complete up to 7 discrete postures, which correspond to regions that cover about 30° each, centered at 0°, ±30°, ±60°, and ±90°. *Rotation* is also usable as a continuous input control for a parameter value, such as the volume of a hi-fi system.

Tilting. During user testing, *tilting* turned out to be the most challenging interaction primitive for users since it requires turning the head in order to follow the device screen. We therefore do not use precise tilting values, but only an indication of the direction ("north", "west", "south", "east", and central position). This results in an input capacity of five postures. It is straightforward to extend this by "north-west", "north-east", "south-west", and "south-east", resulting in an overall input capacity of 9 postures.

Distance. The *distance* is measured during view finder mode and has an input capacity of 8 easily distinguishable distances. Distance is another a good candidate for continuous input.

Stay. The *stay* interaction primitive requires the user to stay in a certain posture. It automatically changes the provided information after a certain amount of time. The time interval can be freely specified, but should depend on the amount of information shown on the device screen. For a few lines of information it would typically be a couple of seconds. This primitive can be combined with the *keystroke* primitive described next, in order to realize a "timeout kill" mechanism as used for multi-tap text entry [14]. The input capacity is unlimited in principle, requiring the user to wait.

Keystroke. Finally, the *keystroke* interaction primitive consists of pressing a button on the device's keypad or using the device's thumb-operated joystick. Our target device has a 12 button numeric keypad and a non-isometric joystick with five states (left, right, up, down, press). The input capacity of this interaction primitive is obviously limited by the number of available keys.

The numbers given for the discernible input capacity of each interaction primitive decrease, if the basic primitives are combined with each other, as shown in the next sections.

4.4   Dynamic Interaction Primitives

There are two kinds of dynamic interaction primitives. With the first, the phone is moved ("swept") across the code in a certain direction while the camera is in view finder mode. The direction of movement is sensed by the mobile device and used as the input parameter. Interaction symbols for this kind of dynamic interaction primitive are not shown on the device display, but printed next to the code. For each possible direction of movement, a label is given, informing the user about the operation that will be triggered when the code is "swept" in the indicated direction. These interaction primitives are suitable for "blind" operation, in which a single operation is selected and immediately triggered after the movement. Sweep primitives can be regarded as the equivalent of a crossing-based interface for visual codes [19]. The input capacity amounts to 4 for both horizontal and vertical movement as well as for diagonal movement. A combination of both movement types seems to be too complex. With current phone hardware, the movement must not be too fast, in order for the codes to be reliably detected at multiple positions in the image. The input capacity and interaction cues are depicted in table 2.

Table 2. Input capacity and interaction cues of *sweep* interaction primitives

Dynamic interaction primitive („sweep")	Input capacity	Interaction cues (printed next to the code)
horizontal or vertical movement	4	
diagonal movement	4	

The second kind of dynamic interaction primitives is based on the optical movement detection algorithm that does not require a visual code in the camera image. It provides relative linear movement and relative rotation. It is not suited for discrete input, but for continuous adjustment of parameter values or for direct manipulation tasks. The corresponding interaction cues can be shown on the device display, printed next to a code, or shown on an electronic display to indicate that its objects can be directly manipulated by movement detection. Table 3 contains the capacities and interaction cues of these interaction primitives.

A *clutching mechanism* is required to prevent incidental motions of the phone from triggering unwanted dynamic interaction primitives. In our system, the relative movement tracking is active while the phone's joystick button is held

Table 3. Input capacity and interaction cues of relative movement interaction primitives

Dynamic interaction primitive (relative movement)	Input capacity	Interaction cues
relative linear movement	4 (continuous)	
relative rotation	2 (continuous)	

down. Releasing the button exits the relative movement detection state. This is also known as a *quasimode* as defined by Raskin in [20]. In Buxton's model [21], pressing the joystick button down corresponds to a state transition between state 1 ("tracking") and state 2 ("dragging"), releasing the button again transitions back to state 1.

4.5   Combinations of Interaction Primitives

The basic interaction cues are designed in such a way that they can be combined to form more complex interaction cues. Table 4 shows the possible combinations of two static interaction cues. When the mobile display shows a combination interaction cue, this means that the user has a choice to select between more than one interaction primitive to reach further information items. The usability of such combinations is discussed in Section 6. Combinations of more than two interaction cues should be avoided in order not to confuse the user. Even with combinations of only two static interaction cues, a large number interaction possibilities results.

Some of the static interaction primitives can be combined with the dynamic *sweep* interaction primitives. Each of the eight directions of movement can be combined with the following static interactions: rotation, tilting, and distance. The idea is to move the camera across the code in the chosen direction while keeping a certain rotation, tilting, or distance. In the case of rotation, for exam-

Table 4. Combinations of two static interaction primitives with example interaction cues

Combination	Interaction cue	Combination	Interaction cue
pointing & rotation	+ highlighted area	rotation & stay	
pointing & tilting	+ highlighted area	rotation & keystroke	
pointing & distance	+ highlighted area	tilting & distance	
pointing & stay	+ highlighted area	tilting & stay	
pointing & keystroke	+ highlighted area	tilting & keystroke	
rotation & tilting		distance & stay	
rotation & distance		distance & keystroke	

ple, it should be easy to hold the phone rotated 90° counterclockwise from the upright position.

Combinations of static primitives and dynamic primitives that sense relative movement seem to be more practical. Even if they cannot be executed simultaneously, performing a dynamic after a static interaction primitive is useful. A user first selects a certain parameter using a static interaction primitive – like tilting – and then uses relative linear movement to adjust the value. The relative movement detection is activated while the user is holding the joystick button down. This kind of combination resembles a "point & drag" transaction in classical GUI interfaces [21].

5   Visual Code Image Maps

In this section, we describe how combinations of interaction primitives can be applied in entire *visual code image map* applications. Visual code image maps consist of a number of areas, which are located close to a visual code and associated with multiple information aspects or specific operations. Areas can cover a certain region in the vicinity of a code, occupy the same space as the code, or even be defined as infinitely large. Area locations and shapes are defined in terms of the coordinate systems of the visual codes located near them. Area-related information is accessed by varying the input parameters provided by the visual code system. The input parameters are abstracted to a set of postures that are easily discoverable and applicable by users. The postures are specified as combinations of interaction primitives in an image map definition.

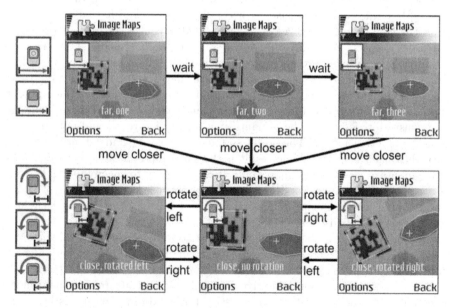

Fig. 3. An example interaction flow in a visual code image map

Figure 3 shows an example interaction flow for a simple image map. To the left of the screenshots, the enlarged interaction cues are drawn. An elliptical region next to a visual code is associated with six information items. At a farther distance (depicted in the upper three screenshots), three different information items are presented. The user just has to stay at that distance. The *stay* user interaction symbol indicates that more information will be displayed by waiting. Moving closer to the code plane, the interaction cue changes and another information aspect is displayed (depicted in the lower three screenshots). In the near distance posture, more information can be accessed by rotating the phone to the left (counterclockwise) and to the right (clockwise). The underlying user interaction model is discussed in more detail below.

When designing overlays over the camera image, design guidelines as described in [22] should be taken into account. The visual context given by the camera image should be maintained as far as possible. A graphical representation should be chosen such that the underlying context is revealed. This avoids the issue that the user has to split visual attention between the camera image (the "context") and the generated graphical overlay. It enables *dual attention*, which is characteristic of see-through tools. In addition, unnecessary information, i.e., information that is not part of the currently pointed area should be hidden. This is especially important for small displays.

5.1   User Interaction Model

The user interaction model determines how a user can browse information or trigger actions in a visual code image map. We use a stateless model that only considers the currently sensed parameters. Each interaction posture is associated with a rule. A rule consists of a condition and a result that is activated when the condition is met. A condition is made up of a set of constraints. A constraint restricts the valid range of a single input parameter. The rules are continuously checked and their results activated if their conditions are met. The visual code image map designer has to ensure that conditions are mutually exclusive. If they are not, the order of execution is undefined. For non-idempotent functions, it is important that they are not activated multiple times. Checking such constraints is part of the semantics of each action result and not specified in the interaction model. The stateless model is easy to understand for users, since they always see the same result if the same input posture is chosen. For image map designers, image map applications are easy to specify in this model. In a completely stateless model, some of the proposed combinations of static and dynamic interaction primitives cannot be realized. It is therefore slightly extended as described below.

State-based models are inherently difficult to understand for users since the system can behave differently on the same input parameters if it has different states. We therefore limited the notion of input state in the system to the relative movement interaction primitives. In order to activate relative movement detection, the user has to hold the joystick button down. The user's last posture receives relative movement updates while the joystick button is held down.

Releasing the button exits the relative movement detection state. This *quasi-mode* scheme ensures that the user is not inadvertently locked in a state. The second notion of state is introduced with the *stay* static interaction primitive. It becomes true when the time stayed in a certain posture is within a predefined time range. The state is thus defined by the set of other constraints of a condition, without the *stay* interaction primitive. A rule containing a *stay* interaction primitive fires when all other constraints have been true for the specified amount of time. The timeout is reset when the rule becomes invalid again.

5.2   Visual Code Image Map Specification Language

Based on the interaction model described above, we developed a visual code image map specification language. The specification language is XML-based. Depending on the visual code value, different measures are taken to retrieve the specification of an unknown image map. The XML description is loaded from the local file system, obtained via Bluetooth or the mobile phone network. It is parsed and the extracted information is used to present information and provide functionality according to the image map. We assume that up-to-date information is inserted into the XML file on the server, e.g. via PHP scripting.

5.3   Information Results

Information results can consist of auditory cues, textual overlay over the camera image, bitmap overlays, and overlays of graphical shapes. Textual overlays can appear at a constant position in the mobile's display, which is the default in the current implementation. The text position can also be tied to specific code coordinates and thus appear as an overlay of an element in the image map. Bitmap overlays can either appear at a constant display position or located at specific code coordinates. As with textual output, free rotation of images is an expensive operation for current mobile devices and can thus not be performed in real time on current devices. The Symbian operating system, for example, only provides functions for rotating text in steps of 90°, which is sufficient for legibility in the case of rotation. Graphical overlays, such as rectangles, ellipses, and polygons are automatically adapted to perspective distortion by using the code coordinate system mapping. It is possible to specify multiple textual and graphical outputs in a single information result.

5.4   Action Results

Triggering an action result consists of starting the requested application on the device and dispatching the provided arguments in the format the application requires. The semantics of the arguments depend on the given application. In the simplest case, the argument string provided in the XML description is simply passed on to the application. In a more complex case, it requires parsing the argument string and calling multiple methods on the phone application. The action result needs to define whether it has to be executed on each image update while the corresponding condition is valid, once as the rule first becomes active, or only when the joystick is additionally held down. Example action results are starting the WAP browser with a specific URL as an argument, storing vCard and vCalendar entries, placing a phone call to the number given in the argument string, invoking the SMS editor, or sending a predefined text message without invoking the SMS editor. Other action results include opening a Bluetooth connection to report relative movement updates and visual code sightings.

5.5   Focus Point Adaptation

A problem with visual code image maps comes from the fact that at least one code needs to be present in the camera view in order to compute the mapping from the image to the code coordinate system. This restricts the radius of action for moving the focus point. This situation is shown in the left section of Figure 4. The focus point is typically indicated to the user with a cross hair that is located in the middle of the display. The reachability problem can be solved in a number of ways. First, multiple codes can be dispersed throughout an image map. This raises aesthetical concerns and restricts the designer of an image map, because more space is occupied by visual markers. This might be mitigated in the future with higher-resolution cameras, allowing much smaller codes to be used. Additionally, with zoom cameras, a wide angle setting can be used to cover a larger part of the image map. Second, there is no reason why the focus point has to be located in the middle of the screen. One option would be to include the most suitable position of the cursor as a parameter in the image map specification. If a visual code is located to the left of a vertical arrangement of areas, for example, the focus point might be set horizontally to the right for easier targeting.

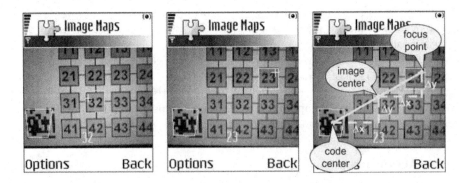

Fig. 4. Central focus point (left) and adapted focus point (middle and right)

A third option is to dynamically adapt the position of the focus point depending on the position of the code center on the screen. This is shown in the middle and right of Figure 4. The focus point is computed as the mirror point of the code center point through the image center point. In usability tests, this smooth adaptation style seemed to be more predictable than another adaptation style, in which discrete focus point positions had been used. The smooth adaptation of the cursor position requires more dexterity than a fixed cursor position, but is manageable after a short time. If no code is present in the image for a certain time, the focus point is repositioned to the display center. If multiple codes are available, the nearest one is chosen for adaptation. If multiple codes are visible in the camera image, the adaptation can be disabled, because the reachability problem is no longer given. With dynamic adaptation, the reachable radius is increased by up to 100% compared to a focus point which is centered on the display.

5.6   Visual Code Image Map Editor and Interpreter

We have developed a visual code image map editor in Java. The editor produces image map specifications from jpg, gif, and png images (typically a picture of the visual code in the real world) so that users can draw areas and specify constraints, interaction cues, and results. The resulting output is an XML file that can be stored on a server and which can be downloaded to the mobile phone.

On the device side, we have developed a generic visual code image map interpreter in C++ for Symbian devices. For each detected code, the interpreter tries to locate the corresponding image map and continuously checks for satisfied conditions in the available rules. As long as the conditions of a rule are satisfied, the corresponding information or external application is shown.

6   Usability Evaluation

6.1   Goals and Design

To understand the strengths and weaknesses of the individual interaction techniques, as well as the approach as a whole, we designed a qualitative usability study. It consisted of a questionnaire, two task execution parts, and a final interview. The questionnaire covered basic biographic data and asked about users' level of experience with mobile phones, text messaging, and playing computer games. The two task execution parts served different purposes. The aim of the first one was to evaluate individual interaction primitives and their combinations independently from the semantics of a specific application. The second one used the campus map scenario outlined in Section 3 to help users understand the implications of using the interaction concepts in a broader context. The dynamic interaction primitives have not been evaluated in this study.

A number of technical factors influence the users' satisfaction with the interaction techniques, such as the size and quality of the display and the response time and reliability of the visual code system. However, we can expect that most of these technical factors are likely to improve. The usability evaluation thus tried to focus on issues that are inherent to the design of the proposed interaction techniques.

The first part of the study consisted of 15 individual tasks. Users employed the various interaction techniques to try and find a secret number and a secret letter in a particular image map. The first few tasks tested the dexterity required for the basic interaction primitives as well as how easily users were able to remember and distinguish between various interaction cues. The remaining tasks tested combined interactions. The second part of the study allowed users to get a feel for a possible real-word application. Lastly, in post-test interviews, users were asked to express their opinion about the overall system, rate the individual interaction primitives, and to give feedback about the presented scenario.

When observing tasks, we used the think-aloud technique. Tasks were performed under quiet, laboratory-like conditions. Our evaluation procedure was adapted from the guidelines proposed in [23].

The execution of the study, including the initial questionnaire and the final interview, lasted approximately one hour per user. Eight users took part in our study, with ages ranging between 17 and 35. All of our users had some experience with personal computers, and all regularly used mobile phones for making phone calls and writing text messages. Some of them were heavy phone users, who often played mobile phone games and accessed information via WAP.

6.2   Findings and Discussion

Our results indicate the most challenging interaction primitive for users to do was *tilting*. The *pointing*, *distance*, and *stay* primitives were rated the best, followed by *keystroke* and *rotation*. For combinations which used *pointing* with other static primitives, we found two groups of people who preferred different user interactions. The first group, consisting of five participants, preferred user interactions that demand less manual dexterity. They favored the *pointing & stay* interaction, followed by the *pointing & keystroke* interaction. The second group, consisting of three participants, preferred the *pointing & distance* and *pointing & rotation* combinations. One possible explanation for this difference is dexterity. Since the first group seemed to have more problems with manual dexterity, they preferred passive user interactions, like *stay*, and well-known interactions, like *keystroke*. The second group, which had less problems with manual dexterity, liked combinations which used *distance* and *rotation* primitives the best because this gave them immediate control over the visual code application. With the *stay* primitive, the system forces the user to pause. This can be problematic, since the user cannot control the duration of each state. The *pointing & tilting* combination was by far the most difficult interaction. The reason seems to be that this combined interaction which asks users to simultaneously focus on an area while keeping a visual code in the camera image and tilting the phone to the required position is very demanding for first time users.

During view finder mode, camera images are continuously sampled and the display is updated accordingly. We provided an "information freezing" feature that stops the view finder mode and shows the information related to the last captured phone posture. Some users used this feature as soon as they reached the correct phone posture. The feature is extremely important in that it provides users with some sense of permanence and stability.

We observed some learning effects during the usability test. In general, participants managed the *rotation* interaction primitive in task 13[1] more easily and more rapidly than in task 3[2] although task 13 was more difficult. Evidently, participants had improved their skills in handling the interaction techniques during the performed tasks and, moreover, the tasks did not seem to exhaust them.

All user interaction cues seemed to be easy to learn and remember. However, two participants first confused the *tilting* and *rotation* interaction cues. But after this first mistake they had no further problems. The interaction cues have been redesigned in the meantime and now use different colors for indicating "rotation" (red) and "tilting" (blue), which should improve distinguishability.

In the second part of the study, users had to look up a building on a campus map that was printed on a poster and attached to the wall. Observation showed that the application was not self-explanatory. Most users needed some instructions on how to use it. The following observations have been made during the second part:

- If the information areas are not clear, users tend to focus on the visual codes since they assume that they contain information items. The observation of this behavior offers two conclusions: first, a visual code image map designer should pay attention to design obvious information areas. Second, in a complex image map application, focusing directly on the visual codes should trigger a help menu or a description of the application.
- Most users tended to read printed information that was captured by the camera and shown on the phone display by looking directly at the printed information. They seemed to avoid the display since the size and quality is not yet good enough. However, users had no problems to read generated textual information and graphical overlays over the camera image directly on the display.
- Two users spontaneously remarked that they find it easier to access information aspects with the information map application on the wall than with the newspaper-like tasks on the table.
- Reading distances differed between users, but all users managed to find a suitable distance between a printed code and the camera after a short time.

7   Conclusions and Future Work

We have used a visual code system to augment camera phones with physical gestures in order to turn them into versatile interfaces to real-world objects. The proposed conceptual framework allows constructing rich interaction sequences by combining a few basic interaction primitives in a flexible way. Even though

---

[1] *rotation* plus *pointing* and only one visual code in range.
[2] *rotation* plus *pointing* and two visual codes in range.

the input capacity of each individual interaction primitive is limited, their combination results in a large number of input postures. The chosen stateless interaction model, or rather its realization as an XML-based specification language, adequately describes visual code information maps, including input postures, phone movements, information results, and action results. An authoring tool and a generic interpreter application for Symbian phones enable the creation and usage of visual code image map applications.

The user evaluation showed that most of the postures are easily and quickly discoverable with the help of graphical and auditory cues. It also showed that users generally like the proposed interaction paradigm. A few undesirable combinations of interaction primitives have been revealed that should be avoided by visual code image map designers.

A possible next step in this research would be to investigate how data found in an image map can be actively manipulated instead of just accessed. Another idea would be to examine if users develop a kind of "posture memory" – in the sense of "muscle memory" – when they repeatedly access the same information items. Furthermore, investigating the proposed interaction techniques in computer-augmented board games would be very interesting.

Acknowledgments

We thank the anonymous reviewers for their valuable comments and suggestions for related work. We also thank Jennifer G. Sheridan (Lancaster University), Rafael Ballagas (RWTH Aachen), Friedemann Mattern, Marc Langheinrich, and Harald Vogt (Institute for Pervasive Computing at ETH Zurich) for constructive comments and discussions. Last, but not least, thanks to our test users.

References

1. Want, R., Fishkin, K.P., Gujar, A., Harrison, B.L.: Bridging physical and virtual worlds with electronic tags. In: Proceedings of the SIGCHI conference on Human factors in computing systems, ACM Press (1999) 370–377
2. Fishkin, K.P.: A taxonomy for and analysis of tangible interfaces. Personal Ubiquitous Comput. **8** (2004) 347–358
3. Fishkin, K.P., Moran, T.P., Harrison, B.L.: Embodied user interfaces: Towards invisible user interfaces. In: Proceedings of the Seventh Working Conference on Engineering for Human-Computer Interaction, Kluwer, B.V. (1999) 1–18
4. Ballagas, R., Rohs, M., Sheridan, J.G., Borchers, J.: Sweep and Point & Shoot: Phonecam-based interactions for large public displays. In: CHI '05: Extended abstracts of the 2005 conference on Human factors and computing systems, ACM Press (2005)
5. Rohs, M.: Real-world interaction with camera-phones. In: 2nd International Symposium on Ubiquitous Computing Systems (UCS 2004), Tokyo, Japan (2004) 39–48
6. Rohs, M., Gfeller, B.: Using camera-equipped mobile phones for interacting with real-world objects. In Ferscha, A., Hoertner, H., Kotsis, G., eds.: Advances in Pervasive Computing, Austrian Computer Society (OCG) (2004) 265–271

7. Kindberg, T.: Implementing physical hyperlinks using ubiquitous identifier resolution. In: Proceedings of the eleventh international conference on World Wide Web, ACM Press (2002) 191–199

8. Fitzmaurice, G.W., Zhai, S., Chignell, M.H.: Virtual reality for palmtop computers. ACM Trans. Inf. Syst. **11** (1993) 197–218

9. Fitzmaurice, G., Buxton, W.: The Chameleon: Spatially aware palmtop computers. In: CHI '94: Conference companion on Human factors in computing systems, ACM Press (1994) 451–452

10. Rekimoto, J.: Tilting operations for small screen interfaces. In: Proceedings of the 9th annual ACM symposium on User interface software and technology, ACM Press (1996) 167–168

11. Harrison, B.L., Fishkin, K.P., Gujar, A., Mochon, C., Want, R.: Squeeze me, hold me, tilt me! an exploration of manipulative user interfaces. In: Proceedings of the SIGCHI conference on Human factors in computing systems. (1998) 17–24

12. Bartlett, J.F.: Rock 'n' scroll is here to stay. IEEE Comput. Graph. Appl. **20** (2000) 40–45

13. Hinckley, K., Pierce, J., Sinclair, M., Horvitz, E.: Sensing techniques for mobile interaction. In: Proceedings of the 13th annual ACM symposium on User interface software and technology, ACM Press (2000) 91–100

14. Wigdor, D., Balakrishnan, R.: TiltText: Using tilt for text input to mobile phones. In: Proceedings of the 16th annual ACM symposium on User interface software and technology, ACM Press (2003) 81–90

15. Hinckley, K., Sinclair, M., Hanson, E., Szeliski, R., Conway, M.: The VideoMouse: A camera-based multi-degree-of-freedom input device. In: Proceedings of the 12th annual ACM symposium on User interface software and technology, ACM Press (1999) 103–112

16. Zhai, S.: User performance in relation to 3D input device design. SIGGRAPH Comput. Graph. **32** (1998) 50–54

17. Brewster, S.A.: Using nonspeech sounds to provide navigation cues. ACM Transactions on Computer-Human Interaction **5** (1998) 224–259

18. Brewster, S., Brown, L.M.: Tactons: Structured tactile messages for non-visual information display. In: Proceedings of the fifth conference on Australasian User Interface, Australian Computer Society, Inc. (2004) 15–23

19. Accot, J., Zhai, S.: More than dotting the i's — foundations for crossing-based interfaces. In: Proceedings of the SIGCHI conference on Human factors in computing systems, ACM Press (2002) 73–80

20. Raskin, J.: The humane interface: New directions for designing interactive systems. ACM Press/Addison-Wesley Publishing Co. (2000)

21. Buxton, W.: A three-state model of graphical input. In: Proceedings of the IFIP TC13 Third Interantional Conference on Human-Computer Interaction, North-Holland (1990) 449–456

22. Tapia, M.A., Kurtenbach, G.: Some design refinements and principles on the appearance and behavior of marking menus. In: Proceedings of the 8th annual ACM symposium on User interface and software technology, ACM Press (1995) 189–195

23. Gomoll, K., Nicol, A.: Discussion of guidelines for user observation. From: User Observation: Guidelines for Apple Developers (1990)

u-Photo: Interacting with Pervasive Services Using Digital Still Images

Genta Suzuki[1], Shun Aoki[1], Takeshi Iwamoto[1], Daisuke Maruyama[1],
Takuya Koda[1], Naohiko Kohtake[1], Kazunori Takashio[1],
and Hideyuki Tokuda[1,2]

[1] Graduate School of Media and Governance, Keio University
[2] Faculty of Environmental Information, Keio University,
5322 Endo, Fujisawa, Kanagawa 252-8520, Japan
{genta, shunaoki, iwaiwa, marudai, acky, nao, kaz, hxt}@ht.sfc.keio.ac.jp
http://www.ht.sfc.keio.ac.jp/

Abstract. This paper presents u-Photo which is an interactive digital still image including information of pervasive services associated with networked appliances and sensors in pervasive computing environment. U-Photo Tools can generate a u-Photo and provide methods for discovering contextual information about these pervasive services. Users can easily find out this information through the metaphor of 'taking a photograph'; the users use u-Photo by clicking on a physical entity in a digital still image. In addition, u-Photo makes managing information more efficient because the still image has embedded visual information. Using u-Photo and u-Photo Tools, we conducted various demonstrations and performed usability tests. The results of these tests show that u-Photo Tools are easy to learn. We also present that the time that expert u-Photo users take to find the object in piles of u-Photos is shorter than the time it take to find the object in piles of text-based descriptions.

1 Introduction

A principal theme of pervasive computing is the interaction between users and pervasive services. Networked devices such as networked appliances, networked sensors, and other computing-enabled everyday objects are becoming more common. This means that there are not only increasing number of devices but also incleasing the pervasive services associated with these devices.

The increase of these pervasive services now requires intuitive ways to discover and use them. Jini [8], and UPnP [14] provide methods to discover networked appliances' services. Directory services [4][21] also supply information about networked services. However, they don't return enough information about the services. Users need to know not only the virtual and networked information (e.g. host names, URLs, types of services) but also the links between the services' physical entities and virtual information because the pervasive services actuate or sense the physical world. Suppose that there are multiple printers in a location. How can visitors tell the network name of a specific printer? It is

H.W. Gellersen et al. (Eds.): PERVASIVE 2005, LNCS 3468, pp. 190–207, 2005.

inconvenient if systems that supply information about the services do not show the links between network names and physical entities of the printers.

Our approach uses interactive, digital still images for intuitive service discovery and use. U-Photo is a digital still image with information of pervasive services. U-Photo uses the simple action of taking a photograph to discover pervasive services and then uses image-based intuitive GUI to use the services. Users can interact with the services anytime as long as they have the u-Photos.

In this paper, we discuss the basic concept of u-Photo, the design of u-Photo Tools for using of u-Photo, and experiments based on the prototype. The rest of this paper is structured as follows: Section 2 describes the challenges faced in our work. In Section 3, we describe the basic concept of u-Photo. Section 4 presents the design of u-Photo media and u-Photo Tools. Details about the prototype appear in Section 5. Section 6 describes the prototype experiments, which included usability tests. Section 7 presents a discussion about u-Photo. We review related work in Section 8. Finally, we present our conclusions in Section 9.

2   Pervasive Services

2.1   Classification of Pervasive Services

We classify our target pervasive services into following three groups: environmental context sensing, appliance control, and personalization.

Environmental context sensing services acquire sensor values from networked sensors. In pervasive computing environment, sensors such as ultrasound sensor, infrared ray sensor, and RF readers have network connectivity. Furthermore, networked small sensor units [3][7] have been developed and they build sensor networks [6]. These sensors will be embedded everywhere in the environment and provide sensing services. We can acquire context information of physical world such as temperature, and brightness from these services. For instance, a user can monitor his/her room temperature from a different location. Since sensors have limited sensing areas, it is important for users to know the locations of sensors and sensing areas.

Appliance control services control networked appliances. A number of networked appliances have already released (e.g., air conditioners, microwave ovens, refrigerators, and lights) and it seems that all appliances will be networked in pervasive computing environment. We can control these appliances from mobile devices, PCs, and other input devices. One example of appliance control is controlling home appliances from the user's office.

Personalization services allow control of arbitrary appliances as if they are ours. Needs for personalization services arise when nomadic users want to reproduce a service to a different device [9][11][17]. Transferring media such as videos and audios is an example of a personalization service. In other words, we can say these personalization services are roaming user's tasks. Personalization service also supports applying personal settings to unfamiliar appliances. For example, the temperature at which a user feels comfortable, can be applied to each air

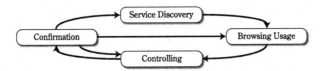

Fig. 1. User operation cycle of pervasive services

conditioner of rooms he/she visits. Personalization services works in two steps: first, users mark off settings and execution states of appliances, and reproduce them in another location.

2.2   User Operation Cycle

When using pervasive services, there is a operation cycle of *Service Discovery, Browsing Usage, Controlling,* and *Confirmation* shown in Fig.1.

– Service Discovery
  At first, a user has to discover the services that he/she wants. This operation is classified to two ways. The first classification is by function. For example, the user would look up a service as "What's the temperature here?" The second classification is by actual device (e.g., "Are there any air conditioners near here?"). In both cases, since the devices have limited actuation or sensing areas, the users have to know the links between the services' physical and virtual information.
– Browsing Usage
  After the service discovery, the user needs to know how to get data from the sensors and control the appliances. In other words, this operation involves finding out how to use the pervasive services. In this case, there are the following two types of information: information for connecting to the service and information about command-to-action binding. The former includes the IP address of the device, the port number, or other information to specify service in the network. Information such as clicking the "ON" button means turning on TV is included in the latter.
– Controlling
  After browsing the usage information, the user actually controls the appliances or sensors.
– Confirmation
  Finally, the user confirms whether the device performed the actions he/she intended. To do so, the user looks at the device or gets to the service state by using service commands. If the results are not as expected, the user goes back to the Service Discovery, Browsing Usage, or Controlling operations.

2.3   Challenges

Our research aims to provide a method that improves the user's operation cycle. To do that, the following three issues must be considered:

- **How to intuitively remind a user of pervasive services?** $\cdots$ How does a user discover the services? In particular, when he/she works with an invisible device such as a sensor embedded in a wall – how to do that? As we mentioned above, information about the services on the network is inseparable from physical entity because each pervasive service has limited actuation or sensor area in the physical world.
- **How to interact with pervasive services easily and instantly?** $\cdots$ After a user finds a pervasive service usage, how does he/she browse the service's usage? When a user wants to get temperature here and now, how does he/she do so? One way is that he/she looks up the information required for using the services such as the URL, and then executes the client application for using the service on his/her PC, and finally, he/she executes the operation. However, this would be difficult for novice users.
- **How to manage pervasive services' information?** $\cdots$ When a user controls a device from a remote location, he/she needs information about the service such as the device name and the location of the device. Moreover, personalization requires storing information about the services' states. However, it is difficult for users to manage a lot of information. When there are many caches of text descriptions of pervasive services, a user would be hard pressed to remember which description applies to which service. The stored information should be easily distinguishable from other information.

3   Concept of u-Photo: Interactive Digital Still Image

Our concept is based on an interactive, augmented still image called *u-Photo*. A u-Photo includes following three types of information about pervasive services:

1. **Physical Entities of Pervasive Services.** A digital still image can show the corresponding physical entities of pervasive services. For example, if an air conditioner in user's home appears in a still image, the image shows that the figure is a physical entity corresponding to the air conditioner service.
2. **Network Information about Pervasive Services.** Client applications for pervasive services require information about services' network. For example, when a user wants to print documents on a networked printer, he/she needs to know network information such as the printer's name, the IP address, and the type of the printer.
3. **State Information of Pervasive Services.** Personalization services need the state information of the source device, in order to transfer them to the destination device. An example of state information is content data and a timecode for playing in the video services.

3.1   Augmented Image-Based Interaction

U-Photo deals with the issue of service discovery in two phases, generating and viewing. The simple action of taking a photograph triggers the discovery of services. Users can easily determine the target to focus on and the time needed

194   G. Suzuki et al.

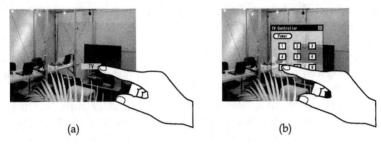

(a)   (b)

Fig. 2. The image-based interaction with pervasive services: (a) User clicks TV icon on a still image, and (b) GUI of TV control application superimposes on the still image

to capture it. Then, the discovered information is saved in a still image such as u-Photo. When a user opens u-Photo, notations such as 'Video Service' and 'Sensor Service' appear on the still image, and the user knows that pervasive services are embedded.

U-Photo also presents an image-based intuitive interaction with pervasive services. Just by clicking on the target objects in the photo image, the pervasive service's client application is superimposed (see Fig.2). There is no need to know the IP address, the URL, or any information about the network.

To address the issue of managing information efficiently, since u-Photo media include still images, users can find the network information by browsing images even if there are a lot of them. Keeping state information is intuitive since the still image shows information about visual state of the services. In addition, digital still images are suitable for carrying and distributing. Once a user takes a u-Photo, he/she can send it to friends by attaching it to e-mail.

3.2 Pervasive Services and Their Eyemarks

Each service must have a physical entity that appears on a still image. We call the physical entity a *service eyemark*. We define three patterns for configuring service eyemarks.

The first pattern occurs when devices are visible and are the service eyemarks themselves (see Fig.3(a)). For example, display devices can be a service eyemark because they are revealed. When one device provides multiple pervasive services, it can be the service eyemark for all services.

In a case where the target devices are embedded, services working at these devices have external service eyemarks (see Fig.3(b)). In particular, sensor devices in a pervasive computing environment tend to be tiny and embedded. Since the appliances/sensors have an actuation/sensing area, users can guess the area being denoted by a service eyemark. For instance, a user can issue "temperature near the plant pot" if the plant pot is configured as a service eyemark.

The last type of service eyemarks is a combination of these two cases. A revealed device doubles with the service eyemark of an other device (see Fig.3(c)). A user would issue "temperature near the TV display" if the TV display is configured as a service eyemark of a sensor that stands near the TV display.

Fig. 3. Models of service eyemarks: (a) Services are working at object (a case where the object is the appliance/sensor). (b) An object has no services but stands near the appliances/sensors. (c) An object has services, and the object stands near other appliances/sensors

3.3   Scenario

In order to clarify our research goals, we present several scenarios using u-Photo.

- Scenario 1: Controlling Devices
  Bob takes pictures of his room, which are stored as u-Photo in his PDA. He goes out to work, forgetting to turn off the room light. After finishing work, he realizes he might have left the room light on. To check whether the light is on or not, he uses the u-Photo Viewer in his PDA and taps the "light icon" displayed on top of the light image in the u-Photo. His u-Photo responds and shows that the room light's state is on. He then taps the OFF button, which is displayed in the u-Photo, to turn off the room light.
- Scenario 2: Discovering Services in an Unknown Environment
  Bob is in a project meeting in a different department and wants to print a document - an easy job as he can just take a u-Photo of the printers he sees there to select one suitable, and to start the print job. The u-Photo automatically configures the printer's entry on his laptop PC.
- Scenario 3: Recording States Information of Services
  One day, Bob and Ann were watching a video at Bob's home, but Bob needed to go out to answer a phone call. Bob stored the state of the video service, such as the content information and the time code, in a u-Photo. He paused and turns off the TV from the control information of the devices. After returning to her home, Ann received an e-mail from Bob with the u-Photo attached. She opens the u-Photo and watches the rest of the video at her desktop computer using u-Photo.

4   System Design for u-Photo

We will describe the system design for our concept. We design u-Photo Tools as systems to create and view u-Photos. U-Photo Tools consist of the *Eyemark Lookup Server, u-Photo Creator*, and *u-Photo Viewer* as shown in Fig.4. Eyemark Lookup Server and u-Photo Creator are systems for generating u-Photo. When a new pervasive service is installed in the environment, the environment developer such as an administrator of a building registers the information about the service to the Eyemark Lookup Server. After the information is registered, users can take a u-Photo of the service. When a user takes a photo using a device with u-Photo

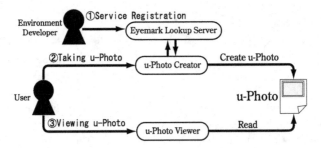

Fig. 4. Overview of u-Photo and u-Photo Tools

Creator installed, the u-Photo Creator looks up the network information in the Eyemark Lookup Server and generates a u-Photo. u-Photo Viewer is u-Photo's viewing application.

4.1   u-Photo Media Design

This subsection describes the visualization model of u-Photo and format of u-Photo Media.

In the u-Photo visualization model, there are three layers in visualizing services (see Fig.5). The *Photo Layer* shows the image of an ordinary photo. The u-Photo overlays two visual layers called the *Tag Layer* and the *Application Panel Layer* on the traditional Photo Layer. In the Tag Layer, service eyemarks are tagged with clickable icons. The Tag Layer will appear on the Photo Layer when a user first opens a u-Photo. Clicking an icon triggers the display of the Application Panel Layer. A GUI of the target service's client application, such as a TV control panel or the GUI for acquiring sensor data, is visualized in the Application Panel Layer. A user decides on a target service by searching the Photo Layer, then invokes application by clicking icons in the Tag Layer, and then uses the service from the client application GUI of the Application Panel Layer.

We will now introduce the u-Photo media format. This format is based on a JPEG, with an XML description of pervasive services in the comment area. Fig.6 shows a DTD of the XML format. `<u_photo>` has three attributes:

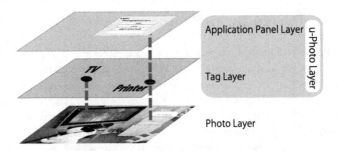

Fig. 5. Visualized layers in u-Photo

```
<?xml version="1.0"?>

<!ELEMENT u_photo (location_info, timestamp, focusing_area)>
<!ATTLIST u_photo xsize CDATA #REQUIRED>
<!ATTLIST u_photo ysize CDATA #REQUIRED>
<!ELEMENT location_info (#PCDATA)>
<!ELEMENT timestamp (#PCDATA)>
<!ELEMENT focusing_area (service_eyemark)?>

<!ELEMENT service_eyemark (coordinate)>
<!ELEMENT service_eyemark (appliance)+>
<!ELEMENT service_eyemark (sensor)+>
<!ATTLIST service_eyemark id CDATA #REQUIRED>
<!ATTLIST service_eyemark name CDATA #REQUIRED>
<!ELEMENT coordinate (x, y)>
<!ELEMENT x (#PCDATA)>
<!ELEMENT y (#PCDATA)>

<!ELEMENT appliance (application_info*)>
<!ATTLIST appliance id CDATA #REQUIRED>
<!ATTLIST appliance name CDATA #REQUIRED>
<!ATTLIST appliance eyemark_type CDATA #REQUIRED>

<!ELEMENT sensor (application_info*)>
<!ATTLIST sensor id CDATA #REQUIRED>
<!ATTLIST sensor name CDATA #REQUIRED>
<!ATTLIST sensor eyemark_type CDATA #REQUIRED>
```

Fig. 6. DTD of u-Photo XML

`<location_info>`, `<timestamp>` and `<focusing_area>`. `<location_info>` shows
the location name, global positioning system (GPS) information, or other location information. The `<service_eyemark>`, which shows the description of
pervasive services, is found in the `<focusing_area>`. The Tag Layer represents the `<service_eyemark>`. For the icons put on the still image, the
`<service_eyemark>` has a service eyemark ID , service eyemark name, a coordinate for the service eyemark on the still image (`<coordinate>`), and one or more
appliances/sensors related to the service eyemark (`<appliance>` and `<sensor>`).
`<appliance>` or `<sensor>` is used to construct the Application Panel Layer. Both
the `<appliance>` and `<sensor>` have a device ID, device name, binding to service eyemark that shows whether the device is at the service eyemark or the
device is near service eyemark, and application information.

    <application_info> is used for describing the network and state information
of pervasive services. Each pervasive service's client application defines the XML
format for *<application_info>*. An XML tag example of the application information is shown in Fig.7. This is a simple application to control the light. In
the XML tag, there is the IP address of the light server, its port number, a
command for controlling the light, and the state of the light at the time the
u-Photo was created. From this description, a simple ON/OFF button GUI of
the light (Fig.8) is created without requiring the users to know the IP address
or any other information.

4.2   Eyemark Lookup Server

To detect service eyemark coordinate in a still image, we adopted image processing because other methods, such as attaching an RF-tag or IR-transmitter,

```
<UI name="Light">
 <state>OFF</state>
 <button name="ON">
  <ip>192.168.10.6</ip>
  <port>12345</port>
  <command>LIGHT_ON</command>
 </button>
 <button name="OFF">
  <ip>192.168.10.6</ip>
  <port>12345</port>
  <command>LIGHT_OFF</command>
 </button>
 <button name="Get Status">
  <ip>192.168.10.6</ip>
  <port>12345</port>
  <get_command>GET_STATUS</get_command>
 </button>
</UI>
```

Fig. 7. XML description of simple light ON/OFF application

Fig. 8. GUI of simple light ON/OFF application

are difficult to use for detecting coordinates in a still image. Processing photo images has two approaches. One approach attaches visual tags and detects the ID from the tag's color, marks, or figures. Another approach picks up the shapes of the target objects without attaching any visual tags. In the latter approach, it is difficult to distinguish objects with the same shape. Thus, we adopted the method that attaches visual tags to each service eyemark.

Next, we discuss how to bind visual tags to the service eyemarks. We assume that there is an Eyemark Lookup Server in each space. The Eyemark Lookup Server has a database of bindings between IDs of visual tags, and service eyemarks in addition to pervasive service's network information assigned to service eyemarks. If a user takes a u-Photo and visual tags are detected in u-Photo image, the tag IDs that are the results of image processing are sent to the Eyemark Lookup Server, and the network information of pervasive services with the information of the service eyemarks is returned. In additional, the Eyemark Lookup Server can issue new visual tags if a new service eyemark is installed in the target space. These mechanisms enable users to update service information from the visual tags.

4.3   u-Photo Creator

The u-Photo Creator runs on the u-Photo Camera, a digital camera with network connectivity. The modules of the u-Photo Creator are shown in Fig.9. There are six steps, as follows, in creating a u-Photo:

1. *Visual Tag Installer* periodically downloads visual tag information for image processing from the Eyemark Lookup Server.
2. *Camera Controller* provides the interface for controlling the camera. When a user presses the shutter button, the captured image will be delivered to the Image Processor.

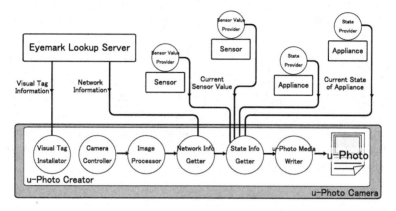

Fig. 9. u-Photo Creator

3. *Image Processor* detects a service eyemark on the photo images. Visual tag IDs and the coordinates in the still image are acquired. This information is delivered to the Network Information Getter.
4. *Network Information Getter* sends visual tag IDs to the Eyemark Lookup Server and obtains pervasive services' network information.
5. *State Information Getter* obtains state information such as the state of an appliance and its current sensor value.
6. *u-Photo Media Writer* transforms the collected information to the u-Photo's XML format and combines the XML data and the captured still image into JPEG format data.

4.4   u-Photo Viewer

The u-Photo Viewer displays both the Photo Layer and the u-Photo Layer. The client application runs on users' computers to perform services. The u-Photo Viewer has three modules as shown in Fig.10:

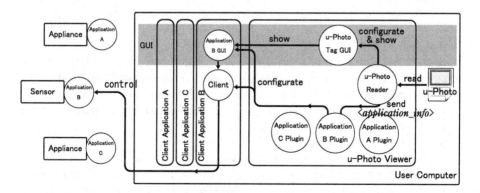

Fig. 10. u-Photo Viewer

1. The *u-Photo Reader* reads the XML data of the u-Photo file when a user opens a u-Photo file.
2. The *u-Photo Tag GUI* displays the Tag Layer using the service eyemark information from the u-Photo Reader module.
3. The u-Photo Reader also passes the XML tag to the *Application Plug-In module*. The Application Plug-In module configures the client application's network information. This module enables users to use client applications without doing any manual configuration. Each Application Plug-In module is downloaded from the Internet on demand according to the *<application_info>*'s XML tag.

5   Prototype Implementation

We used the Sony Vaio typeU with an attached USB web camera (see Fig.11(a)) for the u-Photo Camera. Table 1 and Table 2 present the devices' specification. We used visual markers from the AR Toolkit [10] as tags (see Fig.11(b)). The Image Processor was written with the AR Toolkit Version 2.65 for Windows. The AR Toolkit typically processes real-time streaming video, but we configured it to process images when a user presses a shutter button, as in Fig.11(c). Fig.12 shows the GUI sequence from taking a u-Photo to controlling the devices

Table 1. Specification of VAIO typeU

Model	Vaio type U (VGN-U70P)
Dimensions (WxDxH)	167mm x 26.4mm x 108mm
Weight	550g
CPU	Intel Pentium M 1GHz
Memory	512MB
OS	Windows XP Professional
JAVA	J2SE 1.4.2
Display	800x600(5.0inch)

Table 2. Specification of USB Camera

Model	PCGA-UVC11
Dimensions(WxDxH)	60mm x 33mm x 34mm
Weight	42g
Optical Sensor Type	CMOS - 370,000 pixels
Video Capture Speed	30 frames per second
Resolution	640 x 480

We implemented the following four services and applications: appliance control, sensor information viewer, printing service, and suspendable video service.

- Appliance Control
  A TCP/IP-based power-control box is attached to control a light and an electric fan. Their control application is a simple network application in which the client application sends a control command in text format to IP address and port of the control server. Service eyemarks are configured by the light and the fan themselves.
- Sensor Information Viewer
  For networked sensor units, U.C. Berkeley Mica2s are used. There is a sensor server at a PC that connects to the gateway node of the Mica2. The sensor services' service eyemarks are a light, an electric fan, a printer, and a display near the sensors.

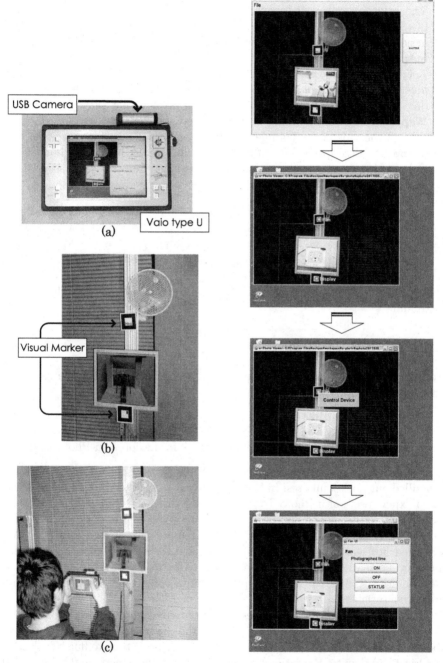

Fig. 11. Prototype implementation: (a) u-Photo Camera. (b) Visual markers of AR Toolkit. (c) Taking a u-Photo

Fig. 12. GUI sequence from taking u-Photo (shown in Top figure) to controlling device using u-Photo Viewer

– Printing Service
The printer application supports not only printing from the printer GUI invoked by clicking the printer image on u-Photo but also a drag-and-drop action, meaning dragging a document and dropping it on the printer image.
– Suspendable Video Service
A QuickTime streaming server provides video services. To realize suspendable video service, we adopt Wapplet framework [9] that deals with media data. When we take a u-Photo of a PC's display that plays a video, the Wapplet framework running on the PC records the the URL and the time code of the video as a Wapplet profile. The Wapplet profile is written as a <wapplet> description (one of the <application_info>) of the u-Photo XML. Other video devices easily resume the same video from the same scene using the u-Photo.

The execution time from pushing the shutter button to displaying a u-Photo is 1.9 seconds. The time for creating a u-Photo is 0.9 seconds. The rest of the time is used to draw a GUI of the u-Photo Viewer.

The difference between the data format of u-Photo and that of normal JPEG file is text data of u-Photo XML. In our experimental applications, data of u-Photo XML description changes JPEG file size from 43 KB to 45 KB at the maximum.

6   Usability Analysis

We performed two tests to measure the following three usability metrics of u-Photo and u-Photo Tools.

– Learnability of u-Photo Tools
– Subjective satisfaction of u-Photo Tools
– Efficiency of managing pervasive services' information as u-Photo media.

In the first test, subjects completed multiple tasks using u-Photo Tools and then filled out questionnaires. In the test, the subjects, including 12 novice users and 5 expert users of u-Photo Tools, had eight tasks to complete. In each task, the subjects either controlled appliances or received sensor data: e.g., turning on a light using u-Photo Tools and getting temperature near a plant pot. We measured how easy u-Photo Tools was to learn to use by comparing the time spent by novice users of u-Photo to finish tasks to the time spent by expert u-Photo users to finish a task. The questionnaire's answers show us the system's subjective satisfaction.

The result of comparing the time presents that using u-Photo Tools is easy to learn. The graphs shown in Fig.13 denote the expert and novices' learnability about the controlling devices. Fig.13(a) shows the time it took to finish each task, and Fig.13(b) denotes the ratio of the time taken by the experts and novices that is shown in Fig.13(a). There is a difference of over ten seconds between the novice users' time and expert users' time for Task1, which is the first task. But there almost be no difference between the expert and novices users after the first task.

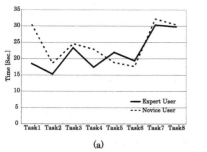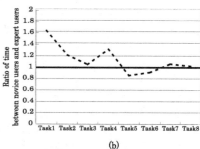

(a)   (b)

Fig. 13. The time spent for controlling devices. (a) Average time that novice users and expert users took for controlling devices in each task. The solid line shows the average time of expert users and the dotted line represents average users' time. (b) Learning curves of novice users

To measure subjective satisfaction, we asked the novice users to fill out our questionnaire after completing the test. The questionnaire uses the Likert scale [12]. The statements and results are shown in Table 3. Users indicated their degree of agreement with each statement on a 1-5 scale for each statement (1 = strongly disagree, 2 = partly disagree, 3 = neither agree nor disagree, 4 = partly agree, and 5 = strongly agree). From the table, we can see that users are highly satisfied about Q1, Q3, and Q6 in both cases of acquiring information and controlling devices. In contrast, users disagree on Q2. The average ratings of the questionnaire are 3.89 for capturing and 3.94 for controlling. To calculate the average rating, the rating of the negative questions (Q2 and Q4) is reversed. The value 3.6 is known as a better estimate of "neutral" or "average" subjective satisfaction [13]. Therefore, the subjective satisfaction with our system is better than average. However, the subjects who agreed with Q2 said that there are two factors that frustrated them: GUI responses occasionally became slow and recognition of visual markers sometimes failed. These are performance issues. Thus, improvement of the prototype's usage could make subjective satisfaction better.

The objective of the second test was to evaluate the efficiency of managing pervasive services information with u-Photo media. We compared the time that

Table 3. Questionairre's results

Question	*1	*2
Q1: It was very easy to learn how to use this system.	4.83	4.83
Q2: Using this system was a frustrating experience.	2.58	2.5
Q3: I feel that this system allows me to achieve very high productivity.	3.92	3.83
Q4: I worry that many of the things I did with this system may have been wrong.	2.17	2.17
Q5: This system can do all the things I think I would need.	3.08	3.17
Q6: This system is very pleasant to work with.	4.25	4.5

*1 Average ratings for capturing information using u-Photo Tools
*2 Average ratings for controlling devices using u-Photo Tools

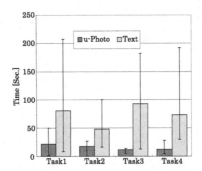

Fig. 14. The time for finding a file

expert users took to find the object in piles of u-Photos with the time it took to find the object in a pile of Wapplet profiles. Wapplet profiles are text format files and include information for personalization. In the test, we had five expert u-Photo users as trial subjects. Each subject downloaded 21 u-Photos and 21 Wapplet profiles to his/her PC and searched for four objects from the files, an air conditioner, a microwave oven, a printer, and a video display. We recorded the time it took to find the correct file by using u-Photo and Wapplet profiles.

The time spent in finding a file is shown in Fig.14. This graph shows the maximum, average, and minimum time spent. In each task, the time spent using u-Photo is shorter than the time spent using Wapplet profile in text format. In Task3 and Task4, in which other files also included printers and video displays information, there was quite a difference of time spent between u-Photo and text information. From these results, we conclude that the efficiency of managing information in u-Photo format is better than the conventional text format.

7   Discussion

Demonstrations at UbiComp2004 [19], and UCS2004 [18] also showed us users' impressions of u-Photo Tools. Over 200 participants used or viewed the system in close up. We found that our approach seemed to attract the participants, but the difference between the shape of u-Photo Camera (shown in Fig.11(a)) and a traditional camera would cause misunderstanding about u-Photo's the use. Therefore, next prototype of u-Photo Camera should be camera-shaped with a traditional shutter button.

Because the visual tags can treat the same devices as different service eyemarks, using visual tags seems to scalable against the number of services. In addition, while there is no global need for unique visual tags, the Eyemark Lookup Server supports unique visual tags. We actually used LED transmitters, which are identified by their color and blinking pattern, in our first prototypes but found them too hard to configure. In contrast, it is easy to generate visual markers in the current prototype. The environment developer simply decides on a unique black-and-white marker pattern, prints it, and attaches it to a service eyemark.

A scalability issue of users arises in the environment that has a lot of users per service. A user authentication module for u-Photo Creator and u-Photo Viewer will be necessary. In addition, u-Photo Viewer also needs exclusive access control for the controlling devices. If two users control the same light at the same time, the light should operate based on only one of the two commands determined by user's authority, location, and so on.

8   Related Work

There have been similar researches that share a part of our motivation. Passage [16] and mediaBlocks [1] use physical objects to transfer information between devices. In Passage, physical objects such as a watch and a key chain are called the "Passenger." When users want to transport digital objects, they only move the Passenger from the source device to the destination device. The media-Blocks, which are electronically tagged wooden blocks, serve as physical icons that transport online media. Using physical objects is useful for the immediate use of personalization service but unsuitable for long-term use of multiple objects. Suppose a user has a great deal of Passengers/mediaBlocks. How can the user know which one has which information? On the other hand, since u-Photo includes the still image, it would be easier to grasp the binding between files and information.

There is a wide variety of systems that visualize environment information. NaviCam [15] displays situation-sensitive information by superimposing messages on its video see-through displays using PDAs, head mounted displays, CCD cameras, and color-coded IDs. InfoScope [5] is an information augmentation system that uses a camera and a PDA's display without any tags on objects. When a user points him of her PDA to buildings or places, the system displays the name of the place or the stores in the building on the PDA. DigiScope [2] annotates an image-using, visual, see-through tablet. In this system, a user can interact with embedded information related to a target object by pointing to the object. Although these researches are similar to u-Photo in terms of annotating an image, the researchers focused on real-time use where a user can interact with a target object in front of the user now. On the other hand, we concentrated on recording pervasive services information and reusing it.

Truong, Abowd, and Brotherton [20] have developed applications in which tasks are recorded as streams of information that flow through time. Classroom 2000, one of their applications, captures a fixed view of the classroom, what the instructor says, and other web-accessible media the instructor may want to present. In this approach, which stream to record or when to record the stream depends on each application. In addition, since the tasks they target on are never executed again, every state of the task needs to be recorded as a stream. On the other hand, the tasks we focused on are reproducible, and we note the states of tasks that are captured only when the user releases the shutter to produce digital photos.

Several products have already been provided that focus on recording contextual information to digital photos. Digital cameras provide states (e.g., focal length, zoom, and flash) and cellular phones provide GPS information. However, the present products and the photo format do not provide methods for noting the pervasive services information and using photos as user interfaces of a target object in the photo.

9   Conclusion

To address the difficulty in discovering and using pervasive services, this paper presented u-Photo, an interactive, digital still image. Taking a photograph also captures information for service discovery. U-Photo, which is generated by taking a photo, becomes a GUI for specifying the target services. We have developed u-Photo Tools for generating and viewing u-Photo. Experiments with the prototypes gave us the following three usability results: (1) After novice users of u-Photo Tools use u-Photo Tools only a few times, they can complete tasks in the same amount of time as expert users. (2) The subjective satisfaction with u-Photo Tools is better than average. (3) Users can find information in u-Photo a file easily more than text-based files. However, we learned that improving the u-Photo Camera hardware will make our system more useful. We also think that a user authentication and device access control will make u-Photo Tools a more scalable and robust system.

Acknowledgements. This work has been conducted partly as part of the YAOYOROZU Project by the Japanese Ministry of Education, Culture, Sports, Science and Technology, and the Ubila Project by the Japanese Ministry of Internal Affairs and Communications.

References

1. H. Ishii B. Ullmer and D. Glas: mediaBlocks: Physical Containers, Transports, and Controls for Online Media. In *Computer Graphics Proceedings (SIGGRAPH'98)*, 1998.
2. A. Ferscha and M. Keller: Digiscope: An Invisible Worlds Window. In *Adjunct Proceedings of the 5th International Conference on Ubiquitous Computing (UbiComp 2003)*, 2003.
3. H.W. Gellersen, A. Schmidt, and M. Beigl: Multi-Sensor Context-Awareness in Mobile Devices and Smart Artefacts. In *Mobile Networks and Applications*, 2002.
4. E. Guttman, C. Perkins, J. Veizades, and M. Day: Service Location Protocol, version 2. In *Internet Request For Comments RFC 2608*, 1999.
5. I. Haritaoglu: Infoscope: Link from Real World to Digital Information Space. In *Proceedings of the 3rd International Conference on Ubiquitous Computing*. Springer-Verlag, 2001.
6. W. Heinzelman, J. Kulik, and H. Balakrishnan: Adaptive Protocols for Information Dissemination in Wireless Sensor Networks. In *Proceedings of the International Conference on Mobile Computing and Networking*, 1999.

7. J. Hill and D. Culler: A Wireless Embedded Sensor Architecture for System-Level Optimization. Technical report, U.C. Berkeley, 2001.
8. Sun Microsystems Inc. Jini technology overview. *Sun White papers*, 1999.
9. T. Iwamoto, N. Nishio, and H. Tokuda: Wapplet: A Media Access Framework for Wearable Applications. In *Proceedings of the International Conference on Information Networking*, 2002.
10. H. Kato, M. Billinghurst, I. Poupyrev, K. Imamoto, and K. Tachibana: Virtual Object Manipulation on a Table-top AR Environment. In *Proceedings of the International Symposium on Augmented Reality (ISAR 2000)*, 2000.
11. T. Kawamura, T. Hasegawa, A. Ohsuga, and S. Honiden: Bee-gent: Bonding and Encapsulation Enhancement Agent Framework for Development of Distributed Systems. In *the 6th Asia Pacific Software Engineering Conference*, 1999.
12. M.J. LaLomia and J.B. Sidowski: Measurements of Computer Satisfaction, Literacy, and Aptitudes: A Review.: *International Journal on Human Computer Interaction* volume 2, 1990.
13. J. Nielsen and J. Levy: Measuring Usability-Preference vs. Performance. In *Communications of the ACM* 37, 1994.
14. Universal Plug and Play Forum. http://www.upnp.org.
15. J. Rekimoto and K. Nagao: The World Through the Computer: Computer Augmented Interaction with Real World. In *Proceedings of Symposium on User Interface Software and Technology*. ACM, 1995.
16. N.A. Streitz S. Konomi, C. Muller-Tomfelde: Passage: Physical Transportation of Digital Information in Cooperative Buildings. In *Proceedings of the Second International Workshop on Cooperative Buildings (CoBuild'99)*, 1999.
17. I. Satoh: A Mobile Agent-based Framework for Location-based Services. In *Proceedings of IEEE International Conference on Communications (ICC)*, 2004.
18. G. Suzuki, D. Maruyama, T. Koda, S. Aoki, T. Iwamoto, K. Takashio, and H. Tokuda: Playing with Ubiquitous Embedded Information using u-Photo. *Demo Session of International Symposium on Ubiquitous Computing Systems*, 2004.
19. G. Suzuki, D. Maruyama, T. Koda, T. Iwamoto, S. Aoki, K. Takashio, and H. Tokuda: u-Photo Tools: Photo-based Application Framework for Controlling Networked Appliances and Sensors. In *Electronic Adjunct Proceedings of The 6th International Conference on Ubiquitous Computing (UbiComp2004)*, 2004.
20. K. N. Truong, G. D. Abowd, and J. A. Brotherton: Who, What, When, Where, How: Design Issues of Capture & Access Applications. In *Proceedings of the 3rd International Conference on Ubiquitous Computing*. Springer-Verlag, 2001.
21. W. Yeong, T. Howes, and S. Kill: Lightweight Directory Access Protocol. In *Internet Request For Comments RFC 1777*, 1995.

Towards Massively Multi-user Augmented Reality on Handheld Devices

Daniel Wagner[1], Thomas Pintaric[1],
Florian Ledermann[2] and Dieter Schmalstieg[1]

[1] Graz University of Technology,
{wagner, pintaric, schmalstieg}@icg.tu-graz.ac.at
[2] Vienna University of Technology,
ledermann@ims.tuwien.ac.at

Abstract. Augmented Reality (AR) can naturally complement mobile computing on wearable devices by providing an intuitive interface to a three-dimensional information space embedded within physical reality. Unfortunately, current wearable AR systems are relatively complex, expensive, fragile and heavy, rendering them unfit for large-scale deployment involving untrained users outside constrained laboratory environments. Consequently, the scale of collaborative multi-user experiments have not yet exceeded a handful of participants. In this paper, we present a system architecture for interactive, infrastructure-independent multi-user AR applications running on off-the-shelf handheld devices. We implemented a four-user interactive game installation as an evaluation setup to encourage playful engagement of participants in a cooperative task. Over the course of five weeks, more than five thousand visitors from a wide range of professional and socio-demographic backgrounds interacted with our system at four different locations.

1 Introduction and Related Work

Augmented Reality (AR) can naturally complement mobile computing on wearable devices by providing an intuitive interface to a three-dimensional information space embedded within physical reality [1]. Correspondingly, the human-computer interfaces and interaction metaphors originating from AR research have proven advantageous in a variety of real-world mobile application scenarios, such as industrial assembly and maintenance, location-based information systems, navigation aides, computer-supported cooperative work, and entertainment.

However, existing AR systems aiming at unconstrained mobility, like the Touring Machine [2], MARS [3], or Tinmith [4] have typically emerged as wearable variants of existing desktop setups. Their creators would commonly package a single (notebook) computer with a variety of sensors and peripheral devices in such a way that users can wear it on their backs, with both arms through shoulder straps. Graphical augmentations were usually shown through

H.W. Gellersen et al. (Eds.): PERVASIVE 2005, LNCS 3468, pp. 208–219, 2005.

Fig. 1. A typical "backpack" setup (left) for Mobile AR versus a lightweight handheld device (right)

an optical see-through head-mounted display (HMD). A typical example of this type of setup is depicted in figure 1.

Although these "backpack" systems have been successful proof-of-concept prototypes within their respective range of applications, they are maintenance-intensive and lack the robustness demanded by permanent deployment outside a constrained laboratory environment. Their prohibitive cost not only prevents the development of a commercial market (and with it widespread availability) for the foreseeable future, but also thwarts researchers in their plans to conduct multi-user experiments exceeding a handful of participants. Finally, there are situations and social contexts in which the unwieldy and rather conspicuous AR "backpacks" seem impractical, or even inadequate.

Part of the usability and scalability issues of these mobile yet monolithic wearable AR systems have been addressed by other lines of research investigating the use of lightweight wearable devices as thin clients supported by a ubiquitous computing infrastructure. Instead of delivering graphical overlays by means of a head-mounted display, those systems convey information using the magic-lens [5,6] property of camera-equipped portable displays, such as keyboard-less personal digital assistants (PDAs) built for pen-computing. Rekimoto used a tethered analog display and a CCD camera in the NaviCam [7] project to track color-coded fiducial markers on a connected workstation. The Batportal [8] by Newman et al. was driven by a remote VNC display server using ultrasonic outside-in tracking, while the AR-PDA project [9] relied on a digital image streaming mechanism in order to outsource machine vision and graphics rendering tasks to an application server. In summary, the inherent infrastructure-dependence of thin-client approaches has confined these projects to restricted working volumes, thereby preventing them from evolving into self-sufficient mobile AR systems.

We believe there is a need for an unconstrained, infrastructure-independent AR system running on lightweight wearable devices to "bridge the gap" in situations where traditional "backpack" systems are too costly and unnecessarily cumbersome, but thin-client implementations exhibit inadequate deployability, scalability or interactive behavior. Particular examples include sporadic use over lengthy time spans, in between which devices must be stowed away, mixed indoor/outdoor use in wide-area environments, and massively multi-user application scenarios. This has motivated us to develop our own software framework targeting lightweight handheld devices.

2   System Architecture

We have identified three distinct classes of commercially available wearable computers as potential candidates for a stand-alone handheld AR platform: cellular phones, PDAs and Tablet PCs. All of these device designs make specific trade-offs between size, weight, computing power and cost. While cellular phones are extremely portable and widespread, their current lack of adequate processing power and local network connectivity renders them a suboptimal platform for rich and meaningful AR applications. Furthermore, their small display size and limited data input capabilities are less than ideal for three-dimensional user interfaces. Tablet PCs do not share the aforementioned drawbacks but are considerably more expensive and too heavyweight for single-handed, or even prolonged two-handed use. Taking into account all of these constraints, we chose the PDA as target platform for our Handheld AR framework. PDAs are a good compromise between processing power, size and weight; they are socially acceptable and their touch screen input mechanism is familiar, which we considered crucial for our planned deployment of AR applications to untrained users.

We have devised a component-based software architecture to accelerate the task of developing and deploying collaborative applications on handheld devices. At its center lies a lightweight variant of the *Studierstube* [10] framework that has been stripped of all the functionality deemed unnecessary for running applications on mobile devices, where computing resources are scarce. Concurrent multi-application execution and application-migration capabilities were among the features we omitted. The blueprint of our framework's design was published in an earlier paper [11], but has since undergone major revisions.

Studierstube extends OpenInventor[1], a scene-graph rendering library, and uses OpenTracker [12], a modular dataflow middleware for pose tracking. Both, *Studierstube* and OpenTracker make use of ACE (the Adaptive Communication Environment)[2] for network communication abstraction. *Studierstube* allows application development in C++ or, more rapidly, via OpenInventor scripts. Alternatively, application developers can choose to use APRIL [13], a high-level descriptive language for authoring story-driven AR presentations.

There are several software libraries that provide hardware abstraction mechanisms on PDAs, however, we considered them insufficient for our purposes as

---

[1] SGI OpenInventor, http://oss.sgi.com/projects/inventor

[2] The ADAPTIVE Communication Environment, http://www.cs.wustl.edu/ schmidt/ ACE.html

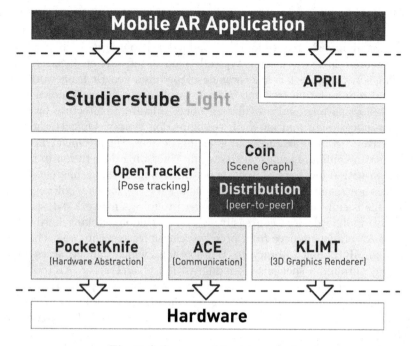

Fig. 2. Software architecture overview

they were primarily intended for 2D game development. Hence, we developed our own tool, called PocketKnife, which resembles a collection of classes designed to facilitate the development of graphical applications on mobile devices.

Since no OpenGL-compatible 3D graphics libraries for mobile devices were available at the time, we developed our own software renderer, called Klimt[3]. Its API is very similar to that of OpenGL and OpenGL|ES. Applications built with Klimt are able to run Coin[4], an OpenInventor-compatible scene-graph rendering library, which we ported to Windows CE. Klimt is able to render up to 70,000 triangles and up to 11 million textured pixels per second on a standard PocketPC PDA with a 400Mhz Intel XScale processor.

Network connectivity is central to any distributed system. Collaborative AR applications share scene- as well as application-specific data. Hence, a reliable, proven communication framework is essential in order that developers can concentrate on higher-level design aspects. ACE includes a wrapper library that provides platform-independent access to system resources, such as network sockets, threads and shared memory. ACE simplifies the development of object-oriented network communication code, shields developers from directly programming the socket API and instead allows concentrating on application-level architecture design.

---

[3] Klimt   an Open Source 3D Graphics Library for Mobile Devices, http:// studierstube.org/klimt

[4] Coin3D scene graph renderer, http://www.coin3d.org

Tracking is an indispensable requirement for every Virtual Reality (VR) and Augmented Reality (AR) system. While the quality of tracking, in particular the need for high performance and fidelity have led to a large body of past and current research, little attention is typically paid to software engineering aspects of tracking software. OpenTracker was developed as a generic framework for accessing and manipulating tracking data. It implements the well-known *pipes & filters* dataflow pattern and provides an open software architecture based on a highly modular design and an XML configuration syntax. OpenTracker incorporates drivers to most commercial tracking devices. Using OpenTracker, AR developers can configure their tracking setup (including data fusion from multiple sources) with a few lines of XML code. Switching between different tracking setups does not require changes to the application code, instead, editing of a single XML file is sufficient. Since OpenTracker provides a network data-transport mechanism, mobile devices can easily access outside-in tracking hardware via Wireless LAN. Independence from pose tracking infrastructure was achieved by porting the ARToolKit[5] library to WindowsCE, which can be accessed in a generic way through a specialized module within OpenTracker. ARToolKit can process up to 150 images per second natively on a PDA equipped with a 624MHz XScale processor (depending on the number and size of the fiducial markers visible in the video image). Alternatively, the processing task can be outsourced to a server.

Programming tools for PDA-development are error-prone, and debugging remains a slow and cumbersome task — even on device emulators. Consequently, developers attempt to write and test most of their code natively on a workstation. All previously described components are available for PDAs running WindowsCE, as well as regular PC-based workstations running Windows 2000/XP, which greatly facilitates the software development process. The hardware abstraction module allows software engineers to develop applications on the PC, while only the final testing is done on the PDA itself. Finally, all of the software described above is available under an open source license. Readers interested in evaluating our framework are invited to obtain further information and a copy of the software from our website[6].

3   Application Requirements

In order to assess the practical deployability and usability of our framework, we considered it imperative to conduct a field test in which as large a number of users as possible would be asked to try their hand at a PDA-based AR application. Ideally, some participants would not have had prior experience with AR interfaces.

The application that we eventually presented to end users in the evaluation was chosen according to several criteria: first and foremost, the application

---

[5] ARToolKit computer vision library, http://www.hitl.washington.edu/artoolkit

[6] The Handheld Augmented Reality Project, http://studierstube.org/handheld_ar

should expose our framework's major features and key properties to the end user while simultaneously allowing us to draw early conclusions about the practical value of our developments. While the application would have to be designed for a high anticipated volume of use, it should not offer a reduced experience to users who would only try it briefly. Finally, the application task should be kept simple and straight forward in order to avoid discouraging participation from non-technical audiences.

While it would have been possible to draw inspiration from a number of marker-based augmented reality applications published by other researchers, none of those met all of our requirements or made use of the unique possibilities gained by bringing marker-based AR to handheld devices. Naturally, we were looking for an interactive application that would allow its users to participate in a collaborative or concurrent task. The application should be distributed, synchronizing state between multiple clients through wireless networking. Many marker-based AR applications that have so far been presented make heavy use of fiducials as tangible interface components, allowing their users to flip through the pages of marker-enhanced "magic books" [14], to use markers as cards in an augmented memory game [15], or to use markers for positioning various objects such as design elements or video surfaces in the user's workspace [16,17].

In contrast to these applications, which focus on the use of fiducial markers as moveable, dynamic parts of the application, we sought to employ the handheld's tracked display itself as the tangible, dynamic interaction element. Therefore, we decided to focus on pen-based touch-screen input as the main interaction technique. A static arrangement of multiple fiducial markers in the environment would enable the PDAs to perform self-tracking from a variety of different angles and distances. Another important requirement was that the application should be sufficiently spatially distributed to give an impression of the properties of our tracked display surface with respect to panning and zooming interactions — users should be required to move in closely with environment to discover important details, and to move the perspective away from the setting in order to gain an overview of the scene. This differs from other applications such as the magic book, which are designed to be fully visible within the field of view of the user, and therefore require no navigational actions from the user. Usually, marker-based tracking techniques are sufficiently accurate for computing a marker's position and orientation relative to a camera, but not to perform inside-out tracking of the camera in relation to the environment. Making use of the multi-marker tracking capabilities of ARToolKit, we could overcome this limitation, using all visible markers in the camera image to average out tracking errors and provide stable tracking of the device with respect to the environment.

Since our application was intended for use by non-expert audiences, and because we also wanted to allow primary school children to participate, we invented a simple game called "The Invisible Train". We specifically chose the game genre because we expected its playful nature of engaging in cooperative tasks would encourage users to participate in our evaluation. Furthermore, we assumed a game would make the concept of AR interfaces more intuitively accessible to

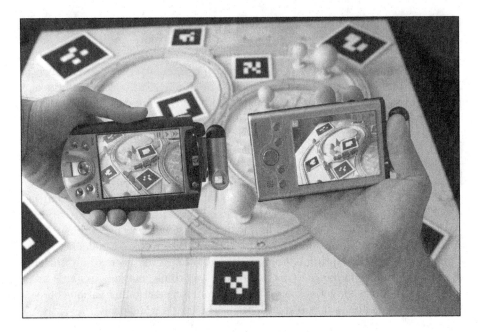

Fig. 3. Two PDAs running the *Invisible Train* game

users without prior exposure to this type of technology. The *Invisible Train* lets players control virtual trains on a real wooden miniature railroad track. We deliberately left the decision whether the game should be collaborative or competitive open. As a result, the game can be played either collaboratively (trying to avoid a collision between trains for as long as possible) or competitively (attempting to crash into the other player's train). Since people were anticipated to use the application for just about a minute each, we omitted a scoring mechanism and left the decision whether to cooperate or compete to the players.

4   The Invisible Train

The *Invisible Train* is a simple multi-player game, in which players steer virtual trains over a real wooden miniature railroad track. These virtual trains are only visible to players through their PDA's video see-through display, since they do not exist in the physical world. Figure 4 shows the game's user interface elements, as seen from a player's perspective.

Users are offered two types of actions: operating track switches and adjusting the speed of their virtual trains, both of which are triggered in response to a tap on the PDA's touch screen. There are two different kinds of track junctions: three-way (Y-shaped) and four-way (X-shaped) interconnections. Both are visualized through semi-transparent graphical icons floating above the physical junction element. These track switch icons serve as clickable buttons and indicate their current state and effect on train routes by their visual appearance (see Figure 5).

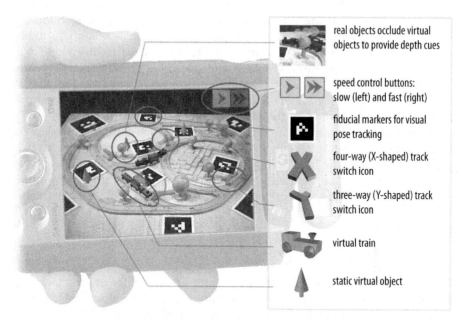

real objects occlude virtual objects to provide depth cues

speed control buttons: slow (left) and fast (right)

fiducial markers for visual pose tracking

four-way (X-shaped) track switch icon

three-way (Y-shaped) track switch icon

virtual train

static virtual object

Fig. 4. User interface elements and graphical features

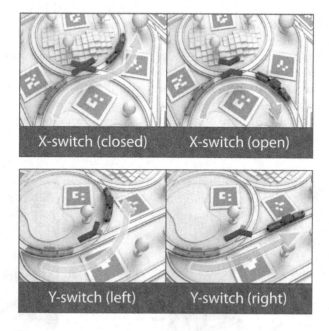

X-switch (closed)   X-switch (open)

Y-switch (left)   Y-switch (right)

Fig. 5. Track switch icons and their effect on train routes

Whenever users activate a track switch, its icon turns fully opaque for one second, during which other track switch buttons become unclickable. This mechanism was primarily intended to provide users with visual feedback, but will also prevent "racing conditions" where multiple users rapidly try to operate the same track switch. Users need not exercise great precision when aiming at their touch-screens: a ray-casting algorithm automatically selects the appropriate track switch depending on the closest virtual track being pointed at.

Virtual trains can ride at two different speeds, which can be controlled via two dedicated buttons in the upper right screen corner. The active button is shown in color while the inactive button is grayed out.

During the game, application state is constantly synchronized between all participants via wireless networking. Whenever a collision occurs, the game ends.

5   Evaluation Scenario

We consecutively deployed the *Invisible Train* at four different locations: the SIGGRAPH 2004 computer graphics convention in Los Angeles (USA), an orientation day for incoming freshmen at Vienna University of Technology, a career information event for secondary school students, and inside the Ars Electronica Center's (AEC) "Museum of the Future" in Linz (Austria).

Over the course of these exhibitions, we gradually moved from expert audiences, who were familiar with AR technology, to a general public (see figure 6) with little or no previous exposure to AR. An estimated five to six thousand visitors have engaged in playing the *Invisible Train* game during the four evaluation cycles, the last of which lasted for over four weeks and was partially unsupervised (with occasional maintenance work done by AEC museum staff). To our knowledge, these quantities lie at least an order of magnitude above comparable informal field tests of mobile AR system, denoting the first time a mobile AR application has successfully withstood a field-test of sizeable proportions.

Fig. 6. Visitors playing the *Invisible Train*

6   Usability Assessment - Lessons Learned

Although we did not perform a formative user study, we solicited user feedback through informal, unstructured (i.e. no specific or predetermined sets of questions were asked) interviews and conducted a summative evaluation of user performance and behavior, which led to small iterative refinements of the game's user interface. More importantly, however, we successfully completed a rigorous stress-test of our system architecture's overall robustness.

Several of our empirical observations, some of which were directly comparable to our past experience involving HMD-equipped "backpack"-style setups, confirmed our generic assumption that handheld devices would generally be more accessible to a general public, and exhibit flatter learning curves, than traditional mobile AR systems: We found that visitors had little to no reservations towards using our system. Several participants figured out how to play the *Invisible Train* on their own by simple trial and error, others would learn the gameplay by looking over another player's shoulder while awaiting their turns — some children would intuitively grasp the concept and outperformed even seasoned computer science professionals. Consequently, our supervision overhead was considerably lower than administrators of traditional mobile AR application would normally experience. On many occasions, we could observe unsupervised user experience in which visitors would pass around the PDAs while explaining the game to each other. Most participants would play at least a single game (averaging roughly 60 seconds) before handing their PDA to the next visitor.

In stark contrast to our past experiences with "backpack" setups, we experienced almost no hardware-related failures, with the exception of a small number of application crashes, whenever users removed the add-on camera from its SDIO slot. These incidents have only further confirmed our observation that wearable devices intended for public deployment must resemble robust monolithic units without any loosely attached parts.

According to user feedback, our application was considered sufficiently responsive for the intended type of spatial interaction: only a negligibly small fraction of players felt their PDA's display update rate and delay would impair their ability to play the game. We measured our system's average performance at 7 frames per second (on devices equipped with Intel's XScale PXA263 processor clocked at 400MHz, and an add-on SDIO camera from Spectec Computer Ltd), while wireless network latency was measured at about 40-50ms. Camera blur caused loss of registration during rapid movements, but was not considered a major problem. Thanks to code optimizations and a new generation of PDAs that feature hardware-accelerated 3d-graphics, we were most recently able to raise our system's overall performance to approximately 12 frames per second.

Another observation we made during the four week evaluation period at the AEC is that some users will eventually try everything to forcibly break the software. Thus, we came to believe it was important for applications to automatically restart in case of a failure, e.g. after a user deliberately presses the hardware reset switch.

The major cause of interruptions arose from our devices' short battery life, which lasted approximately two hours (per 1800 mAh rechargeable Li-ion module), thus requiring regular battery replacements.

7   Conclusion and Future Work

Overall, our large-scale system evaluation yielded very satisfying results. Although we have yet to conduct formal usability testing, empirical evidence suggests that our handheld AR interface was sufficiently intuitive to grasp, enabling untrained users to complete simple collaborative spatial tasks with minimal or no prior instruction. Our system proved exceptionally stable and robust under heavy use conditions. It continued to function without interruption during the final two-week period of unsupervised use by museum visitors.

As a next step, we plan to move from a four-user setup to an application scenario that simultaneously involves dozens of participants in a wide-area setting, which will bring us one step closer to our goal of *"AR anytime, anywhere"*.

Acknowledgements

This research was funded in part by the Austrian Science Fund *FWF* under contract No. Y193.

References

1. Starner, T., Mann, S., Rhodes, B., Levine, J., Healey, J., Kirsch, D., Picard, R.W., Pentland, A.: Augmented reality through wearable computing. Presence: Teleoperators and Virtual Environments **6** (1997) 386 – 398
2. Feiner, S., MacIntyre, B., Höllerer, T., Webster, A.: A touring machine: Prototyping 3d mobile augmented reality systems for exploring the urban environment. In: Proceedings of the First International Symposium on Wearable Computers (ISWC), Cambridge, Massachusetts, USA (1997) 74–81
3. Höllerer, T., Feiner, S., Terauchi, T., Rashid, G., Hallaway, D.: Exploring mars: developing indoor and outdoor user interfaces to a mobile augmented reality system. Computers & Graphics **23** (1999) 779–785
4. Piekarski, W., Thomas, B.H.: Tinmith-evo5 a software architecture for supporting research into outdoor augmented reality environments. Technical report, Wearable Computer Laboratory, University of South Australia (2001)
5. Bier, E.A., Stone, M.C., Pier, K., Buxton, W., DeRose, T.D.: Toolglass and magic lenses: The see-through interface. In: SIGGRAPH '93: Proceedings of the 20st Annual Conference on Computer Graphics and Interactive Techniques, New York, NY, USA (1993) 73–80
6. Viega, J., Conway, M.J., Williams, G.H., Pausch, R.F.: 3d magic lenses. In: UIST '96: Proceedings of the 9th annual ACM symposium on User interface software and technology, Seattle, Washington, USA, ACM Press (1996) 51–58

7. Rekimoto, J., Nagao, K.: The world through the computer: Computer augmented interaction with real world environments. In: UIST '95: Proceedings of the 8th annual ACM symposium on User interface and software technology, Pittsburgh, Pennsylvania, USA (1995) 29–36
8. Newman, J., Ingram, D., Hopper, A.: Augmented reality in a wide area sentient environment. In: Proceedings of the 4th IEEE and ACM International Symposium on Augmented Reality (ISAR'01), New York, NY, USA (2001) 77–86
9. Gausemeier, J., Fründ, J., Matysczok, C., Bruederlin, B., Beier, D.: Development of a real time image based object recognition method for mobile ar-devices. In: AFRIGRAPH '03: Proceedings of the 2nd International Conference on Computer Graphics, Virtual Reality, Visualisation and Interaction in Africa, Cape Town, South Africa (2003) 133–139
10. Schmalstieg, D., Fuhrmann, A., Hesina, G., Szalavári, Z., Encarnação, L.M., Gervautz, M., Purgathofer, W.: The studierstube augmented reality project. Presence: Teleoperators and Virtual Environments 11 (2002) 33–54
11. Wagner, D., Schmalstieg, D.: First steps towards handheld augmented reality. In: Proceedings of the 7th International Symposium on Wearable Computers (ISWC 2003), White Plains, NY, USA, IEEE Computer Society (2003) 127–137
12. Reitmayr, G., Schmalstieg, D.: An open software architecture for virtual reality interaction. In: VRST '01: Proceedings of the ACM symposium on Virtual reality software and technology, Banff, Alberta, Canada, ACM Press (2001) 47–54
13. Ledermann, F., Schmalstieg, D.: APRIL: A high-level framework for creating augmented reality presentations. In: Proceedings of the 2005 IEEE Virtual Reality Conference (to appear), Bonn, Germany, IEEE Computer Society (2005)
14. Billinghurst, M., Kato, H., Poupyrev, I.: The magicbook: a transitional ar interface. Computers & Graphics 25 (2001) 745–753
15. Wagner, D., Barakonyi, I.: Augmented reality kanji learning. In: Proceedings of the 2003 IEEE and ACM International Symposium on Mixed and Augmented Reality (ISMAR 2003), Tokyo, Japan, IEEE Computer Society (2003) 335–336
16. Billinghurst, M., Cheok, A.D., Prince, S., Kato, H.: Real world teleconferencing. IEEE Computer Graphics and Applications 22 (2002) 11–13
17. Barakonyi, I., Fahmy, T., Schmalstieg, D., Kosina, K.: Collaborative work with volumetric data using augmented reality videoconferencing. In: Proceedings of the 2003 IEEE and ACM International Symposium on Mixed and Augmented Reality (ISMAR 2003), Tokyo, Japan, IEEE Computer Society (2003) 333–334

Design Methodology for Context-Aware Wearable Sensor Systems

Urs Anliker, Holger Junker, Paul Lukowicz, and Gerhard Tröster

Institut für Elektronik, ETH Zürich,
Gloriastrasse 35, 8092 Zürich, Schweiz
{uanliker, junker, lukowicz, troester}@ife.ee.ethz.ch

Abstract. Many research projects dealing with context-aware wearable systems encounter similar issues: where to put the sensors, which features to use and how to organize the system. These issues constitute a multi-objective optimization problem largely determined by recognition accuracy, user comfort and power consumption. To date, this optimization problem is mostly addressed in an ad hoc manner based on experience as well as trial and error approaches. In this paper, we seek to formalize this optimization problem and pave the way towards an automated system design process. We first present a formal description of the optimization criteria and system requirements. We then outline a methodology for the automatic derivation of Pareto optimal systems from such a description. As initial verification, we apply our methodology to a simple standard recognition task using a set of hardware components, body locations and features typically used in wearable systems. We show that our methodology produces good results and that a simple example can provide information that an experienced system designer would have problems extracting by other means.

1 Introduction

Wearable computing systems are characterized by their ability to adapt to the user's context. It has been demonstrated that body-worn sensors which are integrated into the user's outfit can be used to facilitate this functionality to a certain extent [1].

From a system point of view the design of on body - distributed context recognition systems is a complex multi-objective optimization problem. It involves a trade-off between user comfort, communication costs, power consumption and recognition performance. The design alternatives include the choice and placement of sensors, the choice of communication and processing devices, the choice of features and classifiers and the communication/computation trade-offs involved in mapping the computation to different nodes. The design space grows exponentially with the number of alternatives, which means that an exact solution is intractable for all but the most trivial problems.

Todays system designers rely on their experience and a trial and error process to solve the optimization problem above. Clearly, as the involved systems

H.W. Gellersen et al. (Eds.): PERVASIVE 2005, LNCS 3468, pp. 220–236, 2005.
© Springer-Verlag Berlin Heidelberg 2005

become more complex and context aware computing moves towards commercial applications, a formal, more automated design framework would be desirable. Building on previous modelling [2] and system optimization work [3] done by our group, this paper constitutes a major step in the direction of such an automated framework. Currently, our design methodology address four points: a formalism to specify the constraints, a formalism to specify the optimization goals adapted from a specific application, a feature selection process based on mutual information, and a genetic algorithm based on multi-objective optimization.

Like most automated system design approaches our framework aims to support rather than replace the human designer. It is a fact that even for very complex problems an experienced human designer can often quickly find reasonable approaches. Thus, the outline of the solutions suggested by our framework is often similar to what such an experienced designer might come up with. However, when it comes to a detailed analysis of specific trade-offs some sort of automated analysis is indispensable. In addition, even for an experienced designer, it is important to have a method for checking his ideas and finding possible improvements. Finally, when body-worn sensors move towards mainstream applications, it is important to have a tool allowing engineers with little experience in this domain to easily integrate such systems into their overall designs.

1.1   Related Work

There are various methods available to explore the computer architecture design space. Only a few references will be given here as it is not the purpose of the paper to advance the state of the art in this area in general. Many known approaches for the design of architectures deal with heterogeneous systems consisting of different sorts of hardware components, e.g. [4, 5, 6, 7, 8]. Some of them particularly deal with conflicting criteria in the optimization process [9, 10]. However, such methods have not been applied to design and evaluation of context-aware wearable sensor systems so far. What we believe needs to be investigated is how existing methods can be extended and applied in order to deal with hardware and context recognition trade-offs. The pervasive computing systems presented have typically been optimized by experience and a trial and error process.

Some aspects of pervasive computing system design have been addressed before. Here, we will state the previous work, which has influenced our framework. Koshizen [11], Junker [12] and Denzler [13] addressed the problem of sensor selection by an information-theoretic based measure. The information-theoretic selection approach allows a sensor selection without implementing a classifier.

Feature combination can be optimized by a genetic algorithm which has been shown e.g. by Yang [14] for feature selection in medical applications, and by Sun [15] for gender classification.

On the system optimization itself Blickle [16] introduced a framework to map an algorithm-level specification onto a heterogeneous hardware/software architecture. An improved version of the framework was later used by Thiele [17] to design network processors. Based on the success of the two applications, we utilize the same genetic optimizer [18] for the work in [2] and the results presented in this paper.

1.2   Paper Contribution

This paper presents a modeling and evaluation methodology to provide design decisions for context-aware wearable computer systems that consist of spatially distributed computing and sensing modules. Our methodology aims at finding optimized architectures for such systems with respect to power consumption and classification performance. To our knowledge this paper provides the following novelties:

- Systematic framework for sensor selection based on power consumption and classification performance for wearable computing applications
- Derivation of design objectives that cope with a heterogeneous, distributed sensor network taking classification performance via mutual information and energy cost for computation and communication into account.

2   Exploration Methodology

In this section, we recapitulate the main properties of the methodology we presented in [2], and describe our extensions to this work.

2.1   Previous Work

The methodology has been designed in a modular way such that different algorithms can be substituted and combined for each design and specification step individually. The exploration methodology consists of three main modules, shown in Fig 1.

- The *problem specification* describes the problem at hand by usage profile, information flow, physical constrains and hardware resources.
- The *architecture model* consists of a generic model which describes the overall types of architectures considered by our methodology and a problem specific model which incorporates the design constrains of the problem at hand. The architecture model can be regarded as the interface between the problem specification and the exploration environment.
- The *exploration environment* generates architectures fulfilling the design constrains implied by the architecture model. Then, the architectures are rated and selected according to the two design objectives. Based on the selection, new architectures are generated. The exploration environment is repeated until a halt criteria is meet.

The next paragraphs recapitulates terms and definitions used later in this paper.

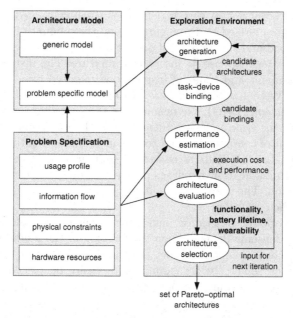

Fig. 1. Modular exploration methodology consisting of three main components: problem specification, architecture model and exploration environment

Architecture Model. The *generic model* consists of a set of computing modules distributed over the user's body. Each module contains devices and communication channel interfaces. The devices can be processors, application-specific integrated circuits (ASICs), sensors or IO interfaces. For *inter-module communication* there exists a set of connections. Each connection consists of one or more physical channels matching the channel interfaces of the corresponding modules.

The *problem specific model* provides a set of constraints on the system topology, the resources available within each computing module, and the assignment of tasks to modules.

- *System Topology:* The system topology determines, which modules the system contains and how they can be interconnected.
- *Module Resource Set:* The module resource set specifies the types of devices and channels that a module can contain.
- *Task Resource Set:* The task resource set describes, on which modules and on which devices a certain task can run.

Problem Specification. The description of a specific design problem involves four steps, which correspond to the four types of design constraints: usage profile specification, information flow specification, physical constraints specification and hardware resource specification.

The *usage profile specification* intends to capture the workload characteristics of the wearable system. The specification is hierarchically structured into tasks, applications and scenarios. A *task* is defined as a self-contained unit of computation that is characterized by three parameters: the amount of input data, the computational load and the amount of output data. To characterize the computational load of a task, we use its instruction mixture. The instruction mixture quantifies the amount and types of instructions required by a task to process the input data. We define an *application* to be a set of tasks in the form of a directed acyclic graph (DAG). We denominate the source nodes of the DAG as input tasks and the sink nodes as output tasks. The task specification determines the amount of computation and communication needed to perform on the wearable system. In a particular *scenario*, these figures are translated into computation and communication requirements by assigning two timing parameters to each application: The repetition frequency R and the maximal latency D_{max} acceptable for the execution.

Batteries and power generation devices or power transmission wires can be more or less burdensome depending on the location of the module. In addition, some body locations provide much better conditions for power generation than others. Large area solar cells for example can easily be placed on the outer, upper back surface of clothing. In contrast, energy generation in glasses is rather difficult. To reflect these considerations, the *power weight vector* $\boldsymbol{w}_P$ as part of the *physical constraints specification* specifies a set of location dependent, problem-specific weights for the power consumption of modules. If a module is placed at a location p, then its power consumption is scaled by multiplying it with the p-th element of the vector $\boldsymbol{w}_P$.

The *hardware resource specification* provides a set of computation and communication channel devices available for the design. Each computing *device* is characterized by execution speed and electrical parameters. For each device, the number of execution cycles for each instruction class is given by the *instruction class execution time vector*. The electrical parameters characterize the power consumption of a device. We consider three operation modes: sleep, idle and execution. The specification consists of the sleep power P_s (sleep mode), the idle power P_i (idle mode), and the energy consumption per cycle E (execution mode). Based on the computation load of a device the power consumption P_d is calculated. A communication channel serves as interface between two modules that consume and generate data. The tasks running on the modules define the communication requirements for these channels. A channel type has a maximum data rate and an end to end delay of data packets. We distinguish between four operation states for each channel type: *transmitting*, where data is transmitted with the maximal data rate B_{max}; *receiving*, where data is received; *idle*, where the modules are still connected to each other but no data is transmitted; and *standby*, where the power consumption is low while the device can still be controlled. We consider two modes: continuous mode, where the channel performs the sequence idle–transmitting/receiving–idle, and burst mode, where we find standby–transmitting/receiving–standby. We suppose that the communication channel chooses the most power efficient mode that still satisfies the delay and bandwidth constraints. Based on the communication load the most power efficient mode is selected and the channel power P_c consumption is calculated.

2.2   Extensions to the Model

Context-aware systems recognize different contexts (such as user activities) by applying a classification engine to preprocessed sensor data.

Comparing the properties of a context with an application introduced in [2], we see similarities. While an application consists of a set of tasks which can be executed on different devices, a context requires preprocessed data from sensors. This preprocessed data is derived from features (see below for feature definition) which can be executed on different devices.

Context. A context is derived using features extracted from sensor data. The context parameters are update rate (f_{rep}) and minimum classification performance $(class\_perf)$. The context specification is added to the *usage profile*, where applications have been specified in [2].

Feature. A feature is a mathematical function, which preprocesses raw sensor data. A feature is defined in a similar way as a task, the characteristic parameters are the amount of input data $(datain)$, the computational load $(instruction\ class\ mix\ vector\ \boldsymbol{I}_F)$ and the amount of output data $(dataout)$. The feature extraction can involve a data reduction, i.e. $dataout \leq datain$.

Sensor. A sensor is an information source with arbitrary complexity. A sensor generates data at a sampling frequency (f_{sample}) with a specific resolution (res). We consider two power states: sampling (P_{sample}) and idle (P_{ilde}). Sensors are specified in the *hardware resource specifications* in an analogous manner as devices.

Mapping and Binding. In our previous work [2] a task resource set was defined as part of the problem specific model. The task resource set describes, on which module and on which device a task can be executed. We introduce a context resource set which describes on which module a classifier can run and which features can be used as input. For each feature, we define a feature resource set which describes on which module and on which device a feature can be executed and which sensor can be used as data source for the feature, shown in Fig. 2.

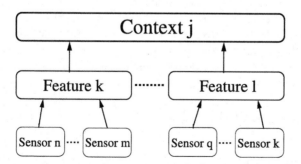

Fig. 2. Data flow: The context resource set defines the input features, the feature resource set defines the raw data sources, i.e. sensors

In the module resource set, we specify types of devices and channels that a module may contain. For the problem at hand, the types of sensors are included in the module resource set.

In the *architecture generation* step, one or more of the specified features are selected for each context. For each feature one or more of the specified sensors are selected. Each context is bound to one of the specified modules. Each selected feature is mapped to one of the specified devices (module). And each selected sensor is placed on one of the specified modules. In the case, where sensors, features and context are not on the same module, communication bandwidth is allocated. The allocated bandwidth between the sensor module and the feature module is

$$BW_{sensor-feature} = datain(feature) \cdot f_{rep}(context) \tag{1}$$

The allocated bandwidth between the context module and the feature module is

$$BW_{feature-context} = dataout(feature) \cdot f_{rep}(context) \tag{2}$$

3 Objectives

3.1 Power Consumption

The first objective we use for our optimization process is the overall power consumption. We first introduce the power consumption of one sensor and then show how the power consumption of one module is calculated. The overall power consumption is then derived by summing up the power consumptions of all individual modules.

The sensor power consumption is calculated in two steps. First, we define the sensor load ($SLoad$) as:

$$SLoad = \frac{max[f_{rep}(context) \cdot datain(feature)]}{f_{sample} \cdot res} \tag{3}$$

The maximum requested data rate of all features assigned to a specific sensor is divided by the data generation rate. The data consumption rate of a feature is determined by the update rate of the contexts to which a feature is bound and the amount of input data of the feature.

In a second step, the sensor power consumption (P_{sen}) is calculated by

$$P_{sen} = \begin{cases} P_{idle} & \text{for } SLoad = 0 \ , \\ (1 - SLoad)P_{idle} + SLoad \cdot P_{sample} & \text{for } 0 < SLoad \leq 1 \ , \\ \text{not valid} & \text{for } SLoad > 1 \ . \end{cases} \tag{4}$$

The module power consumption (P_{mod}) is the sum of the power consumption of all allocated devices, channels and sensors for a specific module (m). This sum is weighed by the module power weight (w_p).

$$P_m = \sum_{devices \in Module} w_P \cdot P_D + \frac{1}{2} \sum_{channels \in Module} w_P \cdot P_C + \sum_{sensors \in Module} w_P \cdot P_{Sen}$$

(5)

The device power consumption P_D, the channel power consumption P_C and module Power weight (w_P) have been affiliated in [2]; the sensor power consumption is given in eq. 4.

3.2   Classification Performance

The second objective that we use for our optimization process is related to the recognition accuracy of the system. In general, this accuracy depends on the feature/sensor combination and on the classification engine used for the recognition task. For our framework, we propose to use the information-theoretic based measure mutual information. This measure allows to evaluate the usefulness of feature/sensor combinations with respect to the recognition accuracy.

In the following, we review the basics of mutual information and explain how the measure is used in our optimization process. A more detailed description on mutual information can be found in a previous work [12], where we used mutual information to derive design considerations of wearable, context-sensing systems.

3.3   Mutual Information - Basics

The mutual information MI between two continuous random variables X and Y is defined as:

$$MI(X;Y) = \int_{x \in X} \int_{y \in Y} p(x,y) log \frac{p(x,y)}{p(x)p(y)} dx dy$$

(6)

The mutual information measures the statistical dependencies between the two variables X and Y and therefore provides a measure of how much information one variable contains about the other. Eq. 6 can be written in terms of the Shannon entropy $H(Y)$ and the conditional entropy $H(Y|X)$ as shown in eq. 7.

$$MI(X;Y) = H(Y) - H(Y|X)$$

(7)

$H(Y)$ measures the uncertainty about Y, and $H(Y|X)$ the uncertainty of Y when X is observed. $MI(X;Y)$ therefore provides a measure for the reduction in uncertainty about Y when X is known.

Assuming Y to be the class variable C and X a feature F, then the mutual information $MI(C;F)$ provides a measure of how much information feature F contains about the class C. Mutual information can also be calculated between multiple variables, allowing the evaluation of the information gained about the class using a set of features rather than a single feature only. The concept of mutual information has already been applied with respect to feature selection problems in classification tasks see [19, 20]. The reason why mutual information directly relates to classification results is expressed in Fano's inequality [21] which is given in eq. 8.

$$Pr(c \neq \hat{c}) \geq \frac{H(C) - MI(C; F) - 1}{log(N_c)} \qquad (8)$$

N_c is the number of classes, and $Pr(c \neq \hat{c})$, the error probability. Thus, eq. 8 provides a lower bound on the error probability, which is decreased if $MI(C; F)$ gets larger.

The calculation of the mutual information between a feature vector and the output class requires the estimation of the joint probability density function (pdf) $p(C; F)$. In this paper, we apply a method proposed by [20] that uses parzen windows to estimate the required joint pdf estimation. The approach allows computation of the mutual information between multiple features and a class vector. Details on the calculation of the mutual information is beyond the scope of this paper, but can be found in [20].

3.4   Mutual Information - Recognition Objective

We define the recognition fitness $R(C_i)$ as

$$R(C_i) = \begin{cases} 0 & \text{for } MI > H(C) \cdot class\_perf \ , \\ \frac{H(C) \cdot class\_perf - MI}{H(C)} & \text{for } MI < H(C) \cdot class\_perf \end{cases} \qquad (9)$$

$H(C)$ represents the entropy of the context set, MI the mutual information of a specific feature/sensor combination, and $class\_perf$ a parameter which defines the percentage of the entropy reduction that has to be reached. Note that $MI \leq H(C)$.

4   Case Study

For initial verification, we have applied our design methodology to derive an optimized system using body-worn sensors to classify three modes of locomotion: level walking, ascending stairs and descending stairs. We start the optimization process with a set of components and sensors, as well as body locations and features typically used for the given classification task.

The choice of a rather simple system design problem is motivated by the necessity to be able to easily judge the quality of the solutions produced by the system. It is a standard, well understood problem for which good solutions are known and which can be compared with the results produced by our approach. While the ultimate objective of the system is to address complex problems which are intractable for experienced designers such a simple example is more desirable for the purpose of initial verification and illustration. At the same time, it can be shown that even in such trivial design task there are parameters and trade offs that are difficult to judge without the help of an automated formal methodology.

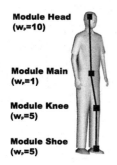

Module Head
(w,=10)

Module Main
(w,=1)

Module Knee
(w,=5)

Module Shoe
(w,=5)

Fig. 3. Location of the four modules and possible communication channels

Table 1. Possible sensor locations (marked with an 'x')

	head module	main module	knee module	shoe module
accelerometer	-	x	x	x
FSRs	-	-	-	x
gyroscope	-	-	x	-
air pressure	x	x	x	x

4.1   System Description

In our experiments, the context update rate (f_{rep}) is set to 10 seconds and the required classification performance $(class\_perf)$ to 90%. The sensor set we used (see Tab. 2) includes accelerometers, a gyroscope, an air pressure sensor and force sensitive resistors (FSRs). For more detailed information on how FSRs can be used to recognize different modes of locomotion the reader is referred to [22]. As features, mean, variance (var), root mean square (rms), interquartile range (IQR), lag (see [22]), cycle-time and slope are defined. The device and channel sets are given in Tab. 3 and Tab. 4.

Figure 3 shows the four different locations allowed for the modules. All four module resource sets include all possible devices according to Tab. 3 and all channels (see Tab. 2). However, depending on the module, only certain sensors are included (see Tab. 1). The main module is directly connected to the knee and head module. The shoe module is connected to the knee module. The module power weights are introduced to represent the difficulty to generate or to carry energy to a specific module location. More information on the power weights can be found in [2]. In our case study, we set the power weight of the main module and the head module to 1 and 10 respectively . The power weights of the knee and the shoe module are set to 5.

In the context resource set, we specify that the classifier will be running on the main module and that all features can be used for all contexts. In the feature resource set, we specify that all features can be calculated on any device on any module. However, only certain features are defined for a specific sensor. Table 2 provides an overview which features are defined for which sensors.

The calculation of the mutual information is based on experimental data. For this purpose we carried out the following experiment [22]. Two 2-dimensional accelerometers (one above the knee of the right leg, one at the back close to the center of body mass), a 2-dimensional gyroscope located above the right knee, an air pressure sensor near the chest, and two force sensitive resistors mounted

Table 2. Sensors devices and defined features for the sensor

Sensor	P_{sample} [mW]	P_{idle} [mW]	f_{sample} [kHz]	res	defined features
accelerometer	1.8	1.8	0.1	8	mean, var, rms, IQR
FSRs	2.0	1.8	0.01	8	lag, cycle-time
gyroscope	75	75	0.1	8	mean, var, rms, IQR
air pressure	1.8	1.8	0.01	8	slope

Table 3. Computing devices, [2]

Device	f_{min} [MHz]	f_{max} [MHz]	E_{max}[a] [nJ]	Type
MSP430F13x	4.15	8	2	low-performance CPU
MSP430C33x[b]	1.65	3.8	4	low-performance CPU
PIC16LF87x-04	4	10	0.7	low-performance CPU
uPD78083, 8bit	–	5	0.55	low-performance CPU
StrongARM SA-1110	59	251	2.8	medium-performance CPU
XScale	150	1000	1.8	medium-performance CPU
SH-4	–	200	7.5	medium-performance CPU
AT91M40807	16	40	3.86	medium-performance CPU
TMS320C55xx (16bit)	–	200	1.7	integer DSP
TMS320VC-150	–	75	2.7	floating-point DSP
ADSP-2116x	–	100	1.9	floating-point DSP

[a] energy consumption per cycle (see [2])
[b] internal multiplier

Table 4. Communication channel types, [2]

Channel Type	P_{tx} [mW]	P_{rx} [mW]	P_i [mW]	P_s [mW]	T_i [ms]	$2T_d$ [ms]	B_{max} [Mbit/s]
RFM TR1000_PIC	39	16	12.8	7.8	100	50	0.115
Bluetooth P2P	151	150	71	17	950	155	0.768
802.11a PC-Card PS[a]	1558	1525	119	93	1000	2	54
802.11b PC-Card PS[a]	390	450	235	225	1000	63	11
100base PC-Card	505	518	389	106	1000	1	100
UART Transceiver (RS232)	125	125	0.99	0.0033	10	1	0.235
USB Bridge	149	149	3.3	3.3	100	1	12
Firewire Bridge	716	716	254	1.5	100	1	400
CAN Bus Controller	33	33	1.2	0.3	100	1	1
I2C Bus Controller	7.5	7.5	7.5	0.012	10	1	0.100

[a] power save mode

under the ball and the heel of the right foot respectively. For collecting the data, a test subject was equipped with the sensors mounted at the described locations on the body and was asked to walk a predefined path in a building that included

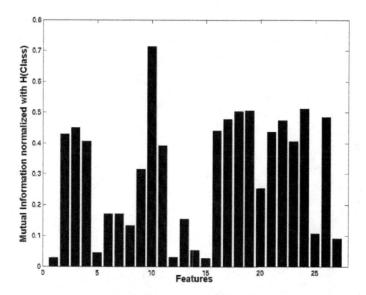

Fig. 4. Normalized MI for the different features. 1 to 8 are features applied to the gyroscope at the knee, 9 is the air pressure slope , 10 is the time lag derived from the FSRs, 11 is the cycle-time derived from FSRs. 12 to 19 arte features applied to the accelerometer at the knee and 20 to 27 are features derived from the accelerometer on the main module

the three described activities. Figure 4 shows the normalized mutual information of the different features based on the recorded data.

4.2   Results

Fig. 5 shows the final population of a design space exploration run together with three selected architectures A, B and C which are summarized in Tab. 5.[1] Although the pareto front is populated by only a few architectures, we see a trade-off between power consumption and classification accuracy.

For architecture A consisting of three modules (main, knee and shoe), the classification objective is lowest (indicating best classification accuracy compared to the other architectures), while its power objective value is highest.

Architecture B with a module located at the knee has medium values for both objectives. Architecture C on the other hand has the lowest power consumption while the value for the classification objective is highest, indicating a poor classification performance.

All three architectures use an accelerometer. Architecture A additionally uses the FSRs. The connections between the modules with allocated bandwidth are

---

[1] The population size and the number of children to be generated in each evolution step were both set to 15.

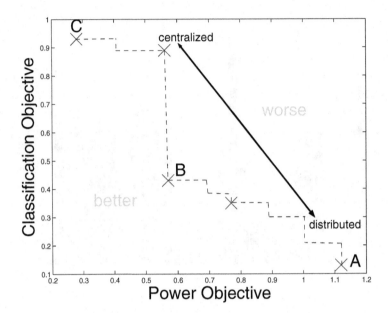

Fig. 5. Final Population of a design space exploration run. The figure also shows three selected architectures (A-C)

Table 5. Example implementations of design points in Fig. 5

Designs:	A	B	C
Devices, Sensors, Features			
main	PIC16LF87x-04	-	uPD78083, Accelerometer, mean, var, IQR
knee	Accelerometer, mean, var, IQR	PIC16LF87x-04, Accelerometer, mean, var, IQR	-
shoe	FSRs, Lag	-	-
head	-	-	-
Connections between modules			
main-head	RS232	RS232	RS232
main-knee	I2C	I2C	RS232
knee-feet	I2C	RS232	RS232

all wire-based and implemented using the I2C-bus. Note that modules not used in a specific architecture (e.g. shoe and head module in architecture B, or knee, shoe and head module in architecture C) are also assigned a communication channel. The reason for this is that we have not defined a 'No connection' interface so far in our exploration environment. Thus, a module that is not used in an architecture will still have a connection to the main module even though no data is transmitted over that channel. In such cases, the exploration environment chooses the communication channel type with the lowest standby power consumption which is in our case RS232.

4.3   Discussion

As mentioned in the previous section, the pareto front is populated by only a few architectures. During the exploration run, the pareto-optimal architectures converge to a few points in the design space. One possible reason for this is that certain features and feature combinations are much more relevant for the recognition task at hand than others, while the computational complexity of all features is very similar. This leads to the fact that only the more relevant features/feature combinations survive during the evolution process, reducing the number of potentially interesting sensor/feature-combinations and thus cutting down the number of potential architectures. If we compare the three architectures A,B, and C we see that all of them use an accelerometer together with the mean, variance and interquartile range features. Note that the architecture on the pareto-front above architecture B is not pareto-optimal since it consumes as much power as architecture B but has a higher classification objective value. This phenomenon may occur because the genetic algorithm SPEA ([18]) tries to find equally distributed points on the pareto-front.

If we compare the properties of the three selected architectures on the pareto-front, we see that architecture A is more distributed than architecture C. Generally speaking, points on the lower right side of the pareto front are more distributed than those on the upper left side. This can be explained as for good classification performance, most of the sensors have to be placed at specific locations on the body to provide relevant data. This applies for both acceleration sensors, the FSRs, and the gyroscope in our case. The air pressure sensor, however is less dependent on a specific location. Since the locations are often distributed over the body, architectures with low classification objective values are likely to be more distributed.

4.4   System Variants

To an experienced system designer the result presented above might seem fairly obvious. This is not surprising since, in the interest of verification, we have chosen an example with tractable, intuitive solutions. However, even in such a trivial example there are aspects where an automatic optimization methodology can provide information that are not obvious. Looking at the 'balanced' system B, consider for example the trade-off between power consumption and recognition rate involved in the choice between the FSR on the foot and the knee mounted accelerometer. It is clear, if the power consumption ratio between the accelerometer and the FSR (including communication costs) increasingly favors the FSR, eventually the accelerometer would be replaced by the FSRs. It is also clear that the FSR would occur earlier than a pure power consumption analysis might indicate, since the FSRs score very well with respect to the classification objective. However, the point at which this change will occur is not obvious. This is where our methodology comes into play. It revealed that up to a power consumption ratio (accelerometer/FSR) of 3, the system stays with an accelerometer while for a power consumption ratio of 4, a system with FSRs is suggested.

The above example illustrates an important aspect of our framework. Apart from systems that are either excessively complex or are addressing exotic problem domains, an experienced system designer may often be able to come up with a reasonable rough system outline. However, when it comes to specific trade-offs between seemingly similar system variants, 'hand optimization' is difficult. In systems dealing with more advanced contexts and more sensors, there is a number of such trade-offs spanning a large design space resulting in considerable performance differences. Especially, in such cases our automatic design space exploration methodology becomes a valuable tool even to an experienced system designer.

5   Conclusion and Future Work

We have described a methodology designed to formalize and automate the choice and placement of sensors and the selection of features for wearable context sensitive systems. The motivation behind our work is to provide a wearable system designer with support and verification tools that would make the design less ad-hoc but a more systematic process such as in other areas (e.g chip layout or communications).

We have concentrated on the trade-off between power consumption and recognition quality. To this end, a formalism for the description of the system constraints and power costs has been devised. To quantify the relationship between recognition performance and sensor/feature choice, the use of mutual information has been proposed. These parameters were then used as input to a genetic algorithm based optimization tool to automatically derive a set of pareto optimal system configurations.

Using a well understood recognition task and a simple system template, we have verified that our methodology produces reasonable results. We have also shown that even in simple scenario where the overall system structure is clear to an experienced designer there are tradeoffs and parameters on which our methodology can provide useful additional information.

In the future, we will apply our framework to more complex case studies and recognition tasks. In addition different extensions of the framework are planned. In a first step, we will implement a 'No connection interface' for modules not used in specific architectures. Furthermore, we plan to add a third design objective to our framework which takes the 'wearability aspect' of the system into account.

Acknowledgments

The authors would like to thank Jan Beutel, Matthias Dyer and Rolf Enzler for their help with the simulation environment and active discussion of the models. This research is supported by ETH Zurich under the Polyproject "Miniaturized Wearable Computing: Technology and Applications".

References

1. J. Mantyjarvi, J. Himberg, and T. Seppanen. Recognizing human motion with multiple acceleration sensors. In *2001 IEEE International Conference on Systems, Man and Cybernetics*, volume 3494, pages 747–752, 2001.
2. Urs Anliker, Jan Beutel, Matthias Dyer, Rolf Enzler, Paul Lukowicz, Lothar Thiele, and Gerhard Tröster. A systematic approach to the design of distributed wearable systems. *IEEE Transactions on Computers*, 53(3):1017–1033, Aug. 2004.
3. Mathias Stäger, Paul Lukowicz, Niroshan Perera, Thomas von Büren, Gerhard Tröster, and Thad Starner. SoundButton: Design of a Low Power Wearable Audio Classification System. In *ISWC 2003: Proceedings of the 7th IEEE International Symposium on Wearable Computers*, pages 12–17, October 2003.
4. W. Wolf. *Computers as Components: Principles of Embedded Computing System Design*. Morgan Kaufman Publishers, 2002.
5. T. Blickle, J. Teich, and L. Thiele. System-level synthesis using evolutionary algorithms. *Design Automation for Embedded Systems*, 3(1):23–58, January 1998.
6. R. K. Gupta. *Co-Synthesis of Hardware and Software for Digital Embedded Systems*. Kluwer Academic Publishers, August 1995.
7. I. Karkowski and H. Corporaal. Design space exploration algorithm for heterogeneous multi-processor embedded system design. In *Proc. 35th Design Automation Conf. (DAC)*, pages 82–87, 1998.
8. J. Liu, P. H. Chou, N. Bagherzadeh, and F. Kurdahi. A constraint-based application model and scheduling techniques for power-aware systems. In *Proc. 9th Int. Symp. on Hardware/Software Codesign (CODES)*, pages 153–158, 2001.
9. G. De Micheli. *Synthesis and Optimization of Digital Circuits*. McGraw-Hill, 1994.
10. M. Eisenring, L. Thiele, and E. Zitzler. Handling conflicting criteria in embedded system design. *IEEE Des. Test. Comput.*, 17(2):51–59, April–June 2000.
11. T. Koshizen. Improved sensor selection technique by integrating sensor fusion in robot position estimation. *Journal of Intelligent and Robotic Systems*, 29:79–92, 2000.
12. H. Junker, P. Lukowicz, and G. Troester. Using information theory to design context-sensing wearable systems. *accepted for publication as an IEEE Monograph on Sensor Network Operations*.
13. Joachim Denzler and Christopher M. Brown. Information theoretic sensor data selection for active object recognition and state estimation. *IEEE Transactions on Pattern Analysis and Machine Intelligence*, 24(2):145–157, February 2002.
14. Jihoon Yang and Vasant Honavar. Feature subset selection using a genetic algorithm. *IEEE Intelligent Systems*, 13:44–49, 1998.
15. Z. Sun, G. Bebis, X. Yuan, and S. Louis. Genetic feature subset selection for gender classification: A comparison study. In *IEEE Workshop on Applications of Computer Vision*, pages 165–170, Dezember 2002.

16. T. Blickle, J. Teich, and L. Thiele. System-level synthesis using evolutionary algorithms. *Design Automation for Embedded Systems*, 3(1):23–58, January 1998.
17. L. Thiele, S. Chakraborty, M. Gries, and S. Künzli. Design space exploration of network processor architectures. In *Network Processor Design 2002: Design Principles and Practices*. Morgan Kaufmann Publishers, 2002.
18. E. Zitzler, M. Laumanns, and L. Thiele. SPEA2: Improving the strength pareto evolutionary algorithm for multiobjective optimization. In *Proc. EUROGEN 2001 – Evolutionary Methods for Design, Optimisation and Control with Applications to Industrial Problems*, 2001.
19. R. Battiti. Using mutual information for selecting features in supervised neural net learning. *IEEE Transactions on Neural Networks*, 5(4):537–550, July 1994.
20. N. Kwak and C. Chong-Ho. Input feature selection for classification problems. *IEEE Transactions on Neural Networks*, Jan. 2002.
21. R.M. Fano. Class notes for transmission of information, course 6.574. Technical report, MIT, Cambridge, Mass., 1952.
22. H. Junker, P. Lukowicz, and G. Troester. Locomotion analysis using a simple feature derived from force sensitive resistors. In *Proceedings Second IASTED International Conference on Biomedical Engineering, 2004*, 2004.

Collaborative Sensing in a Retail Store Using Synchronous Distributed Jam Signalling

Albert Krohn, Tobias Zimmer, Michael Beigl, and Christian Decker

Telecooperation Office (TecO), Universität Karlsruhe

Abstract. The retail store environment is a challenging application area for Pervasive Computing technologies. It has demanding base conditions due to the number and complexity of the interdependent processes involved. We present first results of an ongoing study with *dm-drogerie markt*, a large chemist's retailer, that indicate that supporting product monitoring tasks with novel pervasive technology is useful but still needs technical advances. Based on this study, we uncover problems that occur when using identification technology (such as RFID) for product monitoring. The individual identification struggles with data overload and inefficient channel access due to the high number of tags involved. We address these problems with the concept of *Radio Channel Computing*, combining approaches from information theory, such as the *method of types* and *multiple access adder channels*. We realise data pre-processing on the physical layer and significantly improve response time and scalability. With mathematical formulation, simulations and a real world implementation, we evaluate and prove the usefulness of the proposed system.

1   Introduction

Retail stores are a well perceived application area for Pervasive Computing technology. The processes and workflows involved in a retail store span multiple domains, ranging from physical handling of products for logistics, presentation and check-out to information handling, such as required for marketing and product monitoring. Pervasive Computing technology is by nature an ideal means of improving processes in the physical as well as in the informational world, as it follows the idea of pervading the world with interrelationships between physical objects, information and people.

Recommender Systems are a common example to show how ideas of Pervasive Computing technology have been introduced into the retail area. These systems inform the customer about products and current offers in the store using a display or audio output. Some systems even go one step further by personalizing the recommendation to enhance the shopping experience. But generally, most of the technological efforts aim at reducing the personnel costs in the stores. The most cited example is the automatic check-out without a cashier. These self-check-outs are currently under experiment at e.g. Metro's Future Store [1].

H.W. Gellersen et al. (Eds.): PERVASIVE 2005, LNCS 3468, pp. 237–254, 2005.

To contribute to this complex area with a sustainable novel Pervasive Computing technology, we first conducted a study on the processes and workflows in a retail store. With this study we sought to gain an understanding of the interdependencies of the processes and the real world requirements for workflows in a retail store. It helped us to identify tasks that profit from novel Pervasive Computing technologies and revealed features that such new technology should offer. First results of this ongoing study are presented in this paper. Based on this study we selected one application scenario where we see large gains from introducing pervasive technology – the monitoring of sell-by dates. We also took the existing processes and technologies into account to be able to smoothly integrate the new ideas into existing retail stores.

1.1   Identification and Classification – Tagging on Item-Level

Today, information technology in retail stores is mainly targeted at the *classification* of products. The wide-spread use of EAN (European article numbering system) and UPC (universal product code) barcodes is the reference example for this. Barcodes do generally not identify an individual item but classify it to be e.g. a can of coke. This classification is enough to support tasks in the retail area like ordering or the check-out of customers.

Most of the applications to date that already use the new capabilities of RFID in the retail area only exploit the tagging of groups of products like boxes or pallets, because the individual tagging of products with RFID tags is still too costly, technically not fully matured and not yet completely included in the manufacturing process of packaging of goods etc. Nevertheless, it is widely agreed that RFID has an enormous potential as technological basis for applications in retail stores in the near future.

A drawback that comes along with the *individual* tagging of product is the explosion of data. To take advantage out of the individuality of a single item, an electronic counterpart would have to exist in a data processing system. Handling this mass of data is a complicated task, such that the summarization of local information of single items into groups or classes, in the back end systems, is likely. Further, the potentially huge number of tags communicating in the same radio range severely worsen the problem of access control on the radio channel.

In this paper, we discuss exactly the problems associated with the tagging of products on item level. We see the area of individual identification the most challenging one in the area of RFID technology. The mass of data affecting the radio protocol as well as the processing in data bases is a known issue for the successful future of RFID technology.

In the following, we focus on the application area of product monitoring derived from our ongoing study (section 2). We discuss existing solutions and Related Work in section 3 and summarize the technical requirements in section 3.2. In section 4, we present a novel approach of collaboratively sensing individual information from a large group of goods. Our technical solution is a protocol extension of RFID technology, based on the idea of data pre-processing on the physical layer. We call this approach *Radio Channel Computing*. With the proposed solution we address both mentioned problems of individual tagging: the data explosion and the channel access problem due to the huge number of tags. In section 5, we also present a prototype implementation on wireless nodes and discuss the technical feasibility for the target technology RFID.

2   Processes and Workflows in a Retail Store – A Study

To gain an insight into the workflow of retail stores and their processes, we are conducting a study with one of Europe's leading chemist's companies: *dm-drogerie markt*[1] with more than 1500 chain stores and 20,500 employees in eight European countries. The products offered by *dm-drogerie markt* are manifold, ranging from toiletries and pharmaceutical products, household articles and pet food, to baby and whole food products. Figure 1 shows a typical view of a shelf in a *dm*-store. The study includes interviews with employees on different hierarchical levels. We conducted interviews with four store managers and were supported by six managers at the headquarters giving background information on the supply chain management and an overview on company wide processes. We visited four *dm*-stores of different size and location to gain a representative view on the workflow, complexity and requirements in this retail store environment. The interviews with the store managers included asking predefined questions about the organization, product monitoring, stocktaking and the internal workflow in the company and stores. These interviews were supplemented with short interviews with some shop employees and on-side demonstrations of the relevant work sequences.

Fig. 1. A typical shelf in a *dm*-store

In this paper we focus on handling perishable goods as one facet of the results of this ongoing study that showed very high potential for the application

---

[1] http://www.dm-drogeriemarkt.de

of Pervasive Computing technologies. For chemist's retail stores it is not immediately obvious that monitoring sell-by dates introduces a significant workload. Nevertheless many products, like body lotions and bath additives, in the large assortment of *dm-drogerie markt* carry sell-by dates. To get an idea of how much working time is spent on monitoring, we asked managers of *dm*-stores how product monitoring is organized, how often it is performed and what tasks are involved. In the following section, we present a summary of our study to outline the most important issues in the aspect of monitoring and managing products with sell-by dates.

How often are the shelves checked for perishable products? We learnt that frequent checks that are scheduled on demand by the store manager are in most cases impossible even in small stores with a limited stock. This is due to the number of products with sell-by dates and their distribution throughout the product groups. The headquarter provides predefined schedules for stock maintenance for all *dm*-stores. The checking intervals for product groups range from once every six month to every two months depending on how far the sell-by date is from the production date, how often a product is sold and how large the in-shop stock of a product normally is.

The fixed schedule leads to an unnecessary amount of checks, as in many cases the stock rotation ensures that no products are found that are near their sell-by dates. On the other hand, with fixed check intervals, it is still possible that products that have passed their sell-by dates remain in the shelves until the next scheduled check or a customer discovers them. This could only be avoided if products that reach their sell-by date during the next check interval would generally be removed form the shelves, which is not feasible for products that are only checked every six months. The store managers agreed that it would save a lot of time if the checking could be done on an on-demand basis.

What are the criteria for products to be removed from the shelves? When checking a shelf, the employee removes all products and checks the sell-by dates. Products that reach the sell-by date within the next 8 weeks are removed, reduced in price and put in special sale boxes. Over all product groups that have to be monitored, on average 10 out of 4000 articles are sorted out for sale due to their near expiration. All product monitoring tasks, including continuous stocktaking, are performed during regular opening hours. The store manager schedules the work as short term, depending on the number of customers in the shop and the general workload of the store employees.

How long does it take to check a product group? The checks for sell-by dates are a laborious task. The time needed for checking depends on various factors. Some of them can be influenced by technical aids, some are only connected to the knowledge and experience of the employee performing the check. The product groups in a store can be separated into three classes:

The first class consists only of product groups in which no single product has a sell-by date, such that they require no monitoring.

The second class is made up of the product groups that consist only of products that all have a sell-by date. In this class all products in a product group have to be checked in the monitoring process.

The third class contains product groups in which one can find products with and without sell-by dates. Whenever a product group of this third class is to be checked, the familiarity of the employee with the product group significantly influences the time for the checks. Other important factors on the time necessary are the shape and size of the products and where on the packaging the sell-by date is located. It takes much longer to check small products with tiny printing, like lip sticks, than it takes to check larger products like flour bags. We asked the store managers for the time it takes to check different product groups that significantly differ in their characteristics. In figure 2 we now compare two product groups: *whole food products* (5 shelf segments[2]) and *pharmacological products* (7 shelf segments).

	different products on the shelf	items on the shelf	time to check the shelf	check time per item
whole food products	241	3000	6h	7sec
pharmacological products	487	4000	16h	14sec

Fig. 2. Some numbers on the manual process of checking the goods

How many items are found? An important indicator when analysing the expenditure of product monitoring is the number of items that are actually identified for removal from the regular stock in individual product groups. In our interviews we learnt that many different factors influence these numbers: The location and size of a store influences what products are sold and how many times. To some extent this determines also how exactly the assortment in a given store is made up. Large stores in shopping areas and malls with big parking lots attract more customers that buy bulky and heavy goods. The customers of theses shops tend to be younger than in other areas which is reflected by a higher sales volume in whole food, beauty products and baby products. Stores where the share of elderly people among the customers is high, tend to sell more pharmacological products. Additionally, some products like sunscreen are subject to strong seasonal fluctuations. So it can be safely assumed that no two of the 1500 *dm*-stores offer exactly the same assortment.

It is not feasible to provide each store with an individually optimised schedule for product monitoring. So a general schedule has to be very defensive to make sure that it is applicable for all of the stores. The large variety of assortments and the differences in the turnover in the product groups lead to very diverse numbers of items that have to be removed due to expiration. According to the

---

[2] A shelf segment is 1 m wide and 1,80 m high.

store managers, in around 4000 single items, the number of products with critical sell-by dates can be none, some or up to 40 depending on the store and the checked product group. On average, only 10 out of 4000 items have to be sorted out during a check, while checking of these items takes more than 12 hours.

2.1 Implications and Assumptions – Check on Schedule Versus Check on Demand

The limitations of efficiency using a fixed, centrally prepared monitoring schedule have been discussed in the previous section. As mentioned, schedule-based checking leads to an unnecessary amount of checks introducing high costs due to the expenditure of time for the checks. An alternative to *checking on schedule* would be *checking on demand*, which is more flexible with respect to the individual product group turnaround times as well as to the different store profiles. Checking on demand would improve the intervals between individual checks saving personnel costs. In this context the granularity of the partitioning of products for the checks should be decreased below product group level. Checking individual shelves instead of whole product groups (up to 10 shelf segments) would add to the flexibility and reduce the items involved in one single check down to around 400, based on the figures derived from our survey. For shelves that need higher attention, the check rate could be increased with still lower over-all costs than with using fixed schedules on product group level. Changing the task of sell-by dates checking from *checking on schedule* to *checking on demand* would positively influence the overall efficiency of the workflow in a *dm*-store. Based on this idea, we envision a technical system that allows to change the scheduling of product monitoring by introducing Pervasive Computing technology into the workflow.

Further, as a second result of our study, the store managers are very interested to monitor the changes over time of the sell-by dates of a certain product group or all products of one shelf. For example, consider that after new items have been placed on a shelf a continuous process of selling and reloading of the shelf follows. During that continuous process the products become more and more mixed concerning their sell-by dates, due to activities such as customers taking products from the back of the shelf, personnel placing "fresher" products in front of older ones, and other random re-ordering of the shelf space. The monitoring of the development of the sell-by dates of a defined group of products is a helpful instrument for ordering, advertising and for the optimisation of the range of products.

To enable both tasks – the *check on demand* and the *generation of the overview of sell-by dates* – we propose an extension to existing RFID protocols. The technical details are discussed in the following sections.

3   Collaborative Sensing for Group Profiling

For the previously mentioned tasks of checking the sell-by dates and the generation of the overview of the sell-by dates, we want to support the employees by

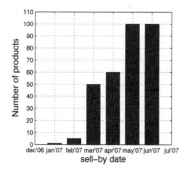

Fig. 3. Profile of sell-by dates of products

Fig. 4. Ordering products

providing a *profile* of the sell-by dates of a given group of items. A *profile* is a histogram showing the sell-by dates of all observed goods.

Figure 3 shows such a profile. The profile does not give information on the individual identification of the products but only gives the number of products with the same sell-by date. For the generation of the desired profiles, the identification is not necessary. The resolution and range of the time axis is a matter of implementation. With this profile, the employee can decide whether a manual check is necessary and can at the same time monitor the development of the sell-by dates. If e.g. all observed goods expire very far in the future, a manual check would obviously not be necessary. Such a profile provides the basis for the on-demand checks mentioned in section 2.1.

The technology that we propose will generate these profiles by *collaboratively sensing* the sell-by date among selected products. It is based on RFID technology. We therefore assume, that all products are tagged with RFID transponders and carry their sell-by date in the tags. To avoid time-consuming additional tasks, we envision combining the process of sell-by date profiling with the inevitable ordering process. When ordering new products, the employee scans a product identification – normally a barcode – on the shelf to trigger the process in a back-end system (see figure 4). While pointing at the barcode to scan, we could evoke a collaborative sensing of the sell-by dates of selected products that are in radio range and generate a profile of their sell-by dates. The radio range for HF/UHF (typically around 1m) would cover 200-300 items. The profiles of sell-by dates could be displayed on the scanner or collected in the back-end for generating a store wide profile.

To seamlessly include the generation of profiles into the ordering process and avoid additional inconvenience, the primary factor is the time needed. The scanning of a barcode for the ordering process would typically need a fraction of a second. Therefore, the included sell-by dates scanning process must be performed in a similar time. If it takes too long, it is not feasible. The task should not produce additional inconvenience and should appear to be real-time – typically faster than 50ms.

3.1   RFID Standards, Prevailing Protocols and Related Work

Smart Shelves. The tracking or sensing of products in stores is an intense discussed topic. One suggested solution is the use of so called *smart shelves*. These shelves have multiple RFID readers embedded and are therefore able to continuously scan all the products placed in them. In [2] even basic interaction of customers with the products can be monitored. Nevertheless, installing an infrastructure, which completely covers all product areas and stocks in a store is a complex and costly task. One out of many problems is that of antenna interference when many readers are installed in a dense setting. Additionally, the readers have to be connected to a power supply and in some cases to a data processing system. This disturbs, for example, frequently changing installations for special offers and needs frequent reorganization of the whole system. While a self-organizing systems approach may be considered as a solution, they increase the complexity.

Active Tags. Several companies have specialized in smart product monitoring in the retail area, with perishable goods being a popular focus for technical solutions. An example where the sell-by date is monitored in a system based on smart tags is marketed by Infratab [3]. Infratab's FreshAlert[TM] tags can monitor the shelf life of perishable goods. The technology is based on active tag technology including a temperature sensor, an indication light and a battery. Infratab proposes a target price of 1$ [4] which we consider to be too high for our target application.

Radio Frequency and Read Range. RFID technology is generally classified by its target operation frequency. The demand for longer read ranges and higher data rates drove the communication frequencies higher and higher. To date, the most common standards in the HF- Band (13 Mhz) are the ISO 15693 [5] and the ISO 18000-3 Mode 1 and 2 [6]. In the UHF band (868/916 MHz) the most important efforts are the ISO18000-6 and the standard contribution from EPC global [7]. For the target application identified in our study, we are especially interested in high data- and identification rates as well as in read ranges in the area of around one meter. Even though a read range of one meter is hardly possible with available HF-band technology, both HF and UHF are considered as state of the art for the target application.

Identification Speed. According to the standards, the fastest identification processes in the HF-band can be achieved with the ISO 18000-3 Mode 2, reaching up to 200 items/s. Other protocol improvements have been achieved and have been contributed to the Mode 5 specification, which is now discontinued due to the high requirements on the hardware. Using this discontinued mode 5, in [8], the authors calculate that an identification of 500 tags including 100 Bytes of data read from each tag should be possible in around 800ms. Nevertheless, both results only refer to an idealized theoretical calculation and give no statistical confidence. According to an article in the RFID journal in June 2003 [9], the latest technology from Magellan Technology Pty Ltd [10] can identify 1200 tags per second using the ISO 18000-3 Mode 2 when tags are sequentially running through a tunnel reader at high speed. This does not mean that 1200 tags can be read in one second in a static setting. Magellan has instead shown another demonstration, where they identify 100 tags within a second in a nearly static setting. The numbers given for identification and read processes have always to be read very carefully to not be misinterpreted. As an example for a realistic estimation of the speed of identification processes, we refer to the work of Vogt in [11]. There an identification scheme (based on slotted Aloha) is statistically modelled under realistic assumption for collisions and optimised for a fast identification of many tags in a static setting. According to his work, the optimal number of slots and cycles for a 99% detection confidence of 200 RFID tags would be higher than $256 * 13$ slots, whereas each slot carries a complete packet. This theory of the identification scheme is generally not limited to a certain target technology (HF or UHF). As a theoretical best-case calculation, we pick values from the most actual physical layers of HF/UHF standards. There, the shortest signals from a tag are $6.25\mu s$ (for UHF) and $14.2\mu s$ (for HF, ISO18000-3 Mode 2). Assuming 64 Bit identifiers, these physical layer parameters and 200 devices, the whole process would still result in more than 3000ms not considering the overhead through messages headers and packets from the reader which are significant.

Identification Protocols. The identification process in the presence of many tags has been discussed widely. A typical approach is the so call *binary search* method. The reader sends out a mask of Bits, the tags compare it with their ID, answer and then the reader sends out the next mask trying to singulate one RFID tag in the read range. This method is explained in detail in [12]. The new standards in the UHF band include mechanisms to speed up the identification process. One approach is e.g. to use a 16 Bit random number for the separation of RFID-tags instead of the complete ID that carries 96 Bit or more. Figure 5 shows such a mechanism. The reader first selects the target group with e.g. filters or masks and then sends a "query" command. This command includes as well how many slots follow from which the tags can pick one randomly. Afterwards, the tags pick a random 16 Bit number and send it in the according random slot. If the reader detects a collision, the process is repeated. If the reader can receive a valid 16 Bit number, it then replies and polls the whole ID and then reads or writes data, deactivates the tag etc. As a best case assumption, the protocol of query, reply, ack and ID-reply for a single tag would take (assuming

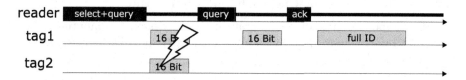

Fig. 5. Using a 16 Bit random number during Identification process

again to date EPC/ISO physical layers) around $2100\mu s$. The random selection is a slotted aloha process know to have a maximum throughput at around 36%. Assuming this and 200 tags, we get something around 1.2 seconds as the process time for reading the IDs of 200 tags. This is of course a very rough rule of thumb calculation but gives a first idea of the timings. This calculation does not include reading or writing of stored data in the tags. It's only the identification!

3.2   Problem Statement and System Requirements

Looking at the examples of the previous section and the target process time of below 50ms, there is a mismatch in technology. As a conclusion of the above analysis of state-of-the-art RFID technology we do not promote a standard protocol for our use case. Smart shelves are too costly, inflexible and complex, while standard RFID tags with mobile readers are not fast enough. To support our target scenario, we propose an extension of existing RFID technology to support the user in her activities rather than completely redesigning the whole workflow which we identified to be too complex and too expensive. We envision a system of *low complexity* and *low hardware requirements* similar to current passive RFID technology where a high number of tags can be efficiently read out in real time. Such a system should also have a *fast and constant response time* (typically faster than 50ms) – even for a large number (1000) of items and should *not need any additional technology or infrastructure*. The constant and predictable response time is a very important point especially for the inclusion of such processes in the normal workflow. With a known reply time, the equipment can work with known delays and the operators do not have to consider the side conditions of the actual task but follow a given scheme without any adaptation to the situation. This is also a big step towards the automation of such a process.

4   Radio Channel Computing

To technically realize a system fulfilling the requirements summarized in section 3.2, we propose a radical new technical approach that we call *Radio Channel Computing*. The idea is, to take advantage of the characteristics of the radio channel itself to perform elementary computation with transmitted data during the transmission on the channel. With this method we can – for the use case discussed in this paper – achieve a *constant, ultra fast* reply time *independent* of the number of tags actually involved in the process.

4.1   Related Work for Radio Channel Computing

The most important ingredients for realizing Radio Channel Computing include early and fundamental ideas of information theory and reach back until the 1940's. The major parts are:

The method of types. In [13], the basic of Shannon's discoveries and formulation of information theory ([14]) is presented in the context of applications.

Roughly spoken, the idea of the method of types is to compress a vector of measurements by partitioning it into subclasses. All elements of the vector are then assigned to an according subclass and only the number of elements in a subclass in then transmitted.

Superimposed codes. In [15] the authors derivate a method to detect codes that have been superimposed on the channel. This idea also dates back to a very early work of Kautz and Singleton ([16]) in which they state: "A binary superimposed code consists of a set of code words whose digit-by-digit Boolean sums $(1 + 1 = 1)$". This idea will be taken over and applied to the area of radio communication with RFID.

Binary adder channels. A fundamental work on the use of superimposed analogue signals for a multi-user binary adder channel can be found in [17]. The authors discuss physical constraints of super positioning of non-orthogonal signals on a channel. The combination of the method of types and multi user adder channels has also been proven to be optimal efficient for distributed detection in [18].

Theory of small samples. It is a common approach in information theory to prove a concept by it asymptotical behaviour. For our case, we are more interested in results that refer to small samples. We apply standard estimation theory and confidence intervals here.

4.2   Multi-SDJS

Multi-SDJS is an extension to Synchronous Distributed Jam Signalling presented in [19]. It combines the above mentioned ideas in a system, that superimposes jam signals on the radio channel. In the context of this paper, the radio channel is supposed to be a binary OR-channel. Two or more simultaneous transmitted signals result in only one in the receiver. In contrast to [17], the receivers are not able to analyse the details (e.g. number) of super positioned signals but only detect the existence of them. This makes the implementation of the system much easier. To achieve the encoding of the sell-by dates into the SDJS scheme, we apply the *method of types* by sub classing the sell-by dates in e.g. units of months. Subsequently, for each subclass representing a certain time interval, the number of goods carrying the according sell-by date are transmitted. The transmission of each of these numbers is done applying the ideas of *binary adder channels* and the *theory of small samples* through the use of the previously developed SDJS theory [19]. Generally, a SDJS scheme is a number of time slots, where devices with radio communication – in our case RFID tags – emit jam signals into randomly selected positions. Using the same principles as the original SDJS [19], the jam signals carry neither a signature nor an identification. The *presence* of signals only inform about the *existence* of products with the according sell-by date. The occurrence of collisions is included in the SDJS theory [19]. For the use-case of this paper, SDJS schemes are used to estimate the number of goods carrying a certain sell-by date. Multiples of these schemes are concatenated to span the entire time-span of sell-by dates. After processing the multi-SDJS scheme, the receiver has an estimated number of goods for each subclass of

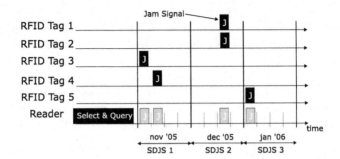

Fig. 6. A Multi-SDJS scheme with three concatenated SDJS schemes

dates – the desired profile can be generated. Figure 6 shows how the Multi-SDJS scheme works. The Multi SDJS-scheme starts with the "select & query" command of the reader containing the filter and masks for the selection of tags. A number of SDJS schemes then follows (in this case three), each representing a certain sell-by date. Each of these sub-SDJS schemes contains a number of slots for the positioning of jam signals. During a single SDJS scheme, e.g. during the scheme for dec '05 in figure 6, the tags randomly select a slot and send a jam signal, when their sell-by date is dec '05. The reader collects theses jam signals and uses them to estimate the number of tags for that date.

4.3   New Aspects for the Estimators of SDJS

For our target application, the SDJS theory of [19] requires significant extension. In this section, we will present two new important aspect for the use of SDJS in this retail scenario. First of all, the maximum likelihood estimator (MLE) will be once more discussed for our target setting. As a second step, we will present a maximum a-posteriori (MAP) estimator that enables us to give confidence intervals for the estimations. The following discussion refers to single SDJS schemes and therefore addresses the estimation of number of products that carry the same sell-by date and participate in the same single SDJS scheme.

Invariance of the MLE. The maximum likelihood estimator of SDJS has the advantage, that the probability distribution $P_k(k)$ of the number of tags k carrying the same sell-by date does not need to be known. Nevertheless, at least the interval $[0, k_{max}]$ of how many tags are possibly there needs to be known. Applying SDJS to the target application, it seems impossible to even only roughly predict the quantity of goods with a certain sell-by date. Fortunately, also this constrain can be loosened when taking a closer look on the ML point estimator. The MLE has an invariance under certain conditions, shown in figure 7. The example is based on a SDJS scheme with $s = 20$ slots. The ML point estimators are given as the three curves. It can be noticed that for all number of received jam signals $a \leq 18$, all three estimators result in the same values even though the preconditions (meaning the range of the number of items) are different. This is due to the nature of the estimator and the underlying process.

The ML-estimator ($\arg\max_k P_{a|k}(a|k)$) only depends on the mapping that SDJS realises. Applying the additional side constraint of an estimation range $[0, k_{max}]$, an estimation $\tilde{k}$ that reaches out of the range $[0, k_{max}]$ has to be corrected to a lower value $\tilde{k} \leq k_{max}$. In figure 7, for $a > 18$, the estimators give different values for the different preconditions $k_{max} = 50, 70, 120$. It is clear that e.g. for the case $k \in [0, k_{max} = 50]$, the estimator can never result in a higher estimation value than 50. Therefore, the estimator curve is limited to $\tilde{k} = 50$. For $s = 20$ and $k_{max} > 59$, the ML-estimations for $0 < a < 20$ will stay invariant of the actual k_{max}. Only for $a = s$ the estimation is always $\tilde{k} = k_{max}$.

Therefore, we can use only one lookup table for different settings as long as we can assume that the upper bound k_{max} of the possible number of devices is above a certain value. This threshold is *only* given through the number of slots s. For our example ($s = 20$), this threshold is $k_{max} = 59$.

MAP Estimation. In the case of a known a-priori distribution, we can improve our estimation by including this knowledge into the estimator. We do this by using a *maximum a-posteriori* estimation (MAP).

$$\tilde{k}_{MAP} = \arg\max_k P_{k|a}(k|a) = \arg\max_k \frac{P_{a|k}(a|k) \cdot P_k(k)}{P_a(a)}$$
$$= \arg\max_k P_{a|k}(a|k) \cdot P_k(k) \tag{1}$$

For each estimation, the probability $P_a(a)$ is identical and can therefore be left out in (1). As mentioned above, it seems impossible to give those distributions of number of goods $P_k(k)$ with equal sell-by dates as an information input to the estimator. For simplicity, we assume an even a-priori distribution ($P_k(k) = const$). Any other more realistic distribution would of course improve the over all result. With this even a-priori distribution we get the same point estimation results as for the ML estimation, as the constant term $P_k(k)$ does not change the maximum of (1). Yet we can now also give confidence intervals for our estimation. We define a *trust level* β (typically $\beta = 0.9$) and can then give a confidence interval $[\tilde{k}_{min}, \tilde{k}_{max}]$ for our estimation with the certainty of β. Figure 8 shows

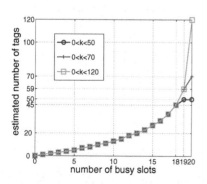

Fig. 7. Invariance of MLE for $s = 20$ and $k_{max} = 50, 70, 120$

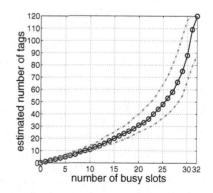

Fig. 8. MAP for $s = 32$ and $k \in [0, 120], \beta = 0.9$

an MAP estimation for SDJS. The dotted lines are the lower and upper limits of the $\beta = 0.9$ confidence interval. This means that e.g. for $a = 15$, the MAP point estimation would give $\tilde{k}_{MAP} = 20$ and statistically, 90% of all possible cases that result in $a = 15$ originate from the interval $\tilde{k} \in [16, 25]$.

4.4   Accuracy Evaluation and Properties SDJS

Primarily, the intention of Multi-SDJS was to create a fast estimation not focused on accuracy but more on speed and scalability. Normally, wireless packet oriented protocols like Zigbee, Bluetooth, RFID, WLAN etc. require more time when the number of information to be transported over the same bandwidth rises. In contrast to this, the speed of SDJS does only depend on the number of slots and not on the number of tags sending. The only draw-back that comes with more tags sending is the decrease in accuracy. This can be seen in figure 8. The confidence interval increases when increasing the number of items. However, for the application scenario, this is exactly what we wanted: a precise estimation for small numbers and a rough idea for the larger groups.

There are different options to increase the accuracy of SDJS. The most obvious possibility is to do multiple SDJS schemes (for the same sell-by date) and combine the measurements in a joint probability distribution $P_{\underline{a},k}(\underline{a}, k)$ and use again an ML or MAP estimation. As the deeper discussion of estimators is not the focus of this paper, we want only to give some idea of the accuracy that can be achieved by using the presented SDJS estimators from section 4.3. We use a MAP estimator and vary the slot numbers s to show how that influences the estimation quality. We are interested in how accurate we can estimate 200 devices. In figure 9, three curves for the estimation of $k = 200$ devices are shown. They represent the distribution of the estimation results for $s = 200, 400, 800$ slots. Even though the estimation results would result in discrete values, we smoothed the graphic with a spline for a better graphical representation. In figure 10, the accumulated error distribution is shown. This figure is based on the real discrete error probabilities of the discrete estimator tables; it therefore carries the steps of the discrete values of the estimators. To read out from figure 10 how big the

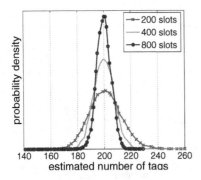

Fig. 9. Distribution of the estimation results for $k = 200$, $s = 200, 400, 800$

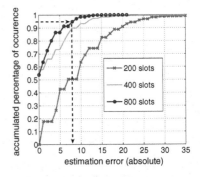

Fig. 10. Error distribution for the estimation of k=200 tags

error (with e.g. a confidence of 95%) for an estimation of 200 devices based on 800 slots is, we have to start at ordinate value 0.95 (see arrow) and then read out at the abscissa, that all errors will be smaller than 8. That means, that for an experiment with 200 tags and 800 slots we expect 95% of the experiments to have an estimation result error of maximum 7 tags.

5   Implementation and Technical Evaluation

To prove the concept of Multi-SDJS we fully implemented SDJS on our wireless sensor platform: the Particle Computers [20]. In our setting (see figure 11), the Particle Computers are configured to behave like passive tags: A "reader" sends out a start signal and then all devices contribute to the Multi-SDJS signalling. For our scenario of monitoring sell-by dates, we use a Multi-SDJS scheme similar to the one explained in figure 6. As a demonstration example, we took a random distribution of sell-by dates and implemented the dates on the Particle Computers. We then performed the Multi-SDJS scheme. The "select & query" command took approx. $900\mu s$, the slot-time was $64\mu s$. In figure 12 the profiles of the real dates and the estimated ones are compared against each other. In this example, we can benefit from the typical characteristic of SDJS that small numbers are estimated better. The three products that expire in February are estimated more precisely than the higher number for June. As we are especially interested in products with critical sell-by dates, which are typically only a few, we get a very good estimation for them.

Future implementations of Multi-SDJS can be realized on RFID hardware platforms, since the operational demands do not exceed those of standard RFID technology. As a speed comparison, we take the same numbers of the best case calculation from section 3.1 and use them now as well for the Multi-SDJS scheme. Assuming a sell-by date time resolution of one month, a total time coverage of 4 years, 100 slots per date, again around $10\mu s$ for a slot and 1ms for the "select & query" command, the Multi-SDJS scheme would take around 49ms – independent of the number of tags present. The speed is within the cognitive bounds

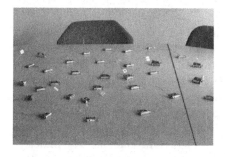

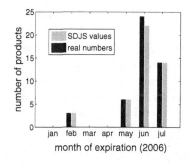

Fig. 11. Prototype implementation of Multi-SDJS on Particle Computers

Fig. 12. Profile of sell-by dates of 50 products

of human, real-time perception and even out-performs the speed requirements give in section 3. As Channel Computing with Multi-SDJS is a very specialized solution for the generation of the mentioned sell-by date profiles, the speed comparison to standard RFID protocols is somewhat improper, given that RFID protocols are not optimized for this particular task and transport unnecessary information. Nevertheless, in the calculation example, Multi-SDJS speeds up the generation of such profiles by 6000% without requiring any additional technological advances. Turnaround times in the tags are not critical as the tags do only one switch to transmission after the query command of the reader. During the slots of the Multi-SDJS scheme, the tags are in transmission state and just pick a slot to transmit their jam signal. The discussion of the best waveforms of the jam signals is not in the focus of this paper. Nevertheless, in the prototype implementation it has already been proven that jam signals can be detected without carrying a packet frame format or preamble or any other signature. Their length was mainly restricted by the sampling speed of A/D conversion and was comparable of the transmission time of 6 Bit of the underlying physical layer. Therefore, the assumption for a SDJS slot time to be in the area of a single RFID Bit-time is in fact realistic. The clock drifts are not critical either. The SDJS-scheme can easily handle a 10% shift of the jam signals. For the given example, this would mean a 10ppm clock, which is a rather high requirement to RFID hardware. Additional (in our case five extra) resynchronisation packets from the reader can easily relax this requirement to 100ppm or less.

6   Conclusion

The ongoing study with *dm-drogerie markt* we presented in this paper provides basic input to our research on novel Pervasive Computing technologies for the retail area. On basis of this study we were able to identify various interesting and promising applications of which we focused on manual monitoring of perishable products by checking sell-by dates. The interviews with the store managers revealed that seamless integration of new technologies and workflows will be essential for their success. We are convinced that in order to assure the real-world applicability of novel Pervasive Computing technology, maintaining close contact with its potential users is necessary.

RFID is widely agreed to be the upcoming technology for logistics and all kinds of workflow and supply chain management in the retail area. Thus it clearly has the potential to be among the novel computing technologies that will pervade our lives. We reviewed state of the art RFID technology and analysed its momentary weaknesses for the deployment in a challenging new application area. This resulted in the proposal of *Multi-SDJS*, an enhancement of existing RFID protocols. We improved response time and achieved constant and predictable scalability and realized a data pre-processing on the radio channel. The underlying idea of *Radio Channel Computing* is the basis for our ongoing research in this area. Many other research areas like data representation and combination, cooperative transmission and distributed estimation flow into this topic. We believe the potential of Radio Channel Computing and also Multi-SDJS in particular goes far beyond the focus of this paper. Being able to sense information in an ad-hoc manner from a large population using a simple and well scaling protocol opens a vast field for new applications like e.g. real time sensor fusion in general. The constant reply time of SDJS is also an ideal pre-requisite for its use in fully automated processes.

Acknowledgements

The work presented in this paper was partially funded by the European Community through the project *CoBIs* (Collaborative Business Items) under contract no. 4270 and by the Ministry of Economic Affairs of the Netherlands through the BSIK project *Smart Surroundings* under contract no. 03060.

References

1. Metro group - future store initiative. Website, accessed: 10/2004. `http://www.future-store.org`.
2. Christian Decker, Uwe Kubach, and Michael Beigl. Revealing the retail black box by interaction sensing. In *Proceedings of the ICDCS /IWSAWC*, Providence, USA, 2003.
3. Infratab Inc. Website, accessed: 10/2004. `http://www.infratab.com/`.
4. RFID Journal. Rfid tags for monitoring shelf life. Website, accessed 10/2004. `http://www.rfidjournal.com/article/articleview/428/1/1/`.
5. ISO/IEC/JTC 1/SC 17. Identification cards - contactless integrated circuit(s) cards - vicinity cards. 2001.
6. ISO/IEC/JTC 1/ SC 31/WG 4. Automatic identification - radio frequency identification for item management communications and interfaces part 3: Physical layer, anti collision system and protocol values at 13.56 mhz mode 2. 2001.
7. Epcglobal Inc. Website, accessed: 9/2004. `http://www.epcglobalinc.org/`.
8. Graham Murdoch and Tim Frost. A comparison of the iso15693 and iso18000-3 mode 5 magellan protocol. 2001.
9. RFID Journal. Magellan unveils tunnel reader. Website, accessed 9/2004. `http://breakwww.rfidjournal.com/article/articleview/445/1/1/`.
10. Magellan Technology Pty. Ltd. Website, accessed: 9/2004. `http://www.magtech.com.au/`.
11. Harald Vogt. Multiple object identification with passive rfid tags. In *IEEE International Conference on Systems, Man and Cybernetics (SMC '02)*, October 2002.
12. Klaus Finkenzeller. *RFID-Handbuch*. Carl Hanser Verlag München Wien, 2000.
13. Imre Csiszár. The method of types. *IEEE Transactions on Informatio theory*, 44(6), 1988.
14. C. E. Shannon and W. Weaver. The mathematical theory of communication. *University of Illinois Press*, 1949.
15. P. de Laval and S. Abdul-Jabbar. Decoding of superimposed codes in multiaccess communication. In *8th European Conference on Area Communication, EUROCON*, 1988.
16. W. H. Kautz and R. C. Singleton. Nonrandom binary superimposed codes. *IEEE Transaction on Information theory*, 1964.

17. I.Bar-David, E.Plotnik, and R.Rom. Limitations of the capacity of the m-user binary adder channel due to physical considerations. *IEEE Transaction on Information Theory*, 40(3):662–673, 1994.
18. K. Liu and A. Sayeed. Optimal distributed detection strategies for wireless sensor networks. In *42nd Annual Allerton Conference on Communications, Control and Computing*, 2004.
19. Albert Krohn, Michael Beigl, and Sabin Wendhack. SDJS: Efficient statistics for wireless networks. In *Proceedings of the 12th IEEE International Conference on Network Protocols*, Berlin, Germany, 2004.
20. C. Decker, A. Krohn, M. Beigl, and T. Zimmer. The Particle Computer System. In *IPSN Track on Sensor Platform, Tools and Design Methods for Networked Embedded Systems (SPOTS). Proceedings of the ACM/IEEE Fourth International Conference on Information Processing in Sensor Networks*, Los Angeles, USA, 2005. to appear.

Parasitic Mobility for Pervasive Sensor Networks

Mathew Laibowitz and Joseph A. Paradiso

MIT Media Laboratory,
20 Ames Street, E15-351,
Cambridge MA, 02139
{mat, joep}@media.mit.edu

Abstract. Distributed sensor networks offer many new capabilities for contextually monitoring environments. By making such systems mobile, we increase the application-space for the distributed network mainly by providing dynamic context-dependent deployment, continual relocatability, automatic node recovery, and a larger area of coverage. In existing models, the addition of actuation to the nodes has exacerbated three of the main problems with distributed systems: power usage, node size, and node complexity. In this paper we propose a solution to these problems in the form of parasitically actuated nodes that harvest their mobility and local navigational intelligence by selectively engaging and disengaging from mobile hosts in their environment. We analyze the performance of parasitically mobile distributed networks through software simulations and design, implement, and demonstrate hardware prototypes.

1 Introduction

1.1 Basic Principle

We are at a point in time where advances in technology have enabled production of extremely small, inexpensive, and wirelessly networked sensor clusters. We can thus scatter large quantities of sensors into an environment, creating a distributed sensor network. Each individual node in the network can monitor its local region and communicate with other nodes to collaboratively produce a high-level representation of the overall environment. By using distributed sensor networks, we can sculpt the sensor density to cluster around areas of interest, cover large areas, and work more efficiently by filtering local data at the node level before it is transmitted or relayed peer-to-peer. [1]

Systems of many small sensors can be deployed to cover large areas of any geometry. By adding autonomous mobility to the nodes, the system becomes more able to dynamically localize around areas of interest and adapt to changes in the sensing landscape. [2] Mobile sensor networks are accordingly well suited to sampling dynamic or poorly modeled phenomena. The addition of locomotion further provides the ability to deploy the sensor network at a distance away from the area of interest, useful in hostile environments. Cooperative micro-robots can reach places and perform tasks that their larger cousins cannot. [3] Mobility also allows the design

H.W. Gellersen et al. (Eds.): PERVASIVE 2005, LNCS 3468, pp. 255–278, 2005.
© Springer-Verlag Berlin Heidelberg 2005

of a system where nodes can seek out power sources, request the dispatch of other nodes to perform tasks that require more sensing capability, seek out repair, and locate data portals from which to report data. [4]

But the creation of mobile nodes is not without a price. Locomotion is costly in terms of node size and power consumption. In dense sensor systems, due to the large quantity of nodes and distributed coverage, it is difficult to manually replace batteries or maintain all nodes. Some researchers [5] have explored using robots to maintain distributed networks, but this is difficult to implement over large, unrestricted environments. Additionally, the added intelligence and processing power required for a node to successfully navigate in an arbitrary environment further increases the power and size requirements of each node. Large nodes, in physical size, complexity, cost, and power consumption, prevent the sensor network from being implemented in most environments. [6],[7]

This research is concerned with exploring a novel type of mobile distributed sensor network that achieves the benefits of mobility without the usual costs of size, power, and complexity. The innovation that allows this to happen is the design of nodes that harvest their actuation and local navigational intelligence from the environment. The node will be equipped with the ability to selectively attach to or embed itself within an external mobile host. Examples of such hosts include vehicles, fluids, forces (eg. selectively rolling down a hill), people, and animals. These hosts provide a source of translational energy, and in the animate cases, they know how to navigate within their environment, allowing the node to simply decide if the host will take it closer to a point of interest. If so, the node will remain attached; when the host begins to take the node farther away from a point of interest, the node will disengage and wait for a new host.

This area of research addresses the intersection between mobile agents, dense distributed networks, and energy harvesting. This paper presents the design and development of hardware and software systems to address the combination of these interests as "parasitic mobility".

Sensor networks are related to and/or encompassed by many larger fields including pervasive computing. The research and project described herein use sensor networks as an example space for developing and understanding the more general idea of parasitic mobility. These ideas are applicable to any field or space that is concerned with the physical distribution and mobility of computational nodes.

1.2   Related Work

Although this research has no direct precedent, it is inspired by systems in nature and human society (discussed in Chapter 2) and it builds upon current work in the encompassed fields of distributed sensor networks and mobile systems.

Wireless sensor networks have become a large area of research, with many universities and institutes contributing. Strategic seed programs begun in the 1990s, such as DARPA's SENSIT initiative [8], have grown into an international research movement.

The Smart Dust Project at UC Berkeley [9] has set a theoretical goal for extremely small nodes in dense embedded sensor networks. While the project itself did not put an actual hardware platform into production, it spun-off into the Mote [10] and more recently the Spec [11]. The Mote is currently the most popular platform for experimenting with compact wireless sensing. It has also served as a building block for many mobile sensor agent projects, all of which essentially involved putting a Mote onto some sort of robot [9]. The Spec is the current result of a project intended to shrink down the Mote to the theoretical goal of the Smart Dust project. While not yet that small, the Spec is around 4mm x 4mm (not including the battery or antenna) and will open the door for many dense sensor array experiments. Similar work is also proceeding at other institutions (e.g. The National Microelectronic Research Center in Cork, Ireland [12]); the research community is congealing around the goal of producing millimeter-sized multimodal wireless sensor nodes. Parasitic Mobility is intended as a means to add mobility to systems built to meet the specifications of these projects with regards to size, power, and node complexity; as the nodes grow smaller, parasitic mobility becomes increasingly feasible and desirable. As the power source remains a problem, current research in energy scavenging [13] and adaptive sensing [14] is very relevant to this initiative. Adaptive sensing is the technique by which sensing capabilities (active sensors, sampling rate, power consumption, bit-depth, transmission, processing) are increased and decreased according to the sensor data itself, never decreasing below a level capable enough to determine when more sensing power is necessary. Such approaches are currently being implemented using the Stack Sensor Platform [15] at the MIT Media Lab. The Networked InfoMechanical Systems research area at the Center for Embedded Networked Sensing at UCLA conducts research and builds systems to investigate adaptive sensing [14] and mobility for distributed sensor networks [16].

And finally, while not distributed sensor networks, there are several mobile sensor devices built by attaching large sensor packages to floating platforms that drift about in ambient flows while collecting data. Some examples include Sonobuoys [17] that acoustically hunt for submarines, drifting instrumentation packages to monitor ocean temperature [18], and balloon-borne modules for surveillance and proposed planetary exploration [19].

2   Examples of Parasitic Mobility

2.1   Parasitic Mobility in Nature

The natural world provides us with many examples of parasitic mobility, including organisms that rely entirely on larger organisms to carry them to habitable locations. Parasitic relationships of this sort are called phoretic relationships from the word phoresis, which literally means transmission [20]. In the context of this paper, these examples are separated into three categories: active parasitic mobility consisting of organisms that attach and detach at will from hosts with their own actuation, passive parasitic mobility consisting of passive nodes that are picked up and dropped off, knowingly or unknowingly, by hosts, and value-added parasitic mobility which consists of either passive or active parasitic organisms that provide symbiotic value to the host in exchange for transportation.

Active Parasitic Mobility. The first such example that comes to mind when discussing parasites in nature is the tick. The tick actively attaches to hosts by falling from trees or by crawling directly onto the host. It remains attached by using an actuated gripping mechanism which it can release whenever it decides to seek food elsewhere. Although the tick is transported to new locations by the host, its primary reason for attachment is to use the host as a source of food. It is therefore not normally considered a phoretic organism. It is still relevant to the topic as the main example of an active attachment mechanism.

Several species of nematodes, a.k.a. round worms, exhibit phoretic behaviors. The Pelodera Coarctata is a nematode that is commonly found living in cow dung. When the conditions in the dung deteriorate and become inhospitable for the nematode, it attaches itself to a dung beetle which will carry it to a new fresh dung pat. [21] Another such nematode is the Onchocerca Volvulus which is infamous as the cause of "River Blindness." This worm attaches itself to Blackflies that in turn bite humans allowing the worm to travel through the skin and infect the host human. These Blackflies themselves are also an example of parasitic mobility. Their larvae require an aquatic stage for growth, so they often attach themselves to freshwater crabs to bring them into the water and protect them. [21]

Marine life is ripe with examples of active parasitic mobility. One example is that of the Remora or Suckerfish. These fish have developed a sucker-like organ that they use to attach to larger creatures such as sharks or manta rays. By attaching to these larger, faster animals the remora covers area faster giving it more access to food. [22]

Passive Parasitic Mobility. Plants often employ parasitic mobility as a means of distributing seeds. A common example of this is the dandelion. The dandelion seeds have a tiny parachute that carries the seed with the wind. This allows the seeds to travel some distance in hopes of landing in an area that provides the requirements of growth. It is completely passive and at the whim of the wind. It is not expected that all the seeds will land in arable areas. This is overcome by the sheer quantity of seeds released into the air. This is more opportunistic than parasitic, but still falls within the conceptual boundaries of this research.

Other plants, with behaviors more aptly described as parasitic, distribute their seeds in bur casings. These prickly cases stick to animals that brush up against them or step on them. They are shaken lose or fall off as a result of shedding, usually at a new location.

Value-Added Parasitic Mobility. Fruit-bearing trees distribute their seeds in a value-added method. Animals gather the fruits as a food source and in turn spread the discarded seed-containing cores. This attraction and provision acts as an attachment mechanism for the seeds. The detachment mechanism is the inedibility of the seeds within the fruit, in other words, when the added value has been used up.

Flowers use their scented petals to attract bees and other insects. The flowers also provide nectar. The bees use the nectar to make honey and carry the pollen from flower to flower. This is an extremely well evolved symbiotic system that has very little wasted energy or resources. [23]

The existence of many such well-evolved systems in nature illustrates the validity of this type of mobility, and justifies investigating further how to use this concept in our research.

2.2   Parasitic Mobility in Society

In human society, many of the systems surrounding us exhibit emergent behaviors that exemplify parasitic mobility. It is important to examine these systems, not only as conceptual examples, but also because it may be possible to embed sensor network technology directly into these existing systems and take advantage of their mobility.

Basic examples, such as people being pulled along by a bus on skateboards, exist throughout society. It is often beneficial to attach to something that can travel in ways that a person cannot. This example further illustrates the economies of parasitic mobility; the people are getting a free ride.

A simple example of parasitic mobility is when a lost object, such as a cellular phone, is returned to its owner. This method of actuation is a combination of the device identifying its destination and a desire for the host to bring it there. Keeping this in mind, it may be possible to design devices that could identify some sort of reward for bringing them to a point of interest to the device. Another example of this behavior is that of a consumer survey (a sensor of sorts) that is redeemable as a coupon when returned.

There are many everyday objects that are only useful for brief intervals. One example of this is a writing utensil. A pen is needed to record information when it is presented or invented; afterwards the pen sits dormant awaiting the next burst of usefulness. During this period where the pen is not deemed useful, it is free to be relocated. It is often relocated by a host requiring its use in another location. As a result, pens generally cover large areas over time, and due to their unlikelihood of being returned, people usually have redundant supplies of pens. Equipping pens with a pervasive computing device is a good way to gain coverage of an environment, particularly an office or academic institutional building.

3   Software Simulation

In order to better examine the concept of parasitic mobility, extensive software simulation was performed. Through the process of designing the software simulator, the proposed systems were examined from the ground up, looking at all the factors that influence a potential sensor network of this type. This was a critical first step into research of this topic. Upon its completion, the simulator was an invaluable asset for testing and examining ideas and algorithms, generation of data identifying expected behaviors, further validating of the overall concept, and providing insights directly used in the design of the hardware system described in Section 4.

3.1   Design Overview

The design of the software simulator can be broken down into three areas: Environmental Simulation, Host Behavior, and Paramor Behavior. "Paramor" is the name given to a parasitically mobile node and is an apt anagram for PARAsitic

MObility Research. On top of these areas, the simulator contains all the necessary hooks for interactively changing behaviors and trying out new algorithms, detailed logging of activity data, and unattended running of multiple simulations with a desired timescale.

The simulator is grid based, and has been tested with maps as large as one million cells. The hosts and paramors participating in the simulation move by transitioning from cell to cell.

Environment Setup. The first step in setting up a simulation is to layout the environment using the Parasitic Mobility Simulator Map Editor. This is the interactive graphical application shown below in Figure 1. The user interface for this tool consists of a window displaying a scrollable, tile-based map, and a control panel for editing the parameters of the selected tile.

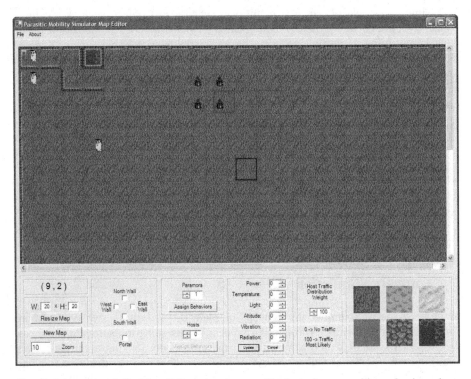

Fig. 1. Screenshot of the Map Editor showing a grid where four parasitic nodes have been deployed, a few hosts have been added, and some walls are being drawn in

Each cell can be assigned levels of environmental properties such as temperature, light, radiation, and the presence and strength of a power source. Basic geographic information can be added in the form of walls and portals.

Each cell in the map can be given a value for the likelihood that a mobile host will pass through it. An example of this would be for an animal-based simulation where locations featuring water and food will have more host traffic than locations without such attractions.

The final action that can be performed in the map editor is populating the map with hosts and choosing deployment locations for the parasitically mobile nodes.

Host Behavior Simulation. In order to accurately simulate parasitic nodes, credible hosts must be designed. It is also necessary to be able to adjust the hosts to simulate different types of real world entities.

A host will essentially stand at a location, list all the possibilities for a new location to travel towards, and randomly select one, with the randomness weighted by the environmental and behavior parameters. The available behavioral parameters in the simulator are stay weight (likelihood that the host will stay in place), stay duration (once a host has decided to stay put this is how long it will stay before reevaluating the situation), covered/uncovered weights (the desire the host has with regards to sticking to places it has already been or exploring new places), portal weight/duration (the likelihood that a host will decide to leave the immediate area and travel through a portal and how long before the host will return), and the speed at which the host travels.

By setting these parameters, hosts can be created that have high levels of randomness or hosts can be created that have no randomness and follow a specific pattern. This implementation allows the simulation of most environments populated with mobile hosts, such as cars, people, and animals. Further enhancements to the host simulation with enable more specifics about the hosts to be simulated, such as the hosts susceptibility to have a parasitic node attach to it.

Parasitic Node Behavior Simulation. The basics behind a parasitically mobile node's behavior are a set of objectives for the node. When a node is idle and a host body comes in range of it, the node attaches to the host. While attached to the host, the node uses the information it can gain from the environment and host's activities to determine if detaching will help it reach its objectives. The objective and behavior of each node can be described by the following parameters: power rate (the rate at which the node uses power), attachment power (additional power needed to attach and detach from a host), power threshold (the level of power reserves below which the node should seek out power as its main objective), battery life (the power capacity of the node), X/Y Goals (a list of 0 or more specific geographic locations that the node should try to reach), goal time (the amount of time the node should spend at a goal location before moving on), sensor thresholds (e.g. light threshold; the level at which the node considers an environmental condition interesting and part of its objectives), coverage (whether or not the node should try to cover as much area as possible), and hops per locale (number of discarded hosts the node is allowed per location, explained more below).

In general, if the node has a set destination, it will try to reach it. If it comes across an area of sensor interest, it will detach, stay for the sensor duration, and then try to continue towards its destination.

If a node is on a path to a destination or trying to go to where is has not been, it needs to hop off when it is on a host that is taking it farther away from its destination, or back into a covered area. This is a matter of calculating the distance to the destination at two points on the trajectory and testing its change or otherwise estimating the host's direction and comparing it to the node's stored coverage map. It is important to allow the node to travel a distance sufficient to sense the host's direction before hopping off. The "hops per locale" parameter is used to prevent situations with nodes being stuck in a spot surrounded by directions where it does not want to go. In a situation like this, the node would continually hop on and immediately hop off every host thinking that the host would take it in an undesirable direction. Using this parameter, the node will only do this a limited number of times until it will choose to stay on any host just to get to a new location and try again.

3.2   Simulation Results

With appropriate parameters, this package can simulate many environments and help test out algorithms and ascertain the requirements for a particular parasitically mobile sensor network. It can also be used to generate numerical data for predicting behavior, such as how long it will take a node to reach a location according to the properties of hosts in the environment, the power usage compared to standard robotic devices, and how many nodes should be deployed to cover an area in a particular amount of time. This section presents some of these results, collected from thousands of hours of simulation time.

Velocity Data. The data shown in Figure 3 results from simulating an environment with a fixed size and host population. The speed of the hosts is also a constant one grid hop per unit of time. The simulation parameters can be mapped to any units provided everything is scaled appropriately. In the next section, this data is used to calculate real-world energy usage values, hence the simulator distance units are related to meters and the timing units are related to seconds. This would mean the hosts travel with a speed of 1 m/s, similar to the walking pace of a human.

The paramor behavior chosen for this test is simply to go to a particular location at a known distance away. The algorithm for attachment and detachment is to attach to every host that comes by, and then decide whether it is bringing the node closer to or farther away from the destination. For a real device to be able to ascertain this information, it must ride the host for long enough to get a fix on the motion or the new location. Based on the GPS and Bluetooth localization systems described in the next chapter, this was set in the simulator as 1/2 of a time unit before the node knows the new location with a resolution of 1/2 of a distance unit.

This simulation was executed 25 times for each distance and the results were averaged. The linearity of this graph is due to the host's random behavior with respect to the node's destination. In other words, at each point (a point being at the end of the node's minimum cycle required to ascertain the direction that the host is traveling) the host is just as likely to turn away from the node's destination as it is to continue moving towards it. Therefore, the average time it takes for a host to take you from one location to the next location that is closer to the destination is the same regardless of how you arrived at the current location. Since the host reassesses its path at each point, the average time it takes a node to find a host going one step closer to the destination and to ride it to the next point, is constant over the entire travel. Hence, the average time it takes to go N number of steps should be N times the average time it takes to go one step, leading to a linear relationship.

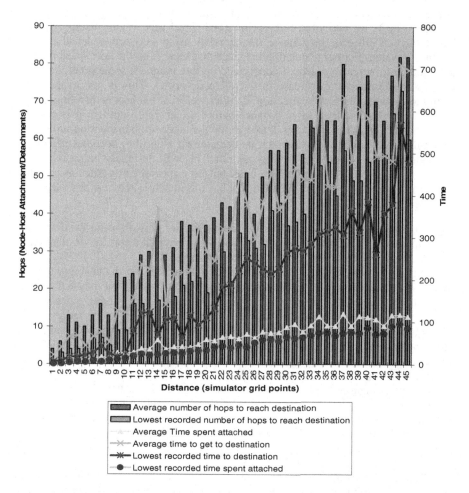

Fig. 3. Graph showing distance versus time data collected and averaged from repeated simulation passes

Besides the total time it took to reach a destination, the graph also shows the time spent attached to a host, in other words, the time spent non-idle and actually traveling. This line is quite smooth; especially in comparison to the total time including time spent idly waiting for a host to pick it up. This smoothness shows that the algorithm is working properly as most of the time is spent waiting for a beneficial host, which varies according to the random flows of the hosts. This randomness is eliminated by the paramor's decision process. The reason that the attached time and distance don't exactly scale with the host velocity is because the nodes still need to attach to the host to ascertain its direction, and even hosts that head towards the destination are not guaranteed to go exactly straight, especially considering the coarse location system of the node.

Many other scenarios have been simulated using this software package. The data collected has illustrated that the total time to destination scales fairly linearly if you change basic environmental properties such as number of hosts. Decreasing the density of hosts increases the slope of the total travel time versus distance traveled, but it there is little or no change in the relationship between attached time and distance traveled. Further simulation indicates that increasing the host speed relates in a proportional increase in overall node speed up to a point. At some point, increasing the host speed causes a decrease in overall node speed. This is due to the node's ability to calculate the host's direction. In other words, if the host is traveling quickly, the node will deviate by a large distance before it can figure out that it is going off track and detach. This identifies that a particular node implementation will have a maximum host velocity above which its detachment algorithm becomes useless and the node's behavior becomes mostly random. This will definitely be an issue when designing real mobile systems where in all but very special cases (such as scheduled vehicular systems like trains) the node will have to attach to the host and ride to find out where it is going.

Coverage Data. Of particular interest to mobile sensor networks and the distribution of ubiquitous devices, is the ability to release nodes without a specific destination and have them attempt to scan or deploy over the entire area.

The first component of the algorithm is to equip the nodes with the ability to record where they have been. When a host takes them back to a location they have already covered, they detach. This proved to be inadequate as the nodes quickly found themselves surrounded by places they had already covered up to the radius of their ability to sense where the host was taking them. Depending on the processing ability of the node, it may be possible to analyze the entire map of coverage and determine general desired directions even if it the node first must travel through an already covered area.

After experimenting with several behaviors, it appears that the key to coverage is to keep moving, even if you might be heading in a direction that has an area in the immediate vicinity that the node has already visited. The chosen algorithm for this simulation is to limit discarded hosts (hosts that are heading to a location already visited) to one per location. In other words, when a host comes by an idle node, the node will attach, and decide if the host will take it to an unvisited location. If not, the node detaches, and waits for the next host. This time it will take the new host without question and ride it until it finds an uncovered location, or at least arrives at a location that has nearby unvisited locations so it can detach and encounter a high likelihood of a host coming by that will go in that direction. It is also important not to attach to a host that already has a paramor attached to it. If two nodes are on the same path, both looking to cover the environment, they will most likely remain together by making the same decisions. Simple broadcast commands sent from individual nodes can aid with the dispersal of mobile sensor nodes. These commands can tell other nodes which areas have been covered and areas of high host traffic.

Energy Usage Calculations and Comparison. By examining the hops, attached/ traveling times, and wait times from the simulator, we can calculate predicted values for the energy consumption rates of a parasitically mobile sensor node. In this section, we introduce the two kinds of nodes designed as the hardware components of this research and compare their predicted power usage statistics to that of two standard mobile robotic sensor devices.

The first device designed for this experiment is a 1 cubic inch node mimicking the passive attachment mechanism of a bur with the ability to actively detach by shaking itself loose. This device is further detailed in Section 4.

Since the attachment is passive and it sticks to every nearby host (bur-like attachment), it requires no additional power, actuation, or sensing during the host discovery and attachment process. When it is idle and waiting for a host, it can remain in a low-power mode and wake up on motion caused by being picked up by a host. The low power mode runs using a 32 KHz clock and keeps alive a comparator on accelerometer data. This low power mode draws around 35 uA. Additionally, the node will wake up once per second and check for a wireless message. This check lasts around 10 ms and uses 16 mA for that duration. However, the power for the communication system will not be included in these calculations because, at this point, we are just looking at the power needed for mobility to compare to standard techniques of moving sensors.

While attached, the semi-passive node can enter a different low-power mode and periodically wake up to check its location, progress, and sense the new surroundings. Assuming that the location system has a resolution of one meter, in the simulation of the environment with the hosts that move at 1m/s, the device will have to wake up and sense once per second of attached time. Depending on the type of location system and sensors, the node could use up to 60 mA for up to 60 ms for gathering data about the location and conditions surrounding it. Two location systems are described in Chapter 4; both systems require less power than this estimate.

And finally, when the node decides that it is time to detach, it needs to activate a detachment mechanism, which in the case of these sticky nodes is a pager motor with a draw of 15mA activated for 500ms to shake loose.

In addition to the semi-passive nodes, an active node was design that adds an actuated method for attachment as well as detachment.

The active node power calculations are fairly similar to those of the semi-passive node. The active node requires 30 seconds, drawing 10mA to wind its spring and execute an attachment or detachment. This node hops at a height of around 6 cm and weighs around 40 grams.

When the active node is not attached it requires more power than the semi-passive node because it needs to identify and locate a potential host to attach to. This requires 30mA of constant power draw to run an IR proximity detection circuit with a fairly high sampling rate. This sampling rate can be reduced, but worst-case ratings are being used for these calculations. Other techniques (e.g. active and passive acoustic sensing, simple vision with a mini-camera) can be used as well, requiring different amounts of power, but with clever adaptive sensor processing [Ari], we assume that 30mA is still in the ballpark.

The first robot chosen for power comparison with parasitic mobility is NASA's Urban Reconnaissance Robot. [24] This robot is equipped with an enormous array of sensors, actuators, and processing power. It is designed to navigate through very tricky environments. Parasitically mobile nodes gain this ability from the hosts they attach to, and these hosts have evolved to navigate their environment in the best way possible. The NASA robot is an ideal comparison as it is a prime example of the power needed to build a device that navigates in a way that parasitically mobile nodes potentially get for free.

This robot draws 145 Watts while moving, sensing, and navigating on flat ground at a rate of 80cm/second. It can also climb stairs using 245 Watts of power. For this comparison, we will assume it is on flat ground. Using this energy consumption rate and speed of travel we can create power versus distance data and compare it to that of the parasitic node.

On the other end of the spectrum from the NASA robot is University of Southern California's RoboMOTE [25]. It is a small wheeled robot measuring less than 6 cubic centimeters in volume. While it does not have the navigation or actuation abilities of the NASA robot, it makes up for it in size, cost, and power consumption. The RoboMOTE exhibits many of the desirable attributes of mobile sensor networks, such as small cheap nodes that can work together. When all the features required for navigation are active, the RoboMOTE uses 1.5 Watts and can travel at a speed of 0.27 km/h.

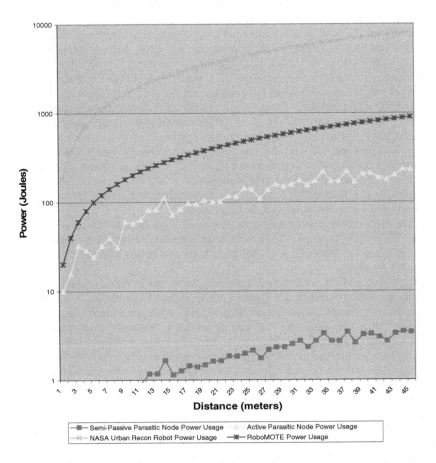

Fig. 4. Energy consumed versus Distance traveled of parasitic and non-parasitic mobile devices. This graph clearly shows the energy usage of parasitically mobile nodes to be an order of magnitude less than that of even the most energy efficient standardly actuated robots

Parasitic Mobility is an attempt to bring the navigational power of the NASA robot into a device the size and cost of the RoboMOTE. That is why these two projects were chosen as points of comparison for the power consumption of these new types of networks. Figure 4, shown above plots the calculated power consumption of the RoboMOTE and the NASA robot along with values observed from the software simulator based on the power rates from the prototype hardware further detailed in Chapter 4. The graph (Figure 4) shows that the power usage of the active node is an order of magnitude less than the RoboMOTE, an energy-efficient robot that uses standard actuation. The power usage of the semi-passive node is an additional order of magnitude less.

Maze Environment. The simulator was also used to simulate many real-world situations and sensor network deployments. Once such set of simulations involved designing a maze-like structure and having the hosts follow particular routes similar to people working in an office environment or vehicles obeying traffic regulations.

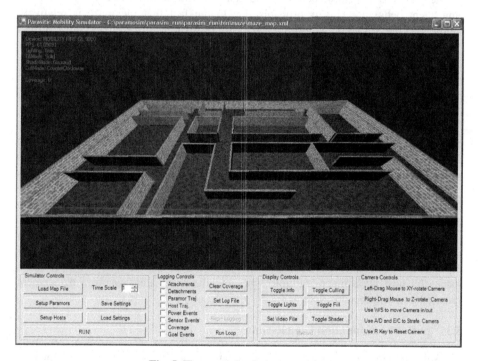

Fig. 5. The maze simulation executing

Three different decision algorithms were tested for the parasitic node behavior: an omniscient algorithm where the node knows the whole map and can pick the best route to get to its destination, a distance algorithm where the node calculates improvements in distance while attached to a host, and a right-hand rule algorithm, a common map solving strategy, where the node always wants to go right at every intersection.

Table 1. Results of maze simulation comparing maze solving algorithms

	Node Behavior 1 (distance algorithm)	Node Behavior 2 (right-hand rule)	Node Behavior 3 (path omniscient)
Total Time	230	600	210
Attached Time	100	300	80
Number of Hops	22	30	12

As expected, the omniscient behavior performed the best, because these nodes will always take the same path, and the number of decision points they will pass is fixed, making their trajectory a probabilistic function of the number of decision points and possible directions that a host can turn at each of these points. It is further helped by the fact that hosts in the test do not turn around, cutting down the number of wrongful directions.

The distance algorithm behavior did not perform significantly worse than the omniscient behavior. This is probably due to the fact that the maze is relatively simple, and the distancing algorithm can easily resolve the situation and more-or-less find the same path as the omniscient node.

Of the three behaviors, the right-hand-rule is the only one that had the potential to get far off track. By the nature of the pattern resulting from this type of behavior, it can take a long time to reach the destination, but it is guaranteed and the coverage of the area is procedural and predictable, which may be desirable for some applications.

In the maze environment, the host velocity and other parameters of the host's behavior have less bearing on the time it takes for the node to reach a destination than the decision algorithms of the node and information that the node has which can help identify the best hosts to ride. In many real-world situations, it may be possible to know many details about the paths that the hosts will take and this information can be fed into the nodes at release, or communicated from node to node as the details are discovered.

The maze simulation is a first attempt to model a particular environment from a geographic and host-flow perspective. The software simulator will be further developed to add more environmental-specific parameters such as probability of a successful host attachment, multiple types of hosts, and areas where a detachment causes the node to become lost.

3.3   Software Simulation Conclusion

The software simulator has proven an invaluable tool with which to experiment with ideas and specific algorithms for implementing parasitic mobility. The experiences with the software simulation and the presence of these types of systems in nature have presented a favorable proof of concept for this type of mobility. The following chapter describes the design and implementation of an actual parasitically mobile sensor network, which takes into account the quantitative and qualitative results from the software simulator.

4   Hardware System

4.1   Electronics Design

A hardware system comprised of electronic nodes equipped with all the necessary elements to implement the specific ideas introduced through the software simulation was designed and built. The nodes required processing, communication, data storage, a location system, a suite of sensors, and an onboard rechargeable power source. The electronics should also facilitate experimentation with different types of attachment and detachment mechanisms.

The electronics were designed as small as could be easily built by hand using easy to obtain components. The design, shown below in Figure 6, is based on stackable layers, each roughly 1 square inch in size. When four layers are stacked, they are less than 1 inch high. More details on the mechanical specifications of the node hardware are given following the breakdown of the individual layers.

Fig. 6. Node hardware shown with 3 of the 4 available layers in place

Power Module. The power module is equipped with a small 3.5 gram Lithium Polymer battery, which can provide 145 mAh at a voltage of around 3.7 V and can discharge at a rate of up to 1 amp. The power module circuit board contains a charge controller to control recharging the battery from any available power source, a hot-swap switch to power the circuit from an external power source (if available) while charging, a gas gauge chip to tell the processor the expected time left before needing a recharge, and an efficient voltage regulator with a battery supervisor circuit.

Processing and Communication Module. The processing module is equipped with a Silicon Labs microcontroller that can run up to 25 MHz using its internal oscillator or go into a low power mode and run off an external 32 kHz crystal. The communication is enabled with a Bluetooth module running an embedded Bluetooth stack that supports Scatternet formations for communication with other nodes. Lastly, this layer contains a 16Mb flash memory for storage of sensor data and map information.

Sensor and Control Module. The sensor layer is equipped with a 2-axis, 2G accelerometer, a microphone, an active infrared proximity sensor, a temperature sensor, a light sensor, an RGB LED, a pager motor to shake off of hosts, and a motor controller for the active attachment mechanism.

GPS Layer. The final layer was a GPS layer designed around a recent embedded GPS chipset, the FSOncore from Motorola. Although this design was tested with sample chips and worked well, even indoors with the assisted mode, the quantity of chips necessary to perform the application test was not yet available. An alternate location system was designed using the Bluetooth radios. This system consisted of deploying enough Bluetooth beacons to cover the test area. By simply checking which beacons were in range, the nodes could tell their position with a resolution depending on how close together the beacons were placed. The maximum resolution of this system was shown to be roughly 3-5 meters with the beacons placed around 5 meters apart. For the actual deployment the beacons were placed farther apart to simplify the environment. This worked well as a temporary solution until the GPS chips could be delivered.

The electronics were then mounted onto one of several different mechanical structures. The first was a hopping mechanism that created an active node which can hop on and off of a nearby host, and attach with a hook. [26]

Fig. 7. Active Node, nicknamed the ParaHop and its hopping actuator

The next two mechanical structures were created by encasing the electronics in a plastic sphere. To make a semi-active or passive node out of this structure, the sphere is then covered with sticky silicone that creates a bur-like device that sticks to anything that comes in contact with it. The semi-passive version can shake itself off once stuck whereas the passive version waits for the bond to wear out.

The sphere can be further enhanced by adding a sticker or other method of instruction for a host to pick it up. This symbolizes the value-added or attraction method of parasitic mobility as described in Section 2. Although they conferred no direct benefit to their hosts, people were amused and intrigued enough to pick up these artifacts.

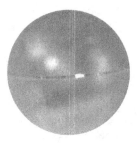

Fig. 8. Electronics encased in 1 inch diameter plastic sphere

4.2   Test Run

Ten such value-added nodes were released into a high traffic hallway of the MIT Media Lab building. All ten were spherical nodes that were labeled with instructions

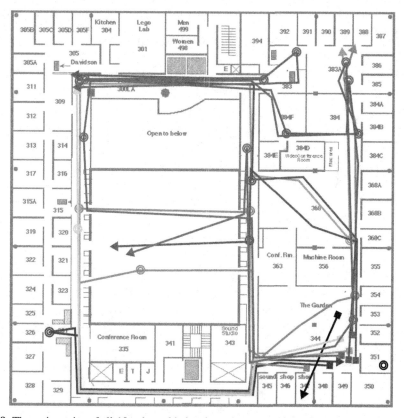

Fig. 9. The trajectories of all 10 value-added style nodes across the test area (third floor of The Media Lab). The squares indicate the deployment point, circles indicate a detachment and reattachment, and triangles indicate their final location. This illustrates that the nodes covered all the public spaces in the test area, indicating that parasitic mobility (with the necessary node redundancy) can be used to deploy nodes to many locations and cover wide regions

to pick them up and to put them down if they shook. The LED also blinked various colors whether it wanted to be picked up, was carried and mobile, or preferred to be stationary. Using these simple methods for attachment and detachment, the nodes were lifted up, carried, and placed down many times throughout the test allowing the basic concept of parasitic mobility to be examined.

The ten nodes were given specific goals to try and achieve. Six of the nodes were programmed to reach different geographic destinations. The remaining four nodes were given specific environmental conditions to look for. Although all ten nodes collected sensor data throughout their tasks, these nodes were programmed with conditions that will cause them to detach upon detecting the desired phenomena. When this happens, the node will try and stay at this location for a pre-determined amount of time or until the sensor condition disappears. If the node is picked up from this state or from a state where it has reached its geographic goal, it will immediately attempt to detach until its allotted time for the goal or sensor point of interest has elapsed.

As an example, we analyze the trajectory (Figure 10) of Node #7 in more depth. Node 7 found a location in the top left corner that it considered interesting, which in this case contained a bright light source, as the node was instructed to seek bright illumination. The data recovered from the node showed that this was indeed the case,

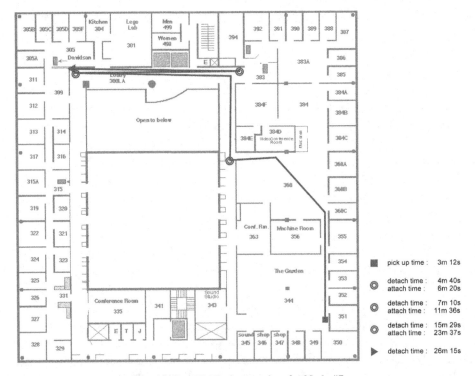

Fig. 10. Specific Trajectory data for Node #7

but that the lighting condition eventually dipped and became uninteresting. Especially how the node winds up being oriented becomes important, since they are spherical, for the light sensor. According to the data from the node, it was picked up but then noted a lighting condition that was below the threshold for it to consider it interesting. In fact, it was far below the level that it had seen before it was picked up. This indicated that the person who picked it up must have covered the light sensor. The node therefore thought that the location was undesirable and did not ask to be put back down. When it returned the second time, it was better oriented and noticed the lighting condition, detached, and remained there for the rest of the test. This took only 26 minutes to happen, meaning that the node was able to fend off hosts picking it up for the remaining hour and a half of high traffic time. The data collected shows 4 attempted pick ups, all successfully ending in the node being placed back in the same location.

Node #7 found a light source and remained there for 4 attempted attachments. This can be seen by looking at the graphs in Figures 11, 12, and 13. The light sensor shows two areas where the light value dropped very low, indicating a bright area. These two areas roughly match the times that the node was in zone 16. During the second stay in zone 16, there were several level shifts in the accelerometer data. These indicate a change in orientation, and the activity in between these levels is due to the node being picked up and vibrating to be put back down because the node liked where it was.

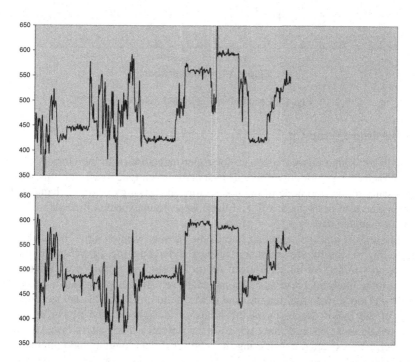

Fig. 11. Accelerometer (X-Axis top, Y-Axis Bottom) data collected from Node #7

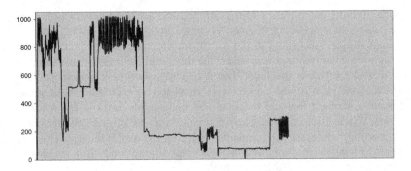

Fig. 12. Light Sensor data collected from Node #7

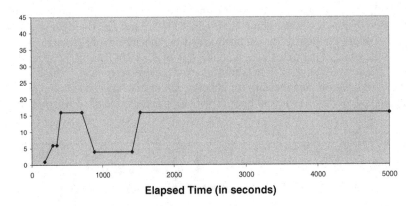

Elapsed Time (in seconds)

Fig. 13. Location data collected from Node #7

4.3   Hardware Wrap-Up

The hardware design proved adequate for experimentation with the concept of value-added/attraction parasitic mobility. The specific prototype used for this test was mechanically robust and none of the nodes stopped working due to mechanical stress. The firmware also performed well and there were no unexpected firmware crashes or missed or mangled data.

One issue was that the sampling rate of the sensors was too slow. It was kept low while testing to simplify development, testing, and debugging, as well as to allow the flash memory to last for the entire test. As the development progresses, the sampling rate will most likely increase and become adaptive. The sampling rate at the time of this test was too slow to pull features out of the audio other than the net amplitude.

One of the major successes of the hardware design was the power supply and power management systems that each node incorporates. The battery lasted as long, if not longer, than expected considering the additional data logging and communication requirements of running such a test. Further development on a clever wakeup system and adaptive sensing [15] can improve this considerably.

The size of the nodes is currently too big to attach to a human or an animal without its knowing. The current size is more than adequate, however, for applications where the hosts are vehicles. This study explored simple proof-of-concept active attachment mechanisms; actual deployed systems would require more work on the host detection, self-righting enclosures, and the attachment and launching mechanism.

The location system, while adequate for this test, was not accurate enough for fine-grained indoor tracking. It would also need to refresh faster and more consistently. Many indoor location systems are under active development [27], hence this situation is rapidly evolving.

5   Conclusion

Through the work described in this paper, a new field of research has emerged. This field sits at the crossroads of distributed sensor networks, mobile systems, pervasive computing, and power harvesting.

Through simulation and initial tests, we have illustrated that it is possible to develop a parasitically mobile sensor network. Our results indicate that they can, in some ways, perform as well as standard robotic mobile sensor networks, but with huge potential savings with regards to power consumption, node complexity, and general robustness due to their relative simplicity. This indicates that it's possible to use parasitic mobility to distribute components of many types of pervasive computing systems throughout a physical space.

More detail is available, including all the collected data, higher resolution images, source code, schematics, and videos in the associated graduate thesis [26] and on the Parasitic Mobility website at http://www.media.mit.edu/resenv/paramor.

5.1   Possible Applications of Parasitic Mobility

In certain environments, parasitic mobility can be used as a replacement for standard mobility for dense, distributed sensor systems. Systems of this sort include applications to sense toxic or hostile areas requiring sensor deployment at a safe distance, dynamically reconfigurable systems such as weather monitoring sensors that need to follow the relative phenomena, and systems where the accuracy of node deployment is minimal, such as for nodes being released in water or from a vehicle.

Going further, parasitic mobility can possibly lead to applications that can only be done (or are better done) with parasitic mobility than standard mobility. Any example where the host behavior is part of what is desired to be monitored would fit this category. In these systems, parasitically mobile nodes would attach to their subjects and would always be at the points of interest.

One application that would be interesting to explore is the idea of a rating system based on breadcrumb trails. Essentially, the parasitic nodes would attach to hosts and pool up in spots of high traffic. These points can propagate through the system and provide information on the popularity of certain pathways and locations. Another similar application would be as a test bed for the spread of entities such as viruses. With a system like this you get data from the viewpoint of the contagion.

Parasitic Mobility can also be used to provide site-specific pervasive technologies. An example would be a system for urban safety where the devices know of areas where crime is abundant and wait at the edges of these locations. When someone enters this area they attach and ride through the dangerous area. The devices can sense an attack to its host and can call for help. If nothing happens and the host leaves the area, the device will detach and wait for the next host.

5.2   Future Work

Our hardware can be further perfected, e.g., a first step would be to increase the performance of the system by increasing the sample rate of the sensors, the onboard processing power, and the resolution and refresh rate of the location system. By increasing the node's capabilities, it will be possible to give the nodes more information about the environment such as onboard databases of map information.

Hooking this research up with actual power harvesting could be a natural fit, allowing self-maintaining, perpetual systems to be developed. These systems can harvest the power from their environment (taking inspiration from the tick, which harvests chemical energy from its host) or from forces acted upon the nodes, such as when they are in the attached state. Smarter power management can be developed, as well as power adaptive sensing, to improve battery conservation.

Also, adding more distributed, node-node communication to the test system would open up some new venues for research. By collaboration, the sensor nodes could optimize their mobility and detachment and attachment algorithms, or maximize network coverage. Such communication could allow nodes to tell other nodes about host-rich locations and other information about the environment.

More experimentation with new types of attachment and detachment mechanisms could lead to new applications of parasitic mobility, e.g. attaching to vehicles. Also, embedding sensor nodes into everyday objects that migrate through a population is an interesting prospect for practical value-added symbiotic mobility. These directions can benefit from smaller nodes. Adding sensors (e.g. camera, motion sensor, and magnetic sensor) can also allow detection and attachment to a larger variety of hosts, as well as a wider range of sensing applications.

The biological inspirations for this research are all from natural systems that have developed over millions of years in synchronicity with their environment and are very niche-dependent. Further conceptual analysis is required to investigate how to map parasitic mobility to particular niches. This analysis would include looking at population density and traffic patterns of various hosts in real world environments. There would also need to be analysis of how effective the attachment mechanisms are with respect to certain hosts and environments. Such investigations would identify where and when parasitic mobility would be advantageous and identify many new applications.

Acknowledgements

This research was made possible thanks to the support of Motorola, Things That Think Consortium, and other sponsors of the MIT Media Lab. The authors would like to acknowledge and thank William Kaiser of UCLA and David Reed of the MIT Media Lab for their helpful advice and involvement, Talia Dorsey for help with node fabrication, and all the "hosts" who happened to be in the Media Lab building during the test deployments.

References

1. Meguerdichian, S., S. Slijepcevic, V. Karayan, and M. Potkonjak. Localized algorithms in wireless ad-hoc networks: location discovery and sensor exposure. In MOBIHOC 2001. Proceedings of the 2001 ACM International Symposium on Mobile Ad Hoc Networking and Computing. 2001. Long Beach, CA, USA: ACM. p. 106.
2. Estrin, Deborah and Cerpa, Alberto. ASCENT: Adaptive Self-Configuring sEnsor Networks Topologies. In IEEE Transactions on Mobilke Comuting Secial Issue on Mission-Oriented Sensor Networks, Vol. 3, No. 3, July-September 2004.
3. Grabowski, R., L. E. Navarro-Serment, and P. K. Khosla. Small is beautiful: an army of small robots. Scientific American (International Edition), 2003. 289(5): p. 42.
4. Howard, A., M. J. Mataric, and G. S. Sukhatme. An incremental self-deployment algorithm for mobile sensor networks. Autonomous Robots, 2002. 13(2): p. 113.
5. LaMarca, A., W. Brunette, D. Koizumi, M. Lease, S. B. Sigurdsson, K. Sikorski, D. Fox, and G. Borriello. Making sensor networks practical with robots. In Pervasive Computing. First International Conference, Pervasive 2002. Proceedings (Lecture Notes in Computer Science Vol.2414). 2002. Zurich, Switzerland: Springer-Verlag. p. 152.
6. Sinha, A. and A. Chandrakasan. Dynamic power management in wireless sensor networks. IEEE Design & Test of Computers, 2001. 18(2): p. 62.
7. Rahimi, M., H. Shah, G. S. Sukhatme, J. Heideman, and D. Estrin. Studying the feasibility of energy harvesting in a mobile sensor network. In 2003 IEEE International Conference on Robotics and Automation (Cat. No.03CH37422). 2003. Taipei, Taiwan: IEEE. p. 19.
8. Chee-Yee, Chong and S. P. Kumar. Sensor networks: evolution, opportunities, and challenges. Proceedings of the IEEE, 2003. 91(8): p. 1247.
9. Kahn, J. M., R. H. Katz, and K. S. Pister. Next century challenges: mobile networking for "Smart Dust". In MobiCom'99. Proceedings of Fifth Annual ACM/IEEE International Conference on Mobile Computing and Networking. 1999. Seattle, WA, USA: ACM. p. 271.
10. Warneke, B., B. Atwood, and K. S. J. Pister. Smart dust mote forerunners. In Technical Digest. MEMS 2001. 14th IEEE International Conference on Micro Electro Mechanical Systems (Cat. No.01CH37090). 2001. Interlaken, Switzerland: IEEE. p. 357.
11. Hill, Jason. Spec takes the next step toward the vision of true smart dust. 2003. http://www.jlhlabs.com/jhill_cs/
12. Brendan O'Flynn, et al, "The development of a Modular Miniaturised Platform for Wireless Sensor Networks," to appear in the Proc. of the Fourth International Conference on Information Processing in Sensor Networks (IPSN 05), Los Angeles, CA, April 25-27, 2005.
13. Paradiso, J.A. and Starner, T., "Energy Scavenging for Mobile and Wireless Electronics," IEEE Pervasive Computing, Vol. 4, No. 1, February 2005, pp. 18-27.
14. Rahimi, Mohammad, Richard Pon, William J. Kaiser, Gaurav S. Sukhatme, Deborah Estrin, and Mani Srivastava. Adaptive Sampling for Environmental Robots. In Proceedings of the 2004 IEEE International Conference on Robotics and Automation. New Orleans, LA. April 2004. pp. 3537-2544.
15. Benbasat, A.Y. and Paradiso, J.A., Design of a Real-Time Adaptive Power Optimal Sensor System. in the Proc. of the 2004 IEEE Sensors Conference, Vienna, Austria, October 24-27, 2004.
16. Pon, R., et al, "Networked Infomechanical Systems: A Mobile Wireless Sensor Network Platform," to appear in the Proc. of the Fourth International Conference on Information Processing in Sensor Networks (IPSN 05), Los Angeles, CA, April 25-27, 2005.

17. Houston, Kenneth M. and Kent R. Engebretson. The Intelligent Sonobuoy System - A Concept for Mapping of Target Fields. In the Proceedings of the Autonomous Vehicles and Mine Counter-Measures Symposium, April 4-7, 1995, Naval Post-Graduate School, Monterey, CA. pp 6-129.
18. Irish, James D., Walter Paul, J. N. Shaumeyer, Carl C. Gaither III, and John M. Borden. The Next-Generation Ocean Observing Buoy in Support of NASA's Earth Science Enterprise. Sea Technology, May 1999. (40): p. 37-43.
19. Kerzhanovich, Viktor V., James A. Cutts, and Jeffery L. Hall. Low-cost balloon missions to mars and venus. In European Space Agency, (Special Publication) ESA SP. 2003. p. 285.
20. Bush, Albert O., Jacqueline C. Fernandez, Gerald W. Esch, and J. Richard Seed. Parasitism: The Diversity and Ecology of Animal Parasites. 2001, Cambridge University Press: Cambridge, UK. p. 391-399.
21. Ibid., p. 160-196.
22. Ibid., p. 306-310.
23. Ibid., p. 6-9.
24. Matthies, L., Y. Xiong, R. Hogg, D. Zhu, A. Rankin, B. Kennedy, M. Hebert, R. Maclachlan, C. Won, T. Frost, G. Sukhatme, M. McHenry, and S. Goldberg. A portable, autonomous, urban reconnaissance robot. Robotics and Autonomous Systems, 2002. 40(2-3): p. 163.
25. Sibley, G. T., M. H. Rahimi, and G. S. Sukhatme. Robomote: a tiny mobile robot platform for large-scale ad-hoc sensor networks. In Proceedings 2002 IEEE International Conference on Robotics and Automation (Cat. No.02CH37292). 2002. Washington, DC, USA: IEEE. p. 1143.
26. Laibowitz, Mathew. Parasitic Mobility for Sensate Media. Thesis, MIT Media Lab. August 2004.
27. Hightower, J. and G. Borriello. Location systems for ubiquitous computing. IEEE Computer, 2001. 34(8): p. 57.

Decision-Theoretic Planning Meets User Requirements: Enhancements and Studies of an Intelligent Shopping Guide

Thorsten Bohnenberger[1], Oliver Jacobs[2], Anthony Jameson[2], and Ilhan Aslan[1,*]

[1] Department of Computer Science,
Saarland University, Saarbrücken, Germany
[2] DFKI, German Research Center for Artificial Intelligence,
Saarbrücken, Germany

Abstract. This paper reports on extensions to a decision-theoretic location-aware shopping guide and on the results of user studies that have accompanied its development. On the basis of the results of an earlier user study in a mock-up of a shopping mall, we implemented an improved version of the shopping guide. A new user study with the improved system in a real shopping mall confirms in a much more realistic setting the generally positive user attitudes found in the earlier study. The new study also sheds further light on the usability issues raised by the system, some of which can also arise with other mobile guides and recommenders. One such issue concerns desire of users to be able to understand and second-guess the system's recommendations. This requirement led to the development of an explanation component for the decision-theoretic guide, which was evaluated in a smaller follow-up study in the shopping mall.

Keywords: Mobile commerce, navigation support, decision-theoretic planning, user studies, recommender systems, explanation.

1   Introduction

A natural and popular application domain for pervasive computing is assistance for shoppers who are shopping in physical environments such as grocery stores, shopping centers, or larger areas such as entire towns.

This paper describes the development of a mobile shopping guide that focuses on one of the many types of assistance that have been explored to date: Given a shopper who wants to find a particular set of products within a limited time, how can the shopper be guided to the possible locations of these products in an order that tends to maximize the likelihood of finding the products while minimizing the time required

---

* This research was supported by the German Science Foundation (DFG) in its Collaborative Research Center on Resource-Adaptive Cognitive Processes, SFB 378, Project EM 5, READY; and by the German Ministry of Education and Research (BMB+F) under grant 524-40001-01 IW C03 (project SPECTER). We thank the six reviewers for their valuable comments.

H.W. Gellersen et al. (Eds.): PERVASIVE 2005, LNCS 3468, pp. 279–296, 2005.

to do so? What makes this problem more than just a navigation problem is the uncertainty that pervades many aspects of it: In particular, there is considerable uncertainty about whether the shopper will find a desired product at a given location and how long she will have to spend looking for it. Despite these uncertainties, the shopper may be under pressure to complete the trip quickly, perhaps even before a fixed deadline.

In the rest of this section, we summarize our earlier work on a decision-theoretic shopping guide that addresses this problem and place it in the larger context of mobile shopping assistants. In the remainder of the paper, we discuss recent significant enhancements to the system and how they have been tested in a real shopping environment.

1.1   A Decision-Theoretic Shopping Guide

Bohnenberger and Jameson [1] introduced the basic idea of a decision-theoretic shopping guide: Given a set of products that a user wants to buy, a set of stores (e.g., within a shopping mall) where she may be able to find them, and estimated times for traveling among the stores, such a system generates a *policy* for guiding the user among the stores: At any given point in time, given knowledge of where the user is and what products she has already found, the system recommends the next store to visit and gives directions for getting to that store. Decision-theoretic planning (cf. Section 2.2) is generally well suited to this recommendation task in that it can take into account not only the costs of visiting particular stores but also the uncertainty about whether the desired product will be found in a given store.

To obtain some initial feedback about the usability and acceptance of this type of guide, we created an initial prototype for a PDA[1] and conducted a study in an artificial mockup of a shopping mall (Bohnenberger et al. [2]): A number of stores were crudely simulated on two floors of a computer science building. Localization was realized with infrared beacons attached to the walls at a number of points, which transmitted identifying signals to the subject's PDA. Each of 20 subjects performed two assigned "shopping" tasks, with the role of the shopkeeper being played in each case by the experimenter, who followed the subject around. Each subject performed one shopping task with the PDA-based guide and the other one with a conventional paper map of the shopping mall that they were allowed to study in advance. Shopping performance with the shopping guide was somewhat better than performance with the paper map, illustrating the basic viability of the method. Even the artificial setting enabled the subjects to suggest a number of improvements to the user interface, which were taken into account in the next version (see Section 2). On a more general level, although the study did not itself create a realistic shopping experience, it did make the functionality clear to the subjects, so that they could offer some speculative comments about their willingness to use a system of this type in a real shopping situation. Their overall attitudes were almost uniformly positive, and they showed appreciation for the system's ability to save them time, cognitive effort, and the frustration of having to replan when the store did not have the product that they had expected to find there. On the negative side,

[1] More precisely: a Compaq iPAQ Pocket PC.

a number of subjects felt that they did not have the "big picture", almost as if they were being led blindfolded through a shopping mall.

On the basis of the user feedback from the study, we developed a version of the shopping guide that included a number of improvements (see Section 2), ranging from minor interface improvements to significant enhancements that address fundamental user requirements. This improved prototype was then tested in a real shopping mall (see Section 3).

1.2   Related Work

Shopping Assistant Prototypes. A large number of systems have been developed since the early 1990s that offer various types of assistance to a shopper. Asthana et al. [3] presented an early portable shopping assistant which, among other functions, helped the shopper to locate particular products within a large store and alerted the shopper to potentially interesting special offers.

ISHOPPER (Fano [4]), like our own guide, assisted the user within a larger geographical area, such as a shopping mall. It alerted a shopper to desired products that were available near his or her current location. This approach is the opposite of the one taken by our guide: Instead of taking the shopper's location as given and recommending products that can be conveniently bought nearby, our guide starts with a list of desired products and guides the user to the locations at which she is most likely to find the products in accordance with an efficient policy.

The more recently developed shopping assistant iGrocer (Shekar et al. [5]) offers a variety of services to a shopper in a grocery store via a mobile phone. In particular, it shows the "quick shopper" the fastest route within the grocery store for picking up the products on the shopping list. This function is similar to that of our shopping guide, except that it does not take into account uncertainty about whether a given product will be found at a given location—a capability that requires the probabilistic reasoning that is characteristic of decision-theoretic planning.

Recently, Cumby et al. [6] have shown how a shopping assistant can predict (and therefore suggest) a shopper's current shopping list on the basis of information about past purchases. Again, this method is complementary to our approach, which presupposes that a shopping list already exists (whether specified entirely by the shopper or with external assistance).

On the whole, existing shopping assistants like these offer functionality that is complementary to that of our decision-theoretic shopping guide. In the long run, it should be possible to integrate various types of functionality offered by different systems into a more comprehensive shopping assistant.

Shopper-Centered Studies. Newcomb et al. [7] have carefully examined the requirements of grocery shoppers for mobile shopping assistants. Some of their results confirm the importance of the goals of our shopping guide: Their survey of 46 diverse shoppers showed that two of the three most widely requested features of a grocery shopping assistant concerned help in arranging the items on the list and in locating the items within the grocery store. The authors also found that shoppers view waiting in checkout lines as a major nuisance in the shopping process; our guide addresses this problem in that it takes into account the expected length of time that a shopper will have to spend in a given store. In a test of their prototype with five shoppers in a grocery store, the authors noted a tendency that was commented on by some of the subjects in our first study: the tendency to focus on getting the products on their list quickly, as opposed to exploring the shopping area.

Taken together with our early results, these results indicate that (a) a decision-theoretic shopping guide can fulfill important requirements that shoppers often have; but (b) it tends to discourage the kind of recreational and exploratory shopping that is in many cases desired by shoppers and store owners. Since this latter fact is sometimes claimed to limit the practical deployability of our approach severely, we should point out that the recreational and convenience orientations to shopping are not as contradictory as they may seem (cf. Kim and LaRose [8]). For example, a shopper who intends to do both some convenience shopping and some recreational shopping in a given visit to a shopping mall may have more time and energy for the recreational shopping if she can finish the convenience shopping quickly and with little effort. And the fact that a given shopping mall has infrastructure that supports efficient convenience shopping (as well as recreational shopping) may constitute a reason for visiting that mall in the first place rather than another one.

Decision-Theoretic Planning for Recommendation. In addition to our own work cited in Section 1.1, other researchers have recently applied decision-theoretic methods to recommendation problems in shopping contexts. Plutowski [9] addresses shopping scenarios very similar to those addressed by our guide, offering new solutions to the complexity issues raised by decision-theoretic planning, which tend to limit the scalability of decision-theoretic methods. New approaches to complexity issues are also presented in the work of Brafman et al. [10] (first introduced by Shani et al. [11]), whose shopping domain is an on-line bookstore, in which the authors were able to test their decision-theoretic recommender in real use.

2   Description of the New Prototype

On the basis of the results of our first user study (Section 1.1) and the related research just summarized, we developed an improved version of the decision-theoretic shopping guide.

2.1   User Interface

Before beginning with her actual shopping, the user must specify to the system in one way or another which products she would like to buy in the shopping mall. In the relatively simple solution that we adopted for this prototype, the shopping list is specified on a larger stationary computing device, on which the computations necessary for the decision-theoretic planning are also carried out.[2] The usability and acceptance of this aspect of the prototype were not evaluated in our study.

---

[2] In a practical deployment, this device might be a computer with touch screens mounted in the walls of the shopping mall.

(a) **(b)** **(c)**

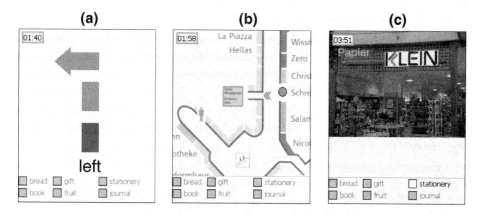

Fig. 1. Three screen shots of the improved shopping guide for the user study in the shopping mall. (a: Animated arrows are used for user-centered navigation recommendations. b: Overview maps show the user's location, the expected next store, and further information about the environment. c: Shortly before the user reaches the expected next store, a picture of the store is shown on the display of the PDA to help the user recognize the destination.)

The main display on the PDA has two parts (see Figure 1): On the bottom of the display, the user can always see the shopping list (which included 6 items in the current user study) with check boxes for indicating to the system which items have been purchased so far. As is shown in screen shot (a), a large animated arrow is used to indicate the direction in which the user should walk whenever she reaches a point at which a choice is available. The animation shows movement from the beginning of the arrow to the end, so as to emphasize that the recommended motion is relative to the user's current orientation. Between one such instruction and the next, an overview map (b) is presented that shows a part of the shopping mall that includes both the user's current location and the next store to be visited. These overview maps were introduced in response to comments of subjects in the first study that they lacked a "big picture" of the shopping mall and wanted to be able to prepare mentally for the next store that they were to visit. When the user approaches the next recommended store, the system displays a photograph (c) of the store, so as to reassure the user that the intended store has been reached.

The user is alerted to each change in the display by an acoustic signal—a feature suggested by users in the first study who wanted to minimize the extent to which they had to attend to the display.[3]

When the user has reached a store, the items available in that store become active in the shopping list, so that the user can check them off if she finds them. Inside a store, the user alone is responsible for finding the right places to look for the desired items. The next navigation recommendation is given to the user when she leaves the store.

---

[3] In the user study, users wore an ear set, which ensured that they heard the signals regardless of the level of ambient noise. It would also be possible to give complete navigation instructions via speech, as several subjects in the earlier study requested.

2.2   Decision-Theoretic Planning

Data Required. For the purpose of this paper, the most important questions concerning the decision-theoretic approach concern (a) the data required by the system and how they can be obtained and (b) the nature of the result of the planning process and the computational resources required.[4]

Table 1. Overview of the types of data about the shopping environment required by the decision-theoretic planner

A topography of the shopping mall that specifies:	For each shop, for each of a set of *product characterizations*:
1. the location of each shop	1. the probability of finding a product fitting that characterization
2. the location of each of a set of beacons, each of which sends an infrared signal to the PDA of the user as she approaches the beacon	2. the typical time spent in the store searching for a product
3. for each beacon, the typical time required to walk between it and each of the neighboring beacons	3. the typical time spent waiting in line after a product has been found

Table 1 gives an overview of the required data. A *product characterization* can have different degrees of specificity. For example, for a bookstore, it might specify the name of a particular magazine; in which case the probability refers to the likelihood that a shopper who enters the store looking for that particular magazine will find it. Or the specification might be more general, such as "sports magazine", in which case the probability refers to the likelihood that a shopper who is looking for either a particular sports magazine or simply some sports magazine that she considers worth buying will end up finding it in this store.

The question of where all of these quantitative estimates might come from in real-life applications of the technology is open-ended, because there are many possibilities (see Bohnenberger [12], chap. 6). Some solutions presuppose a certain amount of cooperation by the vendors in the shopping mall (e.g., some sort of access to their databases). Other solutions would make use of data collected during the actual use of the system to update parameters such as the probability of finding a product fitting a given characterization in a given store, provided that at least some users allowed some data concerning their shopping trips to be transferred to a central computer. A simple, low-tech method was applied for our user study: To determine the time cost of walking from one store to another, the experimenter did the necessary walking and counted the steps required. To estimate the probability of finding a particular type of item in a given store and the time required to find and buy it, the experimenter looked at the number and variety of products offered by the store.

---

[4] For information on technical aspects of the planning process, we refer the interested reader to the brief description given by Bohnenberger et al. [2] and the detailed account given by Bohnenberger [12]. General introductions to decision-theoretic planning are given by Boutilier et al. [13] and Russell and Norvig [14], among others.

Result of the Planning Process and Computational Resources. The result of the planning process is not a single route through the shopping mall but rather a recommendation *policy*: For each possible *state* of the shopping process, the policy specifies a recommended user action, which may involve either walking in a given direction between stores or entering a particular store. A state in the shopping process is characterized by the user's current location, the set of products that the user has bought so far, and (if a time limit has been specified), the amount of time left until the deadline. Note that, if the system generated a fixed plan, it would be determined in advance, for example, how many bookstores the user would visit. With a policy, the user will visit as many bookstores as is necessary to obtain the desired book(s)—unless time runs out first to the point where it is no longer worthwhile to look for books.

Although the resulting recommendation policy covers a large number of possible states, it can be represented and applied on a resource-limited PDA, because the mere application of an existing policy is not computationally demanding. By contrast, the planning process that generates the policy can be highly resource-intensive; for this reason, it may be necessary for this computation to be performed on a larger computing device, as was done for our user study.

3 User Study in a Real Shopping Mall

By testing the use of the prototype in a real shopping mall, we aimed to answer the following questions:

1. Does the shopping guide work as expected in effectively enabling users to find the desired products in an unfamiliar shopping mall and with limited time available?
2. How do potential users evaluate the shopping guide overall, and in what situations would they be inclined to use such a system for their own shopping?
3. What features of the system are well received, and where do users see a need for improvement?

3.1 Method

Realization of Localization. A major practical obstacle to a study in a real shopping mall was the infeasibility of installing localization infrastructure just for the purpose of the study. Therefore, in our study, the experimenter simulated the localization infrastructure of the earlier user study with a second PDA that communicated with the device of the subject. Whereas the subject's PDA would normally receive infrared signals from beacons mounted at various locations in the shopping mall, in our study these signals were transmitted from the experimenter's device via wireless LAN (it is convenient to speak of these signals as coming from *virtual beacons*). The experimenter's device ran a specially written program that automated as much as possible of the task of simulating the beacons.[5]

---

[5] The program exploited the fact that, given knowledge of the mall topology and the current shopping policy, the movements of a user were largely predictable—although on a few brief occasions subjects moved too unpredictably for the experimenter to keep up.

Shopping Mall. The study was conducted in the *Saarpark-Center* shopping mall[6]in the city of Neunkirchen—the largest shopping mall in the German province of the Saarland. The mall hosts about 120 stores on 33,500 m^2 spread over two floors.

Shopping Task. Instead of conventional payment for participation in the study, each subject was given a fixed budget of 25 Euros (about $30) to spend. With this money, the subject could buy (and keep) 1 item from each of 6 categories (some bread, a book, a gift item, some fruit, a magazine, and some stationery). In order to recreate the normal real-life situation in which a shopper has some particular ideas in mind about the product being sought (as opposed to looking for, say, just any magazine) the subject was asked to specify in advance, for each category, some specific characteristics of the product sought (e.g., a particular magazine or a particular type of bread). This measure also introduced some (realistic) uncertainty as to whether the desired product would in fact be found in any given store of the relevant type. Each subject was allowed to shop for at most 20 minutes. This restriction was explained to the subjects with reference to the real-life situations of having to finish shopping before the closing time of the mall or before leaving the mall to go to an important appointment.[7]

Subjects. We recruited 21 subjects (10 female, 11 male),[8] aiming mainly to find subjects who were not familiar with the shopping mall in question (because subjects who are thoroughly familiar with a shopping mall can be expected to benefit relatively little from a shopping guide). Of the 21 subjects, 14 had not been to the shopping mall within the previous 12 months, and none had been there more than 3 times during that period. Only 6 of the subjects had experience with navigation systems, in most cases with car navigation systems. Only 2 subjects had ever used a PDA. The subjects' ages ranged from 21 to 73 years, with a median of 27.

Procedure. Each subject performed the shopping task individually, accompanied by the experimenter. First, the experimenter familiarized the subject with the use of the shopping guide. He then explained the shopping task described above and asked the subject to characterize the specific product to be sought in each category. The subject began at the mall's main entrance and was followed around by the experimenter. Each time the subject's PDA received a signal from a virtual beacon, the shopping guide displayed the navigation recommendation specified by the previously computed policy. When a subject found one of the desired products in a store, he or she checked it off of the list, and the experimenter paid for it. When the 20-minute shopping period was over, the subject filled in a questionnaire and was subsequently asked in a verbal debriefing to elaborate on her answers.

---

[6] http://www.ece.de/de/shopping/center/spn/spn2.jsp

[7] We did not include a control condition in which the subjects shopped without the shopping guide, because (a) we wanted to devote all available resources to the study of the shopping guide in a natural setting and (b) we assumed that subjects already had a great deal of experience in shopping in shopping malls in the normal way.

[8] Since no reliable gender differences were found in the results, the gender variable will not be mentioned again.

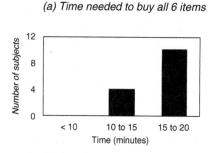
(a) Time needed to buy all 6 items

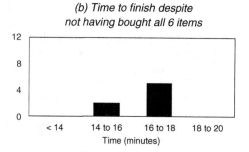
(b) Time to finish despite
not having bought all 6 items

Fig. 2. Time required to finish shopping for subjects who (a) did and (b) did not find all 6 items

3.2   Results

The study proceeded without problems, and the subjects supplied detailed comments on the questionnaire and in the debriefing.

Subjects' Performance with the Shopping Guide. The recommendation policy used by the shopping guide, which took into account the time limit of 20 minutes, did in fact ensure that all subjects reached the mall exit before the deadline had elapsed. This result is not trivial, because of course not all subjects proceeded with the exact speed assumed in the underlying model. Even when a subject walked more slowly than predicted, spent a relatively long time in stores, or simply experienced bad luck in finding the particular products that she had specified, the recommendation policy was able to bring the subject to the exit in time by in effect "giving up" on finding one or more products.

Six of the subjects were guided to the exit although they had managed to find only 5 of their 6 products (or only 4, in the case of one of these subjects). In all of these cases, the shopping guide recommended skipping the (relatively expensive) gift item, which would have been bought at a gift store near the mall exit. When they arrived at the gift store, these subjects had between 2 and 6 minutes left—less than the typical time assumed in the system's model for finding and paying for a gift item. Therefore, the system acted appropriately in advising them to bypass the gift store, given the higher-priority goal of reaching the mall exit in time. But why didn't the policy recommend skipping a less valuable item (such as the magazine) at an earlier stage of the shopping trip, freeing enough time to look for a gift later? In fact, a thorough analysis of the policy reveals that the system exhibits exactly this behavior in some time windows. But if a subject performs well in the early stages of the shopping, the system in effect does not consider it necessary to skip a less important item, expecting that the subject will manage to complete the entire shopping task. If the subject shops more slowly than expected later, the system has no choice but to recommend skipping the last item, even if it happens to be the least desirable one to skip.

Having to skip the gift store was a potentially disappointing result for those subjects who had almost enough time left when they reached this store. If these subjects had understood exactly what was going on, instead of going straight to the exit they could have taken an action that was not represented in the system's model: They could have entered the gift store, seen if they could find a suitable gift especially quickly (keeping an eye on the remaining time) and if necessary left the store without a gift just before the time ran out. It would be possible to enrich the system's model so that it could actually recommend this type of action; but generally speaking situations can often arise in which it is desirable for the user to be able to second-guess the system's recommendation. We will return to this point in Section 3.3.

Subjects' Assessment of the Shopping Guide. Figure 3 summarizes answers that subjects gave to questions concerning their acceptance of the shopping guide. It is generally agreed (see, e.g., Landauer [15]) that subject's expressions of positive attitudes toward a novel system should not be taken at face value, given that the subjects in a study of this type are often biased in favor of a positive evaluation. Still, when we consider all of the frustrations that subjects might conceivably have experienced in this situation, the small overall number of problems and complaints does offer some encouragement.

When asked about conditions in which they thought that the shopping guide would be particularly useful, 16 subjects mentioned unfamiliar environments, 13 referred to situations involving time pressure, and 5 spoke of particularly large shopping malls.

Asked about particularly positive aspects of the shopping guide, 9 subjects mentioned the speed with which they were able to find relevant stores; 4 subjects com-

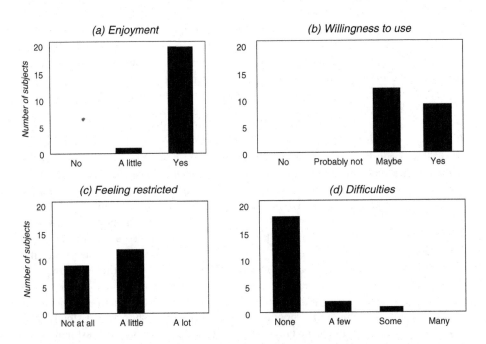

Fig. 3. Subjective acceptance of the shopping guide. The questions were: (a) "Did you enjoy using the shopping guide?" (b) "Would you use such a system in a suitably equipped environment?" (c) "Did you feel restricted by the system? (d) "Did you experience difficulties in using the shopping guide?"

mended the reliability with which they received the recommendations at the right locations; 4 subjects mentioned the photos of the stores that are displayed when a store is
reached; 3 subjects singled out the form in which the recommendations were presented
via the arrows on the PDA's display; and 2 subjects mentioned the overview maps.

Of those who stated that they would "maybe" use a shopping guide of this type in
real shopping situations, 3 subjects urged that for each recommended store, one or more
similar, alternative stores should be presented. On a related note, 2 subjects expressed
a desire to be able to walk in a different direction than the one recommended by the
system. This point will be discussed in Section 3.3.

Whereas the overview maps had been introduced to help subjects to prepare mentally for the next store, 3 subjects pointed out that it would be even better to be reminded
which particular product(s) they would be looking for at the next store.

As Figure 3(d) shows, 3 subjects stated that they had experienced difficulties in
using the shopping guide. One of the specific difficulties mentioned illustrates a more
general issue. It concerned an inadequacy in the system's modeling of products: In
order to look for a gift, one subject would have liked to enter a bookstore; but the
system's modeling had assumed that gifts can be bought only in gift stores. Although a
specific problem of this sort might be corrected post hoc through an improvement in the
modeling, there will presumably often arise situations in which the user's conception
of the relevant products differs from the system's conception. In such cases, it would
be desirable for the user to be able to second-guess the system, choosing an action that
deviates from the system's recommendation.

In the questionnaire, the subjects were also asked if they felt restricted by the use
of the shopping guide. Twelve subjects responded "A little". Most of the complaints
concerned physical restrictions: the need to carry the device in one hand while shopping
(8 subjects) and the wire that connected the earphone to the PDA (3 subjects). But
4 subjects mentioned cognitive restrictions, complaining that the shopping guide took
their attention away from the environment or diminished their freedom of decision about
where to go next. It is noteworthy that another subject considered it to be an advantage
that the shopping guide took his attention away from the environment because as a
result he was not tempted to buy any items that he did not really need.

3.3   Discussion

Taken together, these results indicate three directions in which the tested prototype still
calls for improvement, despite the generally positive feedback:

Further Reduction of Distraction from the Environment. One way in which all
mobile and wearable systems can hamper the natural performance of a user's task is
simply by unnecessarily consuming physical or mental resources that could otherwise
be devoted to the task. Although our efforts to minimize this type of distraction (e.g.,
easy-to-perceive animated arrows; acoustic alerts to changes in the display) were partly
successful, hardware improvements that minimize the need to hold the PDA in one's
hand and to use a wire with the earphone are still called for.

Allowing the User to Second-Guess the System. As we have seen, there are various situations in which a user may have good reason to deviate from the system's recommendation, and several users expressed a desire to do so. The system's modeling of the user's shopping needs, preferences, and capabilities can never be more than a serviceable approximation. In addition to the observed examples mentioned above, the user may, for example, have a strong liking or disliking for a particular chain of stores, which the system is unlikely to know about. In such cases, the user should have the option of deviating from the system's recommendation without sacrificing the benefits of using the system; but she should also be able to judge whether deviation from the recommendation will in fact lead to an improvement or not. The results of the study suggest several specific enhancements along these lines:

1. One reason why subjects felt that they could not second-guess the system is that they had little idea of the consequences of doing so. In reality, the system is quite robust in this regard, much like a car navigation system that computes a new route if the user for some reason leaves the recommended route: Even if the user were to disregard the system entirely for a while and wander around at will, as soon as she began consulting the recommendations again, they would once again constitute an optimal policy in view of her current situation, including the amount of time remaining.[9] In such a case the user's sequence of actions before and including the deviation may no longer be optimal in any sense. On the other hand, if the user's deviation is minor and well-founded (e.g., going into a nonrecommended store because the user sees a desired product displayed in the store window), it is likely that the entire sequence of actions will be more successful than it would have been if the user had followed the recommendations strictly.

Since these basic facts about the system were not clear to the subjects in the study, it is understandable that they were hesitant to deviate from the recommendations even when they saw the desirability of doing so. One strategy for improvement, therefore, is to convey to the users in some appropriate way the necessary understanding of the system's capabilities.

2. Even if users know that they can deviate from the recommendations, it will be difficult for them to do so if they have little information on which to base such a decision. The users in our study could see the stores around them, and the overview maps also showed stores that were not immediately visible. But it was not made explicit what alternative options the user had for finding the desired products. A second strategy for improvement, then, is to give users some sort of preview of what will happen if they take some action that was not recommended by the system.

One possible way of realizing both of the solutions just proposed is to follow a trend that is becoming increasingly popular in the area of recommender systems (see, e.g., Herlocker et al. [16]): providing a mechanism for explaining the system's recommendations. The next section will describe how we designed and implemented a simple explanation component and how users responded to it in a small follow-up study.

---

[9] The system does not even need to recompute its policy in this case, because the originally computed policy already takes into account all possible states that the user might reach, as long as they involve the modeled locations and the relevant time interval.

4   Introduction of an Explanation Component

A well-crafted explanation can convey understanding not only of how a recommendation was arrived at by the system but also of the basic way in which the system works and of how much faith the user should place in it (cf. Jameson [17], section 15.7).

It is not a priori obvious what content should be presented in an explanation of a recommendation based on decision-theoretic planning or in what form the content should be presented. A particular challenge with this type of recommendation is that an individual recommendation may be understandable only as part of a larger recommendation policy.

In order not to rely entirely on our own intuitions, we followed the strategy of Herlocker et al. [16], generating a variety of different types of content and forms of representation and presenting them for feedback to a group of potential users (see Bohnenberger [12], section 7.4, for details). Although these subjects (33 students in a computer science lecture on *Intelligent Environments*) were not representative of the entire population of potential users and were not using the recommendations while performing a real shopping task, they did provide some interpretable feedback on the naturalness and perceived value of various elements of explanations.

4.1   Initial Implementation

In order to see how explanations are used and evaluated in a natural setting, we prepared a relatively simple initial implementation, making use of ideas that had emerged from the questionnaire study.

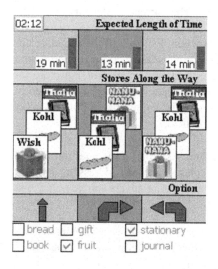 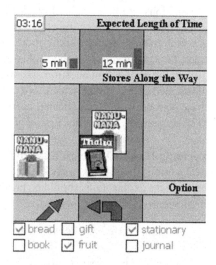

Fig. 4. Screen shots from the initial implementation of the explanation mechanism. (Each store is represented by a rectangle that shows the name of the store and the type of product that it sells. For example, Wish and Nanu-Nana are two alternative gift stores.)

What Is Presented to the User. Figure 4 shows two examples of explanations. The first one might be offered relatively early in the shopping trip used for the study in the mall, when the user has so far found just 2 of the 6 desired products. The (at most 3) walking options with the highest expected utility are always shown, the recommended one being placed in the middle of the screen and highlighted with a more salient background. The information provided about each option concerns two attributes that were judged especially important in the questionnaire study and that were fairly straightforward to implement: the expected length of time until completion of the shopping task if the option in question is followed and the next three (at most) stores that the user can expect to encounter—in both cases, on the (optimistic) assumption that the user will find each product in the next possible store and will proceed with the expected speed. In this example, the user can recognize that the option on the right is quite similar to the recommended option, apparently involving only a different order of visiting the first three stores and a slightly longer expected duration. The user might choose the right-hand option if for some reason she wanted to go to the gift store before the other two stores. The second explanation shown in Figure 4 would be offered a bit later on, after the user had found the bread. Note that these displays "explain" the system's recommendations only in a superficial way, by showing the properties of alternative options in such a way that the user may be able to see why one of them is probably preferable. More generally, we will see shortly (Section 5.1) that the term *explanation* may not be the most apt characterization of the supplementary information provided by our guide—or by other recommender systems.

Necessary Computations. The type of explanation just discussed is so simple that the explanations can be computed on-line on the PDA. The current implementation computes an explanation each time the user arrives at a beacon that corresponds to a location at which the user could walk in more than one direction. For each of the available options, the system simulates the application of the recommendation policy for a user who goes in the direction in question, assuming that every action is successful. For more sophisticated explanations, which took into account the inherent uncertainty involved in these actions, more sophisticated computations would be required (see Bohnenberger [12], section 7.4.3, for a discussion of some possibilities).

Deciding How to Make an Explanation Available. Aside from the question of how explanations should look, a system that can offer explanations must address the question of when the explanations should be presented to the user. A relatively simple policy was implemented for the new prototype:

- When the difference between the overall expected utility of the recommended option is only slightly greater than that of the second best option, the user must tap a button labeled "Explanation" to see the explanation.
- When the difference is of moderate size, the system displays on the normal screen a text explicitly urging the user to consider tapping on this button.
- When the difference is large, the explanation is presented immediately instead of the simpler display with a single animated arrow.

The rationale is that it is especially important for the user to see an explanation when the recommended alternative is much better than the alternatives, in case the user should be considering deviating from the recommendation. Although this rationale is not necessarily the best one, it seemed well suited to eliciting feedback in the study.

4.2   Follow-Up Study in the Shopping Mall

Method. Five subjects were recruited, two of whom had participated in the first study in the shopping mall. The method was the same as for the first study, except for the following additions:

1. When introducing the system, the experimenter demonstrated how an explanation could be requested (and how it might appear spontaneously) and he made sure that the subject understood the information presented in an explanation.
2. The questionnaire presented at the end included several new questions about the explanation mechanism, and the experimenter followed up on them during the debriefing.

Results. Despite the limited number of subjects, the answers given are sufficiently consistent and interpretable to yield a fairly clear picture.

Regarding the overall question of whether the subject found the explanations helpful, 3 subjects answered positively and 2 negatively. The main objection (mentioned even by one of the subjects with a positive attitude) was that under heavy time pressure, a user is not inclined to look at relatively detailed new information but would rather simply trust the system's recommendations.

One question concerned the circumstances under which explanations should be offered spontaneously: when the difference between the recommended and the second-best alternative was especially large or especially small. Of the 5 subjects, 4 chose the former alternative, in effect endorsing the rationale explained above. But one of the same subjects also noted the potential utility of an explanation even in the opposite case: "If the difference [in the predicted remaining duration] is only one minute, the user can decide himself whether he wants to take the longer route, maybe because he considers the fruit more important than the book."

One subject liked the explanations simply because they displayed information about the recommended option that went beyond what was usually displayed (i.e., the predicted remaining duration of the shopping trip and the next three upcoming stores).

Discussion. Despite the roughly even split between positive and negative overall judgments, the following summary statements (which take into account individual comments not mentioned above) seem to reflect the general consensus among the 5 subjects:

1. The appeal of explanations is relatively low in situations involving high time pressure, in which users tend to prefer simple displays that can be taken in at a glance (or better yet, with ambient vision, as is possible with the animated arrows). In addition to the obvious reason that reading explanations consumes scarce time, another reason for this preference may be the subjects' recognition (which is expressed in other comments) that the shopping guide's recommendations are relatively hard to improve on when

time pressure is involved: Given time pressure, the system is exploiting not only its knowledge of the products available in various locations but also its ability to adapt its recommendations continually to the approaching deadline—a task that humans are not especially good at.

2. The subjects do perceive several potential benefits of explanations, but these benefits are due only in part to the explanations' function of clarifying the reasons for the system's recommendations: An explanation can also help simply by conveying additional information about the recommended option and/or the available alternatives, thereby allowing the user to make a well-founded decision to deviate from the system's recommendation and/or to prepare mentally for what lies ahead.

3. Regarding the unrequested presentation of explanations, the strategy implemented in the current prototype is perceived as being basically reasonable, but some subjects would like to exert more control over the presentation strategy (for example, reducing or eliminating spontaneous explanations in the case of extreme time pressure).

5   Conclusions

5.1   Conclusions Concerning the Shopping Guide

The fact that even the follow-up study with the explanation component yielded significant ideas about further improvement of the shopping guide illustrates that the optimal design of a system of this type is not something that can be determined once and for all. Each test involving a new version and/or a new context may yield further ideas for improvement. But this fact is not surprising, since it also applies even to widely accepted software tools like calendar applications.

Our detailed discussion of results calling for improvements should not obscure the overall result that the majority of the subjects found the shopping guide to be an attractive tool for the support of shopping in some types of circumstances, characterized mainly by the unfamiliarity of the shopping environment and the existence of some form of time pressure. Both the basic functionality of the system and many of the specific interface features were found to be well adapted to this type of shopping task.

Aside from some improvements that can be realized straightforwardly, the necessary improvements that came to light concern mostly the need of users for certain types of additional information, ranging from general background information about the basic capabilities and limitations of the system to information that supports particular types of thinking during the performance of the shopping task (for example, deciding whether to deviate from a recommendation of the system). The results yield a good deal of guidance as to how this information should be presented; they also show that the presentation must be selective and subject to control by the user, since users are highly sensitive to the presentation of unnecessary information and since the appropriate amount depends on individual preferences and on situational factors such as time pressure.

With regard to information that conveys a basic understanding of how the system works, one approach currently being explored (see, e.g., Kröner et al. [18]) is to create a special retrospective mode in which the user can interact with the system outside of the natural environment of use. For example, at home at the end of the day, the system might walk the user through some of the day's events, presenting reminders of what happened and explanations of its actions. The idea is that when the user is free of time pressure and attention-consuming environmental events, she will be better able to build up a mental model of how the system works.

With regard to additional information about specific user options and system actions, the main challenge appears to be that of ensuring that the timing and mode of presentation are well adapted to the user and the situation. A good solution will probably involve some combination of (a) specification of long-term preferences by the user, (b) requests by the user for specific information during use, and (c) automatic situational adaptation by the system.

5.2   A More General Lesson

One general theme illustrated by this research concerns a fundamental tension that arises with systems that are employed while the user is interacting in a rich environment. On the one hand, users do not in general want to receive and process much information from a system of this type, preferring instead messages that can be perceived with minimal distraction from their interaction with the environment. On the other hand, users at least sometimes want to use their own knowledge and understanding to second-guess and override the information and advice provided by the system; and doing so will sometimes require getting more information from the system than the user needs in order to take the system's outputs at face value. Finding an acceptable resolution of this tension may be one of the trickiest challenges both for designers of pervasive computing systems and for their users.

References

1. Bohnenberger, T., Jameson, A.: When policies are better than plans: Decision-theoretic planning of recommendation sequences. In Lester, J., ed.: IUI 2001: International Conference on Intelligent User Interfaces. ACM, New York (2001) 21–24
2. Bohnenberger, T., Jameson, A., Krüger, A., Butz, A.: Location-aware shopping assistance: Evaluation of a decision-theoretic approach. In: Proceedings of the Fourth International Symposium on Human-Computer Interaction with Mobile Devices, Pisa (2002) 155–169
3. Asthana, A., Cracatts, M., Krzyzanowski, P.: An indoor wireless system for personalized shopping assistance. In: Proceedings of the First IEEE Workshop on Mobile Computing Systems and Applications. (1994)
4. Fano, A.E.: Shopper's Eye: Using location-based filtering for a shopping agent in the physical world. In: Proceedings of the Second International Conference on Autonomous Agents. (1998) 416–421
5. Shekar, S., Nair, P., Helal, A.: iGrocer: A ubiquitous and pervasive smart grocery shopping system. In: Proceedings of the 2003 ACM Symposium on Applied Computing. (2003) 645–652
6. Cumby, C., Fano, A., Ghani, R., Krema, M.: Building intelligent shopping assistants using individual consumer models. In Riedl, J., Jameson, A., Billsus, D., Lau, T., eds.: IUI 2005: International Conference on Intelligent User Interfaces. ACM, New York (2005) 323–325
7. Newcomb, E., Pashley, T., Stasko, J.: Mobile computing in the retail arena. In Terveen, L., Wixon, D., Comstock, E., Sasse, A., eds.: Human Factors in Computing Systems: CHI 2003 Conference Proceedings. ACM, New York (2003) 337–344

8. Kim, J., LaRose, R.: Interactive e-commerce: Promoting consumer efficiency or impulsivity? Journal of Computer-Mediated Communication **10** (2004)

9. Plutowski, M.: MDP solver for a class of location-based decisioning tasks. In: Proceedings of the First Bayesian Modeling Applications Workshop at the Nineteenth Conference on Uncertainty in Artificial Intelligence, Acapulco, Mexico (2003)

10. Brafman, R.I., Heckerman, D., Shani, G.: An MDP-based recommender system. Journal of Machine Learning Research **6** (2005)

11. Shani, G., Brafman, R.I., Heckerman, D.: An MDP-based recommender system. In Darwiche, A., Friedman, N., eds.: Uncertainty in Artificial Intelligence: Proceedings of the Eighteenth Conference. Morgan Kaufmann, San Francisco (2002) 453–460

12. Bohnenberger, T.: Decision-Theoretic Planning for User-Adaptive Systems: Dealing With Multiple Goals and Resource Limitations. AKA, Berlin (2005) Dissertation version available from http://w5.cs.uni-sb.de/~bohne/.

13. Boutilier, C., Dean, T., Hanks, S.: Decision-theoretic planning: Structural assumptions and computational leverage. Journal of Artificial Intelligence Research **11** (1999) 1–94

14. Russell, S.J., Norvig, P.: Artificial Intelligence: A Modern Approach. 2nd edn. Prentice-Hall, Englewood Cliffs, NJ (2003)

15. Landauer, T.K.: Behavioral research methods in human-computer interaction. In Helander, M., Landauer, T.K., Prabhu, P.V., eds.: Handbook of Human-Computer Interaction. North-Holland, Amsterdam (1997) 203–227

16. Herlocker, J.L., Konstan, J.A., Riedl, J.: Explaining collaborative filtering recommendations. In: Proceedings of the 2000 Conference on Computer-Supported Cooperative Work, Philadelphia, PA (2000) 241–250

17. Jameson, A.: Adaptive interfaces and agents. In Jacko, J.A., Sears, A., eds.: Human-Computer Interaction Handbook. Erlbaum, Mahwah, NJ (2003) 305–330

18. Kröner, A., Baldes, S., Jameson, A., Bauer, M.: Using an extended episodic memory within a mobile companion. In: Proceedings of the Workshop on "Memory and Sharing of Experience" at Pervasive 2004, Vienna (2004)

Integrating Intra and Extra Gestures into a Mobile and Multimodal Shopping Assistant

Rainer Wasinger[1], Antonio Krüger[2], and Oliver Jacobs[1]

[1] DFKI GmbH, Intelligent User Interfaces Department,
66123 Saarbrücken, Germany
{rainer.wasinger, oliver.jacobs}@dfki.de
[2] University of Münster, Institute for Geoinformatics,
48149 Münster, Germany
antonio.krueger@uni-muenster.de

Abstract. Accompanying the rise of mobile and pervasive computing, applications now need to adapt to their surrounding environments and provide users with information in the environment in an easy and natural manner. In this paper we describe a user interface that integrates multimodal input on a handheld device with external gestures performed with real world artifacts. The described approach extends reference resolution based on speech, handwriting and gesture to that of real world objects that users may hold in their hands. We discuss the varied interaction channels available to users that arise from mixing and matching input modalities on the mobile device with actions performed in the environment. We also discuss the underlying components required in handling these extended multimodal interactions and present an implementation of our ideas in a demonstrator called the Mobile ShopAssist. This demonstrator is then used as the basis for a recent usability study that we describe on user interaction within mobile contexts.

1 Introduction

Mobile computing has seen significant advancements in recent years, as applications begin to span multiple and changing contexts. Multimodal user interfaces have also emerged as an integral area of development, as users gradually break free from the stationary desktop computing paradigm and enter the realms of pervasive computing. Multimodal interfaces that provide more intuitive ways to interface the computational power of an environment will gain more and more importance if users start to interact with computationally empowered artifacts that provide no obvious clue on their computational abilities. This is for example true in a shopping scenario where products are electronically identifiable (e.g. through RFID-tags) and where users are able to interact with the products that are on sale to retrieve product information through a shopping assistant. The interaction with the products could be based on speech utterances and performed user gestures (e.g. by picking up a product), however this causes problems relating to the privacy of the request and the presentation of the results, for ex-

H.W. Gellersen et al. (Eds.): PERVASIVE 2005, LNCS 3468, pp. 297–314, 2005.
© Springer-Verlag Berlin Heidelberg 2005

ample if the environment delivers the requested information through a loudspeaker in the user's vicinity. Most of these problems can be overcome by including a personal device in the scenario, which allows users to silently pose requests and receive information from the environment unnoticed by others. In this paper we will present the Mobile ShopAssist demonstrator, which aids a user in finding out product information and product comparison information while shopping in an RFID enabled store. The system accommodates for multimodal input interaction in the form of speech, handwriting, and gesture, which can be performed either on the mobile device or by directly picking up an object from the shelf.

Newcomb et. al. [9] present some interesting design guidelines for a PDA based shopping assistant in a grocery store. They state that one important aspect that has to be regarded during the design process is that shoppers often use their hands to touch the products – something we have tried to incorporate into the design of our ShopAssistant. The authors further highlight the importance to find appropriate breaks in the shopping routine to be able to provide situated assistance. This has motivated us to choose the digital camera domain where normal shoppers usually rely on the help of a shop assistant to make their choice.

To illustrate our ideas, consider the following scenario. A user is interested in buying a digital camera. In possession of a device such as a PDA, the user may enter an electronics shop and start browsing the available range of digital cameras. The store might be crowded, or noisy, and there may also be no shop assistant in sight or available to the user to ask for assistance. Bearing these environment characteristics in mind, the user instead connects to a shelf of interest and downloads the shelf's product database onto the PDA through the use of the Mobile ShopAssist. Upon synchronization, the user will be able to browse both the products that are currently available in the store as well as those that are currently out of stock. With the help of the personal device the user is able to use multimodal queries to obtain information on the different cameras, regardless of whether they are present in the shelf or not. In particular, the system allows the user to pick up a product from the shelf and to then compare it with a product that is displayed on the PDA through the use of spoken natural language (e.g. "*compare this camera to that one*"). After having processed this multimodal input the system provides a comparison chart of both products.

The goal of this paper is to investigate the technical requirements of such a system and to explore the usability issues that arise from the various forms of new modality input combinations that are introduced. In the next section we describe the many modes of interaction that permit flexible user interaction within our shopping scenario. We describe how modality types may be combined on a mobile device, and also extend the modality input combinations to account for interaction with real world environments. In section 3, we describe the key elements required for merging modalities together, the modality fusion module, and include discussion on time-frames and parameters such as confidence values that are used in this process to resolve both non-conflicting and conflicting information sources. In section 4 we describe a usability study that was recently conducted on the Mobile ShopAssist demonstrator, including results on the use of observable modalities within public spaces, modality preference for unimodal and multimodal interaction spanning the virtual and physical world, and modality intuition. Section 5 provides some final conclusions and an outlook on future activities.

2 Multimodal Interaction

Interaction may take place on a unimodal or a multimodal basis, in which unimodal interaction refers to input that is composed of a single modality such as speech or handwriting only (e.g. *"What accessories are available for the EOS 300D"*), and multimodal interaction refers to input that spans multiple modalities such as speech and gesture (e.g. *"Does this <gesture> camera have a wireless control?"*). With respect to time, we suggest that modality information provided by a user can always be categorized as either non-overlaid, overlaid and non-conflicting, or overlaid and conflicting. In more detail, non-overlaid information occurs when input provided to a system does not have any of the same information represented by multiple modalities (e.g. *"What is the price of this <gesture=PowerShot S70>?"*, while overlaid and non-conflicting information occurs when the same information has been represented by multiple modalities, but does not create a conflict (e.g. *"What is the price of the PowerShot S70 <gesture=PowerShot S70>?*), and overlaid and conflicting information occurs when the same information has been provided by multiple modalities and this information conflicts (e.g. *"What is the price of the PowerShot A40 <gesture=PowerShot S70>?*). Finally, with respect to origin, (non-overlaid and overlaid) modality input may originate from devices of the same type or of a different type, in which (e.g. for overlaid information), same-type device input such as speech and speech might arise through the use of both public and private microphones, while different-type device input such as speech and gesture might arise through the use of devices capturing different types of modal input.

2.1 On-device and Off-device Interaction

In contrast to desktop systems that generally make use of devices such as keyboards and the well-established 'Windows, Icon, Mouse, and Pointer' (WIMP) paradigm, we believe that instrumented environments require the addition of new interaction types like speech, handwriting and gesture. This need has arisen through the requirements of scenarios dealing with difficult environment contexts, and contexts in which the user is mobile and/or performing multiple tasks at a single instance in time. It is expected that users will in the future interact directly with artefacts in their surrounding, but will also most likely be aided by personal computing devices. This section outlines on-device and off-device interaction, as found on the Mobile ShopAssist demonstrator.

The Mobile ShopAssist demonstrator accepts modality input of type speech, handwriting, and gesture. Furthermore, user interaction with a set of products can take place either directly on the mobile device, or directly with artefacts in the surrounding environment, i.e. off-device. Interaction may also be part on and off device, as seen in Fig's 1A and B, where a user asks for comparison information on two products via speech, intra-, and extra- gesture.

Speech input in our system is provided by a user via the inbuilt microphone on the PocketPC. We use IBM's Embedded ViaVoice[1] speech recognizer to interpret all or

---

[1] IBM Embedded ViaVoice,
  http://www.ibm.com/software/pervasive/products/voice/vv_enterprise.shtml

part of a user's input. This is done through the use of limited-domain rule grammars that are generally between 50 and 100 words in size, and are dynamically loaded and activated by the system. We consider speech to aid both on and off-device interaction.

Fig. 1. A and B show the combined use of speech, intra- and extra- gesture. C shows feature selection via handwriting, while D shows feature selection via an intra-gesture point on the scrolling text bar

Handwriting input is a typical on-device interaction modality, and requires a user to write on the PocketPC's display through the use of a stylus. We use Microsoft's embedded character recognizer called Transcriber[2], to interpret the user's input as a string of characters, and these characters are then mapped to a valid entry in our corresponding handwriting grammars.

Gesture is a broad term defined in common usage as "motions of the limbs or body, used as a means of expression" [Merriam-Webster dictionary]. As described in [6], gestures are used for everything from pointing at a person to draw their attention, to conveying information about space and temporal characteristics. Current research on gesture ranges from the recognition of human body motion (including facial expressions and hand movements) [13, 1], to pen and mouse based research [12] and sign language. Gesture input within our system is limited to the 'selection' of products, and may be of either type intra-gesture or extra-gesture. **Intra-gestures** are on-device interactions, and occur when a user touches objects displayed on the screen of the PocketPC. The screen coordinates are then mapped internally to the underlying data objects represented as either 2D or 3D graphics. Intra-gestures are provided in the form of stylus or finger input, and can currently be of type "point". **Extra-gestures** are off-device interactions and occur when the user interacts with the physical world around them by physically handling an object. Extra-gestures may be of type "pick-up", or "put-back". Pick-up and put-back actions are evaluated through the use of RFID technology that allows for the detection of objects being either in or out of a given space. In [8], we have experimented with integrating "extra-point" gestures

---

[2] Microsoft Transcriber,
http://www.microsoft.com/windowsmobile/downloads/transcriber.mspx

based on a digital compass from Pointstar[3] in which we map real-world directions to known locations of physical objects, and have also augmented the intra-gesture library to include a "slide" gesture (alongside pointing). In our scenario, typical spaces include shelves that are instrumented with RFID readers and antennas, while typical objects include shopping products that are fitted with passive RFID tags. Within our scenario, intra gestures may also be combined with extra gestures, as shown by the speech utterance: *"Compare this camera <intra gesture> with this one <extra gesture>"* (see Fig. 1). It is this type of on- and off- device interaction that underlies our primary objective of providing interaction possibilities for instrumented spaces.

2.2 Representation of a Modality-Free Language, and Modality Combinations

The task of a modality fusion module is to combine different input streams into a single unambiguous and modality-free dialogue result, as defined by a modality-free language. The different input streams arise through the need for recognizers to use modality-specific grammars to deal with inputs such as speech and handwriting. A simplified version of the modality-free language used within our system is defined as follows:

$$<\text{FEATURE}><\text{OBJECT}>+ \tag{1}$$

The feature and object tags are represented in XML[4] (similar to EMMA[5]) and have a variety of attributes associated with them such as confidence and timestamp information. Valid values for the feature tag include (in reference to digital cameras) 'optical zoom' and 'mega pixels', while valid values for the object tag include 'PowerShot S60' and 'CoolPix 4300'. User input is only considered well-formed or valid if it consists of one feature and at least one object. For this reason, the modality fusion module is only ever activated once a feature has been provided, which can take place via speech, handwriting and/or intra-gesture.

Having defined the two primary constituents of our modality-free language – i.e. FEATURE and OBJECT – it can be stated that although the system accepts speech, handwriting and gesture input, it does not accept all feature and object modality combinations. To demonstrate the extent that such a requirement would place on a system providing speech, handwriting, and gesture input, we would have 9 modality combinations[6] arising from the combination of a single feature and a single object, and 27 modality combinations for a single feature and two object references. These 27 combinations also do not consider the effect that overlaid modality information would have on the size of a full-scale implementation, as in the example: *"How many mega pixels does the PowerShot S60 <G=PowerShotS60> have?"* in which both speech and gesture are used to define the same object referent. Fig. 2 shows the modality combinations that have been implemented in our system so far.

---

[3] Pointstar, http://www.pointstar.dk
[4] W3C Extensible Markup Language, http://www.w3.org/XML/
[5] EMMA: Extensible MultiModal Annotation markup language, http://www.w3.org/TR/emma/
[6] Not differentiating between intra and extra gestures. Also note that extra gestures may only be used for selecting objects.

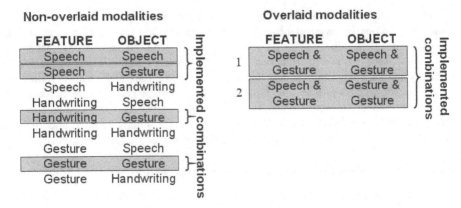

Fig. 2. Non-overlaid and overlaid input modality combinations

3 Modality Fusion

As shown in Fig. 3, our modality fusion component is based on a blackboard architecture. In contrast to the projects QuickSet [3] and SmartKom Mobile [2] in which a heavy reliance existed on distributed and client/server architectures, all of the interaction processing (except for the extra-gesture recognition which is based on RFID technology) is performed locally on the mobile PocketPC device. Indeed the blackboard itself is also located on the mobile device. Recognizable user input is defined by grammars that are associated with product types within the product database. These grammars are dynamically loaded based on the type of products contained

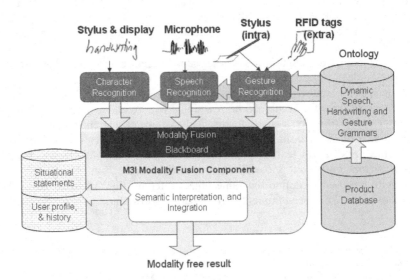

Fig. 3. Modality fusion within the Mobile ShopAssist

within the currently synchronized data container. During user interaction with the system, input is written to the central blackboard in the form of data nodes. These data nodes provide the primary information required for the modality fusion module to make informed decisions about the objects on the blackboard. As described in [14], this information includes the presumed dialog segment (i.e. feature or object), the parent modality group (i.e. speech, handwriting, intra-gesture, extra-gesture), an underlying modality type where appropriate (e.g. point, pick-up, put-back), a confidence value from 0.0 to 1.0, the start and stop times for the dialog segment, a time classification (i.e. past, or present), the raw user input, the matched user input, and the 3-best result matches including confidence scores.

The blackboard is stored on the PocketPC device itself, as too the modality fusion component. This provides the additional benefit that users can disconnect from their surroundings and continue to interact with the system offline. When browsing offline, the user has access to all modalities except extra-gesture, which is based on RFID technology and is recognized by an environment server.

Two important parameters for the modality fusion process – confidence values and timestamps – will be described in the following section. Alongside these types of parameters, we also expect statistical data from user-history log files, and context information in the form of situational statements [5] to further contribute to the modality fusion process. Situational statements refer for example to characteristics of a user (e.g. role, age, gender, walking speed, eye sight), the device (e.g. remaining battery life, working memory, speaker volume), or the surrounding environment (e.g. noisy, crowded, rainy), and are a convenient way of representing context.

3.1 Confidence Scoring

Confidence scoring is the ability to attach a probability to a recognition result in order to measure how confident a recognizer was in matching a result with what was actually inputted into the system. For each of the modalities within our system (speech, handwriting and gesture), we generate an N-best list of results and assign confidence values between 0.0 and 1.0 to each result. This occurs each time a user interacts with the system. "N" in the case of the ShopAssist is equal to 3 and means that the 3 most likely results are returned for a given modality (instead of just one). N-best result lists and their associated confidence values play an essential role in the disambiguation of multimodal input [11]. As an example, user input may be overlapped and conflicting (destructive), or it may be overlapped and non-conflicting (constructive). By keeping a hold of the N-best lists, we are able to store information that a single recognizer such as a speech recognizer might ultimately have thrown away, and are thus able to compare this with results from other recognizers at a later stage (i.e. in the modality fusion module). Confidence values within mobile multimodal systems are also important because the methods used in calculating these values are specific to the individual modalities, and are likely to be affected differently by surrounding environment characteristics. As an example, speech is likely to be affected by background noise differently to gesture, and handwriting will be affected by motion (i.e. while a user is walking) differently to speech.

Confidence values when processing **speech** are generated by matching a user's spoken utterance to a sequence of word hypothesis based on a given language model.

Our language model consists of word-phoneme mappings and grammar files written in a format similar to the Backus-Naur Form (BNF). A current mobile device limitation of our system is that each utterance in the N-best list receives only one confidence value. Speech engines with greater disposable resources are capable of returning confidence values for the individual words in a recognized utterance's word lattice [4]. This limitation means that if a feature and an object are both provided in a single speech utterance, our system will tag both values with the same confidence value. These values may however still be different from one another within the returned N-best list.

The process of generating confidence values for **handwriting** within our system is a two stage process. Written input (see Fig. 1C) is first sent to a character recognizer that converts a user's handwriting input to block characters. The second stage is to then match the recognized input to our own handwriting grammars, which consist of keywords such as "optical zoom", and "mega pixels". This is based on a simple character matching algorithm, which disregards case, punctuation and white space, and performs a sliding character match on the given user input and all entries in the grammar. Grammar entries that are either too long or too short (i.e. +-3 characters in length) are discounted, and grammar entries that start with the same character as the given input are given an additional bias (Val=Val+0.1). The top 3 results are then returned to the modality fusion blackboard.

Intra-gestures are used for the resolution of features and objects on the display of the PocketPC. Objects refer to camera products such as the "EOS 300D" and are provided in the form of graphical pictures, while features refer to keywords such as "price" and are provided as scrolling text on the user's PocketPC display (see Fig.'s 1A and 1D respectively). Regarding object resolution, nine, four, two, or one object rectangles may be displayed on the PocketPC's display at any one time depending on the current mode that the user is in. We generate confidence values by drawing a rectangle around the user's "point" coordinates, equal in size to that of the other rectangles on the screen. The intersection between this Active Area (AA) and each of the Image Rectangles (IR) is then calculated and used to generate the confidence value (AA/IR), which generates a value between 0.25 and 1.0. If the user points to an image rectangle at perfect centre, the rectangles line up and the score is 1.0. If the rectangles only half line up (side by side), the score is 0.5, and if the user points to a corner, the score is 0.25. The 3 best results are then mapped onto the range 0.0 and 1.0 through the use of exponents, for compatibility with the other modalities. For feature resolution, which is based on a user pointing out a keyword from a scrolling text bar at the bottom of the PocketPC's display, we currently allocate the static values 0.8, 0.4, and 0.1 to the 3-best results. 0.8 is assigned to the keyword the user clicked on, while 0.4 and 0.1 are assigned to the keyword to the left and the keyword two to the left of that which the user clicked on respectively. We do not currently consider point coordinates above or below the scrolling text bar when resolving features. We intend in the future, to allow the user to increase and decrease the speed of the scrolling text, and to have access to the font size and direction in which the text flows. These changes would undoubtedly also need to be considered in future confidence scoring techniques for this modality.

All **extra-gestures** are currently given a confidence weighting of 1.0, and no N-best list is returned for this modality in the current scenario. In the case that multiple objects are taken from the shelf (and no "compare" command was given), timestamps are used to resolve the most recent object. The confidence weighting limitation is due to the fact that we do not keep track of the actual physical location of the individual products on the shelf. When compared to a real shopping scenario where each product has a defined position on a shelf (and labeled name and price information), accommodating for a finer resolution would not be difficult to program into our application, and would perhaps allow a modality fusion component to consider products to the left and to the right of the product selected. Information on similar looking product boxes might also be useful for extra-gesture resolution, and thus also confidence scoring.

It should be noted that the generation of adequate confidence values for use by a multimodal system is still an area of ongoing research. Although speech recognizers for example are nowadays built on top of a great wealth of statistical data that has arisen through decades of experience, there is still limited statistical data for determining how best to rate the confidence of modalities such as gesture in different mobile environment contexts. Kumar et al [7] have presented a study that investigates the performance of a multimodal (speech and intra-gesture based) system under field conditions. For this purpose subjects were involved in strenuous activities while performing map-based tasks. The results show that although performance of the single recognizer gets worse with a rising degree of exertion, the overall multimodal recognition results remain stable. A further concern when comparing confidence values between same-type and different-type recognizers is that the confidence weightings may never have been "fair" to begin with, as would result from designers using different statistical models to train their recognizers. As such, an application using multiple recognizers may have to incorporate a penalty-reward system, in which accurate and inaccurate results are used to balance out discrepancies between the different recognizers.

3.2 Time-Frames and Input Synchronization

Dealing with the temporal order in which modal input occurs - often referred to as *multimodal synchronization* [10] - is one aspect of particular importance to multimodal systems. Different input modalities may occur at different times in a dialog act, and each of these possibilities must be correctly accommodated for. As an example, the speech input *"What is the optical zoom of this camera?"* might have a gesture input accompanying it either before, during, or after the actual utterance, and each of these three possibilities would be correct. In our scenario, we use the issuing of a feature to determine our timeframe markers. We distinguish between the period before (a timeframe of up to several minutes), during (a timeframe typically 4 to 5 seconds long) and after (a timeframe of either 0.5, 1.5 or 3.5 seconds long, depending on a user's familiarity with the system) a feature has been issued. If the timeframe values are too small the chances of 'valid' user input being disregarded will be high, and if the values are too large the chances of old or 'invalid' user input being accepted will be high.

Fig. 4 depicts the timeframes within a typical user interaction. Each time a user interacts with an object on the display, it is recorded onto the modality fusion blackboard. In this fashion, a user's interaction may span a timeframe of up to several minutes. However, once the system is aware that the user has started to issue a feature, which is checked each time speech, handwriting or a special subclass of intra-gesture input is provided (as shown in Fig. 1D), the user is given a limited period of time before the modality fusion process begins. This time period depends on whether or not objects with *TimeType* equal to 'present' or 'past' have been selected in the current user-turn, and whether or not the user is familiar or unfamiliar with the system (defined in a user property file). If an object has been selected within the current user-turn, the object will contain a *TimeType* value equal to 'present' and the module will conclude it's processing within 500ms. If however only 'past' objects exist on the blackboard, the user is either referring to an object selected in a previous user-turn, or the user has not yet selected an object. Familiar users are provided with an additional second in this case, while users less familiar with the system are provided with an additional 3 seconds to complete their current dialogue act. The trade-off for extending the timeframe in this manner is that the system appears more sluggish in the case that the user is indeed referring to a past object.

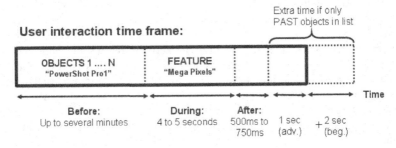

Fig. 4. Input synchronization: 'Before', 'during', and 'after' durations, as used by our system

Initial studies on our system have shown that it generally takes a trained user around 4 to 5 seconds to carry out a complete dialogue act. As an example, these 4 to 5 seconds refer to the time it takes a user to press the talk button once to start talking and once again after having spoken to stop talking for a speech-speech interaction, or the time it takes a user to select an object and to then start and stop writing a keyword on the display of the PocketPC for a gesture-handwriting interaction.

In the case that a feature is found on the blackboard but no object exists, the user is briefly informed and provided with an additional 4 seconds to complete their interaction, after which time the feature is removed from the blackboard. Overlaid and conflicting input can occur for both the feature and object values, however feature conflicts are less frequent due to the restrictive timeframes imposed on the user once a feature input has been initiated. Our system resolves object conflicts by first removing older nodes with similar modality types. We then remove nodes that fall outside a given timeframe (based on the most recent object's timestamp plus a given time-margin), and then recalculate confidence values based on a matching algorithm that considers each remaining node's N-best list (where N=3). Nodes with object values that appear in the N-best lists of multiple nodes have their confidence value increased in this way, and the node with the best overall confidence value is then finally selected.

An initial study on input synchronization in our mobile scenario has been inline with experiments conducted by Oviatt et.al. [10], who shows for example that pen onset usually precedes speech onset, and pointing gestures are integrated with parts of a speech utterance in a natural manner. Regarding speech recognition, we have observed similar to [15] that word-error rates vary directly with speaking style such that the more natural the speech delivery, the higher the recognition system's word error rate. This is more so in our mobile scenario, as we often only provide a single way for users to speak out an utterance that could normally be communicated in one of many ways, e.g. *"what is the price of ..."* and *"how much does ... cost"*. Regarding setting up the RFID technology, we observed that it was sometimes required to tag product boxes multiple times in order for the system to recognize them correctly. In general however, we have found that users were quite content with the performance and accuracy of the system, and it was also observed that the learn-in time (at least for non-overlapped modalities) was acceptable.

4 Usability Study

In this section we describe the results of an exploratory user study that we recently conducted on the Mobile ShopAssist. The primary goal of the usability study was to measure the modality preference of users when interacting with the mobile system. A total of 23 different modality combinations were tested, and these were derived from the three elementary modalities speech, handwriting and gesture. For our modality-free language, <FEATURE><OBJECT>+, the combinations ranged from unimodal to multimodal interaction, and from non-overlaid to overlaid input. Aside from modality preference, we also studied how intuitive the individual modality combinations were to use, and asked users what effect being immersed in a public or private space would have on their use of the three base modality types. A total of 440 user interactions were logged by the system throughout the study, averaging 31 interactions per person. Although we kept a user history of interactions, this study does not delve into aspects of system accuracy or system learnability.

4.1 Method

Our usability study was conducted at the University of Saarland in one of the department's computer terminal rooms. We believe this laboratory setting to differ from a real-world environment in two ways. Firstly, there were few if any other people in the terminal room during the times we conducted the testing (aside from the instructor and the user), and secondly, background noises were kept to a minimum. We conducted the study on a total of 14 people who were either a little familiar or unfamiliar with the system. The study was conducted in English with users that could speak fluent English. 10 of our users were students and lecturers from the computer science department aged between 25 and 37 years, while the remaining 4 users were not from the computer science department and were unfamiliar with the system.

Each user was given a PocketPC device and a headset connected to the PocketPC's audio jack through which the user could speak into and listen to the output from. They were asked to stand in front of an instrumented shelf containing real-world camera boxes. As described in Section 2.2, the users were allowed to mix-and-match modality input combinations when creating their FEATURE-OBECT dialogue inputs, and were also allowed to overlap modalities when communicating with the system. A total of 12 non-overlapped modality combinations and 11 overlapped modality combinations were tested (as shown in Fig. 5). Each test session generally required between 45 and 60 minutes to complete. Users were explained the base modalities that could be used when building feature and object dialogue interactions. They were told that the order of the inputs was irrelevant, i.e. feature then object, or object then feature, and that system errors were to be expected but should not bias their answer as not all modality combinations had been implemented. There were a total of 10 different objects and 13 different features available to the subjects.

The usability study had two parts, the first being an *observation* of each user interacting with the system, and the second being a *written questionnaire*. Within the observation, each user was free to choose their own modality combinations while interacting with the system. Most users managed 4 or 5 different modality combinations within this part before needing to be reminded of the remaining modality combinations. At this point, users were specifically told the order in which they should use the remaining modalities. After each interaction, the user was asked to rate the modality combination by answering the question *"Would you use this modality combination?"*. The rating scale used was a set of preferences that we later mapped onto a scale from 0.0 to 3.0, in which "0=prefer not, 1=maybe not, 2=maybe yes, and 3=prefer yes". Following the practical component, the users were asked to complete a written questionnaire that again asked them to repeat their preference for each individual modality combination, and to also state whether or not they thought the modality combinations were intuitive. Several other questions relevant to mobile and multimodal interaction were then also asked, and the survey ended with the user stating their favourite input modality combination.

4.2 Usability Results

For simplicity, we refer to the individual modality combinations via their abbreviations – speech (S), handwriting (H), intra-gesture (GI), and extra-gesture (GE). As an example, the interaction: <FEATURE modality=speech><OBJECT modality=speech> is analogous to the modality combination SS.

4.2.1 Preferred Modality Combinations

Fig. 5 shows the modality combinations categorized into the groups non-overlapped and overlapped. From the averages shown in the figure, it can be seen that users generally prefer non-overlapped modality combinations (A_v=1.58) to overlapped modality combinations (A_v=0.60). Using a Mann-Whitney U test, this was also shown to be statistically significant in 8 out of 14 subjects: U(12,11)<35, p<0.05, and only 3 subjects had a p>0.12. The non-overlapped combinations have been further grouped according to their start modality, from which it can be seen that the use of speech for the feature (A_v=2.09) is preferred to the use of intra-gesture (A_v=1.39) or handwriting (A_v=1.25) for the feature. Also interesting to note is that within each subgroup of start modalities, the use of the same modality (unimodal) for both the feature and the object referents received the highest or near highest scores (see darkly shaded modality combinations in Fig. 5). Similar to the non-overlapped sub-groups, we categorized the overlapped combinations by their overlapping segment types – feature, object, or both feature and object. It can be seen that users preferred overlapped object information most ($A_v=0.99$) out of all of the overlapped modality combinations. This rating increases to $A_v=1.33$ when speech is set as one of the overlapped modalities and increases to $A_v=1.57$ when handwriting is excluded from the possibilities.

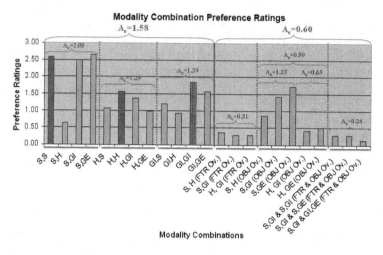

Fig. 5. The 23 modality combinations categorized into the groups overlaid and non-overlaid, and rated according to preference (0=prefer not, 1=maybe not, 2=maybe yes, 3=prefer yes). The darker shaded modalities represent unimodal combinations

Fig. 6 shows all of the modality combinations ranked in order of user preference. It can be seen that SGE is the most preferred modality combination, and that this is very closely followed by SS and SGI. Using the Mann-Whitney U test, the preference for these three modalities when compared to all other modality combinations was significant in 12 out of 14 subjects: $U(3,20)<9$, $p<0.05$. The benefit of allowing a user to provide deictic input can also be seen in that 2 of the top 3 modality combinations, and 7 of the top 9 modality combinations used gesture to identify the object. The successful wedding of the modalities speech and gesture is further exemplified by the overlapped object combinations SGE (rating=1.71) and SGI (rating=1.43), whose preference was shown to be significant in 6 from 14 subjects when compared to the other overlapped modality combinations (U-test, $p<0.36$). As shown in Fig. 6, the modalities have been grouped according to rating point falls between the individual modalities, where the first drop of 0.64 borders on significance (Wilcoxon, $z=-1.807$, $p=0.071$). The first set of combinations are preferred by users ($A_v=2.57$), while the second set of modality combinations ($A_v=1.58$) lie within the category "maybe no" and "maybe yes". The third set of modality combinations has a ranking value directly equivalent to "maybe no", and the fourth set of modality combinations ($A_v=0.36$) is least preferred. The highlighted columns represent those modalities that were not implemented in our system, and although most of these modality combinations exist on the lower side of the ranking scale, the incorporation of the modality combination HH will now be considered for future versions of the demonstrator.

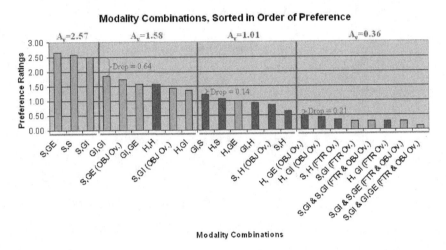

Fig. 6. The 23 modality combinations ranked in order of preference. The darker shaded modalities represent those that have not been implemented in the Mobile ShopAssist

4.2.2 Modality Intuition
We measure each modality's intuitiveness in two separate tests, one conducted during the written component (Fig. 7A), while the other conducted during the practical component (Fig. 7B). Fig. 7A shows the results provided by our subjects to the question: "*Do you feel that this modality combination was intuitive to use?*" ("no", "yes"), while Fig. 7B shows the first 4 modality combinations used by our subjects during the practical component. The modalities in Fig. 7B are weighted exponentially, such that a modality chosen 1st receives a weighting of 1000, while modalities chosen 2nd, 3rd and 4th receive the values 100, 10, and 1 respectively. The resulting weights for the individual modalities are shown in the bottom right of Fig. 7B.

The written component showed that 5 of the 12 non-overlapped modality combinations (SS, SGI, SGE, GIGI, and HH) were rated significantly *intuitive* by our subjects: $Chi^2(1, N=14) > 10.286$, $p < 0.001$. In comparison, 6 of the 11 overlapped modality combinations were rated significantly *non-intuitive* by our subjects: $Chi^2(1, N=14) > 4.57$, $p < 0.33$.

When correlated with the lower graph one can see that the modality combinations SGI, SGE, SS, and GIGI were mirrored as being intuitive. The modality combination HH was however never selected for use by any of our users within their 1st four interactions, despite 13 out of 14 users rating the modality as being intuitive during the written component. The overlapped modality combinations, SGI (overlapped object) and SGE (overlapped object) were also never used within the 1st four modality combinations. Many people commented that handwriting was too slow to use, and perhaps this was a reason why HH was never selected by our users within the practical component. The overlapped modality combinations may also have simply been overlooked by users due to the already wide range of non-overlapped modality combinations to choose from.

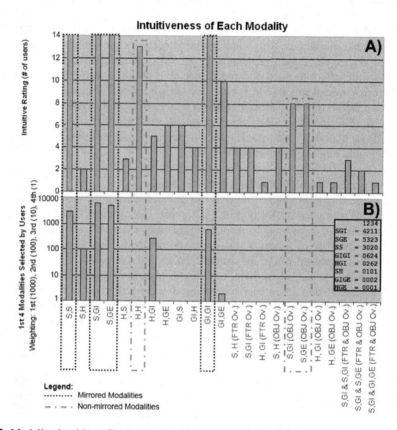

Fig. 7. Modality intuition. Graph A) shows the modality intuition results provided by users during the written component, while graph B) shows the 1st four modality combinations selected by users in the practical component, and their weightings in the bottom right

4.2.3 Public and Private Spaces, and Observable Modality Combinations

One of the questions within our written questionnaire was with respect to how the user would feel using the modalities speech, handwriting, intra gesture, and extra gesture while in a public space (e.g. a shopping mall), and while in a private space (e.g. at home). The choices given to our subjects were "embarrassed", "hesitant", and "comfortable". Chi-square tests show that our subjects would feel comfortable using intra-gesture, extra-gesture, and handwriting within a public environment:

$Chi^2(2,N=14)>8.714$, $p<0.013$. Within a private environment, our users would feel comfortable using all base modalities: $Chi^2(2,N=14)>8.714$, $p<0.013$.

We also compared the group of modalities that are entirely observable by surrounding people (SGE, SS) with those that are entirely non observable by surrounding people (GIGI, HH, HGI, GIH). Excluding modality combinations that are only partly observable (e.g. SGI), it can be seen that within this usability study, users preferred the extrusive modalities ($A_v=2.61$) over the non-extrusive modalities ($A_v=1.43$). SGE (2.64) and SS (2.57) were ranked highest from the entirely observable modalities, while GIGI (1.86), HH (1.57) and HGI (1.36) were ranked highest from the entirely non-observable modalities. This implies that at least within a laboratory setting and for the product type "digital cameras", the feelings of "embarrassment" and "hesitation" had little effect on modality preference. We are now also evaluating usability results from a second round of tests conducted on 28 users at a local electronics store[7], to see what differences might exist between a laboratory and a real-world setting. An average of 13.8 people could be seen from the shelf's location during each of the tests, and our hypothesis that the results will see a modality preference shift towards non-observable modalities appear to be correct.

4.2.4 Subjective Results Obtained from the Study

Several interesting points were raised by our subjects during the study that may serve as a future set of guidelines for interface designers. Our subjects said for example that their preference for a particular modality would change depending on the type of task at hand and the type of products that they were shopping for. Users mentioned that speech and handwriting would for example be a good alternative to gesture if an object was not accessible, not present, or difficult to find on the Pocket PC display or shelf. They noted that in comparison to the extrusive modalities like speech, non-extrusive modalities like intra-gesture would be better suited when dealing with sensitive objects like contraception. Some users also preferred the simplicity of consistent modalities (i.e. unimodal combinations) over mixed modalities, and a further distinction was made between modality combinations that were part loud and part silent such as SH.

Regarding speech, some users found the camera names such as PowerShot S1IS and FinePix A202 non-intuitive to pronounce, despite the system correctly understanding the user and despite the user being told to disregard system failures. Regarding handwriting, users often commented that the feature and object names like "mega pixels" and "PowerShot Pro1" took too long to write. Users also stated that intra-gesture for feature input (i.e. the visual WCIS) would be better if all options could be seen at the one time, rather than needing to wait for the text to scroll into focus, which they said would be problematic if they were stressed for time. With respect to extra-gesture, several users mentioned that pointing to the objects would be an improvement, especially for heavier product types, or for people that had their hands already full with shopping, winter-jackets and the Pocket PC device. These people did however like the ability to touch products as well, and many stated that they liked being able to physically touch a product before purchasing it.

---

[7] Conrad Electronic, Saarbrücken. http://www.conrad.de

5 Conclusions and Future Work

In this paper we have presented a multimodal mobile shopping assistant that integrates interactions on a mobile device and interactions with real world shopping products (i.e. digital cameras). For this purpose, we have incorporated three types of input modalities on a PDA: spoken language, handwriting and intra-gestures, which we have combined with extra-gestures performed with real world artifacts in the user's environment. We have discussed the various multimodal input combinations out of which we have implemented and tested 13 in our prototype. We have discussed how multimodal requests can be resolved by the use of an N-best list and provided some empirical values for an appropriate timeframe to ensure the correct input synchronization of the different modalities.

The results returned by the usability study have highlighted several important facts about mobile multimodal interaction. Most importantly, the study has shown that from the 23 modality combinations offered to our users within the mobile shopping scenario, speech and extra-gesture (SGE) were the preferred choice, closely followed by speech and speech (SS) and speech and intra-gesture (SGI). Indeed, the success of these three modalities is further iterated in that these modes are directly representative of how people interact with other people, and in particular with sales assistants. For future work, we now plan to evaluate a second round of usability testing that has recently been conducted at a local electronics store. We also plan to implement the unimodal combination of handwriting and handwriting (HH), which was ranked higher than expected by our users, and plan to make use of additional context information (e.g. user preferences and user habits) to improve the resolution of multimodal user requests. Such information could be either retrieved from an external user model or by allowing the user to correct the system's false positives through an error recovery procedure.

Acknowledgements

This work was partially funded by the German Federal Ministry for Education and Research (BMBF) under the contract no. 01 IN C02, as part of COLLATE II.

References

1. Baudel, T., Beaudouin-Lafon, M., CHARADE: Remote Control of Objects using Free-Hand Gestures, ACM Journal, Vol. 36, no. 7, 1993, pp. 28-35.
2. Bühler, D., Minker, W., Häußler, J., Krüger, S., Flexible Multimodal Human-Machine Interaction in Mobile Environments, In ICSLP, 2002, pp. 169-172.
3. Cohen, P., Johnston, M., McGee, M., Oviatt, S., Pittman, J., Simith, I., Chen, L., Clow, J., Quickset: Multimodal interaction for distributed applications, Proc. of ACM International Multimedia Conference, 1997, pp. 31-40.
4. Cole, R.A., Mariani, J., Uszkoreit, H., Zaenen A., Zue, V., Survey of the State of the Art in Human Language Technology, Book, Chp1, 1995.

5. Heckmann, D., "Introducing Situational Statements as an integrating Data Structure for User Modeling, Context-Awareness and Resource-Adaptive Computing", ABIS Workshop on adaptivity and user modelling in interactive software systems, 2003.

6. Kendon, A., Conducting Interaction: Patterns of behavior in focused encounters, Book: Cambridge University Press, 1990.

7. Kumar, S., Cohen, P.R., Coulston, R., Multimodal Interaction under Exerted Conditions in a Natural Field Setting. In Proc. of the Sixth International Conference on Multimodal Interfaces (ICMI), 2004, pp. 227-234.

8. Krüger, A., Butz, A., Müller, C., Stahl, C., Wasinger, R., Steinberg, K.E., Dirschl, A., The Connected User Interface: Realizing a Personal Situated Navigation Service, Proc. of the 9th International Conference on Intelligent User Interfaces, 2004, pp. 161-168.

9. Newcomb, E., Pashley, T., Stasko, J., Mobile Computing in the Retail Arena, Proceedings of the ACM Conference on Human Factors in Computing Systems (CHI), 2003, pp. 337-344.

10. Oviatt, S., DeAngeli, A., Kuhn, K., Integration and synchronization of input modes during multimodal human-computer interaction, In Proc. of CHI, 1997, pp. 415-422.

11. Oviatt, S. Mutual disambiguation of recognition errors in a multimodal architecture. In Proceedings of the Conference on Human Factors in Computing Systems, 1999, pp. 576–583.

12. Pastel, R., Skalsky, N., Demonstrating Information in Simple Gestures, In Proc. of the 9th international conference on Intelligent User Interfaces, 2004, pp. 360-361.

13. Wahlster, W., Towards Symmetric Multimodality: Fusion and Fission of Speech, Gesture, and Facial Expression, In. Proc. of the 26th German Conference on Artificial Intelligence, 2003, pp. 1-18.

14. Wasinger, R., Krüger, A., Multi-modal Interaction with Mobile Navigation Systems, In: W. Wahlster (ed.): Special Journal Issue "Conversational User Interfaces", it - Information Technology 46 (2004) 6, München: Oldenbourg Wissenschaftsverlag (ISSN 1611-2776), 2004, pp. 322-331.

15. Weintraub, M., Taussig, K., Hunicke, K., and Snodgrass, A. Effect of speaking style on LVCSR performance. In Proc. of the International Conference on Spoken Language Processing, 1996, pp. 16–19.

AwareMirror:
A Personalized Display Using a Mirror

Kaori Fujinami, Fahim Kawsar, and Tatsuo Nakajima

Department of Computer Science,
Waseda University, Tokyo, Japan
{fujinami, fahim, tatsuo}@dcl.info.waseda.ac.jp

Abstract. In this paper, we propose a personalized display, "*AwareMirror*: an augmented mirror". AwareMirror presents information relevant to a person in front of it by super-imposing his/her image. A toothbrush has been chosen as an identification tool while proximity sensors have been utilized to detect a person's position (in front of the mirror). Also, three types of information that can affect a user's decision have been selected. The mirror has been constructed using an acrylic magic mirror board and ordinal computer monitor. The acrylic board has been attached in front of the monitor, and only bright color from the display can penetrate the board. As a result of preliminary evaluation, we found that the mirror is useful to offer information in an unobtrusive manner while preserving its metaphor.

1   Introduction

Our daily lives and environments are full of computational devices and a heavy amount of information due to the advancement of technologies. Not only traditional computers, but also small palm sized devices like cellular phones and personal digital assistants (PDA) have network connectivity and offer various information like weather forecasting, today's schedule, etc. This allows people to acquire information anytime anywhere. Also, a new variation of traditional displays like ambient displays[15] are installed into our daily living for showing information to a user. However, if these devices do not provide information in an appropriate way, i.e. considering proper timing, location, identity, and intuitiveness, then computation devices cannot offer comfortable services, because people feel inconvenient to their daily living, and the inconvenience makes them confused how to use the technologies. This means that a user requires to have some efforts to acquire useful information. Offering appropriate information in respective situations is a major research topic in ubiquitous/pervasive computing environments, and this is known as *context-awareness*.

To extract contextual information of a person, we propose to use a sensor augmented everyday artefact named "Sentient Artefact" [3]. An everyday artefact has a primary role and functionality(-ies). A system retrieves its user's context from the state of these artefacts, and decides on proper contextual responses. A

H.W. Gellersen et al. (Eds.): PERVASIVE 2005, LNCS 3468, pp. 315–332, 2005.

stationary daily object like a kitchen sink or a mirror stand can offer a user's location. Moreover, the state of personal belongings such as a purse or toothbrush can be utilized to identify its user. Therefore, we prefer to extract the state-of-use context by augmenting everyday artefacts with various sensors. Also, we expect to reduce the uncertainty and availability of higher abstract information by integrating various sentient artefacts.

In this paper, we propose a personalized display, AwareMirror, where we have augmented a traditional mirror with some value added services. Using the mirror as a display while preserving its metaphor provides a user with a feeling of seamless augmentation. The contributions of this paper are that 1) it provides a notion of adding values to our daily objects while preserving its metaphor, 2) it provides a novel displaying technology using a magic mirror, and 3) it allows to change the mode to show detailed information through a user's explicit interaction.

The structure of the paper is as follows: In Section 2, we introduce a notion of mirror augmentation with cyber world. In Section 3, we examine existing work on context-awareness in terms of utilizing a mirror as an interface, and presenting information in a natural way. We describe the design of the mirror in Section 4, and the prototype implementation is shown in Section 5. Section 6 presents the evaluation regarding the selection of display contents and person identification technologies that are gathered by surveying users. An primary usability testing is also shown. In Section 7, we discuss the issues of the current design and implementation that we have found during the development and evaluation processes. Finally, in Section 8, we conclude the paper and show future directions.

2   A Mirror and Its Augmentation with Cyber World

A mirror has been utilized by people since ancient days. It reflects physical objects appearing in front of it. Often we become inquisitive about our physical appearance by looking at a mirror. Moreover, while using a mirror we can also see and comprehend what is happening in the backgrounds, e.g. someone is passing, a kettle is boiling, etc. This reflective nature is essential for a mirror. We usually stay in front of a mirror for a period of time, which suggests the acceptability of presenting information on the surface of the mirror.

We often think about immediate events or something important e.g. schedule of the day, weather forecasting at our today's destination, etc., while performing something else there. We are able to process or comprehend such a variety of information simultaneously while doing another task in front of a mirror, that is usually the main task, e.g. drying hair, brushing teeth, etc., if the information is shown naturally without disturbing the main task (See Fig. 1).

Our hypothesis is that *a mirror which displays information representing people's context can be easily accepted by them because of its nature: reflection.* We call the mirror *AwareMirror*. The mirror utilizes people's prior understandings of a traditional mirror and augments its target to reflect both physical and virtual

Fig. 1. Multi-tasking in front of a mirror

world. This allows a user to be unconscious of its existence although it provides information relevant to them. The important and difficult design principle is that the mirror should be a traditional one first of all. This means that the functionality as a display should not go beyond one as a reflector. Otherwise it becomes a display with a mirror, not a mirror with a display.

3   Related Work

AwareMirror displays information relevant to a person in front of it. The information reflects his/her current or future status, which is often referred to as contextual information or simply context[1]. So, AwareMirror can be considered as a context-aware system.

There is little work regarding the augmentation or using the metaphor of a mirror. Augmented Mirror[7] is an augmented reality system which overlays virtual objects on the mirror. It utilizes a video monitor and a camera to make a *mirror* and shows an application that a person can see him/her with virtual eye-glasses super-imposed on his/her image. Although it uses a metaphor of a mirror, it merely provides an application of image processing technologies. Next, i-mirror[14] is proposed based on the principle that information services and interactive experiences should be offered by enhancing functions of objects in our life space to provide the ease of use with people. It consists of a video camera, magic mirrors, and a video projector to match the line of sight naturally and proposes applications like historical context displays and virtual make-up systems. Its utilization of a magic mirror to super-impose an image on the mirror is close to ours, however, it heavily depends on video capturing technologies which lead to a feeling of privacy violation. Also, it utilizes a very limited notion of contextual information, i.e. past information of the person in front of it. These two systems just use a metaphor of a mirror, but a user does not use them as an ordinal mirror.

Regarding to information representation, an ambient display[15] in the context of tangible user interfaces[5] offers an information using human's peripheral awareness capabilities. Our AwareMirror is also an ambient display in a sense because it allows a person to focus on his/her main tasks while offering information in his/her line of sights. The work of Rodenstein [11] can also be categorized into an ambient display. It applies the opposite notion of a mirror and the biggest characteristic of a window, *transparency*, to overlap information in cyber space, i.e. short-term weather forecast, onto a view of outside. Information visualization with artistic impression like Informative Art [4] and InfoCanvas [13] suggests an "augmented paintings", which can naturally fit into daily living. Their roles are presenting information from the beginning, while AwareMirror has more strict constraints that it should not change its original usage as a mirror while offering additional values, *personalized information.*

The uniqueness of AwareMirror is using low-level sensing technologies and augmenting the notion of a traditional mirror in a natural way. This is expected to take feelings of obtrusiveness away as well as burden of information retrieval and its understanding. AwareMirror suggests how computing capabilities can infiltrate into daily objects. In the next section we describe the requirements for AwareMirror.

4   Design of AwareMirror

4.1   Requirements

As described in Section 2, we must preserve the metaphor of the mirror intact. Additionally, the following requirements need to be satisfied for further value addition.

1. Implicit and natural user identification
2. Minimum feelings of privacy violation
3. Types of information and displaying methods suitable for background processing

Information should appear and disappear automatically to keep its natural usage of a mirror and avoid turning it into mere "display device". So, the user should be identified implicitly as well as naturally. This higher level of contextual information should be extracted without using privacy sensitive sensing technologies. A user usually prefers precise information, but he/she denies to use a service if the service uses the vision-based sensing technology because a camera used in the technology causes a feeling to violate privacy. Mostly the location where a mirror is installed is privacy sensitive by considering actions in the location like changing clothes or making up, etc. Therefore, the privacy requirement should be taken into account. We should also consider the characteristics of tasks conducted in front of a mirror to specify required information and displaying methods. AwareMirror is a mirror first of all, which means that a user primarily does his/her main task, e.g. washing face, and he/she might feel obstructive if irrelevant information appears during the main task. Also, it should not interrupt the task due to understanding information or hiding his/her own figure by super-imposed information.

These requirements are specific to a mirror and installation place. We believe that the development of artefacts should analyze the requirements that depend on each daily object and its location.

4.2   Design Issues

We describe the design issues and approaches of AwareMirror from the several points of view, 1) user detection, 2) display method, 3) contents to show, and 4) modalities of displaying.

Detecting a User: There are several ways to identify a person as follows: 1) face recognition by capturing video images, 2) holding a tag that represents him/her, 3) using biometric information like fingerprint, and 4) acquiring context from everyday artefacts. Biometric-based identification is not appropriate in this case because a user has to put his/her finger explicitly, which might break the first requirement: "implicit and natural identification". The tag-based approach should be rejected due to the same reason. Also, video capturing might provide a feeling of privacy violation.

So, we have utilized the state-of-use of everyday artefacts that are rarely shared with others. Using an everyday artefact's natural functionalities and understanding of people's usage of the artefacts allow an application developer to concentrate on the use of artefacts themselves, rather than the operational environment. Context information can be retrieved from a user's daily activities in a natural way. Such everyday artefacts include a safety razor (an electric shaver), a toothbrush, a comb, etc. We have decided to use a toothbrush for detecting a user because it is gender neutral and utilized by almost everyone.

Three types of information are integrated to detect a user's presence in front of the mirror: 1) the existence of a person in front of a mirror using an infrared range finder, 2) the existence of a toothbrush around the mirror, and 3) the information about the owner of the toothbrush. In Section 6.1, we will discuss the survey of users about alternatives like tag-based, image-based, biometric-based, and artefact-based identifications.

Method of Displaying: We have two options regarding to the method of displaying information on a mirror. One is reflecting on the opposite side of a mirror, e.g. a wall in front of a mirror. The other is penetration behind a mirror. They have both merits and demerits. The *reflection* method does not require a special mirror. We developed this alternative version first, where a 2x4 LED-based abstract display that expresses information through the number of lightning is attached on the front wall of an ordinal mirror (see Fig. 2). However, appropriate positioning of the display was required to avoid the LED display being hidden by a user and other persons crossing behind. Adjusting his/her position to an appropriate position leads the person to feel *"using a system"*. Instead, a

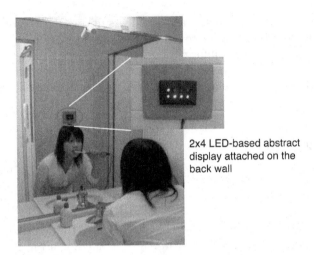

Fig. 2. A mirror with 2x4 LED-based abstract display

flexible projection system like proposed in Steerable interfaces[9] can change the location of presented information dynamically. But it requires a camera-based positioning system and large mechanical settings which are not suitable for our everyday living spaces. Also, the order of picture and text have to be reversed because of the nature of a mirror. On the other hand, the *penetration* method requires a special mirror, by which the image and/or text behind the mirror can be seen through. Of course it also reflects physical objects in front of it at the same time. However, we need not take care of a person's position as well as an order of words and direction of pictures. We have selected this option using a "*magic mirror*". A magic mirror is a translucent panel that reflects things in front of it when the difference of brightness on both sides are large. In other words, things behind the panel can be seen if the brightness difference is small. Therefore, we have utilized this principle to display information.

Types of Information: As introduced in Section 2, we are brushing our teeth, making up, etc., that is normally done in situations where we are considering immediate events or something important over the day to come in the morning. We consider information related to immediate events is useful in such a case. We also often change our decision if someone tells us about weather forecasting, traffic accident, etc. Considering these facts, we have selected the following information to be displayed that can affect our behavior and help decision making.

- Notification and detail information of transportation trouble that the person is going to use by his/her schedule
- Weather forecasting at the destination where he/she will go
- Time to leave his/her home or office for the destination
- Details of the closest event on his/her schedule

These types of information can remind us of taking something required, e.g. umbrella and documents, and offers us the opportunity to take an alternative route to go to the destination, or rush ourselves. Therefore, we consider that it is appropriate for information presented on a mirror.

Two Modalities of Displaying: Although above listed information can be useful, it might disturb a user's primary task if all information appears on the surface of a mirror. Also, privacy sensitive information can be revealed. Therefore, we have decided to apply two phase interactions with the mirror: implicit and explicit.

In the implicit mode, it plays the role of an ambient display, which shows abstract information on the periphery of a user's line of sight. So, in this mode, people use AwareMirror as an ordinary mirror. Abstract information can be represented using images and colors we are familiar with and therefore easy to understand at a glance. This is also a solution that takes into account of the characteristic of the place, *in front of a mirror*, since some people often take their glasses off while brushing their teeth and washing their faces. Therefore, we consider that it is useful for them to be just notified of some important events. In the default mode, the mirror does not display anything, so it just looks like a mirror. However, as described above, if a person appears in front of AwareMirror and a toothbrush is utilized, then AwareMirror turns into the implicit mode. It also returns to the default mode on detecting a user's leaving from the place. These transitions occur automatically.

In the explicit mode, however, it presents detailed information, where they explicitly use it as a display rather than a mirror. It shows information in more detail using text information. This mode of interaction might break our design philosophy if we offer detailed information automatically because it could stop a user's current task whether a person wants to get it or not. Therefore, we provide the flexibility to change his/her mode of the usage of the mirror whenever a user wants to change the modes explicitly. On entering into the explicit mode, the role of AwareMirror turns into an information display, not an ordinary mirror. This is caused by the person him/herself explicitly. Hence, we consider that a feeling of disturbance does not come up in his/her mind. We also consider our approach meets the requirements for ambient displays introduced by Mankoff et al[6].: "Easy transition to more in-depth information".

5   Prototype Implementation

5.1   System Architecture

Figure 3 shows the overall architecture of the AwareMirror system, which consists of four major parts: the physical world information manager, integrated applications, the AwareMirror front end, and the sentient toothbrush.

We consider applications running in a space can share some pieces of information like the location of an object, the state-of-use of the object, its owner(s), etc. Therefore, we have developed a system software called *Bazaar* to manage

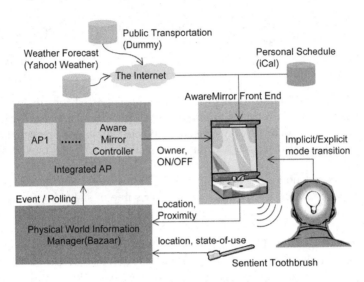

Fig. 3. Overall architecture of AwareMirror

such physical world information separately from each application [2]. Integrated applications that aggregate information from many sentient artefacts are developed on top of *Bazaar*. The applications also control sentient artefacts by using collected information. In this case, one of integrated applications, the AwareMirror controller, is responsible for notifying the AwareMirror front end of requiring operations, i.e. turning on or off the display. This allows the AwareMirror system to replace various identification technologies, i.e. biometric-based, image-based, etc., according to each application's requirements. When the AwareMirror controller receives two types of events: 1) co-location of a sentient toothbrush used by a person with AwareMirror and 2) presence of him/her in front of the mirror, the AwareMirror controller makes the AwareMirror front end to turn on, and passes the ID of the toothbrush's owner to it.

On the AwareMirror front end, the detection of a user, information rendering, and mode transition by him/her are dealt by five software components to be described in Section 5.3. A personal scheduler, public transportation information service, and weather forecasting service are used as external information sources. Finally, a sensor augmented toothbrush, the *sentient toothbrush*, detects the beginning and end of brushing.

An ID is assigned to each sentient artefact, which is detected by some recognition systems like a radio frequency identification(RFID) system, and registered into *Bazaar*. All these components cooperate with each other to offer the implicit and natural interaction between human and augmented artefacts.

5.2 Hardware Settings of AwareMirror

Figure 4 shows an overview and assembling scene of AwareMirror. As described in Section 4, information is projected behind the mirror. An acrylic magic mir-

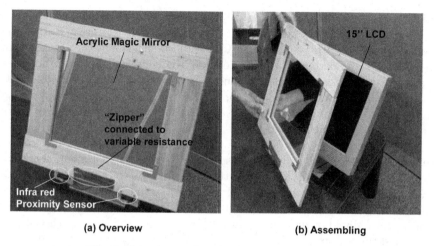

(a) Overview   (b) Assembling

Fig. 4. Overview and assembling of AwareMirror

ror is attached on an ordinal liquid crystal display (LCD) and the information is controlled through a Windows-based PC. A "Zipper" metaphor is utilized to achieve transition from the implicit to explicit mode. When a user opens the zipper, the application's operational mode changes to the *explicit mode* and displays detailed information. The system expects him/her to close the zipper to stop displaying and turn to the default black screen because detailed information may contain highly privacy sensitive information as well as avoid taking mirror's functionalities away. If the user does not open the zipper, the application operates in the *implicit mode*, and the display is controlled by the application itself based on the control information received from *Bazzar*. It starts and stops automatically without a user's intervention. One point to note here about the zipper metaphor is that we have used this notion to make the user to feel "Used To" with the system. As we mentioned previously, we want to develop a mirror with some value added services, not a display. We all know how a zipper works and what interaction it needs to offer its service. So the user does not need to learn a new technology. It is natural for us to open a zipper of some containers to get the things inside, in our case, detailed information. Also, the texture and looks of the zipper remind a person of closing, and thus it contributes to avoid keeping relevant information open. A real zipper is connected to a variable resistance-based input device (slider) which is then attached to Phidget Interface Kit[8]. The distance between the mirror and an object in front of it is measured by two Sharp GP2D12[12] infra-red range finders that provide redundant outputs. The sensing range is from 10 cm to 80 cm, and the field of view is 10 degrees for each. They are also connected to Phidget Interface Kit.

5.3   Software Components on AwareMirror Front End

The AwareMirror front end consists of five components: a) Display Controller, b) Interaction Controller, c) Contents Manager, d) Rendering Controller, and e) Human Detector. Display Controller is the heart of the AwareMirror front end, which controls an application's control flow. It waits for HTTP-based service requests from *Bazzar*. Once received the "Turn On Display" request, it constructs information to be displayed through Contents Manager, and the request is delivered to the Rendering Controller to show the contents. On the other hand, if received the "Turn off Display" request, Display Controller closes the display to turn it into the default mode. Also, it monitors a user's interactions through Interaction Controller which handles a user's input to change the mode from implicit to explicit back and forth.

As described in Section 5.1, three types of information source are utilized. We have used the $Yahoo^{TM}$ Japan's weather service and a simulated transportation information service. Currently, iCalendar [10]-based scheduler service "iCal" runs in a Macintosh Powerbook to offer schedule information. We expect this sort of a scheduler service should be provided in personal devices like cell phones or handheld devices in the future. Based on a user's next schedule's location and time, Contents Manager extracts proper weather and transportation information. Such information can vary according to the time of the day. So, Display Controller manages the timing to display based on a user's preference setting.

Rendering Controller renders the information using $Macromedia^{TM}$ Flash movie because of its aesthetic features and easy to build animation capabilities. An appropriate visual component is selected based on a request from Display Controller. What we need to consider is the color of contents because, due to the characteristics of a magic mirror, dark color is hard to see through the translucent panel.

A user's distance from the two infra-red range finders are transformed into information indicating a user's presence in front of the mirror. So, if a person enters within the sensing range (10 cm to 80 cm), an event is transmitted to *Bazaar*. Also, when a user goes out of the range, the event to notify the absence is delivered.

5.4   Sentient Toothbrush

A sentient toothbrush has been augmented with a two-axis accelerometer connected to Phidget Interface Kit. It can detect the start and end of brushing by detecting its vibration. This is achieved by monitoring the change of the acceleration. It reports its change of the state-of-use to *Bazaar*. Currently, the extraction of the state change is processed on a laptop PC, however, it can be replaced by embedded computers that have wireless connectivities.

5.5   Using the Mirror

Figure 5 shows the results of displaying information related to the person in front of it. In Fig. 5-(a), a girl is brushing her teeth while looking at information on the mirror at the periphery of her line of sights. This abstract representation is what is in the *implicit mode* and initially displayed. In this case, it shows the fact that 1) the weather forecast at her today's destination based on her next schedule is fine with an image of sunshine, 2) the maximum temperature

(a) Implicit mode

Textual expression of the upper image: scrolling from right to left.

Line of sights

Opening "Zipper" to get detail information by herself.

(b) Explicit mode: Scrolling Text

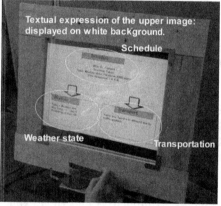

Textual expression of the upper image: displayed on white background.

Schedule

Weather state

Transportation

(c) Explicit mode: black characters with white background

Fig. 5. Usage of AwareMirror, (a) Implicit mode, (b) Explicit mode with scrolling message, and (c) Explicit mode with white background

at her destination is less than 15 degrees Celsius using an image of a girl with gloves and a snow cap, 3) the transportation on the way to her next schedule has some problems indicated with a red car, and 4) time remaining for the next schedule. Her schedule information is utilized as contextual information in the future tense. A screenshot presenting information can be seen in Fig. 6.

If she wants to know more about the information presented abstractly, she will suspend her current task, i.e. brushing her teeth, and open the "Zipper" to get details by herself (Fig. 5-(b)). By opening the zipper, the following textual information scrolls from the right to left repeatedly:

"The next schedule is a meeing with Mr.Fahim to discuss the Pervasive2005 paper in 59 minutes. Today's weather is fine. Maximum temperature is 9 degree's

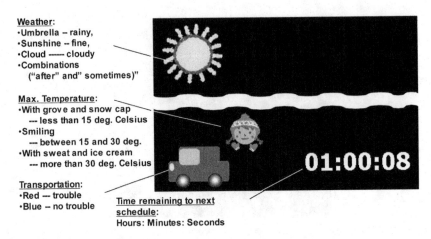

Fig. 6. A screenshot penetrating images from behind

Celsius. The probability of rainfall around your next schedule is 10%. On your way to the next schedule, Yamanote Line is stopped due to an accident."

Also, we have developed another version of the explicit mode, where textual information is presented in black on the white background (see Fig, 6-(c)). It looks like a document on a traditional computer display, which can lose the functionality of a mirror. However, we have expected that a user might accept this because he/she selects it by him/herself in an explicit way. We will discuss on this preference of users in Section 7.

Thus, our AwareMirror provides contextual information with a person, first seamlessly (implicitly) and then explicitly, while preserving its traditional look and interaction mode as much as possible.

6   Evaluation

In this section, we present the results of a user survey regarding the identification methods and display contents. Moreover, we also present the results of user testing. Then, we discuss the requirements and our current design.

6.1   Preference for Identification Technologies

We carried out a survey for investigating preferable identification technologies.

Profiles of Testees: The survey was conducted using questionnaires among 50 people. 34 of them are the members of the authors' laboratory including one professor, four Ph.D students, and 29 master course and undergraduate students where 6 of them are female. Approximately 10 of them work on ubiquitous computing projects. The rest of the testees (16 persons) are people who do not work in our laboratory including five undergraduate students, five housewives, four company employees, and two artists with ages ranging from 20 to 69.

Questionnair: We listed four types of identification mechanisms that include: a) carrying a wireless tag whose detection range is approximately 3m (tag-based), b) face recognition by video captured images (image-based), c) state of an everyday object that is rarely shared with others (sentient artefact-based), and d) fingerprint or voice recognition (biometric-based). Then, we asked testees to compare them and assign a rank from 1 to 4, where 1 for the least preferred and 4 for the most preferred. Also, a person who chooses c) can identify which artefact is desirable.

The Results: The average score for each method is as follows: biometric-based (2.92), tag-based (2.67), sentient artefact-based (2.27), and finally video-based (2.24). This means that the biometric-based identification was most preferable among the four, while the video-based one was preferred least. The biometric-based approach is preferred because it is considered to provide high accuracy and does not require a user to carry anything. However, the method is claimed to require explicit interaction to identify a user. For the tag-based approach, testees liked to control the timing of displaying information, but they disliked the possibilities to forget or lose the tag.

The merit of the artefact-based one pointed by them is its implicit identification by an artefact that is hardly shared with others like a toothbrush. However, the possibilities of intentional or unintentional use by other persons were pointed by participants who specified a lower rank. Finally, the video-based approach was disliked because of its obtrusive feeling of being watched although they know that it requires no input by a user, and also they know that it can extract human activities like looking at a mirror. The characteristic of a washroom is considered to emphasizes that feeling.

In terms of a daily artefact that is hardly shared with others, a toothbrush was listed by most of the participants. A safety razor or electric shaver, towel, hair brush, and cosmetics were also listed.

6.2   Preference for Contents

We also carried out a survey to investigate a user's preference for displayed contents.

Questionnaire: First of all, we made them to understand the notion of AwareMirror. Then, we asked questions about the usefulness of contents to be displayed on the mirror. The testees were allowed to rank the usefulness to 12 imaginary information services, i.e. 1 for "*useless*, 2 for "*weakly useless*", 3 for "*depends on the current situation*", 4 for "*fairly useful*", and 5 for "*very useful*". Also, we provided free space with each question for filling further comments. In addition to the information services that are actually utilized (see Section 4.2), we provided the following ones which can be categorized as information for entertainment and knowledge: fortune teller, level of beer taste, current news, and email contents.

The Results: Table 1 shows the results of the rating, where the second column represents services that were actually utilized. The third column indicates the average number of the rank while the fourth and the fifth mean the type of information and the level of abstraction, respectively. We have found that the testees preferred decision making information rather than ones that fall in the *"knowledge"* and *"entertainment"* category. According to the comments, the reason for the low rating of *"knowledge"* were that getting the information requires the interaction with the mirror, e.g. selecting and reading a number of e-mail one by one, and the interaction is not desirable at the location where the mirror is installed. On the other hand, a user was not interested in *"entertainment"* information in front of the mirror. Other types of preferable information they specified include the states of their health, train time table, etc. Remarkably, several testees expected the flexibility of controlling the level of information details. In Table 1, they preferred detailed information as well, however, they were also worried about the exploitation of privacy sensitive information.

Table 1. Preference of contents regarding usefulness

Name of information	Used	Average rank	Type	Level
Notification of transportation trouble	x	4.69	DM	AB
Details of transportation trouble	x	4.53	DM	DT
Weather forecast at destination with text	x	4.51	DM	DT
Weather forecast at destination with image	x	4.23	DM	AB
Schedule of the day in details	x	3.81	DM	DT
Current news		3.64	KW	DT
Time to departure with image	x	3.59	DM	AB
Notification of change on the current news		3.38	KW	AB
Email contents		2.98	KW	DT
Level of beer taste with image		2.37	EN	AB
Fortune teller with text		2.35	EN	DT
Fortune teller with image		2.10	EN	AB

DM: Decision Making, KW: Knowledge, EN: Entertainment
DT: Detail, AB: Abstract

6.3   Usability Testing

We had a test by one family consisting of 3 members (father, mother, son) to get the feedback of the usability.

Methodology: We had two comparative experiments to investigate the effect of the two phase interaction and presentation in the explicit mode. We have created AwareMirror without the zipper, where only abstract information is displayed. The testees were provided this version of AwareMirror first and then that with the zipper. In the second experiment, two types of presentations, i.e. scrolling text and black characters on white background (see Fig. 5-(b) and (c)), were compared.

The Results: All three testees seleted AwareMirror with the zipper, which indicates they preferred to have the flexibility of controlling the level of information details. However, they complained about the explicit necessity of closing the zipper by themselves. They pointed out the possibility to forget it since they were often in a hurry in front of a mirror. Also, the non-intuitiveness of the zipper was claimed. Instead, they told that they would like to control by a push-button switch like a bell button. The results oppose our initial design described in Section 5.2.

Regarding to the presentation of the explicit mode, they also preferred the version with scrolling text because the white background one gave them obtrusive impression. This suggests that a user regards it as a mirror even if he/she selects to see detailed information. Moreover, there was a request for showing detailed information selectively. Overall, they agreed to the notion of "information perception as secondary task" that AwareMirror is trying to achieve.

6.4   Summary of Evaluation

The notion of augmenting a mirror with context sensitive display was well accepted. The presentation of information triggered by using a toothbrush and standing in front of AwareMirror provides testees with feelings of implicit and natural identification that we were intended. However, testees were worried about the possibility of using these artefacts by others which may hamper their privacy. Information that can affect a user's behavior was preferred because, according to testees' comments, he/she can change the next action considering this information. Regarding to a display, abstract information was preferred due to its unobtrusiveness. The two phase interaction was also desirable because of its flexibility of controlling.

7   Discussions

In this section, we show some issues in designing and evaluating AwareMirror.

7.1   Identifying a Person in Front of a Mirror

We have utilized the state-of-use of a toothbrush for identifying a person. The detection of something in front of a mirror and the co-location of the mirror and toothbrush being used are combined to identify the person in front of the mirror. The sensing technologies used are simple, but this technique may lead to mis-identification. As pointed out in the survey result shown in Section 6.1, an everyday artefact may be used by an unintended person. Also, detecting an artefact status "being used" is difficult. However, these artefacts can be used to start showing personalized information on the mirror without a user's explicit interaction. Also, an assumption that it is utilized in a closed reliable group like a family suppress these issues. Moreover, we flexibly select an appropriate way of the identification since the AwareMirror controller encapsulates it.

7.2 Usability

Mode Transition by Zipper Metaphor: As described in Section 6.3, most of the users liked the two phase interaction, but they did not want to use the "zipper" for mode transition. AwareMirror turns to the black screen (default mode) when it detects a user's absence in the both implicit and explicit mode. Here, we assume that the zipper remains opened. When a new user comes in front of AwareMirror, it displays abstract information. So, he/she needs to close the zipper first if he/she wants to "open" the zipper to change into the explicit mode, which makes them confused. Moreover, as stated by the testees, they often forgot to close the zipper. We consider the reason for this is the statefulness of the zipper. That is, if a "push button" is utilized, a user does not have to bring it to the normal position. Also, we argue that the non-intuitiveness of the zipper for switching modes comes from its multiple roles. It is utilized not only to extract something from inside (digital value), but also to fasten something at a proper position like a zip-up jacket (analog value).

Presentation of Explicit Mode: According to the user testing, scrolling text was desirable as the presentation in the explicit mode. However, it continuously scrolls from the right to left and takes some time to show all information, while the white background-based approach can offer all information at a glance. In the current version, it takes about 40 seconds to show all information as presented in Section 5.5. This makes it difficult to get only desired information rapidly. The problem may be solved by choosing an appropriate information by touching the information on the mirror directly, but the solution causes another problem described in the next paragraph.

Issues in Showing Detailed Information Selectively: The touch panel-based interaction becomes popular for natural input, however it is inappropriate for applying a mirror. If a user touches on its surface, his/her fingerprint remains. Therefore, it makes the functionality of the mirror useless. Additionally, if buttons are used like function keys, it loses the metaphor of a mirror. We need to provide a natural and suitable interaction method for the mirror.

7.3 Possible Issues in Large Sized Version of AwareMirror

The current 15 inches LCD version is small enough to become aware of information displayed. However, in the case of a large mirror, a person might not notice the information if it is displayed on the top and/or bottom corner due to human eye's capability. One option to avoid this is generating sound at the beginning of the display. But the approach requires a user to pay an attention, which might violate our design principle. Therefore, we should consider alternatives while keeping the characteristic pointed in the previous section.

Also, in the current version, the information cannot be seen by others because the body of the subject covers it. However, in turn, the large sized one like Fig. 1 can have the chance, where more than two persons could use it at a time. To show information to an appropriate user, the location should be identified properly. We consider the current location identification mechanism is inappropriate because it utilizes a wide range RFID tag system which can detect tags in 2 to 3 meters. Therefore, it is difficult to match the detection by the infra-red sensor with the detection by the RFID tag reader.

Regarding to the detection of a person in front of the mirror, it is also difficult since an infra-red range finder usually has the narrow range of detection (in case of GP2D12, it is 10 degrees). For detecting with high accuracy, one solution for this is to attach infra-red sensors densely in front of a faucet while loosely at other places, and this leads to better detection. However, the solution might break aesthetic feeling and might be expensive. We are investigating these issues to deploy AwareMirror in public and private washrooms using a 60 inches plasma display in a practical way.

8 Conclusions and Future Direction

In this paper, we have proposed an augmented mirror, AwareMirror. AwareMirror offers abstract and personalized information on a mirror to a person who is in front of the mirror. Our approach preserves the metaphor of a mirror, although the mirror is augmented to offer useful information while a user is washing his/her face or making up. AwareMirror is considered as a new type of ambient displays.

The primary user feedbacks were mostly positive. However, we are working on building and evaluating iteratively through further usability testing. Especially, we need to investigate the usefulness of the explicit mode. Moreover, the size of a display that affects the ease of understanding information, feelings of privacy violation, and sensing technologies should be taken into account in the near future. We have now a 60 inches plasma LCD, and we hope to build a larger augmented mirror to verify the possible issues mentioned above.

Acknowledgments

We would like to thank Ms. Kanako Okada and Mr. Takeshi Kambe for their constant improvements of the AwareMirror system.

References

1. A. Dey, G. Abowd, and D. Salber. A Conceptual Framework and a Toolkit for Supporting the Rapid Prototyping of Context-Aware Applications. *HUMAN-COMPUTER INTERACTION*, 16(2-4):97–166, 2001.
2. K. Fujinami and T. Nakajima. Towards System Software for Physical Space Applications. In *Proceedings of ACM Symposium on Applied Computing(SAC) 2005*, March 2005. (to appear).

3. K. Fujinami and T. Nakajima. Sentient Artefact: Acquiring Context by using Daily Objects. Technical report, Waseda University, 2005(to appear).

4. L. E. Holmquist and T. Skog. Informative art: Information visualization in everyday environments. In *GRAPHITE '03: Proceedings of the 1st international conference on Computer graphics and interactive techniques in Australasia and South East Asia*, pages 229–235, 2003.

5. H. Ishii and B. Ullmer. Tangible Bits: Towards Seamless Interfaces between People, Bits and Atoms. In *Proceedings of Conference on Human Factors in Computing systems*, pages 234–241, 1997.

6. J. Mankoff, A. K.Dey, G. Hsieh, J. Kientz, S. Lederer, and M. Ames. Heuristic evaluation of ambient displays. In *Proceedings of the conference on Human factors in computing systems*, pages 169–176, 2003.

7. S. Naka, H. Kato, and K. Tachibana. Augmented Mirror: Augmented Reality in the Mirror World. Technical Report TR-MVE 2001-10, The Institute of Electronics, Information, and Communication Engineering(IEICE), June 2001. (in Japanese).

8. Phidgets Inc. Web site. URL: ⟨http://www.phidgets.com/⟩.

9. G. Pingali, C. Pinhanez, A. Levas, R. Kjeldsen, M. Podlaseck, H. Chen, and N. Sukaviriya. Steerable Interfaces for Pervasive Computing Spaces. In *Proceedings of the First IEEE International Conference on Pervasive Computing and Communications(PERCOM'03)*, pages 315–322, March 2003.

10. RFC2445. Internet Calendaring and Scheduling Core Object Specification (iCalendar). URL: ⟨http://www.faqs.org/rfcs/rfc2445.html⟩.

11. R. Rodenstein. Employing the Periphery: The Window as Interface. In *Extended abstract of International Conference on Human Factors in Computing Systems(CHI'99)*, pages 204–205, May 1999.

12. Sharp Corporation. Optical System Device. URL: ⟨http://sharp-world.com/products/device/lineup/table/085.html⟩.

13. J. Stasko, T. Miller, Z. Pousman, C. Plaue, and O. Ullah. Personalized Peripheral Information Awareness through Informative Art. In *Proceedings of 6th International Conference on Ubiquitous Computing(Ubicomp2004)*, pages 18–35, October 2004.

14. K. Ushida, Y. Tanaka, T. Naemura, and H. Harashima. i-mirror: An Interaction / Information Environment Based on a Mirror Metaphor Aiming to Install into Our Life Space. In *Proceedings of the 12th International Conference on Artificial Reality and Telexistence (ICAT2002)*, December 2002.

15. C. Wisneski, H. Ishii, A. Dahley, M. Gorbet, S. Brave, B. Ullmer, and P. Yarin. Ambient Displays: Turning Architectural Space into an Interface between People and Digital Information. In *Proceedings of the First International Workshop on Cooperative Buildings (CoBuild'98)*, pages 22–32, February 1998.

Embedded Assessment: Overcoming Barriers to Early Detection with Pervasive Computing

Margaret Morris[1], Stephen S. Intille[2], and Jennifer S. Beaudin[2]

[1] Proactive Health, Intel Research,
JF3-377; 2111 NE 25th Avenue Hillsboro, OR 97124 USA
Margaret.Morris@intel.com
[2] House_n, Massachusetts Institute of Technology,
1 Cambridge Center, 4FL, Cambridge, MA 02142 USA
{intille, jbeaudin}@mit.edu

Abstract. Embedded assessment leverages the capabilities of pervasive computing to advance early detection of health conditions. In this approach, technologies embedded in the home setting are used to establish personalized baselines against which later indices of health status can be compared. Our ethnographic and concept feedback studies suggest that adoption of such health technologies among end users will be increased if monitoring is woven into preventive and compensatory health applications, such that the integrated system provides value beyond assessment. We review health technology advances in the three areas of monitoring, compensation, and prevention. We then define embedded assessment in terms of these three components. The validation of pervasive computing systems for early detection involves unique challenges due to conflicts between the exploratory nature of these systems and the validation criteria of medical research audiences. We discuss an approach for demonstrating value that incorporates ethnographic observation and new ubiquitous computing tools for behavioral observation in naturalistic settings such as the home.

1 Introduction

Baby boomers, the cohort of adults born between 1946 and 1964, will contribute to a growing medical crisis in many industrial countries. As demographics shift and life-spans increase, a larger percentage of adults will require medical care. The rising cost of medical procedures in combination with the greater numbers of people needing assistance will place an enormous strain on healthcare providers. Many diseases that severely limit quality of life are difficult to manage in their later stages, but can be treated more effectively and less expensively if caught early. Early detection, therefore, is increasingly of interest to all parties in the medical system: individuals managing their health, family and medical caregivers, and medical researchers in search of predictive biomarkers.

This paper argues for a new approach to early detection that tightly integrates traditionally separate areas of monitoring, compensation, and prevention (Figure 1). Leveraging synergies in these three areas holds promise for advancing detection of

H.W. Gellersen et al. (Eds.): PERVASIVE 2005, LNCS 3468, pp. 333–346, 2005.

disease states. We believe this highly integrated approach will greatly increase adoption of home health technologies among end users and ease the transition of embedded health assessment prototypes from computing laboratories into medical research and practice.

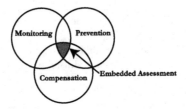

Fig. 1. Health technologies for early detection typically focus on monitoring, compensation, or prevention. We argue that the most powerful interventions may leverage all three areas simultaneously

We derive our observations from a series of exploratory and qualitative studies on ubiquitous computing for health and wellbeing. These studies, outlined in Table 1, highlighted barriers to early detection in the clinical setting, concerns about home assessment technologies among end users, and values of target user groups related to prevention and detection. Observations from the studies are used to identify challenges that must be overcome by pervasive computing developers if ubiquitous computing systems are to gain wide acceptance for early detection of health conditions.

Table 1. The research direction proposed in this paper is based on evidence from ethnographic studies on health needs and a series of concept feedback studies

Study Type	Number of interviews
Ethnographic needs assessment: Household interviews and shadows with older adults and their family members [1]	Full household interviews (44)
Concept feedback studies: Interviews using concept sketches and "informances" (live enactments of proactive health computing capabilities). See [2] for overview of methods.	Boomers (28), healthy elders (35), elders with Mild Cognitive Impairment (12)
Expert interviews: Discussion with researchers and clinicians about early detection, prevention, longitudinal monitoring and EA concepts	13 experts (neurologists, neuropsychologists, nurses, gerontologists)
Participatory design: Interviews using mocked-up data displays and longitudinal monitoring scenarios to elicit feedback about personal health tracking	26 Boomers, 5 elders, 8 professional caregivers (general practitioners, social workers)

2 Barriers to Early Detection

The motivation driving research on pervasive home monitoring is that clinical diagnostic practices frequently fail to detect health problems in their early stages. Often, clinical testing is first conducted after the onset of a health problem when there is no data about an individual's previous level of functioning. Subsequent clinical assessments are conducted periodically, often with no data other than self-report about functioning in between clinical visits. Self-report data on mundane or repetitive health-related behaviors has been repeatedly demonstrated as unreliable [3]. Clinical diagnostics are also limited in ecological validity, not accounting for functioning in the home and other daily environments. Another barrier to early detection is that age-based norms used to detect impairment may fail to capture significant decline among people whose premorbid functioning was far above average. Cultural differences have also been repeatedly shown to influence performance on standardized tests (e.g.,[4]). Although early detection can cut costs in the long term, most practitioners are more accustomed to dealing with severe, late stage health issues than subclinical patterns that may or may not be markers for more serious problems. In our participatory design interviews, clinicians voiced concerns about false positives causing unwarranted patient concerns and additional demands on their time.

Compounding the clinical barriers to early detection listed above are psychological and behavioral patterns among individuals contending with the possibility of illness. Our interviews highlighted denial, perceptual biases regarding variability of health states, over-confidence in recall and insight, preference for preventive and compensatory directives over pure assessment results, and a disinclination towards time consuming self-monitoring as barriers to early detection. Our ethnographic studies of households coping with cognitive decline revealed a tension between a desire for forecasting of what illness might lie ahead and a counter current of denial (see Figure 2) [1]. Almost all caregivers and patients wished that they had received an earlier diagnosis to guide treatment and lifestyle choices, but they also acknowledged that they had overlooked blatant warning signs until the occurrence of a catastrophic incident (e.g. a car accident). This lag between awareness and actual decline caused them to miss out on the critical window for initiation of treatments and planning that could have had a major impact on independence and quality of life. Ethnography and concept feedback participants attributed this denial in part to a fear of being diagnosed with a disease for which there is no cure. They also worried about the effect of this data on insurers and other outside parties. Participants in the three cohorts included in our studies (boomers, healthy older adults, and older adults coping with illness themselves or in a spouse) were much more interested in, and less conflicted about, preventive and compensatory directives than pure assessment.

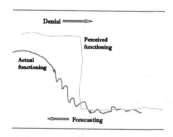

Fig. 2. This heuristic model, published in [1], extends a previous model by Hirsch et al. [5] to illustrate the perceptual and emotional factors that delay assessment

Perceptual biases also appear to impede traditional assessment and self-monitoring. Ethnography participants reported consistently overestimating functioning before a catastrophic event and appeared, during the interview, to consistently underestimate functioning following detection of cognitive impairment [1]. Additionally, we observed probable over-confidence among healthy adults in their ability to recall behaviors and analyze their relationship to both environmental factors and wellbeing. This confidence in recall and insight seemed exaggerated given findings that recall of frequent events is generally poor [3].

As a result of these health perceptions, many of those interviewed felt that the time and discipline required for journaling (e.g. of eating, sleeping, mood, etc.) outweighed the benefits. Additionally, they expressed wariness of confronting or being reprimanded about what is already obvious to them. They would prefer to lead investigations and develop strategies for improving their lives. Interviewees, particularly those in the baby boomer cohort, expressed a desire for highly contextualized analyses of health, posing questions such as "Is quality of time with my kids affected by my deadlines at work?" "Has my posture improved since I started doing yoga two months ago?" "At what time of day do I write the best and how can I schedule my time accordingly?").

Pervasive computing systems may enable this type of integrated, contextualized inquiry if they can also overcome the clinical and individual barriers that might otherwise impede adoption of the new technologies. Table 2 summarizes the *clinical* and *individual* barriers to health assessment and corresponding opportunities afforded by ubiquitous computing technologies that we identified from our interviews.

Table 2. Barriers to early detection and the corresponding ubicomp opportunities

Clinical Barriers to early detection	Opportunities afforded by ubiquitous computing technologies
1. Delayed assessment: Patients and physicians typically do not request assessment until a problem arises and reaches considerable severity (e.g., it is often not until a car accident or fall that a patient's family requests cognitive assessment).	Continuously monitor and use data to encourage patients to seek help.
2. Infrequent assessment: Clinicians lack information about functioning and related behaviors between visits (e.g., cognitive tests are typically administered at most bi-annually, but the significant fluctuation in cognitive functioning -- over the course of a day, week and month -- could inform diagnosis).	Continuously monitor to illuminate patterns and daily variability; provide data directly to patients, who can present patterns to clinicians if they wish.
3. Lack of ecological validity: Clinicians typically lack reliable information about patients' functioning in environments of daily life (e.g., cognitive tests administered in the clinician's office may not reflect functioning in the home, car, or workplace).	Acquire contextually sensitive data to highlight environment-behavior connections and specific incidents that may not be reported in clinical visits.
4. Narrow focus of assessment: Patients and clinicians may overlook early symptoms that are not obviously tied the variable of direct interest (e.g., discoordination, in the case of dementia).	Use implicit sensing to detect subtle changes in manipulation of everyday objects.

5. Avoidance of testing for early detection: Some clinicians limit testing because of time, expense, and poor predictive value (e.g., genetic testing for Alzheimer's biomarkers is sometimes discouraged).	Direct embedded assessment services primarily to end users – *any* individuals interested in monitoring their own health, not only "patients."
***Individual* Barriers to early detection**	**Opportunities afforded by ubiquitous computing technologies**
6. Fear of diagnostic labels: Patients fear diagnosis of illnesses that have no known cure (e.g., Many dread a diagnosis of Alzheimer's disease because there is currently no curative treatment). Patients can also be frustrated by diagnoses that do not explain etiology of symptoms.	Frame feedback in actionable directives for compensatory and preventive health strategies.
7. Avoidance of testing experiences in clinical settings: Clinical assessment can be tiring, intimidating and seem futile. (e.g., Cognitive test batteries are sometimes experienced as a very long "pop quiz" that does not relate to the challenges of everyday life).	Embed assessment into services that have other value propositions. Assessment is woven into everyday routines and devices, assistive services, and mentally stimulating games.
8. Underestimation of health variability and overestimation of insight: Individuals' retrospective accounts and understanding of their own behavior are limited. (e.g., Past research shows that people significantly underestimate food consumption. [6])	Use feedback to highlight variability in health states and point out opportunities to leverage and extend positive health states.
9. Lack of time and discipline required for journaling behaviors and symptoms. (e.g., Patients' compliance with health behavior journals, such as those for tracking diet, tends to drop off quickly).	Automate and embed data capture into everyday activities; request and deliver information at system-detected opportune moments; ensure technology continuously reinforces its value.
10. Discordance between individuals' holistic, integrated view of health and the constraints of most self-monitoring systems. (e.g., Blood pressure cuffs and logs do not reflect the behavioral and environmental factors that influence readings)	Allow people to explore correlations between contextual and behavioral factors.
11. Privacy concerns: Fears about availability of diagnostic information to outside parties. (e.g., Many worry that, if shared, early signs of cancer or dementia may jeopardize medical coverage).	Direct feedback to end users not to caregivers, clinicians, or insurers.
12. Difficulty relating to traditional clinical health metrics and language (e.g., Criteria for mood disorders do not always resonate with individuals' experiences of stress and life dissatisfaction.)	Present tailored and interactive visualizations at appropriate moments related to personal routines.
13. "Proactive" focus on self-improvement, wellness and quality of life: Among Boomers and younger adults, healthful behavior is motivated largely by presentation and performance goals versus strictly defined health goals. Clinicians and current monitoring systems focus on existing problems and preventing high-risk illnesses.	Support users' current concerns, presenting trends of interest, even if these trends may not be directly relevant to clinical care (e.g., Boomers may be more likely to monitor their behavior if they can see its relationship to their immediate productivity and physical appearance versus their risk for cardiovascular disease). Track effectiveness of different cues (e.g., name prompts, posture adjustments from chairs) and feedback displays to inform assessment and self-directed wellness strategies.

3 Advances in Pervasive Computing for Health Management

New approaches to early detection are needed to overcome the significant barriers to health assessment outlined in Table 2. Developments in ubiquitous computing for health and wellbeing have largely been in three separate areas: Monitoring, compensation, and prevention.

3.1 Monitoring

Most prior work on the application of ubiquitous computing technology for healthcare has been in the area of monitoring. Ubiquitous computing researchers have advocated in-home and on-body monitoring to help people to assess their own health and that of their loved ones [7]. Numerous research efforts exist to develop systems that detect activities of daily living (e.g. [7-15]) and specific conditions, such as changes in gait [16]. Sensors embedded in the home are intended to collect longitudinal and contextually sensitive data that can then be processed to automatically detect important changes in behavior patterns caused by the onset of illness. Sensors on mobile devices for detecting patterns of activities have also been proposed [17]. These systems usually collect data continuously or when someone is engaged in a particular activity of interest, such as computer game playing [18].

The focus of much of the prior work on ubiquitous assessment is monitoring, rather than self-awareness – an emphasis that implies a receptive clinical audience. A few clinical trials are currently evaluating in-home monitoring systems (e.g. extensions of [15]), but it is not clear how these studies will address the expectations of medical audiences given their relatively small sample sizes and short (e.g. months) observation periods. Longitudinal, large number of subject studies correlating home and clinical assessment data are not yet feasible for most ubiquitous computing trials. Commercial systems are currently limited to a small number of sensors per dwelling, typically motion sensors, that do not track activities of particular interest, only variation from baseline movement throughout a home (e.g. QuietCare from Living Independently Group). Existing commercial systems provide no compensatory or preventive functionality using the sensors.

3.2 Compensation

Context-dependent information delivery has been explored by a number of researchers to compensate for health problems in later life. Several such systems, designed to help people compensate for cognitive and physical decline [19], are intended to promote independence in and outside the home [17]. Context-aware computer reminding systems have been developed to help people compensate for attentional deficits by reorienting them after they are interrupted from a sequential task such as cooking [19]. Other systems use ubiquitous computing to help people compensate for memory loss by prompting them to take medications [20, 21]. Ubiquitous computing systems have also been proposed to help people remain socially engaged by compensating for impaired recall of names and faces [22], providing visual feedback on social activity to elders and their caregivers [23], and forging connections between people with common interests in social settings [24].

The compensatory systems proposed by ubiquitous computing researchers have typically been demonstrated with prototypes. Few have been tested outside of a laboratory setting or with a plan for gaining acceptance by medical or lay communities.

3.3 Prevention

Context-dependent information delivery has prompted research on preventive health care innovation. "Just-in-time" information delivery systems have been conceptualized to encourage healthy behaviors that either lower the probability of serious illness of those at risk (primary prevention) or help prevent worsening of an illness (secondary prevention) by automatic detection of particular situations or activities [25]. Behavior change is motivated through the delivery of information at key times in the decision making process: points of decision, behavior, and consequence [26]. The promise is to create systems that would, like an effective personal trainer, provide tailored messages at teachable moments – the right place and time when a person is receptive to information – in order to motivate behavior, belief, or attitude change. Ubiquitous computing technologies that simplify data collection and provide summary information may lead to more informed decision making, for example using receipt analysis as a behavioral feedback tool to improve nutritional choices [27].

Many of the preventive technologies developed by medical researchers have been designed for people who are vulnerable to particular illnesses. For example, a number of websites and internet therapies have been tested with people at risk for obesity, diabetes or eating disorders (e.g., [28]). There have also been a number of primary prevention applications designed for the general population, such as desktop applications to help people track their health goals, kiosk-based systems for people to encourage better dietary decision making in supermarkets (e.g. [29]), and the more recent products, such as Sport Brain (SportBrain Holdings, Inc.), that allow people to monitor their exercise. It is our impression, from consumer trends and anecdotal evidence, that the most enthusiastically adopted and effective preventive health systems may be those that are primarily designed for fun rather than health management. For example, the increasingly popular "Dance Dance Revolution" (Konami Corporation), although designed strictly for entertainment, is rich in the social, cognitive and physical stimulation that may prevent diseases such as dementia [30]. Such consumer-oriented games may be especially valuable preventive tools for people who are not already experiencing a serious health issue. Research is needed on the health value of such games and how their capabilities can be extended to assess performance over time, and provide customized programs depending on individuals' agility and health concerns.

4 Embedding Assessment into Daily Life and Wellness Strategies: Integrating Monitoring, Compensation, and Prevention

Evidence from needs assessment and iterative concept feedback studies suggests that assessment will be most sensitive and most well used if it is embedded not only in the home environments but also into individuals' compensatory and preventive strategies.

4.1 Definition of Embedded Assessment

We define the following requirements for *embedded assessment* (EA)*:*

- EA applications should simultaneously serve three purposes: monitoring, prevention, and compensation.
- EA applications should use "extreme personalization" in the way that information is acquired and presented. Monitoring, prevention, and compensation are embedded in the user's everyday physical environments, behavioral repertoires and social milieus. Explicit assessment, which requires conscious engagement from users, occurs at times that make sense during natural activities, and it involves content that is relevant to the end user's life (work, social, family, etc.). Implicit or passive monitoring is integrated into the activities and tools of daily life (e.g., phones that trend changes in the way they are operated, mirrors that capture and reflect subtle changes in appearance).
- EA applications monitor health status by trending the degree and quality of assistance (in the form of hints, prompts, encouragement and adaptive system adjustments) required for particular activities. EA systems search for meaningful patterns that can inform self-directed wellness strategies or medical care.

Monitoring will typically be the least prominent aspect of the user experience in EA. Monitoring is the continuous and contextually sensitive capture of data (physiological, behavioral, or psychological) that are salient to the user and his or her goals. EA monitoring is designed for self-directed inquiry rather than observation by a third party. The data may be only loosely tied to health (e.g., self-presentation, appearance, interpersonal dynamics, posture, etc.) or may be more obviously health related (e.g., eating and sleeping patterns, skin changes, pain). Monitoring can be of normal day-to-day behaviors (e.g., looking for changes in how one operates a remote control, cell phone or VCR) or of performance on tasks that are deliberately undertaken for preventive or compensatory purposes. The data capture is intended for feedback that will allow the end user to explore environment-behavior relationships and develop self-initiated health management strategies.

Compensatory strategies supported in EA are the adjustments a user makes to cope with a health concern. A compensatory strategy can include encoding, rehearsal and organizational strategies to compensate for a memory loss, self-reflection and mindfulness to address negative mood states, medical treatments, dieting, cosmetic procedures, physical therapy, or the use of assistive technologies. EA technologies can be interwoven with these activities, or the technologies themselves can offer the compensatory support. For example, rehearsal exercises and prompts could be offered on a mobile computing device to compensate for memory loss, or the compensatory support could be provided in the form of a visual display of monitoring data intended to invite mindfulness about variability in performance and health. EA technologies can also adjust to help users accomplish a task, such as programming a VCR, or offer graduated prompts for preparing a cup of tea.

Preventive strategies supported in EA are activities that protect against a health concern. Preventive strategies may include cognitive and physical exercise, social engagement, and dietary changes. EA technologies can monitor these activities and provide motivating behavioral feedback. Alternatively, EA applications, such as mentally challenging games presented on a mobile phone, can provide both the interface for the preventive activity and the mirroring of performance trends on this activity.

One example EA application that combines monitoring, preventive activity, and compensatory strategies (that the authors are developing) is a game for families on mobile phone plans. The game is designed to provide *monitoring* by tracking the response times and error rates as family members use the application to send family quiz questions to one another. The quiz items will be structured so that they exercise aspects of memory and reasoning that are typically the focus of cognitive assessment. Trending on users' engagement in this shared activity might provide early indicators of cognitive decline. *Compensatory strategies* will be supported as the feedback from the game helps individuals identify their strengths and weaknesses, along with the cuing and problem solving approaches that are most helpful for them. Additionally, the system will allow people to practice compensatory strategies such as rehearsal, encoding, mental manipulation of information, and drawing on the memory of family members. The game supports *prevention* of cognitive decline by engaging users with mentally stimulating quiz items, encouraging users to author questions and answers that ultimately generate a family knowledge archive, and by increasing social contact with their extended family.

5 Meeting the Demand for Evidence-Based Health Systems: Challenges of Evaluating Embedded Assessment Technologies

To help early detection of disease states, embedded assessment systems will ultimately need to appeal to both end users and medical audiences. Demonstrating value to these two groups will require empirical evidence of their concurrence with standardized measures, predictive power for early detection, and their effectiveness in guiding end users in self-governed health care initiatives. Similar validation challenges are shared by the many pervasive computing researchers who are developing innovative health care technologies (e.g. see [31]) and other applications for the home. The traditional methods for evaluating and validating assessment techniques within social sciences and medicine require longitudinal studies with very large sample sizes. Such studies would examine the concurrent validity of EA with other measures and, through retrospective analysis, the predictive power of EA as a biomarker for particular health conditions.

To establish concurrent validity, the accepted metric in clinical assessment research, individuals' performance on embedded assessment applications would be compared to their performance on standardized clinical measures over a longitudinal study. Participants would engage with embedded assessment tasks on a daily basis and complete standardized clinical tests or measurements at regular intervals. Attention would be paid to general agreement in the trends (e.g., whether steady decline is apparent in both forms of testing) and to agreement between specific measures (e.g., whether declines in ability to accurately dial telephone numbers parallel scores on standardized tests of working memory).

To examine the predictive power of EA prototypes, one might retrospectively compare the embedded assessment performance of people who had started using the prototypes when healthy but then differentially developed disease (e.g. comparing those who developed Alzheimer's Disease to those with normal cognitive aging). Patterns on EA performance that distinguished these two groups would be used to generate hypotheses about early markers. Needless to say, this approach is challenging. It typically requires matching participants on both baseline health status and endpoint diagnosis, and tracing cognitive functioning and other health factors throughout the lifespan.

Home health technology is typically evaluated in a clinical setting and subsequently migrated to the home. Devices such as blood pressure monitors, for example, were extensively tested in hospitals and later adapted for home use. Similarly, defibrillators have recently been shifted into home usage after extensive clinical testing. EA technology, however, by its embedded nature, cannot be evaluated out of context. Furthermore, many EA technologies will require sensor infrastructures in homes that cannot be evaluated in a piecemeal fashion – the *entire* sensor infrastructure must be available to detect baseline health behaviors on embedded tasks. Evaluation of EA technology is made even more complex by the integration of monitoring, preventive activities, and compensatory strategies. The impact of each component may confound experimental studies looking at one outcome variable. Therefore, researchers interested in EA face a classic "chicken and egg" evaluation problem. To make a (statistically) convincing argument that EA systems can provide useful biomarkers of early onset of disease will require studies where EA technology is installed in many homes for long evaluation periods, most likely of months or years. To justify the cost of a sufficient number of installations, however, will require evidence of the preventive health value of the EA systems.

Our interviews suggest that demand from end users for EA technologies may be sufficient to jumpstart adoption. Preliminary evaluation of EA might therefore focus not on biomarker identification, but on the benefits and obstacles experienced by end users. This approach would use a separate set of ubiquitous computing tools to observe usage and effects of EA systems. Key issues are whether systems enable users to determine meaningful patterns in their health and behavior, and whether these patterns drive behavioral change and health improvement. Traditional usability approaches can be used to examine adoption. Iterative open-ended interview questions, structured exercises, and ethnographic observation can illuminate whether the EA systems were effective in influencing awareness of variability in behavior and in mental and physical health. Demonstration of value to end users from compelling pilot studies may ultimately lead to wide-scale adoption of EA technologies. At that time, large-n trials may be undertaken to evaluate long-term effects; results of such trials could reveal bio and behavioral markers from embedded sensing.

Evaluation of the end-user's experience with EA systems should also incorporate observational tools such as live-in labs [32] and in-home sensors [33]. These tools, increasingly employed to evaluate other types of ubiquitous computing technologies, would generate detailed descriptions of EA usage. Users' everyday experience with EA systems will be important to assess, but difficult to gather through retrospective report. Prototype EA systems deployed in live-in labs and a limited number of homes could detect change in some metrics of adoption: usage, elaboration of features and content, sharing, interaction with systems and other people using the systems in the context daily routines. These adoption measures could be examined to make sense of test performance. In highly instrumented environments, the same sensors used to deploy EA prototypes could be used to provide contextual information related to metrics of adoption, such as physical activity levels, time spent in different activities and areas of the home, and interaction among members of a household or social network.

Time-based evaluations, conducted in an instrumented residential lab or home setting, may also provide compelling evidence of value of an EA prototype. Pervasive computing monitoring is intrinsically well suited to demonstrate variability across time and place. Such analyses may illuminate compelling patterns in behavior, cognitive functioning and other aspects of health. Our Boomer interviewees suggested they might be interested in tracking such variability when managing their own health. Any measured variability might also be of interest to medical researchers interested in early markers or outcome assessment and clinicians trying to hone their diagnoses. Based on these observations, pilot studies that can convincingly demonstrate variability that can be partially explained by context or daily routine variables, such as sleep patterns or time of day, are recommended. Such studies might suggest to researchers that they are missing valuable information when only examining health changes over long intervals and may lead the way to funding for larger scale EA studies in real homes. Until EA systems are widely deployed, researchers will lack evidence on which of the many potential embedded measures provides useful, contextual health markers. Tools are needed, therefore, with a battery of potentially valuable sensors ubiquitously installed to provide data for exploratory identification of the most promising marker strategies.

6 Conclusion

The embedded assessment approach emerged from the series of needs gathering and concept feedback studies and interviews involving a total of 171 people, as listed in Table 1. The general approach of embedded assessment arose as a means of resolving conflicting attitudes about early detection. Our early studies indicated that to be tolerable to end users, assessment needed to be embedded not only with the environments of daily living, but also within accepted compensatory and preventive health strategies. For many types of health assessment, such as cognitive assessment, baselines of functioning must be established during middle age. Many useful proactive health applications, therefore, will need to be relevant and stimulating to this cohort. Our work suggests a promising approach for future research would be to embed health assessment within the social unit of the family, in part because interpersonal connectedness is so highly valued to people at all stages of life. A promising approach may be to focus on developing prototype systems for individuals in midlife who are managing their own health. Other potential users, including family and medical care providers and researchers searching for new biomarkers of disease, will most likely respond to interest from these first two groups rather than initiate usage.

We believe individuals in mid life are the most likely adopters of embedded assessment technologies. Nonetheless, researchers must carefully consider the needs and validation metrics of both groups: the boomer's desire for constructive, insightful and motivating feedback on health, appearance, performance, and the medical researcher's desire for identified biomarkers with predictive power for disease progression. Traditional methods of demonstrating test validity and predictive power of embedded assessment for medical audiences are not immediately feasible for pervasive computing trials. In the absence of such metrics, we argue for outcome measures that will demonstrate the effectiveness of embedded assessment systems as health interventions and self-reflective tools. Demonstration of variability in functioning as a function of context (temporal, environmental, behavioral and social) would be compelling to both end consumers and medical communities. To demonstrate this variability and other metrics of interest to target users, we suggest a tiered validation approach that involves in-home trials and focused observations in live-in laboratories. We believe this approach and our more general discussion of evaluation challenges can guide evaluation of the many innovative prototypes generated by the pervasive computing community for health assessment.

Acknowledgments

This research builds upon the three year Proactive Health project at Intel directed by Eric Dishman. Special thanks to the entire Proactive Health team and to Gillian Hayes for her editorial reviews. We thank our interview and study participants for their insightful and detailed feedback and the generous contribution of their time. The work of the MIT authors was supported, in part, by an Intel Corporation AIM Grant and the MIT House_n Consortium.

References

1. Morris, M., et al., *New perspectives on ubiquitous computing from ethnographic studies on cognitive decline*, in *Proceedings of UbiComp 2003: Ubiquitous Computing*, J.F. McCarthy, Editor. 2003, Springer: Berlin Heidelberg. p. 227-242.
2. Lundell, J. and M. Morris, *Tales, tours, tools, and troupes: A tiered research method to inform ubiquitous designs for the elderly*, in *People and Computers XVIII - Design for Life*, Fincher, et al., Editors. 2004, Springer Verlag: London. p. 165-177.
3. Gorin, A.A. and A.A. Stone, *Recall biases and cognitive errors in retrospective self reports: A call for momentary assessments*, in *Handbook of Health Psychology*, A. Baum, T. Revenson, and J. Singer, Editors. 2001, Erlbaum: Mahwah, NJ. p. 405-413.
4. Kennepohl, S., et al., *African American acculturation and neuropsychological test performance following traumatic brain injury.* Journal of the International Neuropsychological Society, 2004. **10**: p. 566-577.
5. Hirsch, T., et al., *The ELDer Project: social, emotional, and environmental factors in the design of eldercare technologies*, in *Proceedings of the Conference on Universal Usability.* 2000.
6. Bingham, S., *The dietary assessment of individuals: methods, accuracy, new techniques and recommendations.* Nutr Abstr Rev, 1987. **57**: p. 705-42.
7. Mynatt, E.D., I. Essa, and W. Rogers, *Increasing the opportunities for aging in place*, in *Proceedings of the Conference on Universal Usability.* 2000. p. 65-71.

8. Munguia Tapia, E., S.S. Intille, and K. Larson, *Activity recognition in the home setting using simple and ubiquitous sensors*, in *Proceedings of PERVASIVE 2004*, A. Ferscha and F. Mattern, Editors. 2004, Springer-Verlag: Berlin Heidelberg. p. 158-175.

9. Philipose, M., et al., *Guide: Towards understanding daily life via auto-identification and statistical analysis*, in *Ubihealth 2003: The 2nd International Workshop on Ubiquitous Computing for Pervasive Healthcare Applications*. 2003.

10. Wilson, D. and C. Atkeson, *Automatic health monitoring using anonymous, binary sensors*, in *CHI Workshop on Keeping Elders Connected*. 2004.

11. Matsouoka, K., *Smart house understanding human behaviors: Who did what, where, and when*. Proceedings of the 8th World Multi-Conference on Systems, Cybernetics, and Informatics, 2004. **3**: p. 181-185.

12. Haigh, K.Z., et al., *The Independent LifeStyle AssistantTM (I.L.S.A.): Lessons Learned*. 2003, Honeywell Laboratories: Minneapolis, MN.

13. Korhonen, I., P. Paavilainen, and A. Särelä, *Application of ubiquitous computing technologies for support of independent living of the elderly in real life settings*, in *UbiHealth 2003: The 2nd International Workshop on Ubiquitous Computing for Pervasive Healthcare Applications*. 2003.

14. Mihailidis, A., et al., *An intelligent environment to support aging-in-place, safety, and independence of older adults with dementia*, in *UbiHealth 2003: The 2nd International Workshop on Ubiquitous Computing for Pervasive Healthcare Applications*. 2003.

15. Barger, T., D. Brown, and M. Alwan, *Health status monitoring through analysis of behavioral patterns*, in *Proceedings of the 8th Congress of the Italian Association for Artificial Intelligence (AI*IA) on Ambient Intelligence*. 2003, Springer-Verlag.

16. Dockstader, S.L., M.J. Berg, and A.M. Tekalp, *Stochastic kinematic modeling and feature extraction for gait analysis*. IEEE Transactions on Image Processing, 2003. **12**(8): p. 962-976.

17. Patterson, D.J., et al., *Inferring high-level behavior from low-level sensors*, in *Proceedings of UBICOMP 2003*. 2003, Springer-Verlag.

18. Jimison, H.B., et al., *Home monitoring of computer interactions for the early detection of cognitive decline*, in *Proceedings of the IEEE Engineering in Medicine and Biology Conference*. 2004.

19. Mynatt, B.D. and W.A. Rogers, *Developing technology to support the functional independence of older adults*. Aging International, 2002. **27**(1): p. 24-41.

20. Pollack, M.E., et al., *Autominder: an intelligent cognitive orthotic system for people with memory impairment*. Robotics and Autonomous Systems, 2003. **44**(3-4): p. 273-282.

21. Floerkemeier, C. and F. Siegemund, *Improving the effectiveness of medical treatment with pervasive computing technologies*, in *UbiHealth 2003: The 2nd International Workshop on Ubiquitous Computing for Pervasive Healthcare Applications*. 2003.

22. 22. Morris, M., J. Lundell, and E. Dishman, *Ubiquitous computing for Mild Cognitive Impairment: A prototype for embedded assessment and rehearsal*, in *The Gerontologist*. 2003. p. 403.

23. Morris, M., J. Lundell, and E. Dishman, *Computing for social connectedness*, in *Proceedings of CHI 2004*. 2003.

24. nTag Interactive, *nTAG*. 2004.

25. Intille, S.S., *A new research challenge: persuasive technology to motivate healthy aging*. Transactions on Information Technology in Biomedicine, 2004. **8**(3): p. 235-237.

26. Fogg, B.J., *Persuasive technologies*. Communications of the ACM, 1999. **42**(5): p. 27-29.

27. Mankoff, J., et al., *Using low-cost sensing to support nutritional awareness*, in *Proceedings of Ubicomp 2002*, G. Borriello and L.E. Holmquist, Editors. 2002, Springer-Verlag. p. 371-378.

28. Winzelberg, A.J., et al., *Effectiveness of an Internet-based program for reducing risk factors for eating disorders*. Journal of Consulting and Clinical Psychology, 2000. **68**: p. 125-138.

29. Anderson, E.S., et al., *A computerized social cognitive intervention for nutrition behavior: Direct and mediated effects on fat, fiber, fruits, and vegetables, self-efficacy, and outcome expectations among food shoppers*. Annals of Behavioral Medicine, 2001. **23**(2): p. 88-100.

30. Fratiglioni, L., P.-B. S., and B. Winblad, *An active and socially integrated lifestyle in late life might protect against dementia*. Lancet, 2004. **3**: p. 343-353.

31. *UbiHealth 2003: The 2nd International Workshop on Ubiquitous Computing for Pervasive helthcare Applications*. 2003.

32. Intille, S.S., et al., *A living laboratory for the design and evaluation of ubiquitous computing interfaces*, in *Extended Abstracts of the 2005 Conference on Human Factors in Computing Systems*. 2005, ACM Press: New York, NY.

33. Intille, S.S., et al., *Tools for studying behavior and technology in natural settings*, in *Proceedings of UbiComp 2003: Ubiquitous Computing*. 2003, Springer: Berlin Heidelberg. p. 157-174.

Author Index

Lecture Notes in Computer Science

For information about Vols. 1–3390

please contact your bookseller or Springer